The New American History

THE NEW

In the series
Critical Perspectives on the Past,
edited by Susan Porter Benson,
Stephen Brier, and Roy Rosenzweig

AMERICAN HISTORY

Revised and
Expanded Edition

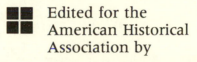

Edited for the
American Historical
Association by

ERIC FONER

Temple University Press

Philadelphia

Temple University Press, Philadelphia 19122
Copyright © 1997 by Temple University.
All rights reserved
Published 1997

Printed in the United States of America

⊗ The paper used in this publication
meets the requirements of American National Standard for
Information Sciences—Permanence of Paper for Printed
Library Materials, ANSI Z39.48-1984

Library of Congress Cataloging-in-Publication Data
The new American history / edited for the American Historical
Association by Eric Foner. — Rev. and expanded ed.
p.   cm. — (Critical perspectives on the past)
Includes bibliographical references.
ISBN 1-56639-551-8 (cloth : alk. paper). — ISBN 1-56639-552-6
(pbk. : alk. paper)
1. United States—Historiography.   I. Foner, Eric.   II. American
Historical Association.   III. Series.
E175.N53 1997
973'.072—dc21   96-52059

Contents

Preface to the Revised and Expanded Edition

IN THE YEARS SINCE *THE NEW AMERICAN HISTORY* WAS PUBLISHED IN 1990, THE study and teaching of history unexpectedly emerged as the subject of intense public debate. For a time, one could scarcely open a newspaper without encountering bitter controversy over the public presentation of the American past. Previously uncontroversial historical anniversaries became occasions for heated debate. The ambiguity that marked the quincentenary of Columbus's voyage to the New World, for example, contrasted dramatically with the unembarrassed celebration of its four hundredth anniversary a century earlier. No one in the 1890s seemed to doubt that 1492 marked an epochal moment in the progress of human civilization, while in 1992, the celebration was tempered by constant reminders of chattel slavery, the decimation of native populations, and other less than glorious consequences. Three years later, a proposed exhibition at the National Air and Space Museum to mark the fiftieth anniversary of the dropping of the first atomic bomb produced howls of outrage from veterans organizations, who charged that initial plans cast the Japanese of the Second World War as innocent victims rather than aggressors. The pressure exerted by these organizations, augmented by the threat of a reduction in congressional funding, forced the curators to rewrite the exhibition script to highlight Japan's wartime atrocities and remove documents revealing that high military officials in 1945 had doubted the need for using the bomb.

Simultaneously, controversy erupted over proposed national standards for history education drawn up with the participation of hundreds of scholars and every major professional association of history teachers. Critics condemned the plan for neglecting great figures of the American past like George Washington, and, more broadly, for adopting an excessively uncelebratory tone in dealing with the nation's history.

Whatever the outcome of these debates—and one hopes that when the smoke has cleared, it will leave behind a heightened public interest in an understanding of history—the transformation of historical scholarship that inspired the original publication of *The New American History* has proceeded apace. This revised edition includes essays on three fields that have undergone extremely dramatic changes of late. The new essays—on intellectual history, Western history, and the history of the family and of sexuality—examine current thinking in three of the most creative subfields in American historical writing. As for the original essays, nearly all have been revised (and some entirely rewritten) to bring the texts and bibliographies up to date. Taken together, the new and revised essays reflect the continuing vitality and creativity of the study of the American past, how traditional fields are being expanded and redefined even as new ones are created.

ERIC FONER

Introduction to the First Edition

IN THE COURSE OF THE PAST TWENTY YEARS, AMERICAN HISTORY HAS BEEN RE-
made. Inspired initially by the social movements of the 1960s and
1970s—which shattered the "consensus" vision that had dominated historical writing—and influenced by new methods borrowed from other
disciplines, American historians redefined the very nature of historical
study. The rise of the "new histories," the emphasis on the experience of
ordinary Americans, the impact of quantification and cultural analysis,
the eclipse of conventional political and intellectual history—these trends
are now so widely known (and the subject of such controversy) that
they need little reiteration. The study of American history today looks
far different than it did a generation ago.

This book comprises essays by thirteen scholars—many of whom
have been at the forefront of the transformation of historical study—
each assessing recent developments in historians' understanding of a period or a major theme in the nation's past. The idea for the collection
originated with a request from the American Historical Association for a
series of pamphlets addressed specifically to high school teachers of
American history and designed to familiarize them with the most up-to-
date historical scholarship. High school teachers, the association believed, sense that the study of history has changed dramatically of late;

overwhelmed as they are with classroom responsibilities, however, they have little time for extensive reading and are unable to keep up with all the trends in research and interpretation.

After a false start or two the proposal, somewhat revised, was adopted by Temple University Press. The project's central purpose remains the same: to provide an introduction to current thinking on key issues and periods of the American experience. The essays that follow will, as planned, be distributed in pamphlet form to high school teachers. But *The New American History* is addressed as well to a far wider audience: students and teachers at the college level and the broad public concerned with the current state of American historical study.

Although the book does not claim to offer a comprehensive view of all the subfields of American history, it is safe to say that no one can deny the centrality of the subjects that *are* included.

Each author was given a free hand in developing his or her reflections; consequently, there is some inevitable overlap in coverage. Leon Fink and Richard McCormick, for example, both touch on the labor politics of the Gilded Age; Thomas Holt, Sean Wilentz, and I all discuss recent literature on slave culture (a reflection of how important the body of scholarship dealing with that subject has been). No attempt has been made to fit the essays into a predetermined mold or impose a single point of view or interpretive framework. Nonetheless, certain themes recur with remarkable regularity, demonstrating how pervasively the "new histories" have reshaped our understanding of the American past.

If anything is characteristic of the recent study of American history, it is attention to the experience of previously neglected groups—not simply as an addition to a preexisting body of knowledge but as a fundamental redefinition of history itself. Women's history, as Linda Gordon shows, has greatly expanded its subject area, moving beyond the movement for suffrage, which preoccupied earlier women's historians, into such previously ignored realms as the history of sexuality. Leon Fink shows how labor history, from a field that defined its subject as the experience of wage workers in factories and the activities of unionized workers, has expanded to encompass the study of slaves, women at home, and the majority of laborers, who in America have always been unorganized.

Even more striking, perhaps, is that Afro-American history and women's history have matured to the point where they are not only widely recognized as legitimate subfields with their own paradigms and debates but are seen as indispensable to any understanding of the broad American experience. These points are made effectively in surveys of the two fields by Thomas Holt and Linda Gordon, but they are evident in other contributions as well. Richard McCormick makes clear that any calculus of Americans' gains and losses in the late nineteenth and early twentieth centuries must take into account the severe reverses suffered by blacks in those years. William Chafe places the civil rights movement at the center of his analysis of social change in post–World War II America. My own essay on the Civil War era argues not only that slavery and emancipation were the central issues in the sectional crisis but that blacks were active agents in shaping the era's history.

Women's history, too, has forced historians not simply to compensate for their previous neglect of one-half of the population but to rethink some of their basic premises. John Murrin explains why the study of family structure is essential to an understanding of colonial society. Linda Kerber delineates how the American Revolution affected prevailing definitions of "manhood" and "womanhood" and how patriarchy itself was restructured as a result of the revolutionary crisis. Leon Fink emphasizes the obvious but long-ignored fact that women have always been part of the country's labor history. Sean Wilentz shows that a key result of economic changes in the Jacksonian era was an ideological division between the public sphere of men and the private sphere of women. And Richard McCormick deals with the Women's Christian Temperance Union and the settlement houses not simply as women's organizations but as exemplars of the kinds of organizations that arose in response to the changes affecting all aspects of late nineteenth-century American life.

Many of the essays also demonstrate the impact of new methods on recent historical study. John Murrin shows how historical demography has yielded a new estimate of the human toll exacted by the colonization of the New World and how epidemiology affects our understanding of the decimation of the hemisphere's original inhabitants. Alice Kessler-Harris outlines the ways in which the "new empiricism" of statistical analysis has helped shape developments in social history. Richard McCormick and Alan Brinkley assess the impact of modernization theory on the study of both the pre– and post–World War I periods.

Despite the apparent ascendancy of social history, these essays do not lend credence to recent complaints that historians are no longer concerned with politics, economics, the Constitution, and intellectual history. Such traditional concerns appear in virtually every essay, although often in forms that earlier historians might find unrecognizable. The old "presidential synthesis"—which understood the evolution of American society chiefly via presidential elections and administrations—is dead (and not lamented). And "politics" now means much more than the activities of party leaders. Some essays devote attention to the broad political culture or "public life" of a particular era; others stress the role of the state itself in American history and the ways various groups have tried to use it for their own purposes. My essay examines the significance of changes in the Constitution and the structure of federalism during the Civil War and Reconstruction (a "traditional" concern) and finds that the mobilization of the black community helped to establish the period's political agenda (a "new" perspective, although one anticipated a half-century ago in W. E. B. Du Bois's monumental *Black Reconstruction in America*).

Other contributors also accord political and intellectual developments a central place. Linda Kerber devotes considerable attention to the political culture of the generation of colonists who made the American Revolution. Sean Wilentz places ideological and political conflicts at the center of his analysis of the Jacksonian era. James Shenton explores the effect of persistent ethnic loyalties and the tensions spawned by immigration on American political alignments. Alan Brinkley discusses the New Deal within the context of the constraints imposed on government by the nature of America's political and economic institutions, and the general impact of the period on the evolution of the American state. And Walter LaFeber shows how the Constitution has helped to shape the evolution of American foreign policy.

Many historians have lamented of late the failure of the current generation of scholars to produce a modern "synthesis" of the American past. Older synthetic interpretations, ranging from Frederick Jackson Turner's frontier thesis to the consensus view of the 1950s, have been shattered, but no new one has emerged to fill the void. Indeed, the very diversity of the "new histories" and the portrait of America they have created seem to have fragmented historical scholarship and impeded the attempt to create a coherent new vision of the national experience. Several of the essays echo this concern, but there is sufficient similarity in their approaches and interpretations to suggest that the fragmentation of historical study may have been overstated. If the essays do not, and by their very nature cannot, produce the widely called-for new synthesis, several do point in that direction. Sean Wilentz, for example, suggests that the social, political, and economic history of Jacksonian America can be integrated into a coherent whole by placing the market revolution at the center of the account. McCormick demonstrates that "public life" can be a flexible, imaginative concept, capable of integrating a variety of social, economic, and political developments.

Taken together, these essays leave the impression that American history is a field of remarkable diversity and vitality. Its practitioners continue to grapple with the most pressing issues and persistent themes of our national experience: definitions of liberty and equality, causes of social change, the exercise of political power. Today, popular knowledge—or lack of knowledge—of the nation's past has once again become a subject of intense public discussion. Certainly, the more all of us—students, teachers, and other citizens—know of our national experience, the better. But as these essays illustrate, American history at its best remains not simply a collection of facts, not a politically sanctioned listing of indisputable "truths," but an ongoing mode of collective self-discovery about the nature of our society.

ERIC FONER
Columbia University

Part I
Eras
of the
American
Past

1

■ BENEFICIARIES OF CATASTROPHE: THE ENGLISH COLONIES IN AMERICA

John M. Murrin

MOST AMERICANS REGARD OUR COLONIAL ERA AS A HEROIC PERIOD. BOLD MEN and women, often fired by a sense of divine mission or by a quest for a fuller and juster life than Europe could offer, braved the severities of an Atlantic crossing, attacked the "howling wilderness," erected their tiny settlements, established large and thriving families, and somehow still found time to create the free institutions that remain even today the basis for our democratic society. Eighteenth-century Europeans saw things differently. The generation that witnessed the American Revolution also debated the moral significance of the discovery of the Americas and the establishment of European trade and settlement in both the East and West Indies. Abbé Guillaume Thomas François Raynal in France and William Robertson in Scotland found little to praise and much to condemn. "I dare to state it," agreed Joseph Mandrillon, a minor philosophe, "the discovery of America was an evil. Never can the advantages it brought about (no matter how one considers or depicts them) compensate for the harm it has caused." To educated and thoughtful Europeans, the opening of the Americas seemed one of the greatest moral monstrosities of all time.

The philosophes estimated that the conquest and settlement of the Americas cost the lives of 20 million people, most of them Amerindians.

3

They admitted that the process led to swift improvements in mapmaking, shipbuilding, navigational techniques, and related skills and that it certainly quickened the pace of European commerce. But, they insisted, most of these positive assets were used only to exchange vices between the hemispheres. Europeans carried greed and cruelty, slaves and enslavement, disease and death to the Americas. They brought back syphilis, gold and silver to fuel inflation and an interminable cycle of destructive wars, and such products as tobacco and sugar to undermine the health of people who never even got close to the New World. Early America was a catastrophe—a horror story, not an epic.

America's revolutionary leaders—such as Benjamin Franklin and Thomas Jefferson, who both served the new republic as ministers to the court of Louis XVI—resented these arguments and the related claim that the environment of the New World was so enfeebling that, over time, it caused all forms of life to degenerate. American plants and animals had less variety and vitality than those of Europe, Asia, or Africa, insisted most careful observers, who were particularly struck by the paucity of large mammals in the Western Hemisphere. Humans who moved to the Americas would surely inflict the same degeneracy upon their descendants, the philosophes warned. Jefferson once met this criticism by persuading a friend to ship a moose to France as a typical example of an American deer. But European sentiment was already beginning to shift by then. Many philosophes readily conceded that the American Revolution might herald a daring new departure for all mankind. Its message of liberty and equality, constitutionalism married to popular sovereignty, reverberated throughout much of Europe. Indeed, the success of the Revolution ended the debate over whether America was a hideous mistake, or at least banished that perception to what is now the Third World. Even historians usually regard this controversy as more amusing than instructive.

Until recently, American colonial history recounted the activities of Europeans in America: the institutions they established, the liberties they fought to secure, the ideas they propounded about God, man, and society. But since the 1960s, as in other fields of American history, scholars have turned to large problems of social history. Who were the settlers? Where did they come from? What sort of communities did they struggle to create? Who was here when they arrived? Where did the colonists get their slaves? What happened when these very different cultures came together?

Research in elementary numbers during the 1970s and 1980s ought to revive the Enlightenment controversy about early America. Reasonable estimates now exist for the flow of people across the Atlantic, including the volume of the African slave trade from the fifteenth through the nineteenth century. Some of the most imaginative scholarship of the past generation has gone into reconstructing the approximate size of the pre-Columbian Indian population in several major portions of the Americas, a necessary prelude to measuring the impact of European intrusion. Together these materials tell a story a good deal more dismal than even the philosophes had quite imagined.

The figure of 20 million dead falls far short of the true total, which was at least double and perhaps triple that number. Of course, many Europeans on both the eastern and western shores of the Atlantic benefited immensely from the settlement process. Most actors on all sides of the transatlantic drama made rational choices in their own best interests, including even enslaved Africans, once they understood what few options they still retained. But using the elementary utilitarian criterion of the greatest good for the greatest number as a crude but revealing way of assessing the overall process, nobody can now make a compelling case that the settlement of the Americas was a net benefit to mankind until sometime in the nineteenth century. In aggregate terms, losers far outnumbered winners until then. Unlike the philosophes, today's historians see what happened in early America not as a moralistic melodrama but as a tragedy of such huge proportions that no one's imagination can easily encompass it all. The truest villains were microbes, whose predations acquired an inevitable momentum that quickly made human motivation all but irrelevant for the deadliest part of the process.

Before 1820 nearly 12 million people crossed the Atlantic from Europe and Africa to the Caribbean, North America, and South America (Table 1). The overwhelming majority, more than 8 million, came against their will—in chains. Africans constituted over two-thirds of the entire migration. And to the 8 million who arrived in the Americas must be added several millions more who died on the cruel middle passage across the Atlantic or in wars of enslavement within Africa. Only in the period between 1820 and 1840 would the number of free passengers landing in the Americas catch up with and then decisively surpass the volume of the Atlantic slave trade. For more than three centuries, in other words, the slave trade was no unfortunate excess on the periphery of free migration. It was the norm.

The situation was less extreme in the English colonies, at least on the mainland, than elsewhere. About 380,000 people left the British Isles for England's North American and Caribbean colonies before 1700. A huge majority came from England and Wales, not Scotland or Ireland. They were joined by 10,000 to 15,000 other Europeans, mostly from the Netherlands and France. During the seventeenth century almost 350,000 slaves, or about 47 percent of the people crossing the Atlantic to the

TABLE 1
Migration Stream to the Americas, 1492–1920

European settlers
    To Spanish and Portuguese colonies ... 1.3 million
    To British America ... 1.9 million
    To other European colonies in the Americas ... 0.3 million
        Total Europeans ... 3.5 million

African slave imports to all European colonies in the Americas before ... 8+ million
  Anglo-American abolition of the slave trade in 1808

Overall pattern: Africans = 70% of total; settlers = 30%

English colonies, left Africa to provide coerced labor for these new societies. Three-fourths of the entire human wave went to the West Indies, which attracted over 220,000 settlers (roughly 56 percent of the Europeans) and nearly 320,000 slaves (about 91 percent of the Africans). The Chesapeake colonies drew nearly 120,000 settlers (32 percent) and over 20,000 slaves (7 percent). The Middle Atlantic region claimed a net of some 20,000 colonists (just over 5 percent) and a few thousand slaves. After subtracting outmigrants, probably fewer than 20,000 Europeans and an insignificant trickle of Africans went to New England.

Patterns changed during the eighteenth century. The African slave trade hit its all-time peak as over 6.1 million people were dragged aboard ships headed for the Americas—nearly 45 percent of them traveling on British or North American vessels. Losses in transit probably approached or exceeded 20 percent until at least midcentury but improved somewhat after that. Africans were not the only unwilling migrants. Between 1718 and 1775 Great Britain shipped 50,000 convicts to North America, most of them to Maryland or Virginia.

Recent estimates indicate that over 150,000 Europeans entered the mainland colonies from 1700 to 1760, fairly close to the probable minimum of 180,000 slaves imported during the same period. Most of the voluntary immigrants came from new sources in the eighteenth century. Between 1700 and 1760 nearly 60,000 Germans and more than 30,000 Irish settlers and servants sailed for the Delaware Valley alone. Thousands of others—Irish, Scottish, English, and German—landed in New York, the Chesapeake, and the lower South. London registration records indicate that the British capital continued to send perhaps 800 indentured servants a year to the colonies from 1718 to 1759. No doubt the capital and the home counties provided other migrants as well. Northern England probably contributed a sizable (as yet untabulated) stream.

After the fall of New France in 1760, immigration exploded: 55,000 Irish, 40,000 Scots, 30,000 English, 12,000 Germans, and 84,500 Africans swarmed into North America. Totaling more than 220,000 people, the newcomers equaled nearly a seventh of the total population of just under 1.6 million people in the mainland colonies in 1760. Their story—where they came from, how they got to America, and where they went after they arrived—has been marvelously told in Bernard Bailyn's Pulitzer Prize–winning study, *Voyagers to the West* (1986). The typical colonist from southern England was an unmarried male in his teens or early twenties who often possessed artisanal skills and brought with him a set of optimistic expectations. He was most likely to settle in Virginia or Maryland, and he probably left home because of the pull of the New World, not out of exasperation with England. The characteristic emigré from north Britain (Ulster, Scotland, and northern England) sailed to America as part of an intact family. The head of the household was typically in his thirties, was frequently a farmer, and carried bitter memories of the social environment he was leaving—heavy taxes, rack-renting landlords, and unemployment or underemployment. He usually led his family to Pennsylvania, New York, or North Carolina.

Statistically, the British colonial world as a whole approximated the dismal norm set by other Atlantic empires in the eighteenth century. Over 1.5 million enslaved Africans crossed the ocean to British colonies in the West Indies and North America, outnumbering by three to one the half million free migrants who sailed for the same provinces. In the islands, however, slave imports overwhelmed free immigrants by about ten to one. On the mainland, slaves probably outnumbered other newcomers in most decades between 1700 and 1760, but for the continent and the century as a whole, free migrants exceeded slaves by a margin of roughly four to three over the entire period, with most of the edge for voluntary migrants coming after 1760.

Settlers and slaves carried with them microbes that were far more deadly than muskets and cannon to Indian peoples with virtually no immunities to smallpox, measles, and even simple bronchial infections. The result was the greatest known demographic catastrophe in the history of the world, a population loss that usually reached or exceeded 90 percent in any given region within a century of contact with the invaders. In warm coastal areas such as the West Indies and much of Brazil, it sometimes approached complete extinction in a much shorter time. By Russell Thornton's careful estimates, the pre-Columbian population of the Americas exceeded 70 million, or about one-seventh of the 500 million people then inhabiting the globe. High estimates for the Americas run to double this number, and low estimates to about 50 million. Mexico probably had more than 15 million when Hernán

Cortés arrived in 1519, Peru between 8 million and 12 million, the Caribbean several millions, the continent north of the Rio Grande close to 8 million (with about 5.7 million in what is now the lower forty-eight states), Brazil over 3 million, and the rest of South America several millions more. By comparison, Europe west of the Urals probably had about 55 million people in 1500—living, to be sure, in a much smaller geographical area. The Indian population of 1492 thus outnumbered all European immigrants to 1820 by a ratio of perhaps fifteen or twenty to one, and all Africans who arrived by at least six and perhaps even nine to one.

Disease demolished these numerical advantages. The Carib Indians had virtually disappeared from the Greater Antilles by 1550. Mexico's 15 million had plummeted to 730,000 by 1620, and Peru's 10 million to 600,000. The Americas were never a "virgin land"; in Francis Jennings's melancholy but telling phrase, they became a "widowed land." By the mid-eighteenth century, Europeans outnumbered Africans except in Brazil, the West Indies, and South Carolina, but nearly everywhere south of Pennsylvania (except in Mexico and a few other locations that did not rely heavily on African slavery) blacks outnumbered Indians within regions of European settlement.

Interaction among the three cultures was extensive. The plants and animals of the Western Hemisphere seemed so strange to Europeans that without knowledgeable occupants to tell them what was edible and how it could be prepared, the intruders would have found far greater difficulty in surviving. The first explorers or settlers to arrive in a region, for instance, nearly always had to barter for food. Indian trails showed them the easiest ways to get from one place to another and where to portage streams and rivers. Indian canoes and snowshoes displayed an ingenuity and utility that Europeans quickly borrowed. Settlers also learned from their slaves. Africans, for example, may well have taught South Carolina planters how to cultivate rice. From their masters, in turn, Africans acquired knowledge of the prevailing European language and, more slowly, Christian convictions. Catholicism also spread to Africa in the fifteenth and sixteenth centuries, especially to the Kingdom of the Kongo where the ruling elite was converted by Portuguese missionaries. By contrast, very few Africans in either hemisphere embraced any form of Protestantism before the late eighteenth century.

For their part, Indians greatly valued firearms whenever they could get them. Those who acquired them early, such as the Iroquois, won huge advantages over neighboring nations. Indian women quickly discovered the benefits of European pots, and soon iron pots as well as textiles found a steady Indian market. Alcohol established an insatiable demand. Almost by itself, it committed Indian men to active participation in the fur trade. It also exacted a fierce toll from peoples who had no prior cultural experience with its intoxicating powers.

Yet Indian society had many built-in immunities to European influences. Although most Indian peoples in North America were agricultural, they also spent part of the year hunting. Their crops gave them a strong attachment to the land but not the European sense of exclusive ownership of individual plots. The need to move every year also prevented Indians from developing large permanent dwellings and necessarily restricted their desire and capacity to consume European goods. Because women erected and controlled the home environment (wigwam, longhouse, tepee, or pueblo in North America), they had no wish to own any more possessions than they were willing to carry from one place to another several times a year. Women also did the routine agricultural labor in Indian societies, a practice that seemed degrading to male European observers. The consequences of their attitudes were significant: however well intentioned, European efforts to "civilize" the Indians by converting warriors into farmers seldom succeeded, for at the deepest cultural level these demands amounted to nothing less than an attempt to turn men into women. When Indians did copy the agricultural practices of the settlers, slavery often provided a necessary intermediating mechanism. Nineteenth-century Cherokee warriors, for instance, were willing to become planters, provided they could force others—African men and women—to work for them in the fields.

War provided a grisly but frequent point of cultural contact, and perhaps no activity did more to intensify mutual misunderstanding. European geopolitical norms had little resonance among Indians who, like Africans, were far more likely to fight for captives than for territory or trade. Aztecs waged continuous war to provide thousands of sacrifices for their gods every year. Most North American Indians practiced analogous rites but on a much smaller scale, and they were far more likely to keep their prisoners. Indeed, Indians often fought in order to replace losses from death, a phenomenon that anthropologists now call "the mourning war." Epidemics, which utterly demoralized some nations, accelerated warfare among others, such as the Iroquois in the northern or the Catawba in the deep southern region of what is now the United States. As the death toll from imported disease climbed at appalling rates, these Indians waged war to replace their losses. These wars became so ferocious that in the seventeenth century they all but depopulated the huge area between the Great Lakes and the Ohio Valley.

In this process Indian societies proved far more openly assimilationist than European colonies were. The Iroquois, for example, seem to have begun by absorbing such similar peoples as the Hurons and other neighbors who spoke Iroquoian dialects. When that supply ran thin, the

Iroquois turned to Algonquian nations. As early as the 1650s or 1660s, most of the people who claimed to be members of the Five Nations of the Iroquois Confederation had not been born Iroquois. They were adoptees. Only in this way could the confederacy preserve its numbers and its strength.

Even this strategy was failing by the 1690s, when New France provided virtually all of the Iroquois' northern enemies with muskets and gunpowder. Suddenly the price of war became heavier than its benefits. In 1701 the Five Nations chose a policy of neutrality toward both the English and the French, and thereafter they usually confined their wars with other Indians to fighting distant southerly tribes, such as the Catawbas in the Carolina backcountry. As the Iroquois wars ceased in the north, many Algonquian peoples returned to the Great Lakes and the Ohio Valley, where they formed new communities, virtually all of mixed ethnic backgrounds.

During the eighteenth century some Indian communities adopted significant numbers of Europeans and granted them and their descendants full equality with other members of their communities. Women usually decided which captives to adopt and which to execute, often after deliberate torture. Most of those tortured and killed were adult men; most of those adopted were women and children, whether Europeans or other Indians. European women who spent a year or more in captivity quite often made a voluntary choice to remain. This decision baffled and dismayed the European men they left behind, including in many cases a husband and children. Adult male settlers found it inexplicable that "civilized" women, some of whom were even church members in full communion, could actually prefer a "savage" life and would not object to toiling in the fields. In fact, Indian women enjoyed greater respect within their villages than European housewives received from their own communities, and Indian women worked fewer hours and participated more openly in making important decisions, including questions of war and peace. Adoptees shared fully in these benefits; some adopted males even became chiefs.

On the other hand, Indian fondness for torture shocked and enraged most settlers. Warriors took pride in their ability to withstand the most excruciating torments without flinching. The ideal brave chanted defiant war songs or hurled verbal abuse at his tormentors until the end. Captured Europeans did not share these values, and they screamed horribly, wept, and begged for mercy until they finally endured a miserable death. The only major exceptions were Jesuit martyrs, who sang the praises of the Lord and forgave their enemies while dying. This courage made them the most effective missionaries in North America. They alone measured up to Indian standards of masculinity. Nevertheless, Europeans won every major war. From an Indian perspective, the weak were indeed inheriting the earth.

Each European empire formulated its own distinctive Indian policy in North America. Catholic Spain and France poured considerable resources into missions, run mostly by Franciscans in northern New Spain and by Jesuits in New France. By 1630 about 86,000 Pueblo, Apache, and Navajo Indians had been baptized in New Mexico, and by 1650 perhaps 26,000 in Florida. Small garrisons of soldiers protected the missionaries, but the Spanish government actively discouraged trade and refused to sell firearms to Indians. The labor demands and severe discipline of the missions, which included the whipping of adults, touched off a massive uprising among the Pueblos in 1680, the most successful Indian revolt in American history. Spanish missionaries and settlers were either killed or driven from New Mexico for a decade. In Florida the English settlement of South Carolina finally undermined the Spanish missions. The English armed their Indian allies with muskets and attacked the missions between 1702 and 1704, enslaving thousands and dispersing the rest. By the early eighteenth century the Spanish presence in North America was marked more by military garrisons than by thriving missions. Yet Spain tried again to establish a mission frontier in Texas in the 1720s and in California in the 1770s.

In New France commerce gained priority over missions after Louis XIV took charge of the colony in the 1660s, although mission activity remained important throughout the colonial era. Frenchmen journeyed far into the continent to swap brandy, muskets, textiles, and pots for beaver pelts. Because the French were always heavily outnumbered in the interior, they learned that only through careful negotiation could they survive at all, much less prosper. By 1700 they had established what Richard White calls a "middle ground" between the Great Lakes and the Ohio, and they helped to direct the process by which that region was resettled. No society, Indian or European, exercised sovereignty over the middle ground. French diplomacy followed Indian customs and, in effect, established the governor of New France as the supreme alliance chief among the Indian nations of the area. According to Indian traditions, the most powerful chief had to be the most generous. Indian presents cost the French government more than the fur trade could return in profits, but the amicable relations of the middle ground enabled the Algonquians to defeat the Iroquois and hold back the English well into the eighteenth century.

Among the Protestant empires, the Dutch emphasized trade even more than the French did but made no effort to convert Indians. The English were quite willing to trade and, especially in New England, a few of them put great energy into missionizing. But within a few years on either side of 1620, both Virginia and Plymouth decided to make land available to virtually all free adult male settlers. Sooner or later, this policy led to wars of conquest against the Indian inhabitants of the continent. In England only the eldest son was likely to inherit land. In North America, all sons expected land, and all daughters hoped to marry young men of a status equal to that of their own brothers. This quest for land made the English mainland colonies distinctive, and it turned the colonial household into British North America's most important institution. Because nearly every head of a household owned land and enjoyed the "independence" that went with it, he could not easily be forced into doing something that displeased him. Social life, including politics, involved an ethic of voluntarism, or voluntary cooperation in public projects. Even colonial wars were usually fought by short-term volunteers.

The English were accustomed to fighting for trade and territory. Unlike Indians, they showed almost no inclination to capture opponents, adopt them, and assimilate them fully into their culture. Their Indian captives became slaves instead and seldom lived long. Exceptions to this pattern did occur, though rarely as a result of war. On Martha's Vineyard and Nantucket, for instance, most Indians did convert to Protestantism in the seventeenth century, and in the eighteenth—until disease radically reduced their number—many of them went to sea as skilled harpoonists on colonial whaling vessels.

Such examples of peaceful cooperation and borrowing did little to mitigate the ferocity of war when it occurred. Because the settlers regarded themselves as "civilized" and all Indians as "savages," they saw little point in observing their lingering rules of chivalry in these conflicts. Often encumbered in the early years by armor and heavy weapons, they could not keep up with Indian warriors in the forests and were not very skillful at tracking an opponent through dense cover. But they could find the Indians' villages, burn them, and destroy their crops. In early Virginia, New England, and New Netherland, the intruders—not the Indians—introduced the tactic of the deliberate and systematic massacre of a whole community, which usually meant the women, children, and elderly who had been left behind when the warriors took to the forest. The intruders went even further. Often women and children became their targets of choice, as in the Mystic River campaign of 1637 during the Pequot War in New England, when Puritan soldiers ignored a fort manned by warriors to incinerate another a few miles away which was packed with the Pequots' noncombatants. The motive for this kind of warfare was not at all mysterious. It was not genocide in any systematic sense; settlers relied too heavily on Indians to try to get rid of all of them. The real purpose was terror. Outnumbered in a hostile land, Europeans used deliberate terror against one Indian people to send a grim warning to any others nearby. As Virginia's Governor Sir William

Berkeley put it in anticipating a war that never quite happened in 1666, "I thinke it is necessary to Distroy all these Northerne Indians for . . . twill be a great Terror and Example of Instruction to all other Indians." He also proposed selling all women and children as slaves to defray the cost of the expedition. These practices struck Indians as at least as horrible and senseless as torture seemed to the Europeans, but they could be cruelly effective. Until the arrival of pacifist Quakers in the Delaware Valley after 1675, the English colonies were all founded by terrorists.

Americans like to see their history as a chronicle of progress. Indeed it is. Considering how its European phase began, it could only improve. The internal development of the settler communities is a story of growth and innovation. Ordinary free families in the English colonies achieved a level of economic autonomy and well-being difficult to match anywhere else at that time. Starvation, for example, was never a problem after the very early years, but it continued to threaten most other communities around the world. The main reason for the contrast was, of course, the availability of land in North America, which made subsistence relatively simple once the newcomers understood what crops to grow.

Before 1700, however, the human cost was immense for most colonists, and it got much worse for Africans in the eighteenth century, the period in which the Atlantic slave trade peaked. The same principle that liberated Europeans enslaved Africans. Cheap land meant scarce labor, and the coercion of outsiders became the most obvious answer to the shortage. Voluntarism prevailed among householders of roughly comparable autonomy, but force governed relations between masters and their servants or slaves. The quest for material improvement motivated the vast majority of settlers and servants who crossed the ocean, and they had few scruples about depriving outsiders of their liberty in order to achieve their own goals. That is, they did in America what they would not have dared try in Europe; they enslaved other people. Even Puritans and Quakers, driven by powerful religious commitments, found prosperity quite easy to bear. To the extent that they resisted slavery, they acted less from principle than from a dislike of "strangers" who might cause them moral difficulties.

Historians have worked with patience and imagination to reconstruct the community life of English North America. Paying close attention to settler motivation, demography, family structure, community organization, local economy and social values, they have uncovered, not a single "American" colonial experience, but an amazing variety of patterns. Current scholarship is now beginning to link the diversity of colonial North America to specific regional subcultures within the British Isles. In some respects the American environment even intensified these contrasts.

The numbers are striking (see Tables 2 and 3), particularly the contrast between those who came and those who survived. Within the English colonies before 1700, the huge majority of settlers that chose the West Indies over the mainland had become a distinct minority by century's end. The 220,000 Europeans and 320,000 slaves who had sailed for the islands left a total of fewer than 150,000 survivors by 1700, and the preponderance of slaves over free colonists, which already exceeded three to one, grew more overwhelming with each passing year. The 135,000 Europeans and at least 25,000 slaves who had gone to the southern mainland colonies before 1700 had just over 100,000 survivors at that date. By contrast, only 40,000 people had gone to the Middle Atlantic and New England colonies in the seventeenth century, but the survivors and their descendants numbered almost 150,000 by 1700, just over 5,000 of whom were Africans. Founded by some 10 percent of the free migration stream and only 5 or 6 percent of the total number of free and enslaved passengers, the northern colonies by 1700 accounted for considerably more than half of all the European settlers in English North America and the West Indies.

This sudden and quite unexpected expansion of the area of free-labor settlement was the greatest anomaly yet in two centuries of European overseas expansion. The Middle Atlantic colonies in particular, which had gotten off to a slower start than New England, were by 1700 poised to become the fastest-growing region on the continent and probably in the world over the next century and a half. One paradox is

TABLE 2
Migration to British America to 1780
(in thousands)

	Immigrated before 1700	Immigrated 1700–1780	Total	
To West Indies				
From Europe	220	101	321	(19.3%)
From Africa	316	1,029	1,345	(80.7%)
Total	536	1,130	1,666	(100%)
To mainland				
From Europe	175	337	512	(62.9%)
From Africa	28	274	302	(37.1%)
Total	303	611	814	(100%)
To all British America				
From Europe	395	438	833	(33.6%)
From Africa	344	1,303	1,647	(66.4%)
Total	739	1,741	2,480	(100%)

TABLE 3
Pattern of Settlement in the English Colonies to 1700
(in thousands)

	Immigrated before 1700		Settled by 1700	
Europeans				
To West Indies	220	(29.8%)	33	(7.8%)
To the South	135	(18.3%)	104	(24.7%)
To the Mid-Atlantic	20	(2.7%)	51	(12.1%)
To New England	20	(2.7%)	91	(21.6%)
Total Europeans	395	(53.5%)	279	(66.2%)
Africans				
To West Indies	316	(42.8%)	115	(27.3%)
To the South	25	(3.4%)	22	(5.2%)
To the Mid-Atlantic	2	(0.3%)	3	(0.7%)
To New England	1	(0.1%)	2	(0.5%)
Total Africans	344	(46.6%)	142	(33.7%)
Grand total	739	(100.1%)	421	(99.9%)

Note: Percentages do not total 100 because of rounding.

striking. Almost certainly, intense religious motivation was underrepresented among those leaving the British Isles. Puritans (and Quakers later on) were a tiny percentage of the transatlantic migration, but their core-religionists who remained at home were numerous enough to generate a revolution and execute a king between 1640 and 1660. Protestant dissent acquired its power in American life not because of its prominence among the migrants in general but because of the amazing ability of this small number of people to survive and multiply.

These enormous differences in rates of population growth stemmed from patterns of migration, family structure, and general health. Among the colonists, sex ratios tended to get more unbalanced the farther south one went. Men outnumbered women by less than three to two among the first settlers of New England, most of whom arrived as members of organized families. In New Netherland the ratio was two to one, and it was probably somewhat lower in Pennsylvania. Early Maryland and Virginia attracted perhaps six men for every woman, a ratio that fell slowly. Because most Chesapeake women arrived as indentured servants, they were not legally free to marry and bear children until they had completed their terms. Most were in their mid-twenties before they could start to raise legitimate families. Not surprisingly, both the bastardy rate and the percentage of pregnant brides were quite high, cumulatively affecting something like half of all immigrant servant women. In the early West Indies, women were even scarcer, sometimes outnumbered by ten or twenty to one. To move from that situation to all-male buccaneering communities, as in Tortuga and parts of Jamaica in the 1650s and 1660s and in the Bahamas later on, did not require a radical transition.

Life expectancy and rates of natural increase also declined from north to south. The New England population became self-sustaining during the first decade after the founding of Boston in 1630. Immigration virtually ceased after 1641, and for the rest of the colonial period the region exported more people than it imported. Yet its population grew at an explosive rate, from fewer than 20,000 founders to nearly 100,000 descendants (including outmigrants to the middle colonies) in about seventy years. New Netherland entered a similar cycle of rapid natural increase in the 1650s. Early New Jersey townships and Pennsylvania's first farming communities were almost certainly demographically self-sustaining from the decade of their founding between the 1660s and 1680s.

By contrast, the Chesapeake colonies took most of the century to achieve natural growth. Although settled longer than any other part of English North America, Virginia remained a colony dominated by immigrants until the decade after 1700, when native-born men (those born after 1680) finally took charge. Immigrants had already survived childhood diseases in England, but their life expectancy as young adults in the Chesapeake was much lower than that of Englishmen of the same age who stayed behind or those who went to more northerly colonies. Men could expect to live only to about age forty-five in Maryland and Virginia, and women died even sooner, especially if they were exposed to malaria while pregnant. This situation improved slowly as, for example, settlers planted orchards and replaced contaminated drinking water with healthy cider, and as a native-born population with improved immunities gradually replaced the immigrants. In the West Indies, life expectancy may have been as much as five years shorter. From the Chesapeake through the islands, even the men in power were often quite young.

These differences powerfully affected family size and structure. Although New England women married only slightly younger than their English counterparts, they averaged about one or two more pregnancies per marriage, fewer women died in childbirth, and families lost fewer of their children to disease. Thus eighteen of Andover's twenty-nine founding families had at least four sons who survived to age twenty-one, and fourteen of these twenty-nine families had at least four daughters who lived that long. The average age at death for the heads of these households was seventy-two years, and a third of them lived past eighty.

As these settlements matured, power gravitated naturally to their founders, who, as respectable grandfathers, continued to run most towns until the 1670s and even the 1680s. They often retained economic control over adult sons by withholding land titles until their own deaths, by which time their oldest children could be middle-aged or even elderly. They retained religious control, at least in the Massachusetts and New Haven colonies, by tying voting rights to church membership and by insisting on a publicly verified conversion experience before granting that membership. Most ministers and magistrates (the Puritan gentry who administered justice) favored a degree of compromise on this question. What later came to be called the Half-Way Covenant, a measure approved by a New England synod in 1662, encouraged second-generation settlers to have their children baptized even though neither the father nor mother had yet experienced conversion. The parents did have to be orthodox in doctrine and willing to accept the discipline of the church. But lay saints—the grandparents who still numerically dominated most churches—resisted the implementation of this policy. They believed in infant baptism, but only for the children of proven saints. Thus very few people took advantage of the Half-Way Covenant until the founding generation began to die and lose control in the decade after Metacom's (or King Philip's) War (1675–76).

In brief, New England families tended to be patriarchal, authoritarian, and severely disciplined at the same time that the region's adult males were becoming a fairly egalitarian community of aging farmers. Few towns were inclined to tolerate any significant degree of religious nonconformity. Those who could not accept local standards often made their way to Rhode Island, where they explored the difficulties of trying to find some basis for unity other than sheer dissent from someone else's values. It took time.

In the Delaware Valley, Quaker families shared many of the demographic characteristics of New England Puritans, but the family ethos was very different. Far less troubled by the doctrine of original sin, Quakers tried to protect the "innocence" of their numerous youngsters and give them a warm and nurturing environment. This goal included the acquisition of enough property to provide each son with a basis for genuine independence at a fairly young age and each daughter with an early dowry. Quakers amassed more land and built larger and more comfortable houses than either their Anglican neighbors or the New Englanders. Those who failed to achieve these goals had difficulty marrying their children to other Quakers. Poor Quakers lost status within the Society of Friends, but if they married an outsider, as many were forced to do, they were "disowned," or expelled from the meeting.

The colonies created largely by Quakers—the provinces of West

New Jersey and Pennsylvania—were far less authoritarian and patriarchal than those in New England. Quakers did not suppress religious dissent except occasionally within their own midst. As pacifists, they objected to any formal military institutions, and the Pennsylvania government created none until the 1750s. But the governor, who had to deal regularly with a war-making British government, was seldom a Quaker. Non-Quaker governors did not easily win deference or respect from the members of the Society of Friends who continued to dominate the assembly, and who insisted on winning for it a body of privileges that greatly exceeded those claimed even by the British House of Commons, though they seldom converted these powers into actual legislation. Quaker assemblymen were far less interested in making laws than in preventing others from using the powers of government against their constituents. Even the court system existed mostly for the use of non-Quakers, and taxes remained low to nonexistent. Pennsylvania acquired its reputation as the world's best poor man's country while almost abolishing everything that the eighteenth century understood by government—the ability to wage war, collect taxes, pass laws, and, to a lesser extent, to settle disputes and punish crime.

Family structure in the Chesapeake colonies differed greatly from either of these patterns. Unbalanced sex ratios before 1700 and short life expectancy even into the eighteenth century meant that almost no settlers lived to see their grandchildren. Among indentured servants arriving during the seventeenth century, many men never married at all, and others had to wait until their late twenties or thirties. Servant women also married late, but as the native-born population came of age and grew in size, its women married very young, usually in their middle to late teens. A typical seventeenth-century marriage endured only seven or eight years before one of the partners died, often leaving the surviving spouse in charge of the property and thus in a strong position to remarry. Death might also dissolve the second marriage before the oldest child by the first one had reached adulthood. Although the experience was not typical, a child could grow up in one household but by age twenty-one not even be related by blood to the husband and wife then running the household. Under these conditions, Chesapeake families tended to spread their loyalties among broader kinship networks. Uncles, aunts, cousins, and in-laws could make a real difference to an orphan's prospects. Even the local tradition of lavish hospitality to visitors may have derived some of its intensity from these imperatives.

Although the organizers of both Virginia and Maryland believed in a hierarchical and deferential social and political order, demographic realities retarded its development. True dynasties of great planters began to take shape only as the seventeenth century faded into the eighteenth.

The slave population became demographically self-sustaining about a generation later than the European and thereafter multiplied almost as rapidly, a phenomenon that made the American South unique among Europe's overseas empires. Only as this process neared maturity could a planter be reasonably certain of passing on property, prestige, and authority to a lineal son. Not even then was he likely to retain significant power over the lives of his adult children. Until the era of the American Revolution, he was not likely to live long enough.

Yet the men who governed seventeenth-century Virginia achieved considerable success in holding the colony to at least an elementary Anglican loyalty. Maryland, by contrast, officially favored toleration under the Roman Catholic dynasty of the Calvert family (the first three Lords Baltimore), until Anglicans finally gained control in the 1690s and established their church. In the West Indies the Church of England also became an established institution, but contemporary commentators thought that its moral hold on the planters was rather weak. Mostly because sugar was a more lucrative crop than tobacco, while the supply of land was much more limited than on the mainland, extremes of wealth emerged early in the Caribbean. Slavery was already becoming well entrenched by the 1650s, and by the end of the century the richest planters were beginning to flee back to England to live affluently as absentees off their island incomes.

Regional differences extended to ethnicity as well. New England may have been more English than England, a country that had sizable Scottish, Irish, Welsh, French Huguenot, and Dutch Reformed minorities. The Middle Atlantic region was more diverse than England. It threw together most of the peoples of northwestern Europe, who learned, particularly in New York, that every available formula for active government was likely to antagonize one group or another. Pennsylvania's prescription of minimal government for everyone worked better to preserve ethnic peace until war with frontier Indians threatened to tear the province apart between 1754 and 1764. The Chesapeake settlers, while predominantly English in both tidewater and piedmont, contained sizable ethnic minorities from continental Europe and, in the back country, large Scottish, Irish, and German contingents. But after 1700 their most significant minority was African. The southern colonies mixed not just European peoples but newcomers from different continents. Slaves came to constitute about 40 percent of Virginia's population in the late colonial era. In coastal South Carolina, Africans had become a majority of two to one by the 1720s, but not even South Carolina approached the huge African preponderances of the sugar islands.

The economies of these regions also varied from north to south. In somewhat different ways, New England and the Middle Atlantic colonies largely replicated the economies of northern Europe in their urban and rural mixture, their considerable variety of local crafts, and their reliance on either fish or cereal crops as a major export. Within the Atlantic colonial world these free-labor societies were unique, but they could not have sustained themselves without extensive trade with the more typical staple colonies to the south. New Englanders learned as early as the 1640s that they needed the islands to sustain their own economy, a process that would eventually draw Rhode Islanders into the slave trade in a major way. Tobacco, rice, and sugar—all grown by forms of unfree labor—shaped Chesapeake, South Carolina, and Caribbean society in profound, almost deterministic ways.

In effect, then, the colonists sorted themselves into a broad spectrum of settlement with striking and measurable differences between one region and its neighbors. All retained major portions of their English heritage and discarded others, but what one region kept, another often scorned. David Hackett Fischer traces this early American regionalism to its origins in British regional differences. East Anglia and other counties on the east coast of England gave New England their linguistic peculiarities, vernacular architecture, religious intensity, and other folkways as diverse as child-naming patterns and local cuisine. Tobacco and slaves aside, the distinctive features of Chesapeake society derived in a similar way from the disproportionate recruitment of planter gentry from England's southern counties. The Delaware Valley, by contrast, drew its folkways from the midland and northern counties and the contiguous portions of Wales that gave shape to the Quaker movement. Beginning about 1718 the American backcountry from New York south took most of its social character from the people of north Britain: the fifteen Ulster, Scottish, and north English counties that faced each other around the Irish Sea and shared both numerous cultural affinities and deep-seated hostilities. These people were used to border wars, and they brought their expectations to the American frontier, where they killed Indians—including peaceful Christian Indians—with a zeal that shocked other settlers, particularly the Quakers.

These contrasts affected not only demographic and economic patterns and an extensive list of major folkways but also religion and government. England contained both an established church and eloquent advocates for broad toleration, mostly among the dissenting population. By the end of the seventeenth century, toleration for Protestants had finally became official policy, and England emerged as one of the most pluralistic societies in Christendom. All these tendencies crossed the ocean, but they clustered differently in particular colonies. Until the middle of the eighteenth century most colonies were more uniform in religion and, certainly in formal policy and often in practice as well, more repressive than the mother country. By 1710 the Church of England had become officially established from Maryland south through the islands, but Virginia was less willing than England to tolerate dissent. In New England, by contrast, England's dissenters became the established church, and the Anglican Church had to fight hard and occasionally share an awkward alliance with Quaker and Baptist dissenters to win any kind of official toleration. But in Rhode Island, Pennsylvania, and for most purposes the entire mid-Atlantic region, the triumph of toleration meant death for an officially established church. Only in the aftermath of the Great Awakening of the 1730s and 1740s did pluralism and toleration take firm hold throughout the entire continent.

Provincial governments also varied along the spectrum. Corporate forms predominated in seventeenth-century New England, where virtually all officials were elected and charters—whether officially granted by the crown or unofficially adopted by the settlers—provided genuine antecedents for the written constitutions of the American Revolution. As of about 1670 the rest of the mainland except Virginia had been organized under proprietary forms, devices whereby the Crown bestowed nearly the totality of its regal powers on one or more "lords proprietors," who organized the settlement and, less easily, tried to secure the cooperation of whatever settlers they could attract.

Because the Caribbean was the most viciously contested center of imperial rivalries, the West Indies in the 1660s and 1670s emerged as the proving ground for royal government, a form in which the Crown appointed the governor and the council, a body that both advised the governor and served as the upper house of the legislature. The governor and council appointed the judiciary, and the settlers elected an assembly to join with the council and governor in making laws. Crown efforts to control these societies led by the end of the century to standardized sets of commissions and instructions and to the routine review of provincial legislation and the less frequent hearing of judicial appeals, both by the English Privy Council. These routine procedures, especially as organized under the Board of Trade after 1696, largely defined what royal government was, and they could be exported to or imposed on other settlements as well. But as late as 1678, Virginia remained the only royal colony on the mainland of North America.

The American continents had taken one exceptionally homogeneous people, the Indians (whose genetic similarities were far greater than those of the people of western Europe or even the British Isles) and transformed them over thousands of years into hundreds of distinct linguistic groups and tribal societies. As the emerging spectrum of settlement revealed, the New World was quite capable of doing the same thing to European intruders, whose own ethnic identities were but a few centuries old. The process of settlement could, in other words, create new ethnicities, not just distinct regions. By 1700 it had already magnified a select number of regional differences found within Great Britain. The passage of time seemed likely to drive these young societies farther apart, not closer together. To take a single example, the institution of slavery, although it existed everywhere in at least a rudimentary form, tended to magnify these regional contrasts, not reduce them. The main counterpoise to increasing diversity came not from any commonly shared "American" experience but from the expanding impact of empire. Only through closer and continuous contact with metropolitan England—London culture and the central government—would the colonies become more like one another. After England and Scotland united to form the single Kingdom of Great Britain in 1707, Scots also had a profound impact on the colonies, taking over most of the tobacco trade and contributing greatly to the North American version of Europe's Enlightenment.

During the last half of the seventeenth century, England discovered its colonies. Unlike the Spanish Empire, which subordinated trade to religious and political uniformity, the English government reversed these priorities. Parliament's interest in these tiny settlements derived overwhelmingly from its determination to control their trade, which, from the Restoration of the monarchy in 1660 to the American Revolution, was indeed the most dynamic sector of London's rapidly expanding commerce and thus a major factor in propelling London past Paris as Europe's largest city. Through a series of laws called the Navigation Acts, Parliament confined all trade with the colonies to English shipping (a major benefit to colonial shipbuilders as well), compelled major staple crops (especially tobacco and sugar) to go to Britain before leaving the empire for other markets, and tried to make Britain the source of nearly all nonlocal manufactures consumed in the colonies and the entrepôt for other European or Asian exports shipped to America. Despite ferocious resistance at first, these policies had achieved an extremely high level of compliance by the early eighteenth century. Later attempts to restrict colonial manufacturing and regulate the molasses trade were much less successful.

Crown efforts to assert political control over the colonies arose mostly out of frustration at early attempts to enforce these mercantilistic policies. Virginia had been a royal colony since 1624, but it drew almost no attention from the home government until Nathaniel Bacon's Rebellion of 1676–77 severely threatened the king's very considerable revenues from the tobacco trade. In subsequent years the Privy Council imposed on Virginia the same kind of close oversight that had emerged in the West Indies after 1660. New England attracted London's interest not because of its religious peculiarities—which seemed to sophisticated Londoners both anachronistic and embarrassing—but because it controlled far more shipping than all the rest of the English colonies. Yankee skippers could undermine the Navigation Acts. To destroy that possibility, England revoked the charter of Massachusetts Bay in 1684, merged all the New England colonies into one enlarged Dominion of New England in 1686, added New York and East and West New Jersey to this union in 1688, and tried to govern the whole in an authoritarian manner without an elective assembly. The model for this experiment came from the autocratic proprietary colony of New York under James, Duke of York and brother of King Charles II. The English conquered New Netherland in 1664, renamed it New York, and, except for a brief interlude from 1683 to 1685, the duke governed his province without an elective assembly. When the duke became King James II in 1685, he saw a way of salvaging these faltering efforts by imposing them on a broader constituency.

He got a revolution instead. After William of Orange landed at Torbay in November 1688, drove James from England, and accepted the throne as King William III, Boston and New York copied this example and overturned James's representatives, Sir Edmund Andros and Sir Francis Nicholson, respectively, in the spring of 1689. A few months later, Maryland Protestants overthrew the proprietary government of the Catholic Lord Baltimore. Thereafter, government by elective assembly was no longer in doubt. Massachusetts had to accept a new charter that imposed a royal governor on the province. Although the two leaders of the New York rebellion, Jacob Leisler and Jacob Milborne, were both hanged in 1691, the upheavals of 1689 permanently discredited autocracy in America. By the 1720s the Crown's only other option for effective control, the West Indian model of royal government, had become the norm on the continent as well. Only proprietary Pennsylvania and Maryland (the latter restored to the Calverts in 1716 when the fifth Lord Baltimore converted to Protestantism) and corporate Connecticut and Rhode Island held out from this pattern. Except for Pennsylvania, even they went formally bicameral, and all of them reorganized their court systems along stricter common-law lines. Throughout North America, government was acquiring structural similarities that it had never had in the seventeenth century.

This absorption into empire dramatically altered political culture in North America. The struggles surrounding the Glorious Revolution persuaded most Englishmen that they lived on an oasis of freedom in a global desert of tyranny. Eighteenth-century political ideology emerged as an effort to explain this anomaly and give it a solid historical foundation. In Britain and the colonies everyone in public life affirmed the "Revolution principles" of 1688, which always meant some variant of the triad of liberty, property, and "no popery." Catholics were disfranchised and barred from office. The English gloried in their "mixed and balanced constitution," which prevented any monarch from corrupting a virtuous Parliament. This theme had both "court" (statist) and "country" (antistatist) celebrants and interpreters, and both crossed the ocean to America. Virginia and South Carolina became the purest embodiments of country ideology. They idealized the patriotic role of the truly independent planter-citizen and allowed virtually no holders of profitable public offices to sit in their assemblies. In New Hampshire, Massachusetts, and New York, by contrast, royal success usually depended—as in Great Britain—on the loyal support of a corps of these "placemen" in the lower house. Especially in New England, the governor gained strength from defense needs, which were much greater there than in the Chesapeake colonies. In this environment, country ideology became the creed only of a minority opposition through the 1750s, but its appeal would expand dramatically after 1763, when the entire imperial establishment came to seem a direct threat to provincial liberties instead of a bulwark for defending them.

Other forces also drew the separate parts of the empire closer together in the eighteenth century. Trade with Britain grew enormously. It did not quite keep pace with per capita population growth in the colonies from the 1690s to 1740, but thereafter it expanded even more explosively. Port cities became a dynamic part of the Atlantic cultural world in a way that had simply not been possible in the seventeenth century when New York City, for instance, regularly received only about half a dozen ships from Europe each year. By the mid-eighteenth century, with these arrivals almost daily occurrences, the colonists tended to divide into two distinct blocs: "cosmopolitans," who nurtured strong contacts with the rest of the world, and "localists," who were relatively isolated from such experiences and often suspicious of what outsiders wished to impose on them. This cleavage would powerfully affect the revolutionary generation.

Almost by definition, colonial newspapers reflected cosmopolitan values. They rarely reported local events in any systematic way. Instead they informed their communities what was happening elsewhere, particularly in Europe. The *Boston Newsletter*, established in 1704 by an enterprising postmaster named John Campbell, became America's first successful paper. By the 1720s all the major northern ports had at least one, and by the 1750s three or four newspapers. South Carolina and Virginia each acquired one in the 1730s, and Maryland a decade later.

By the end of the 1760s every colony north of Delaware had also established its own college, but from Delaware south only William and Mary in Virginia provided higher education for the settlers. This difference was symptomatic. On the whole, northern colonies *replicated* the institutional potential of Europe. With New England setting the pace, they trained their own ministers, lawyers, physicians, and master craftsmen. Plantation societies *imported* them instead, even though white per capita wealth was considerably higher from Maryland south. Northern provinces were already becoming modernizing societies capable of internalizing the institutional momentum of the mother country. Southern provinces remained colonies, specialized producers of non-European crops and importers of professionals and craftsmen who could provide necessary services. But all mainland colonies grew at a prodigious rate. In 1700 they had only 250,000 settlers and slaves. That figure topped one million in the 1740s and two million in the late 1760s.

Among large events, both northern and southern colonies shared in the Great Awakening and the final cycle of wars that expelled France from North America. Some historians like to interpret the Awakening— a powerful concentration of evangelical revivals that swept through Britain and the colonies mostly between the mid-1730s and early 1740s—as a direct prelude to the American Revolution, but even though awakened settlers overwhelmingly supported independence in the 1770s, the relationship was never that simple or direct. "Old Lights," or opponents of the revivals, would provide both the loyalists and nearly all of the most conspicuous patriots. At no point in its unfolding did the Awakening seem to pit Britain against America. It divided both.

By 1763 Britain had emerged victorious from its midcentury cycle of wars with France and Spain, struggles that pulled together most of the trends toward imperial integration that had been emerging since the 1670s. When Britain declared war on Spain in 1739, the Spanish empire proved a formidable enemy. Spain repulsed attacks against Cartagena, Havana, and St. Augustine and brought the struggle into the bowels of the British colonies by offering freedom to all slaves who could escape from their British masters and reach Florida. This news triggered the Stono revolt in South Carolina, the largest slave uprising in the history of Britain's mainland colonies. It was led by Catholics from the Kongo who regarded Spain, not Britain, as a beacon of liberty. Spain's message of liberation also contributed to the New York slave conspiracy trials of 1741, which were touched off by a series of suspicious fires, some of which probably had been set deliberately to provide cover for an interracial larceny ring. But the settlers believed they faced a monstrous "popish plot" to free the slaves, kill all the settlers, and turn New York City over to Spain. Before the trials ended, four whites and eighteen blacks were hanged, thirteen blacks were burned alive, and seventy were banished to the West Indies. Some of the victims were black Spanish mariners who had been captured and enslaved by New York privateers. Apparently their real crime was their insistence that they were freemen.

The last of these wars, what Lawrence Henry Gipson called the Great War for the Empire (1754–63), marked the fourth greatest mobilization and the third highest rate of fatality of any American military struggle from then to the present. (Only World War II, the Civil War, and the American Revolution mustered a higher percentage of the population. Only the Civil War and the American Revolution killed a larger proportion of participants.) This time Spain remained neutral until 1762, too late to accomplish anything through intervention. The British Empire did not have to disperse its resources against multiple enemies but could concentrate its overwhelming manpower against New France, which the British colonies outnumbered by more than twenty to one. Despite widespread friction in the first three years of the conflict, no other event could rival that war in the intensity of cooperation it generated between imperial and provincial governments. Both New Light and Old Light preachers saw nothing less than the millennium issuing from the titanic struggle. The result was more prosaic but still as unique as the effort. Great Britain expelled the government of France from North America and took Havana from Spain. In the Peace of Paris of 1763, Britain won control of the entire continent east of the Mississippi except New Orleans, which France ceded to Spain along with the rest of Louisiana west of the great river. Spain ceded Florida to Britain in exchange for Havana.

The war left several ironic legacies. The Empire did not know how to cope with so overwhelming a victory. To North Americans who had participated, the war seemed a powerful vindication of the voluntaristic institutions on which they had relied for their success. To London authorities, it seemed to demonstrate the inability of North Americans to meet their own defense needs even under an appalling emergency. The British answer would be major imperial reforms designed to create a more authoritarian empire, capable of answering its vast obligations whether or not the settlers chose to cooperate.

Neither side noticed another heritage. During the struggle the Indians throughout the northeastern woodlands had shown a novel and intense distaste for shedding one another's blood. The Iroquois ideal of a league of peace among the Six Nations of the Confederacy (the Tuscaroras had joined the original Five Nations in the early eighteenth century) seemed to be spreading throughout the region, fired by universalist religious justifications for resisting all encroachments from the settlers. The Delawares and Shawnees in the upper Ohio Valley provided most of this religious drive for Indian unity, which had a striking impact as early as Pontiac's war of resistance in 1763–64.

As events would show, it was too little, too late. But for the next half-century, this movement inflicted one disaster after another on the settlers and subjected first the empire and then the United States to a rate of defense spending that would have enormous political consequences. Considering the limited resources on which Indian resistance could draw, it was at least as impressive as the effort toward unity undertaken by the thirteen colonies themselves after 1763. It also suggests a final paradox. Without Indian resistance to seal British commitment to imperial reform, there might have been no American Revolution at all.

BIBLIOGRAPHY

Among many general and unspecialized studies available, these titles have been chosen to complement the topics discussed in the text.

The most satisfactory brief surveys of colonial America are Gary B. Nash, *Red, White, and Black: The Peoples of Early America*, 2d ed. (Englewood Cliffs, N.J.: Prentice-Hall, 1982), which emphasizes interracial influences, and Jack P. Greene, *Pursuits of Happiness: The Social Development of Early Modern British Colonies and the Formation of American Culture* (Chapel Hill: University of North Carolina Press, 1988), though it omits Indians entirely. Several collections of essays also provide outstanding introductions to the subject. Jack P. Greene and J. R. Pole, eds., *Colonial British America: Essays in the New History of the Early Modern Era* (Baltimore, Md.: Johns Hopkins University Press, 1984), summarizes current scholarship through the early 1980s on most relevant topics. Stanley N. Katz, John M. Murrin, and Douglas Greenberg, eds., *Colonial America: Essays in Politics and Social Development*, 4th ed. (New York: McGraw-Hill, 1993), collects recent demographic, social, and political studies. Thad W. Tate and David L. Ammerman, eds., *The Chesapeake in the Seventeenth Century: Essays on Anglo-American Society* (Chapel Hill: University of North Carolina Press, 1979); Richard S. Dunn and Mary M. Dunn, eds., *The World of William Penn* (Philadelphia: University of Pennsylvania Press, 1986); and David D. Hall, John M. Murrin, and Thad W. Tate, eds., *Saints and Revolutionaries: Essays on Early American History* (New York: Norton, 1984), stress, respectively but not always exclusively, the Chesapeake, the Delaware Valley, and New England.

Alvin M. Josephy, ed., *America in 1492: The World of the Indian Peoples before the Arrival of Columbus* (New York: Knopf, 1993), provides a strong introduction to pre-Columbian history. Russell Thornton, *American Indian Holocaust and Survival: A Population History since 1492* (Norman: University of Oklahoma Press, 1987), carefully examines Indian demographics. Alfred W. Crosby Jr., *The Columbian Exchange: Biological and Cultural Consequences of 1492* (Westport, Conn.: Greenwood Press, 1972), successfully achieves a global perspective. Philip D.

Curtin, *The Atlantic Slave Trade: A Census* (Madison: University of Wisconsin Press, 1969), has become indispensable. Other studies of the slave trade and its consequences include John Thornton, *Africa and Africans in the Making of the Atlantic World, 1400–1680* (New York: Cambridge University Press, 1992), and Patrick Manning, *Slavery and African Life: Occidental, Oriental, and African Slave Trades* (New York: Cambridge University Press, 1990). Important studies of settler-Indian relations include Francis Jennings, *The Invasion of America: Indians, Colonialism, and the Cant of Conquest* (Chapel Hill: University of North Carolina Press, 1975); Peter C. Mancall, *Deadly Medicine: Indians and Alcohol in Early America* (Ithaca, N.Y.: Cornell University Press, 1995); James W. Axtell, *The Invasion Within: The Contest of Cultures in North America* (New York: Oxford University Press, 1985); William Cronon, *Changes in the Land: Indians, Colonists, and the Ecology of New England* (New York: Hill & Wang, 1983); Daniel K. Richter, *The Ordeal of the Longhouse: The Peoples of the Iroquois League in the Era of European Colonization* (Chapel Hill: University of North Carolina Press, 1992); Matthew Dennis, *Cultivating a Landscape of Peace: Iroquois-European Encounters in Seventeenth-Century America* (Ithaca, N.Y.: Cornell University Press, 1993); Patrick M. Malone, *The Skulking Way of War: Technology and Tactics among the New England Indians* (New York: Madison Books, 1991); and James H. Merrell, *The Indians' New World: Catawbas and Their Neighbors from European Contact through the Era of Removal* (Chapel Hill: University of North Carolina Press, 1989). A good introduction to the Enlightenment debate on America is Henry Steele Commager and Elmo Giordanetti, eds., *Was America a Mistake? An Eighteenth-Century Controversy* (New York: Harper & Row, 1967).

Bernard Bailyn, *The Peopling of British North America: An Introduction* (New York: Knopf, 1985), provides a broad overview, but only his *Voyagers to the West: A Passage in the Peopling of America on the Eve of the Revolution* (New York: Knopf, 1986), fully reveals both the complexity of the subject and the extraordinary depth of his research. Other studies of migration include A. G. Roeber, *Palatines, Liberty, and Property: German Lutherans in Colonial British America* (Baltimore, Md.: Johns Hopkins University Press, 1993); Aaron S. Fogelman, *Hopeful Journeys: German Immigration, Settlement, and Political Culture in Colonial America, 1717–1775* (Philadelphia: University of Pennsylvania Press, 1996); Jon Butler, *The Huguenots in America: A Refugee People in New World Society* (Cambridge, Mass.: Harvard University Press, 1983); Alan L. Karras, *Sojourners in the Sun: Scottish Migrants in Jamaica and the Chesapeake, 1740–1800* (Ithaca, N.Y.: Cornell University Press, 1992); and A. Roger Ekirch, *Bound for America: The Transportation of British Convicts to the Colonies, 1718–1775* (Oxford: The Clarendon Press, 1987).

Edmund S. Morgan has written the best narrative history of any single colony in *American Slavery, American Freedom: The Ordeal of Colonial Virginia* (New York: Norton, 1975). The most significant recent studies of Chesapeake society are Allan Kulikoff, *Tobacco and Slaves: The Development of Southern Cultures in the Chesapeake, 1680–1800* (Chapel Hill: University of North Carolina Press, 1986); James Horn, *Adapting to a New World: English Society in the Seventeenth-Century Chesapeake* (Chapel Hill: University of North Carolina Press, 1994); and Darrett B. Rutman and Anita H. Rutman, *A Place in Time: Middlesex County, Virginia, 1650–1750* (New York: Norton, 1984). On the deep South, see Peter H. Wood, *Black*

Majority: Negroes in Colonial South Carolina from 1670 through the Stono Rebellion, (New York: Knopf, 1974). For the islands, see Richard S. Dunn, *Sugar and Slaves: The Rise of the Planter Class in the English West Indies, 1624–1713* (Chapel Hill: University of North Carolina Press, 1972).

For colonial New England, the most interesting recent studies are David D. Hall, *Worlds of Wonder, Days of Judgment: Popular Religious Belief in Early New England* (New York: Knopf, 1989); Andrew Delbanco, *The Puritan Ordeal* (Cambridge, Mass.: Harvard University Press, 1989); Virginia DeJohn Anderson, *New England's Generation: The Great Migration and the Formation of Society and Culture in the Seventeenth Century* (New York: Cambridge University Press, 1991); Stephen Innes, *Creating the Commonwealth: The Economic Culture of Puritan New England* (New York: Norton, 1995); Daniel Vickers, *Farmers and Fishermen: Two Centuries of Work in Essex County, Massachusetts, 1630–1830* (Chapel Hill: University of North Carolina Press, 1994); Philip J. Greven, *Four Generations: Population, Land, and Family in Colonial Andover, Massachusetts* (Ithaca, N.Y.: Cornell University Press, 1970); Christine Leigh Heyrman, *Commerce and Culture: The Maritime Communities of Colonial Massachusetts, 1690–1750* (New York: Norton, 1984); and Carol F. Karlsen, *The Devil in the Shape of a Woman: Witchcraft in Colonial New England* (New York: Norton, 1987), an absorbing and innovative study of gender relations that uses witchcraft as a lens.

On New Netherland and New York as a pluralistic society, see Michael Kammen, *Colonial New York: A History* (New York: Scribner, 1975); Joyce D. Goodfriend, *Before the Melting Pot: Society and Culture in Colonial New York City, 1664–1730* (Princeton, N.J.: Princeton University Press, 1992); and Donna Merwick, *Possessing Albany, 1630–1710: The Dutch and English Experiences* (New York: Cambridge University Press, 1990). For an excellent introduction to the Delaware Valley settlements, see Barry Levy, *Quakers and the American Family: British Settlement in the Delaware Valley* (New York: Oxford University Press, 1988). Gary Nash, *Quakers and Politics, 1681–1726* (Princeton, N.J.: Princeton University Press, 1968), is outstanding.

For gender relations in general and the colonial household in particular, see Mary Beth Norton, *Founding Mothers and Fathers: Gendered Power and the Forming of American Society* (New York: Knopf, 1996); Mary M. Schweitzer, *Custom and Contract: Household, Government, and the Economy in Colonial Pennsylvania* (New York: Columbia University Press, 1987); Laurel Thatcher Ulrich, *Good Wives: Images and Reality in the Lives of Women in Northern New England, 1658–1750* (New York: Random House, 1991); Elizabeth Reis, *Damned Women: Sinners and Witches in Early New England* (Ithaca, N.Y.: Cornell University Press, 1997); Cornelia Hughes Dayton, *Women before the Bar: Gender, Law, and Society in Connecticut, 1639–1789* (Chapel Hill: University of North Carolina Press, 1995); and Susan Juster, *Disorderly Women: Sexual Politics and Evangelicalism in Revolutionary New England* (Ithaca, N.Y.: Cornell University Press, 1995).

Three recent studies have vastly improved our understanding of the French and Spanish experiences in North America: Richard White, *The Middle Ground: Indians, Empires, and Republics in the Great Lakes Region, 1650–1815* (New York: Cambridge University Press, 1991); David J. Weber, *The Spanish Frontier in North America* (New Haven, Conn.: Yale University Press, 1992); and Ramón A.

Gutiérrez, *When Jesus Came, the Corn Mothers Went Away: Marriage, Sexuality, and Power in New Mexico, 1500–1846* (Stanford, Calif.: Stanford University Press, 1991). All three recognize that the Indian experience is absolutely central to their story.

On regionalism, see David Hackett Fischer, *Albion's Seed: Four British Folkways in America* (New York: Oxford University Press, 1989). On cultural change, the best recent studies are Richard L. Bushman, *The Refinement of America: Persons, Houses, Cities* (New York: Knopf, 1992); and Charles E. Clark, *The Public Prints: The Newspaper in Anglo-American Culture, 1665–1740* (New York: Oxford University Press, 1994). For the Great Awakening, see Frank J. Lambert, *"Pedlar in Divinity": George Whitefield and the Transatlantic Revivals* (Princeton, N.J.: Princeton University Press, 1994); and Nathan O. Hatch, *The Sacred Cause of Liberty: Republican Thought and the Millennium in Revolutionary New England* (New Haven, Conn.: Yale University Press, 1977). The best introduction to colonial politics remains Bernard Bailyn, *The Origins of American Politics* (New York: Knopf, 1968), although it is now aging. Newer perspectives include Jack P. Greene, *Peripheries and Center: Constitutional Development in the Extended Polities of the British Empire and the United States, 1607–1788* (Athens: University of Georgia Press, 1986), and Alan Tully, *Forming American Politics: Ideals, Interests, and Institutions in Colonial New York and Pennsylvania* (Baltimore, Md.: Johns Hopkins University Press, 1994). For the midcentury wars and upheavals, see T. J. Davis, *A Rumor of Revolt: The "Great Negro Plot" in Colonial New York* (New York: Free Press, 1985), and Lawrence H. Gipson, *The British Empire before the American Revolution*, 15 vols. (New York: Knopf, 1936–70), vols. 6–8. Fred Anderson, *A People's Army: Massachusetts Soldiers and Society in the Seven Years' War* (Chapel Hill: University of North Carolina Press, 1984), is a thoughtful study. On the Indian bid for spiritual renewal, see Gregory E. Dowd, *A Spirited Resistance: The North American Indian Struggle for Unity, 1745–1815* (Baltimore, Md.: Johns Hopkins University Press, 1992).

2

■ THE REVOLUTIONARY GENERATION: IDEOLOGY, POLITICS, AND CULTURE IN THE EARLY REPUBLIC

Linda K. Kerber

THE TALES OF THE REVOLUTIONARY GENERATION ARE AMONG THE CENTRAL LEG-ends of the American community. The midnight ride of Paul Revere, Lexington and Concord, John Hancock signing his name so large that King George could read it without spectacles: these stories have become our basic lessons in citizenship. The founding generation articulated enduring political questions and provided the structures by which we still conduct our political lives. Some of the enduring questions are philosophical: How best can people put limits on power and authority? How can a person be understood to be free and yet at the same time subject to law and to constraint? What is the appropriate relationship between ruler and ruled? Others are historical: Why did the least-taxed people in the Western world make a revolution about a modest increase in taxes? Is the American Revolution best understood as a conservative or a radical upheaval? How did a disparate set of newly independent states stabilize their revolution and create a lasting nation?

At least since 1913, when Charles Beard's *Economic Interpretation of the Constitution* linked support for the Constitution with the Founders' economic self-interest, historians have understood the revolution to have involved class interests as well as political theory. Beard's interpretation was based both on archival research and on his understanding of the politics of his own time; like other Progressives he saw political reality as the clash between special interests on one hand and the people on the other. In the 1950s, however, historians' confidence in Beard's research strategies was undermined. Cold War politics inclined many historians to shift their attention from the struggles within revolutionary society to concerns that Americans of different backgrounds shared. In the last quarter-century, responding in part to the pressing questions of our own time, a new generation of historians have offered their own rich interpretations of the experience of the revolutionary generation. Many of the organizing questions remain the same, but in answering them, the new research has tended to restore *rebellion* to histories of the American Revolution. Historians have stressed the ways in which marginal people—blacks, women, the impoverished—shaped the Revolution and were in turn affected by it. And historians have developed broader conceptualizations of political ideology that permit them to place political theory in an extensive social context. Because much of the new research focuses on narrowly defined aspects of the revolutionary experience, generalizations are hard to make, but one characteristic that unites the recent literature is an appreciation of the unsettled aspects of the society of the early republic, and of the radicalism—both social and intellectual—of the American Revolution.

CHANGING INTERPRETATIONS

American historians of the 1950s (among them Edmund Morgan, Benjamin Wright, and Robert Brown) stressed the Revolution's moderation. It sometimes seemed that there had been no revolutionary generation at all; John P. Roche called the Founders a "reform caucus." In his last major book, Richard Hofstadter pointed out that historians seemed to assume that "somehow the Revolution had to be tamed and naturalized, distinguished from other, more mischievous revolutions." In part, this interpretation emerged inescapably from contemporary evidence. American participants had steadily insisted that the British were the real revolutionaries; the Americans were simply conserving what they had known. Moreover, after the French Revolution (and, later, the Russian) historians could not help being impressed by the Americans' restraint and by the success with which they avoided the cycle of revolution and counterrevolution and continuing violence.

Historians' urge to "tame the Revolution" also reflected their experience of World War II and of subsequent Cold War politics. Encounter with European societies both as enemies and as allies, and the American role in the triumph against Fascism underscored the distinctive stability of American political culture. Cold War politics, especially the desire to repudiate wars of national liberation led by such men as Ho Chi Minh (who claimed to have been inspired by the American example), also encouraged emphasis on the caution and moderation of the American Revolution. Reacting against what they found to be oversimplifications in the work of "Progressive historians" such as Carl Becker and Charles Beard, many writers of the 1950s argued that the themes of class conflict and economic self-interest had been excessively and inappropriately emphasized. More distinctive in American political culture, they argued, were the *limits* of conflict, the wide range of agreement, the moderation that made possible a constitutional consensus.

The neat package fashioned by consensus historians, however, began to come apart almost as soon as John Higham gave the "school" its name in 1962. At least three factors contributed to its demise. First, some historians, notably Merrill Jensen, had continued to work within the Progressive tradition, stressing the volatility of the American political scene and the intensity of class antagonism in the early republic.

Second, the appearance in 1959 of R. R. Palmer's magisterial *Age of the Democratic Revolution*, which stressed the transatlantic nature of the political culture that linked American, French, British, Belgian, and Dutch critics of inherited political systems, undermined the idea of the uniqueness of the American experience. This idea was further weakened by historians, among them Bernard Bailyn and Gordon Wood, who found the roots of American opposition to the Crown in the writing of the British Whig opposition, thus identifying another transatlantic community of resistance to established regimes.

Finally, by the late 1960s the Vietnam War had led many historians to doubt the assumption that American politics was inherently consensual. An early expression of this distrust appeared in the collection *Towards a New Past: Dissenting Essays in American History*, which included Jesse Lemisch's essay "The American Revolution Seen from the Bottom Up." Lemisch called for a view of the revolutionary experience that would be sensitive to the experience of the poor and illiterate, those who did not give speeches, did not write letters and diaries, and were not elected to public office.

The research of the last quarter-century can be distinguished from the work of its postwar predecessors in at least two ways. First, the new scholarship broadens the definition of intellectual history to include not only the ideas of the elite, elaborated in pamphlets, sermons, and books, but also the ideas of ordinary people and the ideologies, or systems of thought, embedded in popular political culture. Second, the new research has reinvigorated the Progressive focus on social conflict between classes and extended it to include the experience not only of rich and poor but of a wide variety of interest groups, marginal communities, and social outsiders. Politics itself was transformed, as Eric Foner has remarked, by "the emergence of mass political participation and the expansion of market relations in the economy and society." Both these trends inspired deep social conflict, exacerbated by political events, which in turn affected the course of the Revolution. Thus, new attention to the intellectual roots and social consequences of the Revolution has been central to the quest for a full and complex portrait of late eighteenth-century American life.[1]

IDEOLOGY

Throughout much of the twentieth century the intellectual history of the early republic was treated separately from the social and political history. Political philosophy was often separated from political experience and regarded instead as part of the history of the Enlightenment (as it was in Carl Becker's book on the ideas of the Declaration of Independence) or the history of law and constitutionalism. Political historians of the 1960s and 1970s argued that ideas and action should not be separated, and that even the illiterate might have highly complex ideas about the appropriate relationship of ruler to ruled or the characteristics of the good society. Recent work has acknowledged that ideas played a central role in the era's history but has demanded that ideas be placed in their full social and political setting.

Republicanism

Thanks to Bernard Bailyn, J.G.A. Pocock, Gordon S. Wood, and numerous other scholars, "republicanism" has emerged as the key to understanding the transatlantic political culture of the late eighteenth century. But "republicanism" is not self-defining. "There is not a single more unintelligible word in the English language than republicanism," John Adams once complained.

American patriots made a revolution in an effort to establish a republic—that is, a government without a king. In a republic, the people retain sovereignty, and the agents of government are accountable—usually by election—to the citizens. Republicanism, scholars used to believe, was simply what monarchism was not: a government that derived its powers from the people and rested intellectually on the image of a social contract freely entered by persons who began "by nature free, equal, and independent of each other." It was long assumed that patriots were most deeply indebted for this outlook to John Locke, especially to the

Second Treatise on Government, in which Locke, writing in the aftermath of England's Glorious Revolution, stressed that legitimate government must be grounded in consent. The classic statement of this understanding was Carl Becker's luminous *Declaration of Independence* (1922). It remained for the revolutionary generation to devise *mechanisms* of consent. Their great contributions to the science of politics were, in R. R. Palmer's words, the concept of "the people as constituent power" and the array of strategies—special constitutional conventions, special ratifying elections—that transformed this idea into practice. They freshly defined the role of the citizen, stressing voluntary and contractual allegiance in return, as James H. Kettner has shown, "for the protection of their fundamental rights." In doing so Americans built on their many years of political experience, especially, as Jack P. Greene argued, in colonial legislatures that had long jealously guarded their privileges against the royal prerogative.

By the 1970s, historians' understanding of republicanism had become considerably more complex—so complex, some thought, as to be almost unintelligible. Historians traced the concept of republicanism from a political vision that had traveled from its invention in ancient Rome to Renaissance Italy and then into the political language of the eighteenth-century English Whig opposition. In this older formulation, republicanism implied more than simply accountable, representative government. It took certain assumptions for granted, among them that the citizen was male, that he was made independent by his control of property, and that he undertook to restrain his passions and selfishness on behalf of the higher interest of the republic. These qualities were the ingredients of "civic virtue," and virtue was understood to be the cement that held the republic together. The integrity of the republican order was fragile, perpetually threatened by corruption. Unlike the Lockean formulations, which stressed individualism, competition, and self-interest, the older variant of republicanism stressed self-sacrifice and self-control in the interest of the common good.

This older version of republicanism had a conservative bias; relying as it did on citizens who controlled property, it restricted active citizenship to the few. It is easy to understand its appeal to the Venetian aristocracy of the sixteenth century and the British country gentry of the eighteenth, and even the Virginia planters.

But a republican understanding of politics could also be a force for change. From the older versions of republican theory the revolutionary generation learned that political corruption could be conquered by civic virtue; they were free to criticize the British upper classes and the political establishment for self-indulgence. They learned from a republican interpretation of history that social change could be controlled. History itself, which had once been thought to be composed of ceaselessly recurring cycles of advance, corruption, and decay, was open to direction, improvement, and progress. Thus, the violent response of Bostonians to the re-invigoration of the customs service in 1763–67, once ascribed primarily to the machinations of Samuel Adams and other "pioneers in propaganda," is now understood to express authentic popular feeling, stemming from a deep and widespread distrust of the corruption of British politics. And the passionate political rhetoric of the era, stretching beyond the revolution into the presidencies of Washington, Adams, and Jefferson, and apparently so out of proportion to many of the actual issues of the day, is now understood to have been inspired by a deeply rooted fear for the fate of that civic virtue essential to the republic's survival.

Republicanism was also related to changing definitions of manhood and womanhood. Along with political ideology, these definitions were reconstructed during the revolutionary era. Although the language usually employed gender-neutral terms, republicanism had different variants for men and for women. It could hardly be otherwise in a culture that had not begun seriously to question the inherited assumption that men and women have different social responsibilities. For men, political institutions—the army, the militia, the state legislatures, the Continental Congress, organizations of artisans—facilitated collective experience. A notable male elite—its patriarchal character encoded in its members' identification as the Founding Fathers—articulated political republicanism and embedded it in successive manifestos and institutions, acting in the name, they said, of all Americans, though they certainly did not formally consult women of any race or class, any black men, or (with rare exceptions) propertyless white men. A political language composed of civic republican terms reserved citizenship for men. It assumed that the sine qua non of citizenship was the independent control of property *and* the ability to bear arms in defense of the republic.

The revolutionary generation nevertheless did devise a variant of republicanism that began to make room for women. In the work of Susanna Haswell Rowson, notably her best-selling novel *Charlotte Temple*, seduction and sexual tyranny are associated with unrepublican behavior; the rake belongs in a monarchy, not a republic. Mercy Otis Warren and Judith Sargent Murray, along with Benjamin Rush and a few other men, claimed for middle-class women of the republic the responsibility of monitoring the behavior of their lovers and husbands, their sons and daughters, in order to guarantee that civic virtue would be sustained in the next generation. Women's private choices as lovers, wives, and mothers were thus understood to have taken on a new element of public obligation. The role of the republican mother was a conservative, stabilizing one, deflecting the radical potential of the revolutionary experience.

But women's consciousness of their civic obligations also meant that old boundaries on their lives were stretched, making room for the questioning of hierarchies both within the family and in the public world. Buttressed by Enlightenment commentary on natural rights and by new definitions of citizenship that stressed voluntary allegiance rather than arms-bearing, republican motherhood could be used effectively by women to claim the independence and self-sufficiency that the Revolution demanded for adult men. "In your new code of laws," Abigail Adams cautioned in a letter, "remember the ladies. . . . Remember all men would be tyrants if they could."

Patriarchy

As Americans enlarged the scope, resonance, and power of republicanism, they simultaneously discounted and weakened the force of patriarchy. In the same letter, Abigail Adams observed, "Do not put such unlimited power into the hands of the Husbands." She had in mind domestic violence as well as domestic hierarchy, and she understood that public and private arrangements were inextricably linked. Colonial Americans lived in a culture that shared with the rest of Western society the assumption that it was natural for communities to be organized along the lines of families consisting of adult men and the people over whom they had power and for whom they had responsibility. These dependents included other adult men, especially sons, all the women in the family, and the apprentices, servants, and slaves, both male and female. Patriarchy was compatible with republicanism; the head of the family represented the family in its relationship to the state.

Yet the American Revolution was preeminently a crisis of authority. A patriarchal family and a democratizing society were discordant; Edwin G. Burrows, Michael Wallace, and Jay Fliegelman have emphasized the challenge the Revolution posed to patriarchal relationships, a challenge dramatically expressed in the excoriation of the father figure of George III in the pages of *Common Sense* and in the ritual pulling down and melting of his statues in the streets.

The men who challenged the patriarchal relationship between king and subject left intact the old law of domestic relations, a system that sustained hierarchy within families and emphasized differences between free women and free men, especially between married women and married men. The tradition rested on the concept of "coverture," the idea that a woman's identity is submerged, or covered, by that of her husband when she marries. The concept is not consistent with republican political theory, but it was sustained nonetheless during the years of the early republic. A married couple became a legal fiction: the pair was a single person with a single will; the will of the pair was always taken to be the same as the real will of the husband. All property possessed by the wife was controlled by her husband, who might use and dispose of it without her consent. Since republican theory emphasized that the right to participate in the management of a political unit was stabilized by the ownership of property, the denial of political rights to women seemed to most men quite logical. By republican logic, the single woman should have met no impediment in the expression of her political choices. In practice, single women could act to protect their property rights, but they were rarely permitted to exercise the political rights that men received when they controlled property. All free men, whatever their race or class, gained legal advantage when they married; few saw any need for reform. Cornelia Dayton has argued that long past the Revolution, the eighteenth century saw the "entranchment of patriarchal authority" in the courts.[2]

Alternatives would not be publicly voiced for nearly a half-century. During those years the pressures of the commercial revolution eroded what few protections the system of coverture provided to women. For example, widows had been entitled to the use of one-third of the lands of which their husbands were possessed at the time of their death, but by the second decade of the nineteenth century, state courts were less likely to prevent men from using in speculative schemes land that had been marked for the "widow's thirds."

Denial of patriarchy infused a popular literature that called on women to assert the right to choose their own husbands and to demand of these men friendship and cooperation within marriage. The "private" roles of wife and mother came to be articulated as having an important political dimension. The republic relied on mothers, it was understood, because it was mothers who socialized the next generation of virtuous citizens.

Many of the first novels written in America, literary critic Cathy Davidson has observed, "emphasized the class, gender, and racial inequities in the new land." Lacking the optimism of Crèvecoeur, Philip Freneau, and Joel Barlow, women novelists such as Susannah Rowson and Hannah Webster Foster stressed the vulnerability of women to seduction and disaster when they tried to act on the "impulses toward independence, action and self-fulfillment" that the ideology of the early republic prescribed for men. The imaginative literature by and addressed to women in the early republic depicted the dangers that awaited them in the new society.

The attack on patriarchy was related to the decline of deferential behavior, a decline frequently lamented by members of the upper class throughout the years of the early republic. David Hackett Fischer and James M. Banner consider the decline of deference to be at once a symptom and a result of the Federalists' waning influence and also of the Democratic-Republicans' growing political success in postwar politics. Historians writing during and after the 1960s were themselves living in a world in which deference was eroding; this perhaps made them sensitive to the extent to which modest changes in daily behavior could be an important index of social change.

EXPERIENCE

As historians have refined their understanding of the ideology of the Revolution, they have also redefined its periodization. Most accounts still begin the story in 1763, when after the Seven Years' War the British reexamined their relationship to empire and redefined the colonists' economic and political obligations. But if we grant John Adams's famous observation that the Revolution began long before the first shot, in the "hearts and minds" of the American people, then it should come as no surprise to find several recent historians looking before 1763 for the moment when Americans began to think of themselves as a distinct people and became restive under English rule. "The roots of the Revolution lay not so much in the changes in British policy as in the changes in American society," writes Gregory Nobles.

The constellations of ideas to which we give the labels of "republicanism" and "patriarchy" arose from and interacted with social, economic, and demographic change. Even had there been no quarrel with England, the last third of the eighteenth century would have been a disorienting time in which to live. Among the rapid changes were accelerating commercial revolution and the early stages of industrialization. A fledgling working class made its appearance. A richer variety of consumer goods became available. Literacy grew markedly; evangelical religious denominations spread; and a startling demographic shift (sometimes called "the demographic transition") took place, resulting in a sharp decrease in average family size accompanied by an apparent, though still not well understood, increase in the frequency of premarital pregnancy.

The transformation of the international economy in the last third of the eighteenth century was deeply unsettling, with implications not only for the economy but for social relations of all kinds. Transatlantic economic relations established in a mercantilist era were bound to undergo severe stress in the wake of the rapid spread of commercial capitalism. It is generally agreed that the standard of living for free white people in the period before the outbreak of hostilities was generally high, perhaps comparable to the average per capita wealth in England, and that, as John McCusker and Russell Menard put it, "the progress of the early British American economy had been sufficient to make independence thinkable by the 1770s."[3] The traditional explanations of the coming of the revolution, which rely on the tension created by the old Navigation Acts and what might be called Britain's unilateral renegotiation of trade relations, remain in place, although historians are likely to stress the modest level of taxation on one hand and the resentment and fears that colonists felt at British interference on the other.

The interaction of changing British politics with a changing colonial economy created severe strains throughout American society. The growth of commerce and the opportunities of empire seriously disrupted a seventeenth-century "corporate" world view, which had assumed that population, money supply, agricultural practice, and forms of business association changed slowly if at all. Historians—among them Kenneth A. Lockridge, Joyce Appleby, and Sean Wilentz—have stressed the eighteenth-century destabilization of the older idea of a corporate community bound together by a web of mutual responsibility and clearly delineated social hierarchies. Economic life was fundamentally reconceptualized and reordered, with a new emphasis on the pursuit of self-interest, heightened expectations of profit, and new market opportunities. The earliest factories for the mass production of textiles—beginning with Samuel Slater's in Pawtucket, Rhode Island, in 1790—employed a work force of women and children and signaled a major shift in employer-employee relations. (In his "Report on Manufactures," 1790, Alexander Hamilton would take for granted the ready availability of impoverished and employable women and children for the first industrial work force.) Corporatist concepts were now challenged by a more individualistic liberalism, which offered a vision of social and economic relations as both free and self-regulating. This new vision was embedded in the "invisible hand" of Adam Smith's *Wealth of Nations* (1776).

The Revolution did not produce an egalitarian economy. One out of five Americans remained enslaved; indentured servitude continued for whites. Recent studies of major cities reveal stunning disparities of wealth *both* before and after the Revolution. In 1800, John Alexander has found, the top 0.5 percent of Philadelphia's taxpayers "owned more in taxable property than the bottom 75%." There has been vigorous disagreement about the extent to which poverty increased before the Revolution and the extent to which immiseration contributed to pre-revolutionary tensions. There is increasing agreement, however, about the seriousness of postwar depression and the slowness of the economy to recover. Evidence of the increased problem of poverty inheres in the development and enlargement of public almshouses in the years of the early republic, and with them the definition of poverty as a permanent civic problem and of the most dependent poor as people vulnerable to institutionalization.

To address these issues of economic change, of wealth and poverty, is in effect to raise anew what is sometimes called the question of "American exceptionalism": that is, the extent to which Americans shared in general trends in the Atlantic world or were insulated from them. Historians have swung back and forth on this matter ever since Frederick Jackson Turner argued in 1893 that free land made America crucially different from Europe. Recent historians, notably Sean Wilentz and Gary Nash, have argued that the commercial revolution and the early stages of the Industrial Revolution undermined traditions of artisan production in somewhat analogous ways on both sides of the Atlantic. Moreover, against the interpretations of consensus historians, who understood the American Revolution primarily as a movement for independence and the creation of republican political institutions, these "neo-Progressive" historians stress social upheaval and the political mobilization of newly politicized groups, "the challenging of gentry control of public affairs, and the proposing of remedies for the social ills that many believed had beset American society." These themes have their counterparts on the European continent from the French Revolution through the upheavals of 1848.

Slavery

The period of the revolutionary generation was a strategic but paradoxical moment in the history of slavery. On one hand, the defense of slavery was shaken in theory by the Revolution's egalitarian principle. "See your Declaration, Americans!!! Do you understand your own language?" demanded David Walker in his powerful *Appeal to the Colored Citizens of the World.*[4] And the institution of slavery was shaken in practice when some blacks served in patriot armies, some fled with the British, and some took advantage of the disruptions of war to shape their own communities. On the other hand, the invention of the cotton gin and the subsequent invigoration of the cotton economy, the opening of the old Southwest to settlement and of the old South to the slave trade until 1808, resulted in an extraordinary *expansion* of slavery in the postwar period. Allan Kulikoff has estimated that at least 250,000 slaves were forcibly moved from the old South to the frontier and at least another 100,000 new slaves were imported during the quarter-century after the Peace of Paris.

The rhetoric of republicanism, with its insistence on the right of self-determination, could not help appearing hypocritical when its advocates denied self-determination to hundreds of thousands of slaves. Indeed, when war came, slaves found that the advocates of "freedom and democracy" offered them little. The British promised more. When the British occupied New York City, they recruited slaves there into their military force as the Black Brigade; they welcomed blacks into the Anglican Church; in 1779 Sir Henry Clinton offered freedom to slaves deserting the "rebells." Lord Dunmore raised an "Ethiopian Regiment" eight hundred strong in Virginia. The British sea-lift of fugitive slaves to Nova Scotia offered the only opportunity in the entire pre–Civil War period for substantial numbers of slave families to escape (both before and after the war, runaways were overwhelmingly men without their children). But fearing to lose the support of slaveholding southern loyalists, the British were only occasionally willing to position themselves as a liberating force. The single major slave rebellion of the revolutionary era was squelched before it could be set in motion. Gerald Mullin, the most careful student of Gabriel Prosser's aborted Conspiracy of 1800, has suggested that it was deeply related to the revolutionary experience. Wartime disruption increased the number of slaves who had experienced life under more than one master and who could therefore make comparisons; it exposed them to language by which they could claim freedom as a right; and it enabled them to dream of getting aid from France in their turn.

Slaves used the war and its aftermath to construct their own freedom by flight to the British, by purchasing other family members out of slavery, or by serving with the patriot army. This last strategy usually but not always resulted in freedom, normally after service was completed. (In Virginia, where slaves were not permitted to join the patriot army, some masters presented slave substitutes to recruiting officers as free men; they assumed that they could reclaim their slaves at the war's end, but in 1783 the Virginia legislature defined such men as free.) Ira Berlin, Gary B. Nash, Philip Morgan, and Jacqueline Jones have begun to delineate the demographic contours of the free black community and its increase through escape, manumission, and purchase, often by other free African Americans. Nash has traced the migration of freed blacks to port cities, especially in the North, which provided economic opportunity for men as mariners and dock workers and for women as domestics. In Philadelphia, Nash has shown, former slaves disdained the names assigned them by their masters, formed a Masonic Lodge, took advantage of what opportunities existed for free schooling, and established independent and substantial churches. Nash also traces a gradual but inexorable narrowing of options for free African Americans in Philadelphia in the two generations following the Revolution.

During the 1780s slavery lost its legal foundations in much of the North. The phrase "all men are born free and equal" was interpreted by the Massachusetts courts as implicitly outlawing slavery.[5] Pennsylvania, Rhode Island, and Connecticut adopted gradual emancipation; New York passed a gradual abolition law in 1799. Since gradual emancipation generally freed the children of slaves, its major impact was delayed for a generation. (In New York, even the children were not freed until they reached the age of twenty-five if female and twenty-eight if male; not until 1827 did a new statute free all blacks still remaining in slavery.) The Northwest Ordinance, one of the last acts of the Continental Congress, forbade slavery in the Northwest Territory. Yet the net effect of these developments was to heighten the social differences between northern society, where slavery was declining, and southern society, where technology and geographic expansion supported the region's "peculiar institution." Manumission was severely constrained in North Carolina in 1777; in 1806 Virginia required all manumitted slaves to leave the state within a year. Congress refused to outlaw slavery in the Mississippi Territory.

Slavery was the most potentially explosive issue at the Constitutional Convention. Northern delegates who hoped for the natural erosion of the slave system settled for the avoidance of the actual term "slave" in the text and for the right to end the slave trade after 1808. A fugitive slave clause embedded in the Constitution, Article IV, section 2, required persons "held to service" to be "delivered up" to those who claimed them if they had fled across state lines. Most important, Article I, section 2, provided that three-fifths of the slave population would be counted for purposes of representation (though not for purposes of taxation, as originally proposed). Thus, slavery and sectional difference were inextricably embedded in the fundamental relationships of the new political order.[6]

Federalists often attacked slavery as an immoral system. They were skeptical of the Louisiana Purchase as an expansion of territory open to slavery, and they generally supported Toussaint L'Ouverture in the democratic insurrection against French rule in Saint-Domingue in 1791. When Thomas Jefferson took office he reversed Federalist policy.

Traditional narratives often dropped the subject of slavery after it was embedded in the Constitution and did not take it up again until 1820, when the Missouri Compromise permitted Maine to enter the Union as a free state if Missouri entered with slavery. But slavery was embedded in American social, economic, and political life throughout the early republic. Gradual manumission laws in some northern states meant that parents might be freed but their children would remain indentured servants until they reached their mid-twenties; this was the experience of Sojourner Truth. Freedom for blacks was not the same as freedom for whites: the Naturalization Law of 1790 welcomed as citizens only free white persons. Although some northern states permitted free black men to vote, they had limitations that did not apply to whites (e.g., in New York, black men had to satisfy a property requirement long after it had been dropped for whites).

Historians of the early republic are increasingly likely to situate U.S. slavery in a transatlantic system that linked the United States with Africa and the Caribbean. A vigorous slave trade persisted for twenty years after the inauguration of the first president. African cultural forms and languages remained vibrant, sustained by the infusion of newly arrived people; the ability to speak languages that owners could not understand sustained ethnic and tribal identities and permitted some intellectual privacy. There remains a journal kept in Arabic by a slave on the Georgia sea islands and preserved by his family. The effort to understand the resistance of enslaved people in the years of the early republic has prompted historians to move past the boundaries of the United States and to consider the northern hemisphere as a whole, tracing former slaves who made their way to Canada under British auspices, or comparing the possibilities of "maroonage"—refugee communities in geographically inaccessible places—on the mainland and the Caribbean islands.

Religious Revival

A generation ago most historians emphasized the secular or deist orientation of the patriots, notably of Samuel Adams, Thomas Jefferson, and Thomas Paine. Now historians are more likely to view deism as exceptional and to stress the religious orientation of most members of the revolutionary generation.

Many historians, notably Alan Heimert, Richard Bushman, and Patricia Bonomi, have argued that the Great Awakening of the 1740s was indispensable to the patterns of thought and behavior that would culminate in the American Revolution. Refusing to take communion in an established church may well have been for many individuals a central psychological experience that made it possible for them to believe there might be other things the state had no right to demand of them. "It was in religious debate," writes Bonomi, "that the colonists refined their understanding of natural rights, which served them so well politically, and sharpened their defense of self-interest, a concept that would underpin the new economic liberalism." Ordinary people might be uncomfortable with the complex language of republicanism but could identify with a biblical language that tapped their sense of identity as a religious and ethical people. Ruth Bloch has traced the rich legacy of millennial thought in America, stressing the extent to which many people understood revolutionary issues as the working out of biblical visions and prophecies. Moreover, so long as the Anglican Church was established by the government with the King of England at its head, political revolution against the king had to be in some measure religious revolution against the church. In areas where the church was solidly entrenched, the inability of local elites to influence high church policy was an increasing source of resentment and contributed to patriot sentiment. "The members of the clergy represented an important source of order and authority. . . . Disorder in the church could easily spread to create a much more general disorder throughout society at large," observes Gregory Nobles. Denominations that were committed to nonviolence, however, like the Society of Friends, could not support the violent disruption of the social order; whether they liked it or not Quakers found themselves aligned with loyalists. Denominations that tended to stress authority and obedience—or individual ministers within more liberal denominations—were gravely discomfited by the rebellion. German Lutherans and many Presbyterians, for example, took a guarded position during the Revolution and watched to see its outcome.

Recognizing the religious orientation of the revolutionary generation has led to a fresh appreciation of the radicalism of the separation of church and state, as expressed in Thomas Jefferson's 1786 "Bill for Establishing Religious Freedom": "Our civil rights have no dependance on our religious opinions. . . . Truth is great and will prevail if left to herself." Leaving to each individual the responsibility for the salvation of the soul was at one end of a spectrum; at the other end was the established church. There were middle-range options, such as the multi-denominational establishment of Massachusetts, in which towns might decide to support a non-Congregational Protestant church. To many patriots, including Patrick Henry, eliminating the established church did not seem the common sense of the matter.

Studies of religious behavior in the early republic increasingly employ gender as an analytical category. Female members of sects and churches often felt and behaved differently from their male coreligionists. An intriguing pamphlet published in 1787, *Women Invited to War*, inveighs against political warfare as a crime against the Creator and calls upon women to join a war against Satan. Recent studies of the Second Great Awakening have stressed that women were already members of churches; the "awakening" occurred when they brought their husbands and children into the church. But as the revitalized churches in their turn sought stability and respectability, they were likely to define women as sources of disruption and instability. Susan Juster has studied gender relations among New England Baptists, finding there "the silencing of women's disorderly voices" and a "tendency to conflate femaleness with deception."

Reading, Writing, and Arithmetic

Simple chronology tells us that the revolutionary era coincided with other major cultural shifts, but it has been difficult to bring these themes together. In the 1980s, historians paid serious attention to long-range patterns of cultural and social change, but they have not yet arrived at a clear summary of how these changes intersected with the political revolution. The years of the early republic were significant for the growth of literacy and the transition to a print culture. An increasingly commercial economy relying on written accounts and contracts meant that more people needed to learn to write and to use arithmetic. Historians of literacy now tend to argue that the availability of print materials—engendering a felt *need* to read, write, and compute in order to carry out one's work, interact with merchants and traders, and connect with society outside one's own family and immediate community—was the most important force for the spread of literacy both in America and in Europe. The establishment of schools *followed* rather than initiated the spread of literacy. The growth of literacy and numeracy seem now to have been due primarily to a commercial revolution that rewarded holders of these skills.

Literacy and numeracy have a psychological dimension as well. The individual who has these skills is less dependent on ministers, teachers, and merchants as sources of information and control. The spread of these abilities therefore may also have contributed to the decline of deferential behavior on which so many contemporary observers remarked. To the extent that these abilities permit control of one's life, they appear to have been factors related to the "demographic transition" that saw a substantial decline in average family size among whites in this period.

Although women's literacy lagged behind that of men of their own race and class, a gradual growth in their ability to read and write meant decreased intellectual dependence on local sources of information such as ministers, parents, and perhaps husbands; they could read broadsides and newspapers for themselves and even subscribe to books and magazines published elsewhere. The literacy gap between white men and white women, substantial in the 1790s, had virtually closed by the time of the national census of 1840, which showed nearly universal literacy among northern whites and no disparity between men and women.[7] Increased access to information interacted with a new understanding of citizenship, which, as we have seen, provided a fresh understanding of the ways in which women were part of the civic community; even the "private" roles of wife and mother came to be articulated as having an important political dimension that required literacy for its fulfillment. Later marriages and the decline of household production, coupled with the increasing availability of consumer goods, made it possible for women to move from teaching only small children to teaching older girls, who as teachers themselves contributed in turn to the expansion of educational activities in the next generation and ultimately made possible the explosion of the common schools in the 1830s.

POLITICS

In recent years, historians have increased the complexity of our vision of the political community of the early republic. Progressive historians were fond of bifurcation: rural/urban, wealthy/impoverished. Consensus historians tended to absorb the vast majority into a middle-class democracy. Introducing more precision leads to multiplicities: "artisans" dissolves into ship carpenters, butchers, barrelmakers, and so on, each group with its own burdens and jealousies. The tenant farmers of upstate New York were a very different political community from the marginal farmers of backcountry South Carolina. The more we know about the disparate microcosms that made up the early republic, the more strenuous seems the challenge the founding generation must have faced in creating a polity of which all could be a part.

Political Mobilization

Following the work of George Rudé on France and Eric Hobsbawm and E. P. Thompson on Great Britain, historians have argued that eighteenth-century crowds were not necessarily irresponsible mobs led by demagogues (as they are portrayed in older works) but rather an essential and surprisingly self-controlled element in the early modern politics of both Europe and America. Before the establishment of regular police, crowds enforced the "moral economy" of the laboring poor, materializing when people felt that community traditions had been disrupted: for example, when merchants charged more than the traditional price for food, or when residents wanted to keep smallpox victims out of town.

Crowd action during the revolutionary era was sustained over an extended period of time and often focused on political and constitutional issues—the Stamp Act, impressment, the landing of tea. These protests expressed an egalitarian ideology and a rejection of deference that would continue to inspire the political demonstrations of the "lower sort" throughout the years of the early republic. Crowd action was generally supported by local elites, which suggests that even the provincial governing class felt itself to be excluded from real power in the imperial system. Women, too, were part of the street crowds; in the 1760s they joined the boycotts of British goods, which were a crucial ingredient of resistance to England.

When the war began, the context of mass resistance shifted from the crowd to the armed forces; many of the participants were surely the same. Military history has traditionally been a stepchild of the profession, the preserve of amateurs on one hand and people with military careers on the other. Recent scholars have shown, however, that military history can deepen our understanding of politics and society. The war itself, in John Shy's words, was "a social process of political education." Men were held in the army less by desperation and fear than by patriotism and commitment. Shy, Charles Royster, and Steven Rosswurm have emphasized the transition from a rebellion undertaken with spontaneity to one sustained by a "pervasive armed organization" in the form of militias and an increasingly professionalized army. It has long been understood that a major reason for the vigor with which conservative authorities squelched both Shays's Rebellion in 1786 and the Whiskey Rebellion in 1794–97 was their fear that having learned to sustain popular militancy, Americans would make it a normal part of life in the new republic. Both rebellions are coming under fresh scrutiny as authentic expressions of popular anger with regressive taxes, deflationary monetary policies, and elite claims of political hegemony.

Despite an antimilitarist tradition and a rhetoric that proclaimed "no standing armies," the national government built a professional army rather than relying on the militia after the Revolution. Federalists used an army against domestic rebellion and against Indian resistance; it became, in James Madison's skeptical words, "a resource for accumulating force in the government." Richard Kohn has traced the development, within twenty-five years, of a military establishment that included fourteen frontier forts, thirteen frigates, and a half-dozen arsenals. Struggle over how the national defense was to be managed became one of the distinguishing features of the debate between Federalists and Jeffersonians, but in the end even the Jeffersonians conceded that relying on the militia—egalitarian and democratic though it might be—risked anarchy and vulnerability. When Jefferson came to power, one of his first acts was to establish a military academy.

Indian Relations

The main use of the army in the early republic was against Indians. Patriot relations with indigenous peoples involved ideology, class, and raw power. The role of Indians in the American Revolution has usually been treated as tangential to the main themes of the war, but this view may be changing. Since the 1970s, historians have come to understand the profound impact that alliance with Britain and subsequent defeat had on tribal cultures, to acknowledge the virtually genocidal aspects of national policy following the Revolution, and to recognize the complexity of political relations between the various tribes and the new national government. Although American Indian history is less developed than the history of other aspects of the revolutionary period, scholars now understand the extent to which federal policy in the early republic was shaped by ambivalence about the future place of indigenous peoples and by resentment of the Indians' ability to maintain control over substantial regions of the new nation, especially the Ohio Valley. Where once historians were likely to assume that Indian cultures were doomed to extinction under the inexorable pressures of "civilization," they are now more likely to emphasize the dynamism of Indian cultures, the vigor of efforts like Tecumseh's to sustain the vitality of Indian alliances, and the military force that would have been required to silence Indian resistance.

As a result, accounts of exploration are ripe for fresh analysis stressing an effort to understand the complexity of Indian societies and the interaction between Indian and white societies. Indians are no longer understood to have been, as James H. Merrell has characterized their description in older texts, " 'scattered' through a 'trackless wilderness,' where—having 'no towns or villages'—they 'roam' across the land."[8] Behavior once explained in terms of Anglo-American social codes can look very different when explanations are sought in the Indians' own terms: James P. Ronda, for example, has pointed out that the willingness of Indian women to make themselves sexually available to the men of the Lewis and Clark expedition must be understood in the context of the understanding of many Plains Indian tribes of "sexual contact as a means of transferring spiritual power from one person to another. . . . In [the Mandan buffalo-calling ceremony] women had intercourse with elderly men, taking the seminal skill of old hunters and passing it on to their husbands. Sex became a kind of conduit for power. In the same way, Arikara women sought sex with Europeans as a way to pass the strength and skill of the outsiders on to their mates. . . . Sex was a means to appropriate that power and place it at their disposal."[9]

The title of Richard White's *The Middle Ground* describes both a place—the Great Lakes region between Lake Erie and the Ohio River—and a process—the negotiation of relations among native peoples, the French, the English, and their Anglo-American successors. Instead of relating simple narratives of conquest, White emphasizes that as long as the British struggled for empire, first against the French and then against the Anglo-Americans, native peoples could engage as parties—sometimes equal, sometimes sought after—in dynamic and complex political and imperial relations. But when the French and English were expelled from the region, the Indians were left to face violent European American settlers. By 1815 the Indians had virtually nothing with which to negotiate; the precarious relations of accommodation were succeeded by the collapse of native cultures before invaders.

White is among many historians who are seeking to give equal attention to all parties when examining the multicultural encounters throughout the West. In this vision, the early republic is deeply embedded in an international imperial struggle. In this vision, it is inappropriate to pay attention only to the thirteen original colonies and their successor states; it becomes important to situate the early republic in an expansive international political context. These historians of the early republic do not wait for regions to become U.S. territories and states before taking up their history. The most eloquent of the new work is by Ramón Gutiérrez. His study of Pueblo Indians, Spanish officials, and the Church in northern New Spain (contemporary New Mexico) show how conquest involved European intervention in the politics of marriage and the shaping of gender relations.

The Federal Constitution

In 1959 R. R. Palmer emphasized the originality of the revolutionary generation's conceptualization of a separation between constitutional law and statutory law, and their invention—with state constitutions as laboratories—of practical strategies by which the theoretical concept of "the people as constituent power" might be put into effect: the constitutional convention chosen independently of the standing legislature, the submission of draft constitutions for popular ratification, the embedding of an amendment process into the text itself. In contrast to Progressive historians, who sharply contrasted the politics of the Articles of Confederation against the Constitution, recent authors have usually emphasized the gradual evolution of the political system of the Confederation as it confronted the practical challenges of the revolutionary situation: waging war, maintaining foreign relations, constructing the states into a unified political entity. Fresh attention is being paid to the great constitutional statement of the Confederation years, the Northwest Ordinance. The immediate purpose of the ordinance was to legitimize settlement in the Ohio region; its larger significance lies in the fact that it offered a regular and genuinely original mode by which new settlements could be absorbed into the republic. From its beginning the United States defined itself as an empire that would expand without colonialism.[10]

Historians writing about the Constitution in recent decades have tended to stress the point that despite their bitter debates, both Federalists and anti-Federalists believed themselves heirs to an authentic republican tradition. Taking this belief seriously has led some historians, notably Gordon Wood, to conclude that the Federalists were without conscious hypocrisy when they took the position that a Bill of Rights was unnecessary, that a truly sovereign people need not worry about the reversion to rulers of rights unclaimed by contract. Other historians have argued that even when anti-Federalists bargained hardest for a Bill of Rights, they never really intended to reject the Constitution. Interpretations such as these reduce the potential for real disagreement and are variations on consensus themes. It is therefore worth emphasizing that in their resistance to the Constitution, in their insistence that there are things that even majorities may not do, anti-Federalists forced the Federalists to confront the need for protection of minority rights, giving to the new political order perhaps its most distinctive and important characteristic.

American society in the years of the early republic—once defined as 1783–1815—is increasingly likely to be understood as a postrevolutionary society. The Constitution was a formula for institutionalizing the Revolution, the development of political parties the practical device by which it was done. Study of what is sometimes called the "first party system" abated in the 1980s, but it was a lively and vigorous field of research in the 1960s and early 1970s. Historians were fascinated by the paradox that a generation of politicians whose rhetoric was infused with a suspicion of political parties was itself responsible for the construction of modern political parties. Indeed, in other times and places it has been normal for the victors in a revolution to define themselves as congruent with the state and to define political opponents as counterrevolutionary. Certainly that happened in France in the 1790s; it has been true in many postcolonial African nations and in the Soviet Union, eastern Europe, and China in the twentieth century. It almost happened in America, too, during the party battles of the 1790s. Jeffersonians defined their opponents as "monarchists"; Federalists called their opponents "seditious."

But the postwar consensus that established the federal Constitution did not unravel into a repeated cycle of revolutions. In the course of several decades of electoral struggle, Americans turned theory into practice, each side learning with great pain how to be an opposition party without becoming a revolutionary one. Instead of dividing into pro- and antirevolutionary factions, American political parties groped toward a theory of legitimate opposition and modern political parties well before it was articulated elsewhere. A wide range of new offices to be filled either by election or by patronage drew new men into politics. Open public voting very slowly gave way to the secret ballot (though it was not firmly established until the 1850s). Property requirements for voting eroded: by 1800, South Carolina, Pennsylvania, New Hampshire, and Delaware had granted the vote to virtually every adult white male taxpayer, and Vermont had granted universal manhood suffrage. Elsewhere the depreciation of paper money meant that many who had once been unable to qualify to vote could now do so; moreover, property requirements were often circumvented by collusion or fraud. It is important to recognize how very slow and spotty this extension was; for decades after the close of the war, property requirements meant that many who had borne arms still could not vote. The Constitution left the qualifications for suffrage open to the states; only as states broadened their suffrage did the national electorate expand.

The founding generation had no word for what we call political parties; in the *Federalist Papers* Madison referred only to factions. But in the last thirty years a substantial number of historians have developed a carefully nuanced picture of the invention of political parties and the way they shaped themselves out of lingering wartime alignments and postwar interest-group politics. One of the richest of these studies is Alfred F. Young's on New York, in which the complex strands of experience and interest that went into shaping Federalists and Democratic-Republicans, not only in New York City but also throughout the state, are sensitively reconstructed.

A "complex economic politics . . . competed with the politics of constitutionalism," John Brooke has written. Brooke, Alan Taylor, and Jean Lee have stressed the severity of the social and economic dislocations resulting from the Revolutionary War and stretching long past it. In backcountry Maine, Taylor traces "the steady erosion of the republic of roughly equal small producers, the republic sought by the American Revolution," and the increasing concentration of wealth; he finds similar trends in upstate New York. Simultaneously Joyce Appleby finds small entrepreneurs seizing opportunities in an expanding market economy. The political economy of the early republic was built out of these competing visions.

Throughout the new nation, political parties were supplemented by an array of voluntary societies, which took up political issues like slavery, social welfare, and women's rights. These societies would become characteristic of the American political scene; among the earliest were manumission societies and female benevolent societies.

CONCLUSION

"Early national America" can now be understood to have been a postrevolutionary society; it had to resolve problems of instability not unlike those that have faced postrevolutionary societies in other times and other places as they emerged from profoundly disruptive struggles. Early national America must also be understood as a society caught in the later stages of a commercial revolution and the early stages of industrialization: a society, that is, in the throes of becoming what we would now call modern. It was a society committed to maintaining slavery and deferential patterns of relations between the races, yet it was also a society developing a radically new political system and at the same time adjusting to new modes of communication, new styles of consumption, new patterns of family relations, and newly negotiated relations between the sexes.

A field of study that may have seemed well-mined in 1960 retained its vitality for the next quarter-century and beyond. The old questions have not been resolved, but their answers seem ever more complex. The least-taxed people in the world made a revolution about a modest increase in taxes in part because they had come to believe that the taxes were a sign of an unhealthy imperial relationship and in part because a complex range of anxieties about their society made them edgy. To a story once told in terms of political officeholders, lawyers, and pamphleteers we have added artisans, farmers, working women, middle-class women, and Indians. We add fears of conspiracy and of inexorable historical cycles, the experiences of slaves and of free blacks.

The revolutionary generation began to write its own history in the books of such contemporaries as David Ramsay and Mercy Otis Warren. Moreover, it left extraordinary resources for those who would write its history—in political pamphlets and printed sermons, in private letters and newspapers, in the archives of legislatures, in the decennial census that it initiated. Perhaps most significantly, by constructing a political system that required constant recourse to a single constitutional text, it ensured that subsequent generations would always feel a need to understand ever more richly the society and context in which that central document was written.

NOTES

1. Alongside the new work another major development in scholarship should be noted: the publication of multivolume editions of the complete writings of many members of the founding generation: Washington, Adams, Jefferson, Madison, Hamilton, Franklin, Jay, and Burr. Because these projects make the content of rare manuscripts readily accessible, accompanied by voice-over commentary from knowledgeable historians and editors, they have been a strong foundation for research and reinterpretation.

2. Cornelia Hughes Dayton, *Women before the Bar: Gender, Law and Society in Connecticut, 1639–1789* (Chapel Hill: University of North Carolina Press, 1995), 67. On the refusal to change the old law of domestic relations, see Linda K. Kerber, "The Paradox of Women's Citizenship in the Early Republic: The Case of *Martin vs. Massachusetts*, 1805," *American Historical Review* 97 (1992): 349–78.

3. John J. McCusker and Russell Menard, *The Economy of British America, 1607–1789* (Chapel Hill: University of North Carolina Press, 1985), 352.

4. Cited in David Brion Davis, *Slavery and Human Progress* (New York: Oxford University Press, 1984), 150.

5. *Commonwealth v. Jennison*, 1783. In the census of 1790 there were no slaves in Boston. The same phrase appears in the Virginia state bill of rights. In 1806 a Virginia slave attempted to claim her freedom by the same logic and actually won her case in a lower court, but the decision was overturned in the state supreme court (*Hudgins v. Wright*, Virginia, Supreme Court of Appeals).

6. The first new slave state, Kentucky, was admitted in 1792.

7. Local differences, however, were important and still require study; literacy was much lower in the South. One of the areas with the highest levels of literacy in the early republic was Chester County, Pennsylvania, where the Quaker influence was strong. "Between 1775 and 1830," writes Joan Jensen, "white women moved from less than 50 percent literacy to complete literacy and black women to 60 percent literacy" (*Loosening the Bonds*, 181).

8. James H. Merrell, "Some Thoughts on Colonial Historians and American Indians," *William and Mary Quarterly* 46 (1989): 96.

9. Ronda, *Lewis and Clark among the Indians*, 63.

10. It is also notable that the Northwest Ordinance required the property of those who died without a will to be distributed to children in equal portions without regard to gender. It recognized and accepted a multicultural civic order by legitimizing French inheritance law already in effect in the region. Drawing on state precedents, it included many of the elements of the Bill of Rights and demanded respectful and fair relations with Indians. The final provision outlawed slavery but ordered inhabitants to return fugitive slaves. Property requirements were provided for both officeholding and suffrage.

BIBLIOGRAPHY

For further reading in the history of the early republic, the following titles are suggested.

Alexander, John K. *Render Them Submissive: Responses to Poverty in Philadelphia, 1760–1800.* Amherst: University of Massachusetts Press, 1980.

Appleby, Joyce O. *Capitalism and a New Social Order: The Republican Vision of the 1790s.* New York: New York University Press, 1984.

———. "The Popular Sources of American Capitalism." *Studies in American Political Development* 9 (1995): 437–57.

Bailyn, Bernard. *The Ideological Origins of the American Revolution.* Cambridge, Mass.: Harvard University Press, 1967.

Banner, James M. *To the Hartford Convention: The Federalists and the Origins of Party Politics in Massachusetts, 1789–1815.* New York: Knopf, 1970.

Beeman, Richard, Stephen Botein, and Edward C. Carter II, eds. *Beyond Confederation: Origins of the Constitution and American National Identity.* Chapel Hill: University of North Carolina Press, 1987.

Berlin, Ira, and Ronald Hoffman, eds. *Slavery and Freedom in the Age of the American Revolution.* Charlottesville: University Press of Virginia, 1983.

Bloch, Ruth H. "The Gendered Meanings of Virtue in Revolutionary America." *Signs* 13 (1987): 37–58.

———. *Visionary Republic: Millennial Themes in American Thought, 1756–1800.* New York: Cambridge University Press, 1985.

Bonomi, Patricia. *Under the Cope of Heaven: Religion, Society, and Politics in Colonial America.* New York: Oxford University Press, 1986.

Breen, T. H. "Narrative of Commercial Life: Consumption, Ideology, and Community on the Eve of the American Revolution." *William and Mary Quarterly,* 3d ser., 50 (1993): 471–501.

Brooke, John L. *The Heart of the Commonwealth: Society and Political Culture in Worcester County, Massachusetts, 1713–1861.* New York: Cambridge University Press, 1989.

Burrows, Edwin G., and Michael Wallace. "The American Revolution: The Ideology and Psychology of National Liberation." *Perspectives in American History* 6 (1972): 167–308.

Bushman, Richard. *From Puritan to Yankee: Character and the Social Order in Connecticut, 1690–1765.* Cambridge: Harvard University Press, 1967.

Cohen, Patricia Cline. *A Calculating People: The Spread of Numeracy in America.* Chicago: University of Chicago Press, 1982.

Cott, Nancy F. "Passionlessness: An Interpretation of Victorian Sexual Ideology, 1790–1850." *Signs* 4 (1978): 219–36.

Countryman, Edward. *A People in Revolution: The American Revolution and Political Society in New York, 1760–1790.* Baltimore, Md.: Johns Hopkins University Press, 1981.

Cunningham, Noble E. *In Pursuit of Reason: The Life of Thomas Jefferson.* Baton Rouge: Louisiana State University Press, 1987.

Dann, John C. *The Revolution Remembered: Eyewitness Accounts of the War for Independence*. Chicago: University of Chicago Press, 1980.

Davidson, Cathy N. *Revolution and the Word: The Rise of the Novel in America*. New York: Oxford University Press, 1986.

Davis, David Brion. *The Problem of Slavery in the Age of Revolution, 1770–1823*. Ithaca, N.Y.: Cornell University Press, 1975. (Includes a useful "Calendar of Events," 23–36.)

Dayton, Cornelia Hughes. *Women before the Bar: Gender, Law and Society in Connecticut, 1639–1789*. Chapel Hill: University of North Carolina Press, 1995.

Ditz, Toby L. "Shipwrecked; or, Masculinity Imperiled: Mercantile Representations of Failure and the Gendered Self in Eighteenth-Century Philadelphia." *Journal of American History* 81 (1994): 51–80.

Elkins, Stanley, and Eric McKitrick. *The Age of Federalism*. New York: Oxford University Press, 1993.

Fischer, David Hackett. *The Revolution of American Conservatism*. New York: Harper & Row, 1965.

Fliegelman, Jay. *Prodigals and Pilgrims: The American Revolution against Patriarchal Authority, 1750–1800*. New York: Cambridge University Press, 1982.

Foner, Eric. *Tom Paine and Revolutionary America*. New York: Oxford University Press, 1976.

Formisano, Ronald. *The Transformation of Political Culture: Massachusetts Parties, 1790s–1840s*. New York: Oxford University Press, 1983.

Frey, Sylvia R. *Water from the Rock: Black Resistance in a Revolutionary Age*. Princeton, N.J.: Princeton University Press, 1991.

Gilje, Paul A. *The Road to Mobocracy: Popular Disorder in New York City, 1763–1834*. Chapel Hill: University of North Carolina Press, 1987.

Gilmore, William. *Reading Becomes a Necessity of Life: Material and Cultural Life in Rural New England, 1780–1835*. Knoxville: University of Tennessee Press, 1989.

Greene, Jack P. *Peripheries and Center: Constitutional Development in the Extended Polities of the British Empire and the United States, 1607–1788*. Athens: University of Georgia Press, 1986.

Gross, Robert. *The Minutemen and Their World*. New York: Hill & Wang, 1976.

Gutiérrez, Ramón A. *When Jesus Came, the Corn Mothers Went Away: Marriage, Sexuality, and Power in New Mexico, 1500–1846*. Stanford, Calif.: Stanford University Press, 1991.

Higham, John. "Beyond Consensus: The Historian as Moral Critic." *American Historical Review* 67 (1962): 609–25.

Hofstadter, Richard. *The Idea of a Party System: The Rise of Legitimate Opposition in the United States, 1780–1840*. Berkeley: University of California Press, 1969.

Isaac, Rhys. *The Transformation of Virginia, 1740–1790*. Chapel Hill: University of North Carolina Press, 1982.

Jensen, Joan M. *Loosening the Bonds: Mid-Atlantic Farm Women, 1750–1850*. New Haven, Conn.: Yale University Press, 1986.

Juster, Susan. *Disorderly Women: Sexual Politics and Evangelicalism in Revolutionary New England*. Ithaca, N.Y.: Cornell University Press, 1994.

Kammen, Michael. *A Machine That Would Go of Itself: The Constitution in American Culture.* New York: Knopf, 1986.

———. *A Season of Youth: The American Revolution and the Historical Imagination.* New York: Knopf, 1978.

Kerber, Linda K. *Federalists in Dissent: Imagery and Ideology in Jeffersonian America.* Ithaca, N.Y.: Cornell University Press, 1970.

———. *Women of the Republic: Intellect and Ideology in Revolutionary America.* Chapel Hill: University of North Carolina Press, 1980.

Kettner, James H. *The Development of American Citizenship, 1608–1870.* Chapel Hill: University of North Carolina Press, 1978.

Kohn, Richard. *Eagle and Sword: The Beginnings of the Military Establishment in America.* New York: Free Press, 1975.

Kulikuff, Allan. *Tobacco and Slaves: The Development of Southern Cultures in the Chesapeake, 1680–1800.* Chapel Hill: University of North Carolina Press, 1986.

Lee, Jean Butenhoff. *The Price of Nationhood: The American Revolution in Charles County.* New York: W. W. Norton 1994.

Lemisch, Jesse. "The American Revolution Seen from the Bottom Up." In Barton J. Bernstein, ed., *Towards a New Past: Dissenting Essays in American History,* 3–45. New York: Knopf, 1968.

———. "Jack Tar in the Streets: Merchant Seamen in the Politics of Revolutionary America." *William and Mary Quarterly,* 3d ser., 25 (1968): 371–407.

Lockridge, Kenneth A. *Literacy in Colonial New England: An Enquiry into the Social Context of Literacy in the Early Modern West.* New York: Norton, 1974.

Maier, Pauline. *The Old Revolutionaries: Political Lives in the Age of Samuel Adams.* New York: Knopf, 1980.

Main, Jackson Turner. *The Social Structure of Revolutionary America.* Princeton, N.J.: Princeton University Press, 1965.

McCoy, Drew. *The Last of the Fathers: James Madison and the Republican Legacy.* New York: Cambridge University Press, 1989.

McDonald, Forrest. *Novus Ordo Seculorum: The Intellectual Origins of the Constitution.* Lawrence: University Press of Kansas, 1985.

Merrell, James H. *The Indians' New World: Catawbas and Their Neighbors from European Contact through the Era of Removal.* Chapel Hill: University of North Carolina Press, 1989.

Middlekauff, Robert. *The Glorious Cause: The American Revolution, 1763–1789.* New York: Oxford University Press, 1982.

Morgan, Philip D. *Cultivation and Culture: Labor and the Shaping of Slave Life in the Americas.* Charlottesville: University Press of Virginia, 1993.

Morris, Richard B. *The Forging of the Union, 1781–1789.* New York: Harper & Row, 1987.

———. *The Peacemakers: The Great Powers and American Independence.* New York: Harper & Row, 1965.

Mullin, Gerald W. *Flight and Rebellion: Slave Resistance in Eighteenth-Century Virginia.* New York: Oxford University Press, 1972.

Mullin, Michael. *Africa in America: Slave Acculturation and Resistance in the American South and the British Caribbean, 1736–1831.* Urbana: University of Illinois Press, 1992.

Nash, Gary B. *Forging Freedom: The Formation of Philadelphia's Black Community, 1720–1840*. Cambridge, Mass.: Harvard University Press, 1988.

————. *The Urban Crucible: Social Change, Political Consciousness, and the Origins of the American Revolution*. Cambridge, Mass.: Harvard University Press, 1979.

Nobles, Gregory H. *Divisions throughout the Whole: Politics and Society in Hampshire County, Massachusetts, 1740–1775*. Cambridge: Cambridge University Press, 1983.

Norton, Mary Beth. *Liberty's Daughters: The Revolutionary Experience of American Women, 1750–1800*. Boston: Little, Brown, 1980.

Onuf, Peter S. "Reflections on the Founding: Constitutional Historiography in Bicentennial Perspective." *William and Mary Quarterly*, 3d ser., 46 (1989): 340–75.

Palmer, R. R. *The Age of the Democratic Revolution: A Political History of Europe and America, 1760–1800*. 2 vols. Princeton, N.J.: Princeton University Press, 1959, 1964.

Pocock, J. G. A. *The Machiavellian Moment: Florentine Republican Thought and the Atlantic Republican Tradition*. Princeton, N.J.: Princeton University Press, 1975.

Quarles, Benjamin. *The Negro in the American Revolution*. Chapel Hill: University of North Carolina Press, 1961.

Rakove, Jack. *The Beginnings of National Politics: An Interpretative History of the Continental Congress*. New York: Knopf, 1979.

Ronda, James P. *Lewis and Clark among the Indians*. Lincoln: University of Nebraska Press, 1984.

Rosswurm, Steven. *Arms, Country, and Class: The Philadelphia Militia and the "Lower Sort" during the American Revolution*. New Brunswick, N.J.: Rutgers University Press, 1987.

Rothman, David J. *The Discovery of the Asylum: Social Order and Disorder in the New Republic*. Boston: Little, Brown, 1971.

Royster, Charles. *A Revolutionary People at War: The Continental Army and the American Character, 1775–1783*. Chapel Hill: University of North Carolina Press, 1979.

Salmon, Marylynn. *Women and the Law of Property in Early America*. Chapel Hill: University of North Carolina Press, 1986.

Shy, John. *A People Numerous and Armed: Reflections on the Military Struggle for American Independence*. New York: Oxford University Press, 1976.

Silverman, Kenneth. *A Cultural History of the American Revolution: Painting, Music, Literature, and the Theatre in the Colonies and the United States from the Treaty of Paris to the Inauguration of George Washington, 1763–1789*. New York: Thomas Y. Crowell, 1976.

Slaughter, Thomas P. *The Whiskey Rebellion: Frontier Epilogue to the American Revolution*. New York: Oxford University Press, 1986.

Smith, Daniel Scott, and Michael Hindus. "Premarital Pregnancy in America, 1640–1971: An Overview and an Interpretation." *Journal of Interdisciplinary History* 5 (1975): 537–70.

Taylor, Alan. *Liberty Men and Great Proprietors: The Revolutionary Settlement on the*

Maine Frontier, 1760–1820. Chapel Hill: University of North Carolina Press for the Institute of Early American History and Culture, 1990.

———. *William Cooper's Town: Power and Persuasion on the Frontier of the Early American Republic.* New York: Knopf, 1995.

Tomlins, Christopher L. *Law, Labor, and Ideology in the Early American Republic.* New York: Cambridge University Press, 1993.

Wallace, Anthony F. C. *The Death and Rebirth of the Seneca.* New York: Knopf, 1969.

White, Richard. *The Middle Ground: Indians, Empires, and Republics in the Great Lakes Region, 1650–1815.* New York: Cambridge University Press, 1991.

Wilentz, Sean. *Chants Democratic: New York City and the Rise of the American Working Class, 1788–1850.* New York: Oxford University Press, 1984.

Wood, Gordon S. *The Creation of the American Republic, 1776–1787.* Chapel Hill: University of North Carolina Press, 1969.

———. *The Radicalism of the American Revolution.* New York: Knopf, 1992.

Young, Alfred F. *The Democratic Republicans of New York: The Origins, 1763–1797.* Chapel Hill: University of North Carolina Press, 1967.

———. "George Robert Twelves Hewes (1742–1840): A Boston Shoemaker and the Memory of the American Revolution." *William and Mary Quarterly,* 3d ser., 38 (1981): 561–623.

3

▚ SOCIETY, POLITICS, AND THE MARKET REVOLUTION, 1815–1848

Sean Wilentz

FOR MANY YEARS, AMERICAN HISTORIANS HAD LITTLE DIFFICULTY FINDING LABELS to describe the period from 1815 to 1848. To some it was the age of Jackson, dominated by Old Hickory and the Democratic party; to others, the era of the common man, a time of sweeping democratic ferment and reform. Today such phrases sound quaint. Two decades' worth of revisionist work has made political historians wary of the old presidential synthesis of American history; less attention is now paid to the specific details of Jacksonian electioneering and policy-making, and more to such broad themes as the changing structure of party organizations and the rise of new political ideologies. Likewise, an outpouring of work by social historians—much of it on groups previously slighted—has dramatically changed basic assumptions about the period and raised new, often disturbing questions: How can the years that brought the rise of the Cotton Kingdom and the spread of slavery reasonably be called the era of the common man? What was the role of women in this phase of American history? Were not at least some of the democratic advances of the time won at the murderous expense of Native Americans?

By exploring these and other issues, recent studies have moved well beyond the familiar chronicles of political and social elites. They have cast serious doubts on those "consensus" interpretations that assumed that nineteenth-century Americans, whatever their differences, shared an attachment to liberal capitalist ideals. Unfortunately, recent work has fragmented our understanding into a host of academic sub-specialties. It has also led, in some instances, to a denigration of formal politics and policy, as if such "traditional" matters as the Bank War or debates over the tariff were unimportant. The job of connecting the pieces—and especially of recombining social and political history—has only just begun. That job is made difficult by persisting scholarly dis-agreements over all sorts of interpretive issues. Still, one theme does seem to unite Jacksonian historians of various persuasions and suggest a way of once again viewing the period as a whole: the central importance of the market revolution, which, in one way or another, touched the lives of all Americans. As part of that revolution there arose new forms of social life, consciousness, and politics. These, in turn, prepared the way for the Civil War.

THE MARKET REVOLUTION

The extraordinary economic changes of the early nineteenth century have never failed to impress historians. Between 1815 and 1850 Ameri-cans constructed elaborate networks of roads, canals, and early railroad lines; opened up wide areas of newly acquired land for settlement and trade; and began to industrialize manufacturing. What had been in Thomas Jefferson's day a backward rural nation on the fringes of world economic development had by midcentury established many of the pre-conditions necessary to its becoming a major economic power.

In the 1950s George Rogers Taylor wrote what remains the author-itative account of these changes and dubbed them, collectively, Amer-ica's "transportation revolution." Since then, historians have done less to challenge Taylor's interpretation than to reexamine some of its impli-cations. Social historians in particular have stressed that economic change radically disrupted existing systems of production and old social hierarchies, replacing them with entirely new opportunities and depen-dencies. Behind the technological and institutional innovations Taylor discussed was a deeper revolution in human relations, linked to the emergence of new markets in land, labor, and produce.

Much of the scholarly work on this market revolution has concen-trated on northeastern cities as key sites of economic development. In-tense mercantile activity there, of course, long antedated 1815. Yet be-tween 1815 and 1850 eastern urban capitalists dramatically accelerated the pace of economic change. Often working hand in hand with state and local governments, these merchant capitalists were at the forefront of transportation improvements and the growth of regional and inter-regional marketing; they made great strides in expanding credit and financing resources and in imposing some order on currency and banking; above all, they hastened the erosion of the old artisan handicraft system and the rise of new manufacturing enterprises.

Compared to later periods in U.S. history, industrial growth between 1815 and 1848 was modest; by 1850, the majority of the nation's population still lived in rural areas and worked in agriculture, while only about 14 percent of the labor force worked in manufacturing. Nevertheless, the rate of industrial growth was impressive, especially in the Northeast. The most spectacular examples of early industrialization were the new textile mills of New England, financed by leading established seaboard merchants. Yet as labor historians have shown, mechanization and factory construction constituted only one of several strategies used to revamp manufacturing. In once bucolic single-industry towns (for example, the shoemaking center, Lynn, Massachusetts) merchant capitalists altered production by dividing up craft skills and putting out as much work as possible to country girls living in outlying rural communities. Entrepreneurs in the major seaboard cities and in newer inland settlements such as Cincinnati likewise divided up artisan crafts and relied on underpaid outworkers—women, children, poor immigrants—to produce work for low piece rates. The deployment of these different methods of production brought a rapid increase in the output of raw materials and finished goods, at lower prices and of a higher quality than Americans had ever enjoyed. Simultaneously, however, the new order disrupted the customary artisan regime of masters, journeymen, and apprentices and left thousands of workers dependent on the caprices of the wage-labor market.

Changes in northeastern manufacturing were closely related to a deepening crisis in northeastern rural life. Traditionally, historians slighted the extent of social change in the American countryside before the Civil War. Although improvements in transportation and increased commercialization obviously enlarged the productive capacity of American agriculture, historians tended to assume that most family farms were small capitalist enterprises from at least the mid-eighteenth century on. Recent scholarship, however, has focused on the variety of social pressures, beginning in the 1750s and continuing through the 1840s, that undermined a distinct way of life, one geared more to barter exchange and quasi-self-sufficiency than to the production of cash crops for market. At first, the major impetus for change was demographic, as the mounting population of the settled rural Northeast began to outstrip the available supply of land, leaving rural patriarchs unable to pass on sufficient acreage to their sons. By 1815 these straitened circumstances had led to a steady decline in family size and to an increase in westward migration; it had also heightened farmers' need for cash to buy additional land, thus encouraging them to shift into cash-crop production. The transportation improvements of the next thirty years facilitated that shift and brought to the countryside (at steadily decreasing prices) manufactured articles previously unavailable in the hinterland. By 1850 the vast majority of northeastern farmers had reorganized their production toward cash crops and were depending on country merchants for household items and farm implements once produced at home.

Few historians would dispute that the market revolution brought substantial material benefits to most northeasterners, urban and rural. But the new abundance was hardly distributed equally. Studies of property holding have confirmed that in small country towns and in large cities alike, a tiny proportion of the northeastern population came to command the bulk of the newly created wealth. Those who benefited most from the market revolution—merchants and manufacturers, lawyers and other professionals, and successful commercial farmers, along with their families—faced life situations very different from those known to earlier generations. The decline of the household as the locus of production led directly to a growing impersonality in the economic realm; household heads, instead of directing family enterprises or small shops, often had to find ways to recruit and discipline a wage-labor force; in all cases, they had to stay abreast of or even surpass their competitors.

Perhaps the most profound set of social changes confronting this new middle class involved the internal dynamics of family life. As Nancy Cott, Mary Ryan, and others have explained, the commercialization of both city and countryside removed women from the production of goods, including goods for strictly household use. The world of the propertied began to separate into two spheres: a male public sphere of politics, business, and the market, and a female private sphere of domestic duties and child rearing. By 1850 a new romantic standard of rights and responsibilities within middle-class families had replaced the more severe patriarchal regime of the eighteenth century—a "cult of domesticity" that vaunted women's supposed moral superiority while it restricted women's place to the home, as wives, mothers, and domestic guardians.

Less fortunate northeasterners faced a very different reality, dominated by the new dependencies created by the market revolution. For those at the bottom—immigrant and black day laborers, outwork seamstresses, the casual poor—a combination of overstocked labor markets and intense competition among employers kept wages and earnings near or below subsistence levels. Even in New England, farm girls who went off to work in factories expecting decent situations and high wages found that mill conditions had deteriorated by the mid-1830s. Those small independent artisans and well-paid craft workers who survived faced the real possibility of falling into similar distress, victimized as they were by an increasingly volatile business cycle and by the downward pressures on earnings and real wages in various important trades. By the 1830s a new working class was beginning to carve out its own identity in a variety of trade unions and in political efforts aimed at redirecting the course and consequences of American economic expansion. Marginal small farmers, their old networks of barter exchange undone, saw their livelihoods threatened by competition from western areas opened by canal development and by the middlemen's downward pressure on prices. To all these people, middle-class respectability and the cult of domesticity meant little when measured against the struggle to achieve or preserve their economic independence—or barring that, simply to make ends meet.

Far less is known about the market revolution's social impact in the Old Northwest and the western territories, although some fine recent work has started to redirect the field. Studies of migration suggest that rural northeasterners who could not make a go of it tried to avoid entering the urban wage-labor market; the largest single supply of urban workers (at least by 1850) consisted of immigrants and their children, among them hundreds of thousands of new arrivals escaping hard times in Ireland and Germany. Native-born rural northeasterners, joined by migrants from the South, headed west instead, most of them hoping to reconstruct the independent yeoman communities that had crumbled back home. Accordingly, they bought up as much cheap western land as they could to ensure that they would be able to provide for their families and their descendants.

This new yeomanry faced numerous obstacles. First, the removal of Native Americans from the land had to be completed; federal and state authorities willingly complied, using fraud and violence as necessary. Once the lands were open, settlers found themselves pitted against speculators eager to convert the virgin land to capitalist development. As the proportion of public land sold to speculators dramatically increased, would-be settlers and squatters had to battle hard to get the land they wanted. Once settled, farmers usually had to enter into some sort of economic relations with land speculators or bankers, either taking out mortgages or borrowing money to pay for farm improvements.

Despite these hardships, the vast majority of settlers eventually owned their farms outright. Most of them managed, for a time, to set up a facsimile of the yeoman regime. But it was not to last. Hoping to develop markets for their surplus crops, the western yeomen for the most part supported the extension of new east-west transport routes after

1820; the impact of their innovations quickly surpassed early expectations. By 1850 northwestern farm operators were almost fully integrated into commercial markets; specialized production of grain, livestock, or dairy products became the norm for successful commercial farmers. Under the pressure of reorganization, attempts to recreate the old order of yeoman independence collapsed. Although still dominated by small farmers, the Old Northwest emerged as one of the leading areas of cash-crop agriculture in the world, displacing New England and the mid-Atlantic seaboard as the supplier of eastern and overseas markets.

The opening of the market brought prosperity and rising profits to those farmers who secured sufficient acreage and learned to handle the new rules of credit and competition. Like eastern businessmen (and western businessmen in the new cities along the transport routes), western commercial farmers reordered their public and private lives in accord with the standards of eastern middle-class domesticity. Yet like the Northeast, the Northwest had its dispossessed and those who faced imminent dispossession. Not only were the Native Americans removed from their lands, but so too a substantial number of white settlers suffered from the revolution in marketing. Those unable to get sufficient credit to improve their operations or unwilling to learn capitalist agriculture methods wandered on the periphery of the most concentrated settlement, squatting on unimproved land or purchasing new land—often only to lose it. Those who could not sustain themselves and could not travel farther on fell into the ranks of agricultural wage labor. In all, the rise of capitalist agriculture in the Northwest, as in the Northeast, produced new classes of independent and dependent Americans.

The South experienced the market revolution quite differently, though just *how* differently has been the subject of continuing debate. The outstanding feature of southern economic and social history after 1815 was, of course, the rise of the Cotton Kingdom and the westward expansion of plantation slavery. Since the mid-1950s an outstanding literature on slavery has completely overturned the old sentimentalized, racist interpretation of the plantation as a benevolent institution, supposedly designed as much to civilize "inferior" blacks as to reap profits for the planters. Such recent historians as Eugene D. Genovese, Herbert G. Gutman, Lawrence W. Levine, and Albert J. Raboteau have paid especially close attention to the slaves' own experiences and discovered that a distinctive Afro-American culture took shape under slavery, a culture based on religious values and family ties that gave the slaves the power to endure and in certain ways resist the harshness of bondage. Far from a benign world of social harmony, the plantation South was an arena of intense day-to-day struggles between masters and slaves.

Much more controversial has been the argument, advanced most forcefully by Genovese, that the expansion of slavery led to the creation of a distinctive, noncapitalist southern civilization. As Genovese sees it, the southern slaveholders' attachment to land and slaves as their chief forms of investment guaranteed that the South would fail to achieve sustained economic development. To be sure, the slaveholders were linked to the wider world of capitalist markets and benefited from the improvement of American commerce and finance; like all men of business, they were acquisitive and at times greedy; and, especially for the cotton nabobs, slavery created some outstanding fortunes. But, Genovese contends, the master-slave relationship—so unlike labor relations in the North—created a unique mode of social organization and understanding. At the heart of these arrangements was what Genovese calls paternalism, a system of subordination that bound masters and slaves in an elaborate network of familial rights and duties. Plantation paternalism was fraught with conflict between master and slaves, although (Genovese insists) it did help contain the slaves' rebelliousness. Above all, the slaveholders as a class—and the South as a region—did not share in the possessive individualism and atomistic liberalism that were coming to dominate northern life.

Genovese's interpretation has been extremely influential, though it has also been challenged on various fronts. In particular, historians have questioned Genovese's contention that slavery precluded southern economic development, and that the planters exercised ideological hegemony over their slaves. Generally, however, scholars today agree that the market revolution had the effect of widening the differences between northern and southern society and culture. As historians examine the worlds of southerners who were neither masters nor slaves, southern distinctiveness seems all the more apparent; at the same time, these studies have heightened our appreciation of the complexities of the slave South.

Perhaps the most interesting work of recent years concerns the nonslaveholders who constituted the majority of the southern white population before the Civil War. Far removed from the old settlements of the Tidewater and the rich soils of the Black Belt, there lived relatively isolated communities of white householders and their families who produced mainly for their own needs and had only occasional contact with the market economy. While their way of life distinguished these southern yeomen from the commercial farmers of the North, it also set them apart from the wealthier, less egalitarian planters of their own region; jealous of their personal independence and local autonomy, the southern yeomen resented any perceived intrusion on their political rights. White supremacy and the yeomen's acquiescence in slavery softened these class differences, but throughout the 1820s and 1830s the southern yeomen remained deeply suspicious of the planters' wealth and power, and the possibility that the planter elite might pursue local development policies to the detriment of the backcountry.

The rediscovery of the persistent southern yeomen—in contrast to the declining northern yeomen—has reinforced the argument for growing social divergence between North and South before 1850. But in a different sense the southern yeomen's dilemmas also point out certain commonalities in the history of commercialization throughout the country, which in turn help us understand the market revolution as a national process. At one level, commercialization—as overseen by the nation's merchant capitalists, manufacturers, commercial farmers, and planters—created a hybrid political economy by introducing capitalist forms of labor and market agriculture in the North, and by fostering a different slave-based order in the South. Viewed more closely, the market revolution can also be seen to have produced new and potentially troublesome social conflicts within each major section of the country. Entrepreneurs and wage earners, middlemen and petty producers, masters and slaves, planters and yeomen all found themselves placed in unfamiliar positions, arrayed against one another in fresh struggles for power and legitimacy. In the long run the divergences between free labor and slavery would dominate other differences. Before then, however, new social relations and conflicts *within* the various sections generated social tensions that came to the fore in politics.

The most recent and comprehensive effort to understand the Jacksonian era in terms of expanding market relations is Charles Sellers's *Market Revolution*, which has triggered a new debate over the links between social and political change. Sellers, who began lecturing and writing on the concept of the market revolution in the early 1960s, draws on the latest scholarly literature as well as on his own pathbreaking research, and offers the fullest interpretation of the period since Arthur M. Schlesinger Jr.'s *Age of Jackson*. In a sense, Seller's effort marks the completion of a scholarly cycle, by focusing, much as Schlesinger did, on the economic and social conflicts that inspired the Jacksonian movement. Yet *The Market Revolution* is hardly a recapitulation of *The Age of Jackson*. Whereas Schlesinger saw the emerging struggle between capital and labor as the key to understanding Jacksonianism, Sellers describes a broader popular insurgency of yeoman farmers and urban workers, pitted against what he describes as the Arminian, individualist, profit-maximizing world of the encroaching capitalist market. A similar argument appears in Harry L. Watson's concise survey of Jacksonian politics, *Liberty and Power*.

Seller's interpretation has not won universal assent. In the latter sections of his account of the American Revolution and its legacy, Gordon S. Wood suggests that the democratic agitations of the Jacksonian years arose primarily from the crass commercial ambitions of ordinary Americans. Although Wood insists that the Revolution was a radical event, he sees the rise of American democracy primarily as a rejection of the Founders' elitism, by a footloose population that was driven by a rage for individual prosperity. In a similar spirit, Daniel Feller has described Jacksonian Americans as united by a confident faith in expansive market relations but divided over the best means to pursue economic progress. On somewhat narrower grounds, other historians, above all, Winifred Barr Rothenberg, have argued that the transition to a capitalist market economy occurred much earlier and much more smoothly than Sellers and others have claimed. Central to the debate over these matters is the question of how usefully the commercial relations that arose in the eighteenth and early nineteenth centuries can be described as "capitalist." Given that the Jacksonians' targets included an emerging but not yet dominant class of capitalists, their political critique of "associated wealth" would still seem to have carried a great deal more ideological force than historians like Wood and Feller allow. A useful review of these and related matters—and an attempt to reconcile competing viewpoints—appears in Allan Kulikoff's *Agrarian Origins of American Capitalism.*

Despite the demurrers, historians are much more inclined than they were twenty years ago to agree with Sellers's and others' basic arguments about the economic and social tumults of the age, and their importance to Jacksonian politics. Yet some have argued that, on various specific points, Sellers has simplified matters and failed to connect adequately the spread of market relations to the political events of the 1820s and 1830s. A number of interesting challenges and defenses, along with a reply by Sellers to his critics, appears in Melvyn Stokes's and Stephen Conway's *Market Revolution in America,* a collection of essays drawn from a Commonwealth Fund Conference held in London in 1993.

The appearance of multiculturalism has, not surprisingly, had a noticeable impact on very recent studies of the period—as have, increasingly, ripostes to multicultural scholarship. Without denying the importance of economic change, the multiculturalists have emphasized the racial and ethnic character of the era's conflicts. In Edward Countryman's view, the Jacksonians come off rather poorly, as the defenders of Southern slavery and the fomenters of wild-eyed, bloody expansionism—although the Whigs do not come off much better. Even harsher in their assessments of the Jacksonians—and particularly of the Jacksonians' northern working-class supporters—are Alexander Saxton and David R. Roediger, who argue that the racial privileges accorded white workingmen helped to define an ideology of "whiteness" that, in turn, disfigured the Jacksonians' political appeals.

As history, like so many other fields in the humanities, has become even more fragmented, it is often difficult to get a handle on any major lines of disagreement and discussion. But study of the Jacksonian period of American history may be an exception to the present rule. To be sure, with the proliferation of so many different approaches to the past—including, of late, attempts at postmodernist readings of Jacksonian political texts and efforts to introduce "cultural studies" to the 1830s—it may seem as if the field is spinning off in a dozen directions at once. But thanks to Charles Sellers's bold and authoritative statement of his thesis in *The Market Revolution,* Jacksonian historians at least have a common frame of reference for debate that historians in other areas lack. Sellers's is not the last word on the subject, by any means, but scholars will be fruitfully disputing and affirming his arguments for some time to come.

In doing so, they will also continue various debates over how Americans of different classes, races, and regions experienced the enormous structural changes that confronted them, and how they acted upon those new understandings. Few historians today would argue that economic interest alone determined people's views of the world. Jacksonian historians have found that Americans understood the market revolution as a cultural and political challenge, not simply an economic transformation. These findings have led to a thorough revision of key aspects of American intellectual history after 1815, especially on the contours of political ideology and social consciousness.

IDEOLOGY AND SOCIAL CONSCIOUSNESS

Much of the most important recent work on ideology and social consciousness after 1815 has focused on Americans whom previous generations thought of as "inarticulate"—including women, slaves, and workingmen. Combined with the history of the market revolution, efforts to study ideas "from the bottom up" have revealed far deeper and more complex divisions between various groups of Americans than were once supposed to have existed. Yet the most profound changes in our understanding of popular ideas have come from a larger reorientation in the ways historians approach early American social and political thought—above all, republican political ideas and the social meanings of evangelical Protestantism.

Studies of early nineteenth-century republicanism owe a great deal to some outstanding work, begun in the 1960s, on eighteenth-century politics and the origins and consequences of the American Revolution. After surveying American political discourse at the nation's formation, such scholars as Bernard Bailyn, Richard L. Bushman, J. G. A. Pocock, and Gordon Wood found it difficult to sustain the widespread assumption that America's revolutionary ideology was essentially a pragmatic, legalistic variant of liberal capitalist ideas, derived mainly from John Locke. When late eighteenth-century Americans spoke of politics, they referred to a broad set of principles that they subsumed under the heading of republicanism.

Formulated in a world of monarchs and aristocrats, American republicanism was a radical, nearly utopian vision. Five interlocking concepts formed its key elements: first, that the ultimate goal of any political society should be the protection of the common good, or *commonwealth;* second, that in order to maintain this commonwealth, citizens had to exercise *virtue,* the ability to subordinate private ends to the public good when the two conflicted; third, that to be virtuous, citizens had to be *independent* of the political will of other men; fourth, that to guard against the rise of tyranny, citizens had to exercise their *citizenship* and be active in political life; fifth, that all citizens were entitled to *equality* under a representative, democratic system of laws. Some Americans emphasized certain of these concepts more than others; different groups interpreted them to mean different things; still, current historians argue that Americans drew primarily on these ideals in denouncing Old World inequality and in defining themselves as a nation.

The rediscovery of republicanism has sparked several debates with enormous implications for U.S. history after 1815. Joyce O. Appleby, for one, has warned against ignoring the prominence of liberal ideas about natural rights in early American political thought—ideas that Appleby thinks opened the way for a new capitalist order. Others have stressed the importance of plebeian democratic notions of the republic as spread among urban artisans and backwoods farmers—notions at odds in several respects with both traditional republican thought and with emerging capitalist liberalism. Still others have argued that republican ideas did not long survive the American Revolution as the mainspring of U.S. political thought. Lately, however, it has seemed that the demise of republican politics has been greatly exaggerated. Historians studying the nineteenth century have found that at least through the 1850s, republican political language proliferated throughout the United States. Rather than giving way to a kind of undifferentiated market liberalism, republicanism, it now seems, became a reference point of struggle as emergent classes identified their own interests with the survival and well-being of the republic itself.

Recent labor historians, for example, have found that many of the protest movements of the early nineteenth century proclaimed a distinct working-class republicanism, which combined republican ideals and the labor theory of value to touch the deepest emotions of the rank and file. At the heart of the matter was the question of whether the market revolution and its new forms of wage labor advanced or undermined republican ideals. To northern businessmen, commercialization was the handmaiden of republican progress: by increasing national wealth, they believed, entrepreneurs would widen opportunities for all honest and diligent workingmen to achieve virtuous independence. But to a growing number of workers, the market revolution seemed to vitiate republican ideals—by creating new forms of potentially awesome, undemocratic private power such as banks and corporations, by disrupting the supposedly mutualist regime of the artisan workshop, and by threatening workers with permanent dependence on wages and the capitalist labor market. At stake, organized workers argued, were not simply their own material interests (although these were important) but the fate of the republic in a land they thought had been overrun by purse-proud, nonproducing aristocrats and their political allies.

Similar themes appeared in very different settings as Americans interpreted their new, often bewildering circumstances in terms of the republican political legacy. Yeomen and would-be yeomen in the Northeast and the West attacked land speculators and bankers as an elite money power out to deprive farmers of their hard-won independence. Small producers in the South eyed both planters and merchants in southern cities as wealthy incipient aristocrats and tried to expand the political power of ordinary white men. By the 1830s this crisis of republican values, born of the market revolution, had produced popular movements for labor's rights, land reform, debtor relief, expansion of the suffrage, hard money, and numerous other causes. In response, northern businessmen, western speculators, and southern planters attempted in various ways to link their own favored position with the vindication of democratic republicanism.

Alongside these political divisions a deep spiritual and religious crisis also developed, loosely referred to as the Second Great Awakening. The theological implications of the evangelical revivals of the early nineteenth century and the decline of Calvinist orthodoxy was not lost on earlier generations of researchers; the religious ecstasy unleashed by the evangelicals' camp meetings have long fascinated social historians. But except in the work of a few pioneering scholars such as Whitney Cross, the larger social meanings of the revival were usually described— vaguely—as manifestations of an alleged Jacksonian democratic spirit. Historians today are much more exact; the rise of evangelicalism in its many forms seems to have been critical to the social and ideological transformations that accompanied the market revolution.

Nowhere did the revivals have a more profound impact than in those commercializing rural areas of the North and West familiarly known as the Burned-Over District. Building on the work of Cross, Paul E. Johnson and Mary P. Ryan have carefully reconstructed the sociology of northern evangelicalism. Focusing on Charles Finney's revival in Rochester, New York, Johnson found that it was initially a movement of and for businessmen, commercial farmers, and their families. In the new measures and liberalized doctrines of conversion of the Finneyites' free churches, Johnson argues, these people discovered both religious explanations for the breakdown of old interpersonal community relations and a new vision of man and God, consonant with the middle-class virtues of regular industry, sobriety, and self-reliance. Ryan, in a study of Utica, New York, pays closer attention to the gender dimension of the revivals and emphasizes that the majority of evangelical converts through the 1830s were the wives and daughters of businessmen; while serving as "the cradle of the middle class," Ryan concludes, the revivals had the more immediate consequence of helping to forge a religious view of sexual gentility and female spiritual worth in line with emerging forms of domesticity and middle-class respectability. The evangelical awakening seems to have provided a means whereby the new northern middle class forged the moral imperatives that defined them as a class. And once they did that, the evangelized converts (especially women) attempted with uneven success to bring the rest of society into the fold by means of urban missions, Bible societies, and a host of other religiously inspired moral reform efforts.

The revivals came even earlier to the South than to the North and had, if anything, a more pervasive influence—but their social significance was rather different. Slaveholders, particularly those born outside the established eastern upper crust, found in the teachings of various Baptist, Methodist, and New School Presbyterians a promise of spiritual rebirth and a potential instrument for "civilizing" (and thus further subordinating) their slaves. As Donald Mathews and other scholars have explained, however, the social meaning of southern evangelicalism steadily diverged from that of the northern churches—and, in an important respect, from the slaveholders' own original intentions. Northern evangelicals, with their bedrock insistence on human equality before God, the sinfulness of human coercion, and individual responsibility, generated passions that easily took on antislavery connotations. Southern planters could not accept such views and did not permit them in their churches. Instead, southern evangelicalism came to accept the inferiority of blacks and to emphasize the slaveholders' supposed civilizing mission as a form of Christian stewardship. The slaves, however, although drawn to evangelical Christianity, did not take from it the submissive message the slaveholders thought they would. On the contrary, they blended the biblical motifs of exodus and redemption with surviving West African religious customs and made of them a foundation of their own sense of dignity and community.

Taken together, the continued fragmentation of American republicanism and the ferment of the revivals reveal an intricate series of social and ideological redefinitions. Armed with these views, Americans struggled over the basic issues raised by commercialization, interpreting their conflicts as battles for the very soul of the nation. These struggles shaped the political tumults and innovations associated with the age of Jackson.

POLITICS

It is in the area of politics that the current historiography of the Jacksonian era may seem the most confused. In the 1960s, revisionist political historians were heralding a revolution in methodology and interpretation. Using formidable statistical hardware and the sociological tools of multivariate analysis, the "new" political historians proclaimed as their major finding that, contrary to then prevailing interpretations, economics and class had played only limited roles in shaping political alignments. Ethnicity, culture, and religion, it turned out, were the keys to understanding Jacksonian politics.

These revisionist accounts swept away the mechanistic, often one-dimensional instrumentalism that had marred earlier social interpretations of Jacksonian politics. Yet in the years since this academic revolution began, historians (including some of the "new" political historians) have had second thoughts. Their conclusions did not work for every area of the country; even where they appeared to be valid, the divorce of class factors from culture and ethnicity began to seem artificial. A few efforts at correcting such problems have tried to combine the worthy findings of the "new" political history with those of recent social historians, and out of this work have come more convincing appraisals of the overlapping effects of class, culture, and political ideology. Even more important, these studies have broadened the scope of political history to cover not simply electoral contests and voting returns but the entire way in which power was structured and restructured after 1815.

An important early development in this new social history of politics was a full reevaluation of the origins of professional parties, notably in Richard Hofstadter's 1969 book on changing concepts of party from the framing of the Constitution through the 1820s. Inspired partly by the rediscovery of eighteenth-century republican political discourse, Hofstadter demonstrated how deeply the Founding Fathers abhorred the idea of permanent party divisions, regarding them as factionalized solvents of the commonwealth. Even Thomas Jefferson, head of the first national opposition party in American history, had no intention of making party divisions permanent. Jefferson's celebrated remarks at his first inaugural—"We are all Republicans, we are all Federalists"—meant that in his view only one party, his own, was needed. This anti-party animus lasted down to the 1820s, only to be challenged by a new generation of political upstarts, among them future Jacksonian strategists such as Martin Van Buren. Drawn largely from outside the traditional elite gentry families, this new breed of politicians believed that without regularly organized parties the nation would fall into either unceasing civil strife or oligarchy. Political conflict, they insisted, was inevitable in a nation so diverse as the United States; to deny the expression of that conflict through regular, legitimate channels was both foolhardy and dangerous. Only a forthrightly competitive system of organized parties, each responsible to a broad white male electorate and a party rank and file, and each led by professional politicians, could insure political stability and legislate the popular will.

The emergence of these new kinds of politicians helped to ventilate the political system, at both local and national levels, by encouraging the expansion of the suffrage and important reforms in representation in states still attached to eighteenth-century property requirements. By 1830 the vast majority of the states had either adopted or moved decisively toward universal adult white male suffrage. This process of democratization—discriminating and oppressive as it was to women and free blacks—did not, however, proceed simply from the idealistic or benevolent efforts of new and emerging political elites. Considerable pressure at the grassroots—particularly from the plebeian backcountry— often instigated democratic reform; once organized, this pressure from below often pushed the politician-reformers to proceed well beyond what they initially expected to achieve.

Shifts in national policy, meanwhile, further exacerbated popular discontent. With the demise of the Federalist party after the War of 1812, it appeared to many as if Jeffersonian principles of frugal government and strict construction of the Constitution had at last been vindicated. Yet partly as a result of the mobilization for the war, elements within the Jeffersonian coalition more friendly to government-supported economic development had begun to gain the upper hand. By the mid-1820s many of these men, joined by ex-Federalists, had started to coalesce in a loose-knit way as what would soon be called National Republicans—shorn of much of the belligerent, elitist animus of the old Federalist party but interested in using national institutions (including the Second Bank of the United States, chartered in 1816) to expand the market revolution. In the presidential election of 1824, John Quincy Adams, a leading figure in this group, emerged the winner—though only after the election was thrown into the House of Representatives, where it was beclouded with charges of backroom deals and corruption. Suddenly—or so it seemed to some observers—a revamped form of New England Federalism had captured the White House.

In the aftermath of Adams's election, most of the new party professionals gravitated toward the oppositional presidential aspirations of Andrew Jackson; as much as anything, Jackson's eventual election to the presidency in 1828 amounted to a triumph for the professional vision of party politics. It was to prove only the beginning of a tremendous political transformation. Although known to be unfriendly to various National Republican measures, Jackson ran for the White House on his popularity as a military hero rather than on any clearly defined issues. Even as he was sworn into office, it was not altogether clear where he and his newly formed party would stand on the various political controversies of the day. Nor was it clear how Jackson's adversaries would respond, except to announce their opposition to the professional party idea and their distrust (in some cases, detestation) of Andrew Jackson.

The events that shaped the new political alignments—what historians have dubbed the second of the nation's "party systems"—were directly connected to the social tensions of the market revolution. They came with extraordinary rapidity in the years immediately before and after Jackson's election. Labor conflict hit the Northeast on an unprecedented scale as workers and their radical friends organized the first national labor movement—initially with a string of locally based workingmen's parties, then in centralized urban unions and a national trades' union. Employers responded to union activities with their own organizations and with legal prosecutions aimed effectively at denying workers the right to strike. In 1831 the northern revival reached a crescendo with the Finneyite eruption in Rochester; throughout the decade, evangelized middle-class northerners joined churches and religious moral reform societies by the hundreds of thousands. Western small farmers and squatters pressed for reform of public land policy to widen and guarantee their access to the land. Nat Turner's slave rebellion in 1831 touched off a wave of legal repression in the South to prevent any further such insurrections and to uproot antislavery opinion. Southern yeomen joined popular movements demanding further democratization of the suffrage and wider eligibility for officeholding in some of the older slave states.

Against this background the Jacksonians assembled their party constituency and ideology. Jackson himself was a central figure in this process, if only as a popular symbol; current historians have hotly debated exactly what Jackson stood for. In a study heavily influenced by Freudian insights, Jackson's fiercest critic, Michael Rogin, has portrayed the Old Hero as a deeply disturbed man whose need to supplant the generation of the revolutionary fathers bred a pathologically violent character, its violence directed in particular at Native Americans. In contrast, Jackson's most thorough biographer, Robert V. Remini, has presented him as a politician and statesman who in many respects deserves to be remembered as a man of the people. Yet despite their clashing interpretations, Rogin and Remini (and historians generally) agree that Jackson and his party drew upon the old republican language and reworked it into a powerful political appeal.

Essentially, Jacksonianism developed as an expression of the fears and aspirations of those petty producers and workers threatened by commercialization, as well as of voters in outlying areas not yet integrated into the market revolution. This did not mean, historians are now quick to add, that the Democracy was simply a farmer-labor party, organized as a clearcut opposition to merchant speculators and wealthy planters. Wealthy men (such as Jackson himself) commanded key party posts throughout the country; among them were men who helped to further the market revolution. Significant numbers of petty producers and wage earners, meanwhile, voted for the Democracy's opponents. Like all successful national parties in U.S. history, both the Democrats and the Whigs were coalitions of diverse social groups. For the most part, though, the Democracy tapped into the attitudes—and won the votes—of northern petty artisans and workers, marginal and middling farmers in the Northeast and Northwest, and southern yeomen. Democrats assumed that there was an inherent conflict between "producers" and "nonproducers," in which entrenched "nonproducers" would seek to use the power of the state to their own advantage. The Democrats' professed aim was not, therefore, to end all economic improvement and expansion but rather to keep the hands of established wealth and privilege off the levers of state power, thereby preventing the creation of a new and permanent monied aristocracy.

Jackson's war on the Second Bank of the United States was a turning point in the building of his party's constituency and identity; his veto message brilliantly rearticulated the old republican discourse into a ringing defense of small producers against the alleged schemes of merchant capitalist financiers and foreign investors to subvert the Constitution and equal rights. Jackson's veto of federally sponsored internal improvements, along with Democratic congressional efforts for comprehensive land reform, likewise arrayed the "bone and sinew" against those private interests that would bend government to enhance their private power.

Jackson's enemies had difficulty organizing a coherent national opposition to this democratic appeal. Several studies have stressed that the anti-Jacksonians inherited the once prevalent distrust of political parties, which naturally hampered their responses to the Democrats. More important, as John Ashworth has pointed out, anti-Jacksonians tended to distrust electoral democracy altogether as a potential form of demagogic tyranny. Only in the late 1830s did the anti-Jacksonians finally learn to adapt to the realities of mass democratic politics and pull together as a national political force—the Whig party. Once organized, the Whigs completed a major shift in American political conservatism.

Central to Whig thinking was the desire for an orderly and regulated consolidation of the market revolution. Updating ideas elaborated by the Hamiltonian Federalists and the National Republicans, Whig leaders expected that with the prudent aid of an active, paternalist government (through banking policy, tariffs, and corporate charters), private capital would flourish, making the American economy truly independent of the Old World. Not surprisingly, this stance won considerable approval from northern businessmen, western capitalist farmers, and the larger southern planters. But what turned the Whigs from a poorly organized band into a powerful national party was the larger social and moral vision they attached to their prodevelopment economics and promulgated in their new party organization.

Rejecting the Democrats' claims of an inherent conflict between producers and nonproducers, the Whigs asserted that a basic harmony of interests united all Americans in a kind of mutualist whole. The enlargement of national wealth, they contended, would eventually bring greater opportunity for all. Since the United States, unlike Britain and Europe, was a classless society, they insisted, all those who exhibited thrift, industry, and self-reliance could expect to earn their personal independence. Poverty and inequality, according to the Whigs, stemmed from individual moral failings, not from any flaws in existing political or economic structures. Reflecting both the ethical injunctions of the Second Great Awakening and the discourse of democratic republicanism, the Whigs' argument effectively presented the political and social consequences of the market revolution as the fulfillment of America's republican destiny. It won them considerable popular support from aspiring northern and western small producers, more fortunate wage earners, and some smaller southern planters and entrepreneurs.

By 1840 the clash between Democrats and Whigs had developed into a new party system of two fairly evenly matched national organizations. The politics of economic development remained at the center of their electoral and legislative battles—yet as recent work has emphasized, these battles expressed intense cultural conflicts as well. In the Northeast, for example, the Whigs' combination of economic and moral appeals struck home with Protestant workers and small producers, particularly those caught up in the revivals. Catholic immigrants, especially Irish Catholics at the bottom of the new labor market, were repelled by the Whigs' cultural politics and stuck with the Jacksonians. In the Northwest and the South the clash between the Democracy's emphasis on equal rights and the Whigs' emphasis on respectability set voters enmeshed in the semi-autonomous world of the yeomen's communities against those country and city voters more thoroughly integrated into the commercial world. Particularly in the North, these strains surfaced in battles over all sorts of "cultural" issues without any apparent economic logic—nativism, temperance, sabbatarianism, common schooling—with the Whigs taking up the banner of moral reform. Throughout, however, the lines of class, religion, ethnicity, and subregion tended to converge; cultural identities in politics—the Whigs' entrepreneurial moralism versus the Democrats' stress on personal autonomy and equal rights— were inseparable from the ways in which the market revolution was threatening old ways of life, creating new ones, and setting large groups of Americans at odds.

As it happened, these battles were to be overshadowed by the even deeper struggles that emerged in the 1840s and eventually destroyed the second party system. The essential issue was the expansion of slavery; since 1970, historians have greatly enhanced our understanding of how slavery and antislavery came to dominate the political agenda. Numerous studies have established that both the Democrats and the Whigs understood the need to keep issues associated with slavery out of national affairs in order to insure national party stability. The Constitutional Convention of 1787 and the Missouri Crisis of 1819–21 had shown that this was not always easy to do; the social consequences of the market revolution made the task even harder. The rise of the cotton South and the consolidation of planter power made that region increasingly touchy about any perceived threats to the peculiar institution, especially as the perceived common interest of planter and yeoman in the perpetuation of slavery became the most powerful bond for white southerners across the lines of class and party. In the North, meanwhile, the moral reform efforts that stemmed from the Second Great Awakening and the formation of the new middle class dramatically changed the thrust of antislavery opinion. Out of the maelstrom of reform emerged a new form of antislavery dedicated to "immediate" abolition—a far more radical prospect than anything proposed by the preceding antislavery organizations. Benefiting from the organizational structure of what one historian has called the benevolent empire of reform, and borrowing from propaganda techniques of the revivalist churches, the immediatist abolitionists began to win hundreds of thousands of converts in the most rapidly expanding areas of northern development.

The potential divisiveness of these events did not become fully apparent until after 1840. Before that, party leaders had successfully turned away attempts by both sides to inject slavery into national affairs, using compromise where possible, the threat of force when necessary (as in Jackson's handling of the Nullification Crisis of 1832–33), and parliamentary repression (as in the adoption of the gag rule in 1836).

Two political developments helped alter the situation. First, one wing of the abolitionist movement rejected the position of William Lloyd Garrison and others who held that reformers should remain outside politics. Members of this wing entered party politics for themselves and began to adapt their antislavery views to broader public opinion. Second, internal disputes within the Democracy set the northern and southern wings of the party at odds, amid claims that southern interests (led by the sectional firebrand John C. Calhoun) intended to take over. Both developments made it difficult for party leaders to return to the kinds of issues that had given rise to the second party system. In the mid-1840s the entire system was shaken when debates over Texas annexation and the Mexican War reopened the kinds of territorial issues that had always been rife with sectional antagonism. By 1848 sectional passions dogged the nation's politics on an alarming scale—passions emblematized when the antislavery Free Soil party ran on its national ticket two leading figures of the political establishment: the Democratic former president, Martin Van Buren, and the Massachusetts Whig (and son of a former president, John Quincy Adams) Charles Francis Adams.

It would, of course, take another six years before the second party system finally fell apart, and six more after that before the nation was severed. The political generation of Jackson was able to reconstruct intersectional party alliances, at least in Congress; antislavery northerners and southern sectionalists still had a long way to go in building sectional majorities. Yet by 1848 the political impetus behind the Jacksonian party system was quickly exhausting itself. The social and ideological transformations that had given birth to the Jacksonian Democracy and the Whigs continued—but their significance changed as the deeper sectional implications of economic development became paramount.

Here lay the ultimate paradox of the age. The market revolution, having disrupted old social relations and created new ideological and spiritual crises, encouraged the emergence of a new form of mass democratic party politics. Once in place, the second party system revolved around certain intrasectional issues of class and culture linked to the impact of commercialization. Yet the market revolution also widened the social differences between the free-labor North and the slave South. Once those differences entered national politics—agitated by sectional politicians skilled in the techniques of mass democracy—they threatened the very existence of the second party system. The nation's politicians could not forever contain struggles over the meaning of such grand concepts as equality, independence, and individual autonomy in ways that circumvented the fundamental problems raised by the expansion of slavery. In the 1850s and 1860s, Americans would reap the whirlwind.

BIBLIOGRAPHY

This list covers only some of the noteworthy books published since the mid-1970s, plus a few key works from the 1950s and 1960s. Books that might prove useful in the classroom are marked with an asterisk.

Appleby, Joyce O. *Capitalism and a New Social Order: The Republican Vision of the 1790s.* New York: New York University Press, 1984.

Ashworth, John. *"Agrarians" and "Aristocrats": Party Ideology in the United States, 1837–1846.* Wolfeboro, N.H.: Longwood, 1983.

Bailyn, Bernard. *The Ideological Origins of the American Revolution.* Cambridge, Mass.: Harvard University Press, 1967.

Berlin, Ira. *Slaves without Masters: The Free Negro in the Antebellum South.* New York: Pantheon, 1974.

Blassingame, John W. *The Slave Community: Plantation Life in the Antebellum South.* Rev. ed. New York: Oxford University Press, 1979.

Boyer, Paul. *Urban Masses and Moral Order in America, 1820–1920.* Cambridge, Mass.: Harvard University Press, 1978.

Bridges, Amy. *A City in the Republic: New York and the Origins of Machine Politics.* New York: Cambridge University Press, 1984.

Bushman, Richard L. *King and People in Provincial Massachusetts.* Chapel Hill: University of North Carolina Press, 1985.

Cole, Donald B. *Martin Van Buren and the American Political System.* Princeton, N.J.: Princeton University Press, 1984.

———. *The Presidency of Andrew Jackson.* Lawrence: University Press of Kansas, 1993.

Cooper, William J. *The South and the Politics of Slavery, 1828–1856.* Baton Rouge: Louisiana State University Press, 1978.

Cott, Nancy F. *The Bonds of Womanhood: "Woman's Sphere" in New England, 1780–1835.* New Haven, Conn.: Yale University Press, 1977.

Countryman, Edward. *Americans: A Collision of Histories.* New York: Hill & Wang, 1996.

Cross, Whitney. *The Burned-Over District: The Social and Intellectual History of Enthu-*

siastic Religion in Western New York. Ithaca, N.Y.: Cornell University Press, 1950.

Dawley, Alan. *Class and Community: The Industrial Revolution in Lynn*. Cambridge, Mass.: Harvard University Press, 1976.

Douglas, Ann. *The Feminization of American Culture*. New York: Knopf, 1977.

Doyle, Don H. *The Social Order of a Frontier Community: Jacksonville, Illinois, 1825–70*. Urbana: University of Illinois Press, 1978.

Dublin, Thomas. *Women at Work: The Transformation of Work and Community in Lowell, Massachusetts, 1826–1860*. New York: Columbia University Press, 1979.

Faler, Paul G. *Mechanics and Manufacturers in the Early Industrial Revolution: Lynn, Massachusetts, 1780–1860*. Albany: State University of New York Press, 1981.

Feller, Daniel. *The Jacksonian Promise: America, 1815–1840*. Baltimore, Md.: Johns Hopkins University Press, 1995.

Foner, Eric. *Politics and Ideology in the Age of the Civil War*. New York: Oxford University Press, 1980.

Formisano, Ronald P. *The Transformation of Political Culture: Massachusetts Parties, 1790s–1840s*. New York: Oxford University Press, 1983.

Foster, Lawrence. *Religion and Sexuality: Three American Communal Experiments in the Nineteenth Century*. New York: Oxford University Press, 1981.

Genovese, Eugene D. *Roll, Jordan, Roll: The World the Slaves Made*. New York: Pantheon, 1974.

Ginzburg, Lori D. *Women and the Work of Benevolence: Morality, Politics, and Class in the Nineteenth-Century United States*. New Haven, Conn.: Yale University Press, 1990.

Gutman, Herbert G. *The Black Family in Slavery and Freedom, 1750–1925*. New York: Pantheon, 1976.

———. *Work, Culture, and Society in Industrializing America: Essays in American Working-Class History*. New York: Vintage, 1977.

Hahn, Steven. *The Roots of Southern Populism: Yeoman Farmers and the Transformation of the Georgia Upcountry, 1850–1890*. New York: Oxford University Press, 1983.

Hofstadter, Richard. *The Idea of a Party System: The Rise of Legitimate Opposition in the United States, 1780–1840*. Berkeley: University of California Press, 1969.

Horwitz, Morton J. *The Transformation of American Law, 1780–1860*. Cambridge, Mass.: Harvard University Press, 1977.

Howe, Daniel Walker. *The Political Culture of the American Whigs*. Chicago: University of Chicago Press, 1979.

Jensen, Joan. *Loosening the Bonds: Mid-Atlantic Farm Women, 1750–1850*. New Haven, Conn.: Yale University Press, 1986.

*Johnson, Paul E. *A Shopkeeper's Millennium: Society and Revivals in Rochester, New York, 1815–1837*. New York: Hill & Wang, 1978.

Kelley, Robert L. *The Cultural Pattern in American Politics: The First Century*. New York: Knopf, 1979.

Kulikoff, Allan. *The Agrarian Origins of American Capitalism*. Charlottesville: University Press of Virginia, 1992.

Laurie, Bruce G. *Working People of Philadelphia, 1800–1850*. Philadelphia: Temple University Press, 1980.

*Levine, Lawrence W. *Black Culture and Black Consciousness: Afro-American Folk Thought from Slavery to Freedom*. New York: Oxford University Press, 1977.

Lindstrom, Diane. *Economic Development in the Philadelphia Region, 1810–1850*. New York: Columbia University Press, 1978.

Mathews, Donald G. *Religion in the Old South*. Chicago: University of Chicago Press, 1977.

Oakes, James. *The Ruling Race: A History of American Slaveholders*. New York: Knopf, 1982.

Pessen, Edward. *Riches, Class, and Power before the Civil War*. Lexington, Mass.: Heath, 1973.

Peterson, Merrill D. *The Great Triumvirate: Webster, Clay, and Calhoun*. New York: Oxford University Press, 1987.

Raboteau, Albert J. *Slave Religion: The Invisible Institution in the Antebellum South*. New York: Oxford University Press, 1978.

Remini, Robert V. *Andrew Jackson and the Course of American Democracy, 1833–1845*. Vol. 3. New York: Harper & Row, 1984.

Roediger, David R. *The Wages of Whiteness: Race and the Making of the American Working Class*. New York: Verso, 1991.

Rogin, Michael. *Fathers and Children: Andrew Jackson and the Subjugation of the American Indian*. New York: Knopf, 1975.

Rorabaugh, W. J. *The Alcoholic Republic: An American Tradition*. New York: Oxford University Press, 1979.

Ross, Steven J. *Workers on the Edge: Work, Leisure, and Politics in Industrializing Cincinnati, 1788–1890*. New York: Columbia University Press, 1985.

Rothenberg, Winifred Barr. *From Market-Places to a Market Economy: The Transformation of Rural Massachusetts, 1750–1850*. Chicago: University of Chicago Press, 1992.

Ryan, Mary P. *Cradle of the Middle Class: The Family in Oneida County, New York, 1790–1865*. New York: Cambridge University Press, 1983.

Satz, Ronald N. *American Indian Policy in the Jacksonian Era*. Lincoln: University of Nebraska Press, 1975.

Saxton, Alexander. *The Rise and Fall of the White Republic: Class Politics and Mass Culture in Nineteenth-Century America*. London and New York: Verso, 1990.

Sellers, Charles. *The Market Revolution: Jacksonian America, 1815–1846*. New York: Oxford University Press, 1991.

Smith-Rosenberg, Carroll. *Disorderly Conduct: Visions of Gender in Victorian America*. New York: Knopf, 1985.

Stansell, Christine. *City of Women: Sex and Class in New York, 1789–1860*. New York: Knopf, 1986.

*Stewart, James B. *Holy Warriors: The Abolitionists and American Slavery*. New York: Hill & Wang, 1976.

Stokes, Melvyn, and Stephen Conway, eds. *The Market Revolution in America: Social, Political, and Religious Expressions, 1800–1880*. Charlottesville: University Press of Virginia, 1996.

Taylor, George Rogers. *The Transportation Revolution, 1815–1860.* White Plains, N.Y.: M. E. Sharpe, 1951.

Thornton, J. Mills, III. *Politics and Power in a Slave Society: Alabama, 1800–1860.* Baton Rouge: Louisiana State University Press, 1978.

Wallace, Anthony F. C. *Rockdale: The Growth of an American Village in the Early Industrial Revolution.* New York: Knopf, 1978.

*Walters, Ronald G. *American Reformers, 1815–1860.* New York: Hill & Wang, 1978.

Watson, Harry L. *Jacksonian Politics and Community Conflict: The Emergence of the Second American Party System in Cumberland County, North Carolina.* Baton Rouge: Louisiana State University Press, 1981.

———. *Liberty and Power: The Politics of Jacksonian America.* New York: Hill & Wang, 1990.

Wiebe, Robert H. *The Opening of American Society: From the Adoption of the Constitution to the Eve of Disunion.* New York: Knopf, 1984.

Wilentz, Sean. *Chants Democratic: New York City and the Rise of the American Working Class, 1788–1850.* New York: Oxford University Press, 1984.

Wood, Gordon S. *The Radicalism of the American Revolution.* New York: Knopf, 1992.

4

■ SLAVERY, THE CIVIL WAR, AND RECONSTRUCTION

Eric Foner

NO PERIOD OF OUR NATION'S HISTORY HAS PROVED AS PERENNIALLY FASCINATING to Americans as the era of the Civil War. And in the past generation, none has been the subject of so outstanding a body of new historical writing. Like their counterparts studying other periods of American history, Civil War scholars have devoted increasing attention to the everyday lives of ordinary Americans. Under the impact of this redefinition of the study of history, old questions about the period have yielded new answers; and new concerns such as regional variations in the institution of slavery, the impact of the Civil War upon non-slaveholding whites, and the role of blacks in the sectional crisis have come to the forefront of scholarship. If new research seems at times to fragment history into the diverse experiences of individual groups, and historians continue to differ on key points of interpretation, a synthesis is now emerging that sees slavery as the most crucial problem of ante-bellum American life and the fundamental cause of the Civil War, and the myriad consequences of emancipation as the central themes of the war and Reconstruction.

SLAVERY AND THE ORIGINS
OF THE CIVIL WAR

Arguably the finest body of literature produced by American historians since 1960 has been the work reappraising the South's "peculiar institution." But before new views could take hold, the traditional interpretation that had dominated the field until the mid-1950s had to be swept away. Shaped by the assumption that slavery was a civilizing institution made necessary by the racial inferiority of Afro-Americans, previous histories sketched a congenial portrait of plantation life: decent living conditions for all, only the lightest of punishments, and a general system of give-and-take between master and slave. In this view, slavery—usually unprofitable—was maintained for racial and cultural reasons, rather than economic self-interest, and might well have died out peacefully had the Civil War not intervened.

Not until the era of the modern civil rights movement, which profoundly affected the ways historians viewed race relations in the past, did a full-scale refutation of the traditional interpretation appear. This was provided by Kenneth M. Stampp, who perceived that once one abandoned the notion that slaves were an inferior race in need of civilizing influences, the entire edifice of the traditional viewpoint must fall to the ground. Stampp depicted the plantation as an arena of persistent conflict between masters concerned mainly with maximizing their income and slaves in a constant state of semirebellion.

If Stampp cleared away old delusions about slavery, it was Stanley Elkins who drew attention to his generation's major concern—the nature of the slave experience itself. Impressed by studies arguing that other societies that had known slavery, such as Brazil. were marked by significantly less racial prejudice than the United States (an argument subsequently challenged by other scholars), Elkins asserted that bondage in this country had taken a particularly oppressive form, for which the best analogy was the Nazi concentration camp. A more devastating critique of American slavery could hardly be imagined, but Elkins was less concerned with the physical conditions of slave life than with the psychological impact of "total institutions" upon their victims, whether white or black. He concluded that the culture and self-respect of the slave had been stripped away, leaving an "infantilized" personality incapable of rebellion and psychologically dependent upon the master.

More than any other scholar, Elkins redefined the *problématique* (to borrow a term from the French philosopher Louis Althusser) of historians of slavery: that is, the underlying preoccupations that shape the questions scholars ask. His comparative approach inspired subsequent historians to place the South's peculiar institution within the broad context of the hemisphere as a whole, thus counteracting the insular "American exceptionalism" that underpins so many accounts of this nation's history. At the same time, comparative analysis has underscored the unique qualities of the old South's slave society in which, unlike that of the Caribbean, the white population considerably outnumbered the black. But most strikingly, even though few subsequent writers agreed entirely with his conclusions, Elkins pushed to the forefront the issue of "slave culture," which has dominated scholarship ever since. A generation of historians set out to demonstrate that rather than being transformed into "Sambos" entirely dependent upon their masters, slaves had created a viable, semiautonomous culture among themselves. Scholars delved into sources hitherto largely ignored—slave songs, spirituals, folklore, narratives written by fugitives, the reminiscences of former slaves interviewed during the 1930s by the Works Projects Administration (WPA), marriage registers dating from just after emancipation—to demonstrate that slaves possessed their own values, aspirations, and sense of identity. Their work formed a major component of the broader effort in the 1960s and 1970s to rewrite American history "from the bottom up." The study of slave culture continued to dominate writing on slavery in the 1980s, although Peter Kolchin, in a work comparing American slavery with Russian serfdom, argues that scholars must not lose sight of the authority that planters exercised over every aspect of the slaves' lives, and the obstacles to the creation of real independence within the slave community.

Two institutions of slave life have attracted the most intense scrutiny—the church and the family. The vitality, outlook, and distinctive patterns of worship of slave religion underscore the resiliency of the African inheritance and the degree to which blacks managed to resist the dehumanizing implications of the South's peculiar institution. Blacks rejected the interpretation of Christianity promoted by their masters, which emphasized obedience, humility, and release from suffering in an afterlife rather than in this world. Instead, they came to see themselves as a chosen people akin to the Children of Israel, their bondage and eventual freedom parts of a preordained divine plan. From the Bible they drew favorite images of those who had overcome adversity: Daniel escaping the lions' den, David slaying Goliath, and especially Moses leading his people to a promised land of freedom. In religion blacks found a vehicle for surviving the experience of enslavement with their dignity intact, and in the church an arena for developing a leadership independent of white control. Preachers were key organizers of the nineteenth century's major slave conspiracies, those of Gabriel Prosser (1800), Denmark Vesey (1822), and the religious exhorter Nat Turner (1831). Simultaneously, studies of folktales emphasized the slaves' imaginative reversal of everyday power relations: in the Brer Rabbit stories, for example, weaker creatures get the better of the strong by relying upon their wits. In black religion and folkways, scholars have found solid evidence that slaves understood their own exploitation and believed in the inevitability of their release from bondage.

Similarly, studies of the slave family have shown that an institution once thought to have been destroyed by enslavement not only survived but did so with a set of distinctive values, demonstrating again the partial autonomy of the slave community. Herbert G. Gutman, who has produced the most comprehensive investigation of this subject, acknowledges that black family life faced the constant threat of disruption because of the frequent sale of slaves. Yet he also presents convincing evidence that most slaves lived in "traditional" two-parent families, that many slave marriages were of long duration, and that naming patterns revealed an awareness of family ties going back one or two generations. Subsequent scholars have brought the insights of women's history to bear upon the slave family. Investigating the "internal economy" of slave life—how slaves managed their own time when not at work for their masters—they have discovered a sexual division of labor in which women were generally assigned the tasks of child rearing, cooking, and cleaning, while men hunted, fished, and did outdoor chores. Rather than being the "matriarchy" described in much traditional literature, the slave family was as much influenced by tendencies toward male primacy as the white families around it.

Most recently, historians have moved beyond broad generalizations about the South as a whole to explore the regional variations that gave rise to distinctive forms of antebellum slavery. It has long been recognized that slavery in the cities, where many bondsmen worked as skilled artisans and enjoyed considerable independence from white supervision, differed substantially from the institution in the countryside. But only lately have scholars investigated in detail how rural slavery outside the Cotton Kingdom produced distinct ways of organizing labor, affecting the lives of white and black alike. In the sugar and rice regions, where agriculture required enormous capital investment to support elaborate irrigation systems and grinding and threshing machinery, there arose planter elites whose wealth placed them at the apex of antebellum society. And in both, slaves enjoyed a modicum of day-to-day autonomy: those in the rice fields set their own work pace under a system of individual tasks rather than gang labor; on the sugar plantations, as in the West Indies, black families were allotted individual garden plots. In both cases, slaves used their free time to grow and market crops of their own and were able to accumulate personal property, thus developing a far greater familiarity with the marketplace than those in the cotton region could acquire. In the upper South, moreover, a shift from tobacco to wheat production lessened the need for a resident year-round labor force, leading to the manumission of increasing numbers of slaves. In Maryland, for example, half the black population was already free by 1860.

Attention to regional diversity has also enriched our understanding of the South's free black population. Those in the upper South, employed primarily as agricultural workers or unskilled urban laborers and often linked by family ties to persons in bondage, found their lives closely intertwined with the slave community. Far different was the situation in the port cities of the deep South, particularly Charleston and New Orleans, where there arose a prosperous group of light-skinned free persons of color. Occupying a middle ground between slave and free, black and white, they created a flourishing network of schools, churches, and other institutions and had little in common with the slaves around them. But this free elite would come to play a major role in the turbulent politics of the Civil War and Reconstruction.

Initially, the new focus on the social and cultural aspects of plantation life was accompanied by a neglect of nonslaveholding whites, the majority of the region's population. To a considerable extent, geographical divisions within the old South paralleled those of class and race, and in the predominantly white upcountry a society developed that was distinct in many respects from that of the Black Belt, where most planters and slaves resided. Only recently have historians begun to illuminate this world. The work of Steven Hahn depicts a largely self-sufficient white yeomanry owning few or no slaves, living on the periphery of the market economy, and seeking to preserve the autonomy of their small, local communities. Among other things, Hahn's book adds a new dimension to the continuing discussion of the degree of difference and similarity between northern and southern societies. The world of these yeomen differed profoundly from that of the market-oriented farmers of the Middle West, suggesting that commercial values had penetrated antebellum southern society far less fully than the contemporary North.

The view that slavery was the foundation of an economic and social order differing in fundamental respects from that of the antebellum North can be found in most sophisticated form in the writings of Eugene D. Genovese, his generation's most influential interpreter of the old South. Genovese argued that slavery, although embedded within a capitalist world economy, spawned a unique form of social relations. More than simply an economic investment, it served as the foundation of a distinct way of life, which grew increasingly separate from that of the North as time went on. Slavery gave rise to a hierarchical society based on paternalism, an ideology linking dominant and subordinate classes in a complex pattern of mutual responsibilities and obligations. The slave-holders' outlook differed profoundly from the competitive individualism and acquisitiveness so powerful in the contemporary North. Slavehold-ers saw themselves as responsible for the well-being of an extended "family" of dependents, including not only slaves but white women and children on the plantations. The work of Elizabeth Fox-Genovese shows that planters' wives accepted and reinforced these paternalist, familial values.

The portrait of the old South as a social and economic backwater reminiscent of the semifeudal European periphery did not, however, win universal assent. An entirely different point of view was adopted by historians who believed that the antebellum South adhered to, rather than diverged from, the main trends of nineteenth-century develop-ment. This interpretation was most closely associated with the work of "cliometricians" Robert Fogel and Stanley Engerman, whose writings embodied two major departures in historical methodology: the compu-terized analysis of quantitative evidence, and the application of modern neoclassical economic theory to historical problems. The first greatly ex-panded the possibilities for finding definitive answers to statistical ques-tions (Fogel and Engerman demonstrated, for example, that slavery was a profitable institution, which was not likely to disappear for economic reasons). The second reduced the distinctiveness of the old South to a nonproblem by assuming that slave society functioned according to the same market assumptions as those that prevailed in the North.

Inferring the values and motives of blacks and whites alike from the aggregate economic data, Fogel and Engerman concluded that planters and slaves behaved toward one another in terms of rational calculation: the former concerned primarily with maximizing produc-tion, efficiency, and profit; the latter, equally imbued with the capitalist ethic, aspiring to social mobility within the slave system (for example, the ability to rise from field hand to driver). Other historians argued that antebellum North and South shared not only a common value structure but also the common experiences of territorial expansion and (for whites) political democratization. This emphasis on shared values made the Civil War itself rather difficult to explain, but the actual degree of southern distinctiveness remains a point of continuing debate.

No scholar has yet succeeded in synthesizing the new insights into a coherent account of American slavery's historical evolution from the colonial period through the era of "King Cotton." Nonetheless, the cu-mulative impact of the recent literature has been enormous. For one thing, it leaves little doubt about the centrality of slavery to the course of nineteenth-century American history. Scholars of slavery were among the first to challenge the consensus interpretation of the American experience that dominated writing in the 1950s but which, as its leading practitioner Richard Hofstadter later acknowledged, could hardly encompass the stark reality of the Civil War. It is no longer possible to view the peculiar institution as some kind of aberration, existing outside the mainstream of American development. Rather, slavery was intimately bound up with the settlement of the Western Hemisphere, the economic development of the antebellum nation, and the structure of national politics. And as Lincoln observed in his second inaugural address, everyone who lived through that era understood that slavery was "somehow" the cause of the war.

Not all historians, however, agree with Lincoln's assertion. For example, the Republican party's rise to power, which provided the immediate cause of secession and war, has inspired sharp differences of interpretation concerning the importance of antislavery within northern politics and culture. Paralleling, in a sense, the emphasis some writers placed on the basic similarities between the two sections, a number of historians have insisted that the slavery issue had little impact on the decisions of northern voters. Practitioners of the "new" political history, such as Michael Holt, have argued that the cultural clash between competing ethnic and religious groups, rather than diverse ideological positions on national issues, formed the basis of grassroots northern voting alignments. In this view, the Republican party appears as the instrument whereby New England reformers sought to impose their cultural norms (including temperance and opposition to immigration and Catholicism as much as antislavery) upon the nation as a whole, while the Democratic party united those—including southern slaveholders and northern immigrants—committed to maintaining local autonomy and resisting the cultural encroachment of New England Puritanism.

Those historians who, by contrast, see slavery as the foundation of a society fundamentally distinct from that of the contemporary North, tend also to view Republicans as carriers of an antislavery ideology deeply rooted in the small-town and rural North. This "free-labor ideology" affirmed the superiority of northern society to the "backward" slave South, and viewed the expansion of slavery as a threat to northern laborers' prospects for achieving the economic independence that was ostensibly a right for all members of "free society." Lincoln's own critique of slavery rested firmly on a free-labor ideology, for he saw the institution as violating the right of workers to the fruits of their toil and denying them the opportunity to improve their condition in life through hard work. For the "new" political historians, Lincoln's election in 1860 posed no real threat to the South, and secession resulted from an irrational "crisis of fear." Those who stress the ideological conflict of two fundamentally different societies see in secession the reflection of a reasoned appraisal of the dangers posed by the coming to power of a political party hostile to the South's way of life.

THE CIVIL WAR

Apart from works primarily military in orientation, recent studies of the Civil War carry forward themes dominant in the new interpretation of antebellum history. If slavery was central to prewar American life, it is now clear that emancipation transformed the nature of the war itself. Attention to the experience of slaves, nonslaveholding whites, and free blacks has altered our understanding of the war's course and impact. Moreover, historians are increasingly aware of how the war transformed the warring sections internally, deepening existing divisions and inspiring new social conflicts. Although the terms "North" and "South" continue to be employed as an unavoidable shorthand, it is no longer possible to describe either the Union or the Confederacy as unified monoliths.

The steps by which Congress and President Lincoln moved from an initial policy devoted entirely to the preservation of the Union to embracing the end of slavery as a war aim have often been chronicled. Most Americans, of course, identify the end of slavery almost entirely with the Emancipation Proclamation of January 1, 1863. But it is now clear that the proclamation only confirmed what was already happening on farms and plantations throughout the South. Whatever politicians and military commanders might decree, blacks from the outset saw the Civil War as heralding the long-awaited end to their bondage, and the strength of the community forged under slavery enabled them to seize the opportunities for freedom that now presented themselves. As the Union army occupied territory first on the Confederacy's periphery and then in its heartland, slaves by the thousands abandoned their owners and headed for the Union lines. Some who escaped then made the hazardous journey "home" to lead their families away. Reports of "demoralized" and "insubordinate" behavior on the plantations mounted, especially after the arrival of Union troops in a neighborhood. Slavery, wrote a northern reporter in November 1862, "is forever destroyed and worthless, no matter what Mr. Lincoln or anyone else may say on the subject."

In many ways, nonetheless, the Emancipation Proclamation, rather than the battles of Gettysburg and Vicksburg, marked the war's turning point, for it transformed a struggle of armies into a combat of societies, affirming that Union victory would result in a social revolution within the South. As Philip S. Paludan shows in the most recent study of the Civil War presidency, Lincoln came to merge the goals of preserving the

Union and freeing the slaves into a seamless, coherent purpose, rather than seeing them as distinct goals between which the nation could choose. In such a struggle, compromise was impossible; the war had to continue until the unconditional surrender of one side or another. Moreover, the proclamation authorized for the first time the large-scale enlistment of black soldiers. By the war's end some 180,000 blacks had served in the Union army—over one-fifth of the black male population of the United States between the ages of eighteen and forty-five. As demonstrated in a remarkable documentary collection edited by a group of scholars headed by Ira Berlin, the enrollment of black troops breathed life into the promise of emancipation. This development was especially significant in Maryland, Kentucky, and Missouri, which remained in the Union and were therefore unaffected by the Emancipation Proclamation; there, enlistment for a time constituted the blacks' only route to freedom.

Within the army, blacks were anything but equal to white soldiers. They served in separate units, initially received less pay than white recruits, were generally assigned to fatigue duties, and suffered abuse from white officers. Yet by the end of the war their service had transformed the nation's treatment of blacks, and blacks' conception of themselves. For the first time in American history, large numbers of blacks had been treated as equals before the law—if only military law—and former slaves had for the first time seen the impersonal sovereignty of the law supersede the personal authority of their masters. It was in military service that large numbers of freedmen first learned to read and write, and out of the army would come many of the articulate leaders of black politics during Reconstruction.

If the war severed the bonds that had connected master and slave, it also widened divisions within southern white society. As in the case of the antebellum South, the experience of nonslaveholding whites during the Civil War has only recently been chronicled in detail. There is little doubt, however, that increasing discontent among upcountry yeomen fatally undermined the Confederate war effort. From the outset, disloyalty was rife in the southern mountains. A region of self-sufficient farmers cut off from the rest of Virginia by the Blue Ridge Mountains, seceded from the state in 1861 to become West Virginia, and the yeomen of eastern Tennessee likewise remained loyal to the Union. Elsewhere, the impact of the war and Confederate policies awakened antiwar sentiment and social conflict. With slavery increasingly weakened by black actions, the Confederate government molded its policies to protect the interests of the planter class, and these policies in turn sundered white society.

Many nonslaveholding whites became convinced that they bore an unfair share of taxation, especially direct impressment of goods by the army and the hated tax-in-kind, which undermined the ability of up-country small farmers to feed their families. Above all, the conscription law convinced many yeomen that this was "a rich man's war and a poor man's fight." Provisions that a draftee could avoid service by producing a substitute and that one able-bodied white male would be exempted for every twenty slaves were deeply resented in the upcountry. The result, by 1863, was widespread draft resistance and desertion—a virtual civil war within the Civil War, which sapped the military power of the Con-federacy and hastened its defeat. Moreover, as portions of the upcountry lying at the war's strategic crossroads were laid waste by the march of opposing armies or by marauding bands of deserters, the war experience redrew the economic and political map of the white South. Much of the upcountry was plunged into poverty, thereby threatening the yeo-manry's economic independence and opening the door to the postwar spread of tenancy. And counties in areas such as eastern Tennessee and western North Carolina would defy southern voting patterns for de-cades, remaining Republican long after the rest of the white South had united within the Democratic party.

The war also severely tested the gender relations inherited from the old South. Indeed, among the most significant recent studies of the war's social history are works that introduce gender as a significant cate-gory of analysis. Gender, of course, is a category that embraces men as well as women. Men of all social classes in the old South formed a bond of unity, Stephanie McCurry argues, through the shared experience of domination over their wives. Here, a gender analysis sheds new light on a proverbial conundrum—why the yeomanry, at least initially, ral-lied to a war to preserve a planter-dominated political and social order. Drew Faust questions the popular image of the romantic, heroic south-ern lady selflessly sacrificing for the Confederate cause. Instead, she in-sists, their very commitment to the wellbeing of their families led south-ern women to resent the death, destruction, and economic hardship caused by the war, and eventually to withdraw their support. To the myriad traditional answers to the question of why the South lost, there-fore, Faust adds another: women's disaffection undermined the Confed-eracy.

For the Union as well as the Confederacy, the war was a time of change. Although historians differ about the conflict's precise impact on economic growth, there is no question that most branches of industry prospered, and that agriculture flourished as farm machinery replaced rural laborers drawn into the army. Even more important, however, the war tied the fortunes of an emerging class of industrialists to the Repub-lican party and a national state whose power had been greatly enhanced by the conflict. The economic policies of the Lincoln administration—high protective tariffs, a transcontinental railroad, a national currency (the "greenbacks"), and a new national banking system—shifted the terms of trade against agriculture in favor of industry and centralized control of credit in the hands of leading New York banks. As in the South, however, wartime policies also galvanized opposition that threatened to disrupt the war effort. The enrichment of industrialists and bondholders appeared unfair to workers, who saw their real income devastated by inflation. The expanding powers of the federal government clashed with cherished traditions of local autonomy. And the vast changes in race relations implied by emancipation stirred ugly counterattacks by proponents of white supremacy.

Although not as widespread as in the South, these elements of opposition to the war and its consequences came together for a few terrifying days in July 1863 in the New York City draft riots, the largest civil insurrection in American history apart from the South's rebellion itself. Originating in resentment against conscription (the Union draft, too, allowed individuals to buy their way out of military service), the riot quickly developed into a wholesale assault upon all the symbols of the new order being created by the Republican party and the Civil War. Its targets included government officials—especially draft officers and policemen—factories, docks, the homes of wealthy Republicans, and above all, the city's black population, uncounted numbers of whom were lynched or driven out of the city.

The riots revealed the class and racial tensions lying just below the surface of northern life and raised troubling questions about the war's ultimate meaning. Could a society in which racial hatred ran so deep secure a modicum of justice for the former slaves? This issue acquired new urgency as the end of the war approached. Recent writings emphasize the impact of black military service on Republicans' evolving racial attitudes and locate the origins of the party's Reconstruction commitment to black civil rights in the closing months of the Civil War. But it was not the actions of Congress or the president that forced black suffrage to the center stage of politics at this time. That was accomplished by the political mobilization of the free blacks of New Orleans, who compelled the nation's political leaders to grapple with the question when Louisiana, under a reconstructed government organized at Lincoln's behest, sought readmission to the Union.

If before the war Louisiana's free blacks had thought of themselves as having little in common with the slaves, developments in 1864 propelled them down a radical road. They were shocked by the refusal of Louisiana's Constitutional Convention of 1864, which abolished slavery in the state, to extend political rights to the free black community. And they resented the labor system established by the Union's General Nathaniel Banks, which coerced freedmen into signing labor contracts on the plantations and made no distinction between free blacks and former slaves in applying new "vagrancy" statutes. Increasingly, the free black leadership of New Orleans demanded that the right to vote be given to both free blacks and the new freedmen.

Their complaints against the Louisiana government received a sympathetic hearing in Washington. Black suffrage became a live issue in the Congress that assembled in December 1864. When Congress adjourned in March, the issue remained unresolved. But the impasse led Lincoln, in his last speech, for the first time to call publicly for suffrage for black soldiers and "the very intelligent." Hardly a ringing endorsement of black rights, the speech nonetheless suggested that blacks would have a role to play in shaping the political course of the Reconstruction South. With Lincoln's death and the accession of Andrew Johnson, affairs took a very different course. Indeed, the most recent study, by LaWanda Cox, of Lincoln's attitude toward slavery and race during his presidency refutes the familiar claim that the two presidents' plans for Reconstruction were essentially the same (a notion that originated with Johnson himself, although he never showed the same flexibility on the question of blacks' rights as Lincoln).

Historians today are less inclined to regard the Civil War as the settlement of the issues that had divided Americans than to emphasize that the conflict's most significant achievements—the preservation of the Union and the abolition of slavery—bequeathed to the postwar world a host of unanswered questions. They also stress that the wartime corollaries of these accomplishments, a more powerful national state and a growing sense that blacks were entitled to a still-to-be-defined measure of civil equality, produced their own opposing tendencies. In both North and South, the war's end left continuing conflict over the legacy of emancipation.

RECONSTRUCTION

No period in American history has undergone a more complete reevaluation since 1960 than Reconstruction. As with slavery, scholars began by dismantling a long-dominant one-dimensional view and then proceeded to create new and increasingly sophisticated interpretations. According to the portrait that originated with nineteenth-century opponents of black suffrage and achieved scholarly legitimacy early in this century, the turbulent years after the Civil War were a period of unrelieved sordidness in political and social life. Sabotaging Andrew Johnson's attempt to readmit the southern states to full participation in the Union immediately, Radical Republicans fastened black supremacy upon the defeated Confederacy. An orgy of corruption and misgovernment followed, presided over by unscrupulous carpetbaggers (northerners who ventured South to reap the spoils of office), scalawags (southern whites who cooperated with the new governments for personal gain), and ignorant and childlike freedmen who were incapable of responsibly exercising the political power that had been thrust upon them. After much needless suffering, the South's white communities banded together to overthrow these "black" governments and restore "home rule" (their euphemism for white supremacy).

Resting on the assumption that black suffrage was the gravest error of the entire Civil War period, this traditional interpretation survived for decades because it accorded with firmly entrenched American political and social realities—the disfranchisement and segregation of blacks, and the solid Democratic South. But the "Second Reconstruction"—the civil rights movement—inspired a new conception of the first among historians, and as with the study of slavery, a revisionist wave broke over the field in the 1960s. In rapid succession virtually every assumption of the old viewpoint was dismantled. Andrew Johnson, yesterday's high-minded defender of constitutional principles, was revealed as a racist politician too stubborn to compromise with his critics. By creating an impasse with Congress that Lincoln surely would have avoided, Johnson effectively destroyed his own presidency. Radical Republicans, acquitted of vindictive motives, emerged as idealists in the best nineteenth-century reform tradition. Their leaders, Charles Sumner and Thaddeus Stevens, had worked for black rights long before any conceivable political benefit could have flowed from such a commitment. Their Reconstruction policies were based on principle, not mere political advantage or personal gain. And rather than being the concern of a small band of extremists, the commitment to protecting the civil rights of the freedmen—the central issue dividing Congress and the president—enjoyed broad support within the Republican party.

At the same time, the period of "Black Reconstruction" after 1867 was portrayed as a time of extraordinary progress in the South. The rebuilding of war-shattered public institutions, the establishment of the region's first public school systems, the effort to construct an interracial political democracy on the ashes of slavery—all these were commendable achievements, not elements of the "tragic era" described by earlier historians.

The villains and heroes of the traditional morality play came in for revised treatment. Former slaves did enjoy a real measure of political power, but "black supremacy" never existed: outside of South Carolina blacks held only a small fraction of Reconstruction offices. Rather than unscrupulous adventurers, most carpetbaggers were former Union soldiers seeking economic opportunity in the postwar South. The scalawags were an amalgam of "Old Line" Whigs who had opposed secession in the first place and poorer whites who had long resented the planters' domination of the region's life and saw in Reconstruction a chance to recast southern society along more democratic lines. As for corruption, the malfeasance of Reconstruction governments was dwarfed by contemporary scandals in the North (this was the era of Boss Tweed, Credit Mobilier, and the Whiskey Ring) and could hardly be blamed on the former slaves. Finally, the Ku Klux Klan, whose campaign of violence against black and white Republicans had been minimized or excused by earlier historians, was revealed as a terrorist organization that beat and killed its political opponents to deprive blacks of their newly won rights.

By the end of the 1960s the old interpretation had been completely reversed. Most historians agreed that if Reconstruction was a "tragic" era, it was so because change did not go far enough; it fell short especially in the failure to distribute land to the former slaves and thereby provide an economic base for their newly acquired political rights. Indeed, by the 1970s this stress on the "conservative" character of Radical Reconstruction was a prevailing theme of many studies. The Civil War did not signal the eclipse of the old planter class and the coming to power of a new entrepreneurial elite, for example. Social histories of communities scattered across the South demonstrated that planters survived the war with their landholdings and social prestige more or less intact.

The denial of substantive change, however, failed to provide a compelling interpretation of an era whose participants believed themselves living through a social and political revolution. And the most recent work on Reconstruction, while fully cognizant of what was not accomplished, has tended to view the period as one of broad changes in southern and national life. In the first modern, comprehensive account of the period, Eric Foner portrays Reconstruction as part of a prolonged struggle over the new system of labor, racial, and political relations that would replace the South's peculiar institution. As in the study of slavery, moreover, some scholars of Reconstruction have sought to place this country's adjustment to emancipation in the broad context of international patterns of development, and to delineate what was and was not unique about the American response. Neither slavery nor emancipation was unique to the United States, but Reconstruction was; it stands as a dramatic experiment, the only instance in which blacks, within a few years of freedom, achieved universal manhood suffrage and exercised a real measure of political power.

Like recent studies of slavery and the Civil War, current writing on Reconstruction is informed by a recognition of the extent to which blacks themselves helped shape the contours of change. In a kaleidoscopic evocation of black response to the end of slavery, Leon F. Litwack has shown that freedmen sought to obtain the greatest possible autonomy in every area of their day-to-day lives. Institutions that had existed under slavery, such as the church and family, were strengthened, and new ones sprang into existence. The freedmen made remarkable efforts to locate loved ones from whom they had been separated under slavery. Many black women, preferring to devote more time to their families, refused to work any longer in the fields, thus contributing to the postwar "labor shortage." Continuing resistance to planters' efforts to tie black children to long periods of involuntary labor through court-ordered "apprenticeships" revealed that control over family life was a major preoccupation of the freedmen. Blacks withdrew almost entirely from white-controlled churches, establishing independent religious institutions of their own; and a diverse panoply of fraternal, benevolent, and mutual aid societies also sprang into existence. And though aided by northern reform societies and the federal government, the freedmen often took the initiative in establishing schools. Nor was black suffrage thrust upon an indifferent black population, for in 1865 and 1866 black conventions gathered throughout the South to demand civil equality and the right to vote.

As in every society that abolished slavery, emancipation was followed by a comprehensive struggle over the shaping of a new labor system to replace it. The conflict between former masters aiming to recreate a disciplined labor force and blacks seeking to carve out the greatest degree of economic autonomy profoundly affected economics, politics, and race relations in the Reconstruction South. Planters were convinced that their own survival and the region's prosperity depended upon their ability to resume production using disciplined gang labor, as under slavery. To this end, the governments established by President Johnson in 1865 established a comprehensive system of vagrancy laws, criminal penalties for breach of contract, and other measures known collectively as the "Black Codes" and designed to force the freedmen back to work on the plantations. As Dan T. Carter shows in a study of Presidential Reconstruction, the inability of the leaders of the white South's "self-Reconstruction" to accept the implications of emancipation aroused resentment in the North, fatally weakened support for the president's policies, and made Radical Reconstruction inevitable.

Out of the conflict on the plantations, new systems of labor emerged in the different regions of the South. Sharecropping came to dominate the cotton South. In this compromise between the blacks' desire for land

and the planters' for labor discipline, each black family worked its own plot of land, dividing the crop with the landlord at the end of the year. In the rice-growing areas, with planters unable to attract the outside capital needed to repair wartime destruction and blacks clinging tenaciously to land they had occupied in 1865, the great plantations fell to pieces, and blacks were able to acquire title to small plots and take up self-sufficient farming. And in the sugar region, gang labor survived the end of slavery. In all regions, blacks' economic opportunities were limited by whites' control of credit and by the vagaries of a world market in which the price of agricultural goods suffered a prolonged decline. Nevertheless, the degree to which planters could control the day-to-day lives of their labor force was radically altered by the end of slavery.

The sweeping social changes that followed the Civil War were also reflected in the history of the white yeomanry. Wartime devastation set in motion a train of events that permanently altered these farmers' self-sufficient way of life. Plunged into poverty by the war, ravaged by war casualties, they saw their plight exacerbated by successive crop failures in the early Reconstruction years. In the face of this economic disaster, yeomen clung tenaciously to their farms. But needing to borrow money for the seed, implements, and livestock required to resume farming, many became mired in debt and were forced to abandon self-sufficient farming for the growing of cotton. A region in which a majority of white farmers had once owned their own land was increasingly trapped in a cycle of tenancy and cotton overproduction and became unable to feed itself.

The South's postwar economic transformation profoundly affected the course of Reconstruction politics. As the Black Codes illustrated, state governments could play a vital role in defining the property rights and restricting the bargaining power of planters and laborers. Not surprisingly, when Republicans came to power—largely on the basis of the black vote—they swept away measures designed to bolster plantation discipline and sought to enhance the status of sharecroppers by giving them a first claim on the growing crop. They also launched an ambitious program of aid to railroads, hoping to transform the region into a diversified, modernizing society with enhanced opportunities for white and black alike. But as Mark W. Summers has shown in an investigation of the program, railroad aid not only failed to achieve its economic aims but produced a sharp increase in taxes, thus exacerbating the economic plight of the yeomanry (attracted in some measure to Reconstruction in its early days by the promise of debtor relief) and preventing the Republican party from broadening its base of white support. Railroad aid also generated most of the corruption that undermined the legitimacy of the

Reconstruction governments in the eyes of southern opponents and northern allies alike.

To blacks, however, Reconstruction represented the first time they had ever had a voice in public affairs, and the first time southern governments had even attempted to serve their interests. Recent studies of black politics have stressed both the ways black leaders tried to serve the needs of their constituents and the obstacles that impeded them from doing so effectively. The signal contribution of this new literature has been to reject the idea that Reconstruction politics was simply a matter of black and white. In a broad reevaluation of South Carolina politics, Thomas Holt has argued that many statewide leaders derived from the old Charleston free elite, whose conservative economic outlook rendered them unresponsive to the freedmen's desire for land; studies of Louisiana politics have reached similar conclusions. Free blacks, at the cutting edge of demands for civil and political equality during the Civil War and Reconstruction, failed to find ways of combatting the freedmen's economic plight.

At the local level, however, most black officeholders were former slaves. Although the arduous task of analyzing the local politics of Reconstruction has barely begun, it appears that men who had achieved some special status as slaves—such as ministers and artisans—formed the bulk of black officials. Their ranks were augmented by the little-studied "black carpetbaggers," who looked to the Reconstruction South for opportunities denied them in the North. The presence of sympathetic local officials often made a real difference in the day-to-day lives of the freedmen, ensuring that those accused of crimes would be tried before juries of their peers, and enforcing fairness in such prosaic aspects of local government as road repair, tax assessment, and poor relief. All in all, southern Reconstruction represented a remarkable moment in which the old white elite was stripped of its accustomed political power. It is hardly surprising that its opponents responded not only with criticism but with widespread violence, or that local Republican officials were often the first victims of the Klan and kindred groups.

Recent scholars, indeed, have not only emphasized the role of pervasive violence in the eventual overthrow of Reconstruction but have shown how the problem of law enforcement exposed growing resistance to the expanded federal powers generated by the Civil War. In the war's immediate aftermath Republicans altered the nature of federal-state relations, defining for the first time—in the Civil Rights Law of 1866 and the Fourteenth Amendment—a national citizenship and a national principle of equality before the law, and investing the federal government with the authority to enforce the civil rights of citizens against violations by the states. Then the Fifteenth Amendment prohibited states from infringing upon the right of suffrage for racial reasons, and the Enforcement Acts of 1870–71 gave the federal government the power to protect the civil and political rights of the former slaves against acts of violence.

These were profound changes in a federal system in which the states had traditionally determined and protected the rights of citizens. Yet Reconstruction failed to establish effective means for securing its lofty precepts. The burden of enforcing the new concept of equality before the law was placed upon the federal courts, and it was unrealistic to assume that the courts—even when supplemented on occasion by federal marshals and the army—could bear the major burden of putting down violence in the South. By the 1870s, moreover, many Republicans were retreating from both the racial egalitarianism and the broad definition of federal power spawned by the Civil War. As localism, laissez-faire, and racism—persistent themes of nineteenth-century American history—reasserted themselves, the federal government progressively abandoned efforts to enforce civil rights in the South.

Thus, a complex dialectic of continuity and change affected the ways Americans, black and white, responded to the nation's most profound period of crisis. By the end of the period, slavery was dead, the Union preserved, and both North and South transformed. The social structure populated by masters, slaves, and self-sufficient yeomen was evolving into a world of landlords, merchants, and sharecroppers, both black and white. Indeed, the most recent general history of the Civil War era, by Jeffrey R. Hummel, identifies as the war's most enduring legacy the creation of an oppressive "leviathan" state. Also fading into the past was Lincoln's America—a world dominated by the small shop and family farm—as a rapidly industrializing economy took hold in the North. Yet the aspiration galvanized by the Civil War for a society purged of racial injustice had yet to be fulfilled. The end of Reconstruction thrust former slaves into a no-man's-land between slavery and freedom that made a mockery of the ideal of equal citizenship. Scholars, indeed, have yet to assess fully the significance of Reconstruction's failure. That it was a catastrophe for black America is clear, but it also affected the entire structure of American politics, creating a solid Democratic South whose representatives increasingly aligned with northern conservatives to oppose every effort at social change.

As the nation retreated from the ideal of equality, the war itself took on a new meaning in retrospect. In recent work, how Americans have remembered the Civil War has emerged as an important focus of study. The retreat from Reconstruction went hand in hand with broad acceptance, North and South, of a romantic image of the Civil War as a family quarrel among white Americans, in which both sides fought valiantly for noble principles. In this view, the war's greatest legacy was the preservation of the Union, while the destruction of slavery was worthy of note essentially for removing a cause of dissention among whites. As always, forgetting some aspects of the past was as much a part of historical understanding as remembering others.

It is hardly likely that recent writing represents the final word on slavery, the Civil War, or Reconstruction, for that era raised the decisive questions of America's national existence: the relations between local and national authority, the definition of citizenship, the meaning of equality and freedom. As long as these issues remain central to American life, scholars are certain to return to the Civil War period, bringing to bear the constantly evolving methods and concerns of the study of history.

BIBLIOGRAPHY

Slavery, the Old South, and the Coming of the Civil War

Ashworth, John. *Slavery, Capitalism, and Politics in the Antebellum Republic, 1820–1850*. New York: Cambridge University Press, 1995.

Berlin, Ira. *Slaves without Masters: The Free Negro in the Antebellum South*. New York: Pantheon, 1974.

Blassingame, John. *The Slave Community: Plantation Life in the Antebellum South*. Rev. ed. New York: Oxford University Press, 1979.

Clinton, Catherine. *The Plantation Mistress: Woman's World in the Old South*. New York: Pantheon, 1982.

Elkins, Stanley. *Slavery*. Chicago: University of Chicago Press, 1959.

Fields, Barbara J. *Slavery and Freedom on the Middle Ground: Maryland during the Nineteenth Century*. New Haven, Conn.: Yale University Press, 1985.

Fogel, Robert, and Stanley Engerman. *Time on the Cross: The Economics of American Negro Slavery*. Boston: Little, Brown, 1974.

Foner, Eric. *Free Soil, Free Labor, Free Men: The Ideology of the Republican Party before the Civil War*. New York: Oxford University Press, 1970.

Fox-Genovese, Elizabeth. *Within the Plantation Household: Black and White Women of the Old South*. Chapel Hill: University of North Carolina Press, 1988.

Genovese, Eugene D. *The Political Economy of Slavery*. New York: Pantheon, 1965.

———. *Roll, Jordan, Roll: The World the Slaves Made*. New York: Pantheon, 1974.

Gienapp, William E. *The Origins of the Republican Party, 1852–1856*. New York: Oxford University Press, 1987.

Gutman, Herbert G. *The Black Family in Slavery and Freedom, 1750–1925*. New York: Pantheon, 1976.

Hahn, Steven. *The Roots of Southern Populism: Yeoman Farmers and the Transformation of the Georgia Upcountry, 1850–1890*. New York: Oxford University Press, 1983.

Harding, Vincent. *There Is a River: The Black Struggle for Freedom in America*. New York: Harcourt Brace Jovanovich, 1981.

Harris, J. William. *Plain Folk and Gentry in a Slave Society: White Liberty and Black Slavery in Augusta's Hinterlands*. Middletown, Conn.: Wesleyan University Press, 1985.

Holt, Michael. *The Political Crisis of the 1850s*. New York: Wiley, 1978.

Jones, Jacqueline. *Labor of Love, Labor of Sorrow: Black Women, Work, and the Family from Slavery to the Present*. New York: Basic Books, 1985.

Joyner, Charles. *Down by the Riverside: A South Carolina Slave Community*. Urbana: University of Illinois Press, 1984.

Kolchin, Peter. *American Slavery, 1619–1877*. New York: Hill & Wang, 1993.

———. *Unfree Labor: American Slavery and Russian Serfdom*. Cambridge, Mass.: Harvard University Press, 1987.

Levine, Bruce. *Half Slave and Half Free: The Roots of Civil War*. New York: Hill & Wang, 1992.

Levine, Lawrence W. *Black Culture and Black Consciousness: Afro-American Folk Thought from Slavery to Freedom*. New York: Oxford University Press, 1977.

McCurry, Stephanie. *Masters of Small Worlds: Yeoman Households, Gender Relations, and the Political Culture of the Antebellum South Carolina Low Country*. New York: Oxford University Press, 1995.

Potter, David M. *The Impending Crisis, 1848–1861*. New York: Harper & Row, 1976.

Silbey, Joel H. *The Partisan Imperative: The Dynamics of American Politics before the Civil War*. New York: Oxford University Press, 1985.

Stampp, Kenneth M. *The Peculiar Institution: Slavery in the Antebellum South*. New York: Knopf, 1956.

White, Deborah Gray. *Ar'n't I a Woman? Female Slaves in the Plantation South*. New York: Norton, 1985.

The Civil War

Berlin, Ira, et al., eds. *Freedom: A Documentary History of Emancipation*. New York: Cambridge University Press, 1982– .

Bernstein, Iver. *The New York City Draft Riots: Their Significance for American Society and Politics in the Age of the Civil War*. New York: Oxford University Press, 1989.

Berry, Mary F. *Military Necessity and Civil Rights Policy: Black Citizenship and the Constitution, 1861–1868*. Port Washington, N.Y.: Kennikat Press, 1977.

Clinton, Catherine, and Nina Silber, ed. *Divided Houses: Gender and the Civil War*. New York: Oxford University Press, 1992.

Cox, LaWanda. *Lincoln and Black Freedom: A Study in Presidential Leadership*. Columbia: University of South Carolina Press, 1981.

Escott, Paul D. *After Secession: Jefferson Davis and the Failure of Southern Nationalism*. Baton Rouge: Louisiana State University Press, 1978.

Faust, Drew. *Mothers of Invention: Women of the Slaveholding South in the American Civil War*. Chapel Hill: University of North Carolina Press, 1996.

Hummel, Jeffrey R. *Emancipating Slaves, Enslaving Free Men: A History of the American Civil War.* Chicago: Open Court, 1996.

McPherson, James M. *Battle Cry of Freedom: The Civil War Era.* New York: Oxford University Press, 1988.

Montgomery, David. *Beyond Equality: Labor and the Radical Republicans, 1862–1872.* New York: Knopf, 1967.

Paludan, Philip S. *A People's Contest: The Union and the Civil War.* New York: Harper & Row, 1989.

———. *The Presidency of Abraham Lincoln.* Lawrence: University Press of Kansas, 1994.

Thomas, Emory M. *The Confederate Nation, 1861–1865.* New York: Harper & Row, 1979.

Reconstruction

Benedict, Michael L. *A Compromise of Principle: Congressional Republicans and Reconstruction, 1863–1869.* New York: Norton, 1974.

Brock, W. R. *An American Crisis.* New York: Harper & Row, 1963.

Carter, Dan T. *When the War Was Over: The Failure of Self-Reconstruction in the South, 1865–1867.* Baton Rouge: Louisiana State University Press, 1985.

Foner, Eric. *Nothing but Freedom: Emancipation and Its Legacy.* Baton Rouge: Louisiana State University Press, 1983.

———. *Reconstruction: America's Unfinished Revolution, 1863–1877.* New York: Harper & Row, 1988.

———. *A Short History of Reconstruction.* New York: Harper & Row, 1990.

Gillette, William. *Retreat from Reconstruction, 1869–1879.* Baton Rouge: Louisiana State University Press, 1979.

Holt, Thomas. *Black over White: Negro Political Leadership in South Carolina during Reconstruction.* Urbana: University of Illinois Press, 1977.

Jaynes, Gerald. *Branches without Roots: Genesis of the Black Working Class in the American South, 1862–1882.* New York: Oxford University Press, 1986.

Litwack, Leon F. *Been in the Storm So Long: The Aftermath of Slavery.* New York: Knopf, 1979.

Perman, Michael. *The Road to Redemption: Southern Politics, 1869–1879.* Chapel Hill: University of North Carolina Press, 1984.

Rabinowitz, Howard N. *Race Relations in the Urban South, 1865–1890.* New York: Oxford University Press, 1978.

Rable, George C. *But There Was No Peace: The Role of Violence in the Politics of Reconstruction.* Athens: University of Georgia Press, 1984.

Ransom, Roger L., and Richard Sutch. *One Kind of Freedom: The Economic Consequences of Emancipation.* New York: Cambridge University Press, 1977.

Summers, Mark W. *Railroads, Reconstruction, and the Gospel of Prosperity: Aid under the Radical Republicans, 1865–1877.* Princeton, N.J.: Princeton University Press, 1984.

Trefousse, Hans L. *The Radical Republicans: Lincoln's Vanguard for Racial Justice.* New York: Knopf, 1969.

Wiener, Jonathan M. *Social Origins of the New South: Alabama, 1860–1885*. Baton Rouge: Louisiana State University Press, 1978.

Williamson, Joel. *After Slavery: The Negro in South Carolina during Reconstruction, 1861–1877*. Chapel Hill: University of North Carolina Press, 1965.

5

◨ PUBLIC LIFE IN INDUSTRIAL AMERICA, 1877–1917

Richard L. McCormick

IN THE YEARS BETWEEN THE COLLAPSE OF RECONSTRUCTION AND WORLD WAR I, virtually every man, woman, and child in America had to face the unsettling consequences of industrialization. Railroad and telegraph (and later, telephone) lines penetrated the countryside, factories multiplied in size and number, millions of migrants from the farms of America and Europe found their way to our cities, and the United States made its economic and military might felt throughout the world. Scarcely a person remained unaffected; scarcely anyone's daily life was untouched. Many people made their peace with these developments—or failed to make it—in individual, private ways, most of which are forever lost to history. Their opportunities, their pains, and their choices can be guessed at only from aggregate statistics and an occasional diary or letter. But others supplemented their private decisions with public efforts to withstand and, where possible, benefit from the new economic and social forces around them. They joined organizations, issued pronouncements, attracted followers, and tried to enact laws. Many succeeded in

The author thanks the following persons for the advice and suggestions they provided in reacting to an earlier version of this essay: Eric Foner, Robert Johnston, Suzanne Lebsock, Richard P. McCormick, William L. O'Neill, and David M. Oshinsky.

using public, political means to respond to the conditions they faced; others failed. This essay sketches some of the dimensions of the public life these men and women created. My approach is not the only way to view American history from 1877 to 1917, but its angle of vision brings together much of the social and political history that has been written in recent years.

Like many subjects in American history today, the response to industrialism in the late 1800s and early 1900s lacks a coherent synthesis. Elements of older interpretations remain, but no new viewpoint has appeared that incorporates and replaces them. The "progressive" synthesis, positing a clear-cut battle between the "people" and the "interests," has long been rejected as too simple a framework for an extraordinarily complex era of political and social change, although elements of that viewpoint have reemerged in more subtle forms. Even less useful today is the "consensus" interpretation that appeared in the 1950s, a vision of the past that could never successfully encompass a period when the United States seemed to be coming apart under the strains of economic and social change.

Somewhat more helpful is the concept of "modernization," the notion that America was transformed from a land of "island communities" (in Robert H. Wiebe's phrase) to a nation where organized, cosmopolitan interests held sway. First implicitly suggested by Samuel P. Hays over forty years ago, this interpretation received brilliant, definitive statement in Wiebe's *Search for Order, 1877–1920* (1967). Thirty years later, that study still remains the most convincing synthesis of the history of industrializing America. In the meantime, however, an outpouring of historical research has added enormously to our knowledge of the years that Wiebe covered. Some of that research supports the modernization perspective; other studies suggest the unplanned, haphazard nature of social and political change; still others are too specialized to contribute to (or refute) *any* general interpretation. But this much seems true: we now know much more than Wiebe could have known about the groups that employed public, political methods to try to bring order and justice to modernizing America. The job of organizing that knowledge into a new synthesis remains.

When that synthesis is written, it will probably recognize that many organized endeavors to cope with the consequences of industrialism produced unexpected results. Virtually every feature of American life was being transformed, and no one could have anticipated where the changes would lead. Consider the popularity of the muckraking journalists of the early 1900s. Today their treatises seem boring, and it is hard to understand the emotional reactions their articles provoked— except by remembering that in 1900 Americans did not know how their new society operated: what businessmen actually got when they bribed congressmen, how the Standard Oil Company was built, how badly children were injured in factories. People read the muckraking journals not only to entertain themselves but also to gain some understanding of how modern America worked. It is little wonder that when some men and women ventured into public life to shape their society's choices, they made mistakes, predicted incorrectly, and sometimes contributed to results they ultimately abhorred. The point is not to pardon them all for their mistakes but to recognize the ironies that attended their efforts.

THE GILDED AGE: PARTY VOTING AND CREATIVE ALTERNATIVES

It seems fair to speculate that almost all adult Americans in the late 1800s would have *liked* to influence the choices made by their society—to encourage the building of a local railroad line, for example, or to stop it; to protect their group's religious practices against interference; to obtain higher wages for their labor; and to shape myriads of other decisions vital to their daily lives. Most people confronted variations on a common problem: the defense of their families and communities against outside forces emanating from industrial growth and the increasing heterogeneity of the population. Americans faced that problem, moreover, within a common environment: a rapidly expanding economy that was causing massive dislocations, frequent depressions, and widespread unemployment. Yet whatever the commonalities, these conditions were experienced by diverse, often antagonistic groups with unequal capacities for shaping public choices.

Getting and using influence in the public sphere was not easy, and the task was complicated by ingrained habits, restrictive rules, and social mores. Most men could at least vote, although their choice was usually restricted to the candidates offered by the leaders of the two major parties. Except in a handful of western states, women were denied the vote and were restrained, as well, by a deep and lingering prejudice against practically any form of female involvement in the often sordid public worlds of politics and business. Some economic groups, particularly among the commercial and industrial sectors, were well organized and enjoyed regular access to government officials. But for factory workers and farmers—and, even more, for domestics and unskilled laborers—organization and influence were difficult to achieve. Despite it all, men and women from virtually every segment of society plunged into public life to advance (or defend) their private values. Torchlight paraders rallied the party faithful in Connecticut; women crusaded for temperance in Ohio; cotton farmers organized in Texas; business-minded elites "reformed" New York City; workingmen ran for office in Richmond; angry mobs lynched alleged rapists in South Carolina. Their actions defined the public life of the Gilded Age.

The place to begin an account of that life is with voting, the most widespread means of political participation. To a greater degree than today, the ballot symbolized the "democracy" of American society, and its possession signified inclusion within the political community. Highly prized by the majority of white men who enjoyed it, the right to vote was avidly sought by many women and tenaciously defended by black men, who were encountering increasing barriers at the ballot box. Recent historians have done much to explain what voting meant to late nineteenth-century Americans: why most of those who had the right to vote exercised it so regularly, why some men rejected the major parties so bitterly, and why the question of who could vote was contested with such passion.

Party loyalties ran deep in the Gilded Age—and for good reasons. Appealing to voters on the basis of the same values they learned in their homes and churches, party leaders reminded men of their ethnic and religious identities, of their community's history, and, perhaps above all, of the Civil War—still a vivid memory for most Americans. Republican stump speakers observed that theirs was the party of morality, the party that had abolished slavery and saved the Union, the party of Lincoln. Sometimes Republican candidates in the North might also remind local audiences that theirs was the party of native-born Protestants, the party that would purify the community by imposing right behavior upon its members. Democratic speakers had equally good arguments for their party's faithful. Had not the Democracy defended states' rights against an overweening national government, protected the people's personal liberties against moral fanaticism, and stood for white supremacy? These were powerful appeals, powerfully supported by the spectacular campaigning techniques of the age. Whatever the other choices, when election day came, the vast majority of men cast their ballots for the Democrats or the Republicans. Voting data reveal that virtually every segment of the electorate mobilized in nearly equal proportions—rich and poor, immigrant and native-born alike. Most of those who voted probably cast their ballots for the same party in election after election.

A number of studies published during the late 1960s and 1970s challenged the older "progressive" assumption that party divisions in the late 1800s chiefly reflected class conflicts. Electoral data gathered by such historians as Paul Kleppner and Richard Jensen suggest that at least in the North and Midwest, ethnicity and religion were often the most important determinants of party choice. While the ethnoreligious interpretation of voting behavior has seldom been applied directly to the South, most historians agree that the majority of black voters continued to support the Republican party, which had won their loyalty during Reconstruction, and that the majority of southern whites were Democrats. As historical research on late nineteenth-century voting behavior continues, it is becoming clear that no simple generalizations—whether based on class or ethnicity or religion—can encompass the extraordinary diversity of electoral choices. A town's history, its settlement patterns, its role in the Civil War, a key event in its history such as a strike or a natural disaster, and innumerable other factors could all influence how the men who lived there voted. But of this much we can be certain: they *did* vote, and voting meant more to them than it does to us today.

The strivings of those who were denied the ballot and of those whose right to vote was endangered testify to the real and symbolic importance of voting in late nineteenth-century America. As early as 1848, a handful of women (together with some male supporters) had demanded enfranchisement. Linked to the abolition crusade from which it had sprung, the early woman suffrage movement was based on a belief in the natural rights of all people—male and female, white and black. Although this ideology drew support from the hallowed words of the Declaration of Independence, woman suffrage was in fact a radical demand in the middle and late nineteenth century. As Ellen Carol DuBois has observed, the very idea of woman suffrage suggested that women had public interests as individuals, separate from the interests of their husbands and families. In an age when a woman's sphere was believed to be the home and her husband (or father) was regarded as the home's ambassador to the outside world, woman suffrage was an astonishing notion. Its advocates not only risked the insults of the majority but also fashioned an increasingly full critique of American politics and government, a critique that would be commonplace by 1912 but was quite remarkable in the 1870s. The rowdiness and corruption of male party politics, the need for organization and expertise to solve problems, even the reliance upon social science methods: all these were among the themes of Gilded Age suffragists. Decades before the twentieth-century woman suffrage movement took its pragmatic turn, suffragists had been arguing that women would vote and govern differently from men. The streets would be cleaner, schools would be better, and organized public agencies would tackle social problems—especially in the cities—that government had long ignored.

To the dismay of suffragists, the granting of the vote to black men after the Civil War not only failed to bring a corresponding victory for women but actually set back their cause, because the word "male" was written into the United States Constitution for the first time. Out of this defeat, as DuBois has shown, an independent woman suffrage movement emerged. Divided between rival organizations, often split on strategy and ideology, and, above all, facing determined opposition, the woman suffrage movement of the Gilded Age achieved few victories. But its devoted leaders did succeed in keeping the question alive until another generation of women—having more organizational resources at their disposal and a less hostile political environment in which to operate—could take up the cause and guide it to victory.

Black men had secured the right to vote, and during Reconstruction they had put that right to good use in shaping public decisions on such matters as land, labor, and schools. But blacks had to struggle to maintain the suffrage, a task that grew more difficult with each passing year. In the South, where the great majority of blacks lived, most whites had accepted black suffrage only reluctantly, and many were determined to use whatever means were necessary to control and curtail it. Fraud and violence thus became regrettably common features of southern elections: thousands of blacks were frightened away from the polls, some were murdered for their efforts, and great numbers of them cast Democratic ballots unwillingly. Against these odds it is remarkable how many black men continued to vote for the Republican party or for other anti-Democratic coalition parties. J. Morgan Kousser has estimated that in the presidential election of 1880 a majority of black men voted in every southern state except Mississippi (where violence was rampant) and Georgia (which had already adopted a poll tax)—and most of them voted Republican. But these relatively high levels of black voting were not to last. Beginning in the late 1880s a wave of intense racism swept the white South, bringing with it a renewed determination to insure white supremacy through both violence and restrictive legislation. Lynchings became frequent; legal measures also contributed to keeping blacks in their prescribed places—and away from the ballot box. Yet despite the ferocity with which whites expressed their racism, thousands of blacks joined with whites in voting defiantly for the Populist party in the 1890s.

Rejection of the major parties was not an exclusively southern phenomenon in the late 1800s. In every part of the country, some men were dissatisfied with the Democrats and Republicans, and they poured great energy into independent movements of every stripe. In northern cities, elite reformers denounced the corruption of the political machines—with their seeming hordes of immigrant supporters—and made "independence" from the parties a badge of honor. More numerous if less socially prominent than the Mugwumps (as the city reformers were sometimes called) were those who joined the third parties of the Gilded Age, especially the Prohibition party and the various Greenback and Labor parties of the late 1870s and 1880s. Seldom, however, did the insurgents make much headway against the popular major parties; in presidential elections (the symbolic center of American politics) the third parties were practically invisible.

Perhaps the most promising moment for third parties came in the late 1880s when workingmen made what historian Leon Fink has termed their "single greatest push for political power." Aroused by some brutal defeats in the strikes of the mid-1880s and by the widespread anti-labor sentiments that followed the Haymarket Riot of 1886, the Knights of Labor plunged into local elections across the country. Under various party labels the labor movement fielded tickets in at least 189 towns in 34 states between 1885 and 1888, and a significant minority of its candidates won; in some places the labor party achieved dominance for a few years. But, as Fink has shown, labor's political goals were often vague. Although workers made mighty efforts to curtail state repression of their movement, the workingmen's parties usually "did not set out to do anything dramatically unconventional with political power." Within a few years their organizations had suffered the usual fate of third parties in America.

Electoral politics was not the only way to influence developments in the public sphere, as the proliferation of extraparty groups and associations attests. Businessmen's movements, labor unions, farmers' alliances, and women's organizations abounded during the 1880s. Each group sought to press upon the public the private wants and values of its members. In practice, however, the same social elements that had greatest reason to be content with governance by the major parties also enjoyed the readiest access to other means of influence.

Take first business and financial interests. Although it is hazardous to generalize about so diverse a body of men—from small-town merchants to Wall Street financiers—most of them could be satisfied with the general direction of public policy. Party government was most successful in performing precisely the task for which businessmen looked to government: namely, the distribution of resources and privileges to promote economic growth. In countless ways, from levying protective tariffs to encouraging railroad construction, governments at every level carried out this function while doing little to regulate the economic enterprises they assisted. When wealthy men and corporations gave generously to the political parties, they usually got their money's worth. But even businessmen could not be fully satisfied with party government. Who should get which of the limited available resources was always a controversial question. Even more frightening were the workers' and farmers' organizations that seemed to be trying to change the whole direction of American government. Within the cities, corrupt machines appeared to be pandering to immigrant masses at the expense of business interests. Economic elites thus turned to extra-party organizations: to trade associations whose lobbyists could influence key legislators, to pools and trusts whose combined might could bring order to a chaotic economic environment, to urban reform clubs that challenged the city machines. By no means always successful, businessmen's organizations still surpassed all others in economic resources and in the respect they commanded from government officials.

Industrial workers and farmers had a harder time of it, but they too made creative public responses to their problems. Far more than the business elite (virtually all of which was white, male, and Protestant), the industrial work force was highly segmented. Made up of men and women, blacks and whites, Europeans, Asians, and native-born Americans, Protestants, Catholics, and Jews, the working class was fractured further by the unequal skills of its members, by the diversity of conditions under which they labored, and by the constant geographical mobility of many workers. Not surprisingly, they encountered great difficulties not simply in organizing to improve the conditions of life and labor but even in agreeing what the goals of organization ought to be. Should workers accommodate to industry or resist the "time discipline" of modern factory life? Should each group give priority to organizing its own members or try to forge ties across the boundaries of race, culture, gender, and skill? Following leads first suggested by Herbert G. Gutman in the 1970s, labor historians have made significant advances in explaining how workers answered these questions.

They answered in diverse ways and, in Alan Dawley's phrase, took several "paths to power." One road led, as we have seen, toward electoral politics, another toward revolutionary forms of direct action, and a third toward efforts to establish a cooperative commonwealth of all producers. The Knights of Labor, the largest labor organization of the era, best exemplified this third approach. Acting on the basis of inherited republican ideas—now turned to a penetrating critique of the existing industrial order—the Knights opposed the "wage system" of labor and set out to restore an older set of economic relations based on the solidarity and equality of all producers. Accordingly, the Knights conducted organizing drives within local communities, enrolling skilled and unskilled workers alike; they mounted massive educational campaigns; they lobbied public officials for such measures as the eight-hour day. Unlike most of the national trade unions of the era, the Knights welcomed women and blacks into their ranks. By 1886, membership had grown to approximately 750,000, mainly as a result of some highly successful strikes the previous year. This would be the Knights' peak of strength. Weak leadership, competition from the craft-oriented American Federation of Labor (AFL), and a growing hostility to unions among the middle and upper classes soon destroyed the order. But the Knights' legacy of communitywide organizing and their far-reaching critique of industrial America lived on.

Compared to factory workers, the nation's farmers had some signal advantages when it came to organizing: they enjoyed far more cultural homogeneity (most were native-born Protestants), and their conditions of life and labor, while varied, derived commonality from the land they worked. Yet the economic problems confronting farmers were monumental. Over the course of the late 1800s the prices of staple crops (cotton, wheat, and corn) declined almost steadily. Technological advances may have increased farm productivity, but worldwide overproduction decreased farm income. Nowhere were the economic ills felt more intensely than in the cotton South, where white and black families, landowners and tenants alike, struggled to repay the merchants who held liens on their crops. And nowhere was the effort to organize farmers so successful, at least in the short run, as in the South, home of the Farmers' Alliance.

Spearheaded by dozens of lecturer-organizers who fanned out across the region in 1887, the Alliance grew to over a million (white) members by 1890. In the same years, the Colored Farmers' Alliance enrolled perhaps 250,000 black farmers. From humble beginnings as a secret fraternal order on the west Texas frontier, the Alliance became a mass movement to organize, educate, and politicize previously powerless people. Although rooted in the fabric of their communities, whose social mores they largely shared, local alliances boldly challenged the status quo by establishing cooperatives for buying and selling and by making unprecedented demands upon government. Chief among the Alliance's proposals was the subtreasury system, a plan for short-term government loans to increase the money supply and raise crop prices.

Middle-class women also organized to shape public choices in the late 1800s. Although denied the ballot and considered unfit for the rough and tumble of public life, women increasingly found that protecting "their" sphere of home and family compelled them to take roles outside the home. Especially in a town or city, a woman's ability to raise her children, prepare decent meals, and keep a clean and healthy house depended upon communitywide decisions about schools, water supplies, public health, and innumerable other matters. Women discovered, too, that as long as they confined—or appeared to confine—their attention to subjects that were traditionally considered within their own sphere, few objections would be raised when they organized for action. In consequence, the 1870s and 1880s saw an explosion of single-sex associations, including church groups, literary circles, mothers' clubs, and temperance societies, all of which drew their members at least partly into public life.

By far the largest and most important of these organizations was the Woman's Christian Temperance Union (WCTU). Founded in 1874, it expanded into every region of the country during the following decade and by the early 1890s boasted 150,000 members, most of whom were white, Protestant, and middle class. Although the WCTU's concerns were far broader than its name suggests, temperance was a uniquely compelling cause to rally women and a perfect platform from which to launch related crusades to purify the home by reforming men. Under the charismatic leadership of Frances Willard, the WCTU undertook a "Do Everything" program that included prison reform, aid to homeless children, promotion of the kindergarten movement, sex education, assistance to working women, and woman suffrage. By the late 1890s the WCTU's membership was still growing, but its program was narrowing to the single issue of temperance, and that goal was still far from achieved. Yet no other organization had ever done so much to arouse middle-class women about social problems or to draw so many of those women into public life.

It is tempting to conclude, as some historians have done, that Gilded Age Americans who sought public influence outside the major parties largely failed. Tempting, too, is the even harsher judgment that they deserved to fail because of their unwillingness to cooperate with one another and their disturbing tendency to seek superficial solutions for the problems of their age. To our modern ears, the Knights' notion of a "cooperative commonwealth" sounds like a pipe dream, and the word "temperance" brings to mind prudish and intolerant old ladies. The indictment of these groups is not completely without merit, but it ignores the realities of public life in the late nineteenth century and slights important accomplishments.

Certainly the Knights of Labor, the Farmers' Alliance, and the WCTU could not match the popularity or the power of the Democrats and Republicans. Nor did they achieve their leading policy objectives, much less shift the general course of American governance. Electoral politics was alluring, the major parties enjoyed great legitimacy, and party officials held the reins of power. If these disadvantages were not enough, the insurgent groups' economic enemies possessed formidable material and organizational strengths and commanded great influence within the parties. So it is hardly surprising that the Knights, the Alliance, and the WCTU attained few of their goals. But it is difficult to sustain the judgment that they brought about their own failure. For one thing, these groups were not averse to working with one another; the Knights and the Alliance cooperated in support of the great Southwest railroad strike in 1886, just as the WCTU and the Knights worked together on problems of common concern. For another, their analyses of the conditions they faced were far from superficial. All three insurgent organizations developed broad interpretations of the social problems of the day, and they increasingly offered not panaceas but full-blown agendas for social and political change. They failed because their enemies were more powerful than they and because party voting (by men) was still considered the only fully legitimate means of influencing public decisions.

In a larger sense they succeeded. Although no one could have anticipated such a development, by organizing millions of men and women the three groups were giving Americans early notice that the golden age of the political parties would not last forever. And indeed it did not. By the early twentieth century, hundreds of mass organizations were at work in the public sphere, while the parties were encountering staggering blows to their popularity and legitimacy. At the same time, government was reshaped along the activist, interventionist lines suggested by the Knights, the Alliance, and the WCTU. During the Gilded Age, the quest for electoral offices had occupied the center of the public stage, and the major parties had their day. Within a generation, winning offices would give way to influencing governmental policies as the main preoccupation of public life, and the natural successors of the Knights, the Alliance, and the WCTU were well positioned to take advantage of the shift. First, however, Americans would have to endure some crises that threatened and transformed virtually everyone's hopes for public life.

THE 1890S: A TIME OF CRISIS IN AMERICAN LIFE

Historians now regard the 1890s as a momentous turning point in American history. Within a single decade, immigration from southern and eastern Europe emerged as one of the greatest forces in the long history of the peopling of America. A new culture of leisure and consumption that would dominate twentieth-century life made its first tentative appearance. The movement toward consolidation in business and industry took long strides toward permanently transforming the nation's economy. The political parties went through their most dramatic realignment since before the Civil War. And the United States burst onto the world stage, soon to be a major power. Of course, these statements are possible only with the historian's hindsight. Many Americans living during the 1890s probably were at least dimly aware of these fateful developments, but most people experienced those years as a time of crisis, of economic depression, and perhaps even of severe personal disorientation. The consequences for American public life were cataclysmic.

No depression had ever been as deep and tragic as the one that lasted from 1893 to 1897. Millions suffered unemployment, especially during the winters of 1893–94 and 1894–95, and thousands of "tramps" wandered the countrysides in search of food. Although many cities and states stepped up their appropriations for relief, there was seldom enough. Under President Grover Cleveland the federal government remained aloof from the economic misery. When Jacob S. Coxey dramatized the government's insensitivity by leading five hundred of the unemployed on a march from Ohio to Washington, D.C., in 1894, armed police prevented them from entering the Capitol and herded them into camps. That same year, Cleveland employed the military and judicial might of the national government to crush striking railroad workers in Chicago.

Amid hard times, many Americans questioned the adequacy of their institutions and wondered whether democracy and economic equality were possible in an industrial society. Answering these questions with hope and hard work, some men and women began to experiment with new methods for solving the problems at hand. Hundreds poured their energies into settlement houses where they lived and worked among the urban poor. From their pulpits a new generation of ministers sought to make Christianity relevant to this world, not only the next, by aligning their churches actively on the side of the disadvantaged. Across the country the movement for municipal reform entered a new phase as businessmen and professionals tried to reach beyond their own ranks and enlist broad support for varied programs of urban improvement. Women's clubs increasingly turned their attention from discussing literature to addressing social problems. Although these middle- and upper-class endeavors would not reach a peak of strength for another decade, the seeds of Progressivism were planted during the depression of the 1890s.

Yet the most important movement to change the direction of American life during that troubled decade came not from the urban middle class, or even from industrial workers, but from farmers. Depression had come early to agricultural America and would stay late. For farm families trying to survive by planting cotton, wheat, or corn, it must have seemed that crop prices were always falling, railroad rates rising, and banks foreclosing. Tens of thousands of rural Americans migrated to the cities in search of work, but millions remained on the land, uncertain what to do. During the 1880s, as we have seen, the Farmers' Alliance provided some answers (as well as a welcome antidote to the loneliness of country life), but many of those answers depended upon government. Not surprisingly, the Alliance turned to politics, and from it emerged the Populist party of the 1890s.

Long a subject of interest to historians, the Populist movement has received intensive scrutiny since the mid-1970s. On the whole, the newer studies have improved the image of the Populists by rescuing them from charges of nativism and ideological backwardness and by emphasizing their movement's humane and radical opposition to the institutions and ideas of corporate capitalism. Richard Hofstadter's *Age of Reform* has been the principal victim of the recent historiographical warfare over Populism, and Lawrence Goodwyn has provided the dominant modern interpretation of the movement. Where Hofstadter regarded farmers as small businessmen and criticized the Populists for perpetuating myths that obscured economic reality (the idea of a golden age, a conspiracy theory of history, and a two-class view of society), Goodwyn is much more sympathetic to the language of Populism and sees in the farmers' "movement culture" a cooperative, democratic challenge to an inegalitarian money system and to corporate control of politics. Although Goodwyn has been criticized for excluding from true Populism those who do not fit his interpretation, his *Populist Moment* stands as the most influential recent treatment of the farmers' movement.

Central to the problem of interpreting the Populists is understanding the challenge they posed to the reigning economic and political ideas of the day. There is reason to think that Populism actually had a divided mind on the tenets of a capitalist, industrial society. Some evidence for this comes from the party's national platform of 1892, in which a harsh critique of the nation's political and economic institutions was followed by specific proposals designed to bring economic benefits to farmers. "We meet in the midst of a nation brought to the verge of moral, political, and material ruin," intoned the platform's preamble. The demands that followed included government ownership of the railroads, a flexible national currency, a graduated income tax, postal savings banks, and the free and unlimited coinage of silver. Enactment of these measures would have significantly expanded the government's role in the economy but would not have transformed the capitalist system into something else. The platform suggests that while Populism included a potential for what Goodwyn calls "structural alteration of hierarchical economic forms," it also appealed to farmers on the basis of concrete but moderate changes within the existing system.

A related problem on which historians have disagreed concerns the reluctance of urban industrial workers to rally to Populism and make common cause with farmers. Although the 1892 Populist platform celebrated "the union of the labor forces of the United States," that union was never consummated. Most factory workers turned their backs on the Populist party and continued to vote for the Democrats and Republicans. According to Goodwyn, the American labor movement had not been schooled in the "movement culture" of Populism and "was simply not yet ready for mass insurgent politics." Other historians have offered a simpler explanation for the division between workers and farmers: their contrasting economic interests. In Melvyn Dubofsky's words, "Farmers saw their economic salvation in free silver, cheap money, and inflation; wage workers preferred cheap food, hard money, and high wages." That the Populists were unable to extend their mass base into the cities goes a long way toward explaining their demise. Absorbed by the Democrats (against the will of many southern Populists) and branded as dangerous radicals by middle- and upper-class Americans, the Populists faded after their electoral defeat in 1896.

They had, however, contributed to a profound upheaval in American public life—to the realignment of the political parties and to a significant expansion of popular expectations for government. Where national elections in the Gilded Age had been closely contested and party lines had remained largely unchanged from year to year, the Populist insurgency and the economic depression of the 1890s brought a swift succession of shifts in party fortunes. The ultimate victors were the Republicans, who triumphed decisively in 1896 and (except for the years of Woodrow Wilson's presidency) remained in national power for more than a generation.

But the political upheaval went far beyond the improvement of one major party's position at the other's expense. Partisan loyalties, so firm for a generation, had received a severe blow from the successive electoral changes of the 1890s. Voters soon showed themselves far less interested than before in the vibrant party campaigns typical of the late nineteenth century. Because most areas of the nation were now firmly dominated by one party or the other (the Democrats in the South and the Republicans in the North and West), there was less incentive to vote than before; in consequence, electoral turnout would soon begin a downward slide that continued through the 1920s. For some voters, departure from the ballot box was not a matter of choice. Frightened by the interracial Populist crusade, elite southern Democrats took steps to disfranchise those blacks who had remained active voters through the 1890s, and, by design as well as accident, many poorer southern whites also lost the vote. The results of these developments were not felt fully until the early 1900s, but the party system would never be the same again. Nor would party voting ever again enjoy the privileged position in public life that it had during the nineteenth century.

Already in place were some of the groups and organizations that would fill the void being created by the decline of the parties. The Anti-Saloon League was formed in 1895 as an interest organization devoted to the prohibition of alcoholic beverages. Women's groups set to work in the cities, assisting laboring women and undertaking a multitude of tasks to make the "home" (broadly defined) a decent place to be. Urban reform movements were on the threshold of their most vigorous campaigns to transform city governments. Soon to be organized was the Socialist Party of America, led by Eugene V. Debs. Like the Populists, these and other related groups believed in a strong and active government. They disagreed mightily about what the government ought to do; they had unequal access to power; and all of them experienced disappointments with the results of the changes they inspired. But together they were poised to transform American public life in the early 1900s.

PROGRESSIVE AMERICA: THE NEW SHAPE OF PUBLIC LIFE

The concept of "Progressivism" still dominates the interpretive literature on the early twentieth-century United States, although not all historians are happy with the term. Many have pointed to the disunity of the Progressive movement and the contradictions within it. Others have observed that its democratic rhetoric often was not matched by democratic results. Still others are uncomfortable with a term that connotes "goodness," "enlightenment," and "farsightedness"—features that Progressivism in practice by no means always possessed. Whatever its limitations, the concept is inescapably embedded in the language of contemporaries and the writings of historians.

Within recent years, students of Progressivism have produced an outpouring of studies documenting the varied, fervent efforts to solve the problems caused by urbanization and industrialization. Virtually every group in American society is now known to have had a hand in those efforts, but the spirit and methods of Progressivism unquestionably emanated from the native-born, urban middle and upper-middle classes: from doctors, lawyers, ministers, businessmen, editors, schoolteachers, librarians, college professors, engineers, social workers—and from their spouses. To be sure, not all the members of these groups became Progressives, and no historian has yet solved the riddle of what personal, social, or psychological factors distinguished Progressives from conservatives. Admittedly, too, Progressivism often received crucial support from rural Americans, from the immigrant working class, and from the top leaders in business and finance. But the Progressive ethos—rooted in evangelical Protestantism, now turning to the task of delivering the cities from sin; committed to social science methods because they could eradicate social conflicts; opposed to the worst evils of big business but accepting of capitalism itself; devoted to collectivist, interventionist solutions, confident they would not destroy individualism—was distinctively native, urban, and middle class. By the early 1900s, men and women who shared some version of that ethos were pouring into public life, independent of the parties, to shape social and political decisions.

Progressivism owed much of its success to a distinctive method of reform, variations of which were adopted by the leaders of nearly every cause. They typically began by organizing a voluntary association, investigating a problem, gathering relevant facts, and analyzing them according to the precepts of one of the newer social sciences. From such an analysis a proposed solution would emerge, be popularized through campaigns of education and moral suasion, and—as often as not, if it seemed to work—be taken over by some level of government as a public function. Behind this method of reform lay a confidence that social science offered the means for remedying the conflicts of an industrial society. If the facts were gathered and properly understood, reforms could be found that genuinely benefited everyone. The Progressives' approach also reflected their growing faith that government could be trusted to solve problems. Most reformers did not initially set out to enlarge the government; they placed their faith first in private organizations. Over time, however, they looked increasingly to public agencies to carry out their programs.

These tactics were pioneered in many cases by women, a fact that historians have recognized only recently. The beginning of the twentieth century coincided with the maturation of a remarkable generation of American women. They had fewer children than their mothers and were increasingly freed from full-time housework by laborsaving devices and by society's absorption of some of the family's traditional economic and educational functions; many thus had time to devote to activities outside the home. They also had the inclination to do so. Better educated than any previous cohort of American women, many had gained familiarity with the insights of sociology and psychology and saw the possibilities for new ways of tackling social problems. Of even greater importance, women recognized that in an urban, industrial setting, care of the home and family was no longer just a private matter. One thing, however, had not changed for these women: most men still gave little encouragement to female participation in public life. And so it fell to women to invent their own means to improve the world.

Still lacking the vote, activist women turned naturally to voluntary organizations. Women's clubs, continuing the turn toward civic affairs first seen in the 1890s, campaigned for child labor laws, assisted working women, encouraged the establishment of kindergartens, and supported a multitude of other reforms to make industrial life decent and livable. A parallel movement among black women dealt with many of these issues but also addressed matters of special concern to members of their race, none more important than the crusade against lynching. Beyond the club movement, single-issue women's organizations applied Progressive methods to the problems of intemperance, unsafe factories, disease, prostitution, and many other ills. By banding together with others of their sex, the women who labored in these causes grew increasingly conscious of the problems and prejudices they encountered as women. Out of this consciousness came an astoundingly fertile confluence of feminism and Progressivism.

Perhaps the most creative products of the women's movement (and its male allies) were the settlement houses, of which approximately four hundred had been established in cities across the country by 1910. Writing in the early 1890s, Jane Addams gave the classic explanation for the founding of these institutions in "The Subjective Necessity for Social Settlements." Young women and men, seeking outlets for their urge to be socially useful, turned to the settlements, whose purposes and methods Addams described eloquently on the basis of her experience at Hull House in Chicago. What Addams might well have mentioned, too, is that settlement work offered women the opportunity to move beyond their assigned "sphere." There was no aspect of human life to which settlement workers were not exposed, no social problems completely foreign to their experience. Equally important, settlement women (many of whom remained unmarried) were relatively free of the constraints of husbands and families. For men and women alike, the settlements served as training grounds. From them, residents moved into every conceivable Progressive social reform: the improvement of tenement houses, the public playground movement, the crusade to abolish child labor, the demand for better hours and wages for working women, and many more. In bringing help to urban neighborhoods, settlement workers also brought their own middle-class (usually Protestant) views of decent life and right behavior. Often their values and activities must have seemed alien to the immigrant working people whom they sought to assist. But no other Americans in the early 1900s tried so hard or so successfully to devise solutions for urban, industrial problems as did the women and men of the settlement movement.

In taking roles on the stage of public life, Progressive women experienced a political awakening and gained unprecedented experience in the hard work of shaping public choices. Not surprisingly, they intensified their demand for the vote—both because it was their natural right and because it was an essential tool for accomplishing the social and political missions women had assumed. This time they succeeded. Using the familiar Progressive methods of organization, education, and lobbying, the reunited suffrage movement conducted disciplined drives for the vote in state after state and for a national amendment enfranchising women. Helped along by the direct-action tactics of more militant suffragists and by women's well-recognized participation in World War I, the suffrage cause achieved complete victory with the ratification of the Nineteenth Amendment in 1920.

Yet while the story seems straightforwardly heroic, woman suffrage still inspires controversy among historians, especially on the matter of the movement's ideology. Baldly put, the question is this: How conservative did suffragism become on the way to victory? Thirty years ago Aileen S. Kraditor opened up the subject by suggesting that the final phases of the suffrage movement saw a pronounced shift from arguments based on women's natural rights toward a rationale grounded in expediency. According to Kraditor, twentieth-century suffragists played down the radical challenges to existing forms of marriage and family life that had characterized the nineteenth-century movement and instead demanded the vote for more practical and conservative reasons: to defend the home and to improve the quality of the electorate by increasing the proportion of voters who were native born and white. In a sense, Kraditor's argument is unassailable, for no "radical" movement has ever achieved victory in America without significantly accommodating to the prevailing social values of the middle class. Early in the 1900s those values undeniably included the maintenance of traditional family life, plus goodly measures of racism and nativism. As Kraditor's critics have observed, however, the suffrage movement had always comprised a mix of arguments based on both justice and expediency. In Nancy Woloch's words, the early 1900s saw "not a sharp break but rather a tilt, a reformulation." Still open is the question of what that reformulation meant to the women involved. Was it tactical or sincere? Did it represent a repudiation of feminism or something else altogether?

Like the settlement workers and the suffragists, organized professionals also put Progressive methods to work on behalf of goals they defined as reform. In the 1960s Robert H. Wiebe first suggested that members of a "new middle class"—confident, cosmopolitan, and educated—had sought "to remake the world upon their private models," and subsequent historians have largely sustained Wiebe's view that such people placed a distinctive stamp upon Progressivism. Medical doctors, confident that they possessed socially useful knowledge, undertook public campaigns to eradicate hookworm, dysentery, cholera, tuberculosis, and venereal disease. Psychiatrists organized a mental hygiene movement and took their expertise into schools and prisons. Social workers, many of them former settlement-house residents, used the new method of differential casework to treat each client within his or her own social setting. Educators, criminal justice experts, city planners, and engineers also used their special skills to deal with social problems. In return for their labors, organized professionals demanded recognition as experts within their fields of competence, and they won the power to compel compliance with their methods. Like the settlement workers, that is, they imposed their own values as a condition for doing good. Compared to the settlement workers, however, the professionals frequently enjoyed much more authority to work their will on others.

More coercive still were those Progressives who set out to use legal means to control the racial and ethnic groups they hated and feared. No one fared worse than southern blacks, for whom the early 1900s brought nearly complete exclusion from politics, legal segregation of virtually all public and private facilities, and a sickening explosion of race riots and lynchings. In what sense was the racial radicalism of the white South in the early twentieth century part of the "Progressive" movement? In no sense at all, some historians have argued; the real Progressive spirit in race relations was expressed by the National Association for the Advancement of Colored People (founded in 1909), which appealed to the nation's conscience for political equality and a cessation of violence. Other historians, however, have discerned important connections between Progressivism and racism. As C. Vann Woodward put it, "The typical progressive reformer rode to power in the South on a disfranchising or white-supremacy movement." Similar (if far less violent) expressions of Progressivism may be found in the movements to "Americanize" European immigrants and to halt their continued entrance into the United States. The exclusionists, in particular, employed the quintessentially Progressive methods of organization, data gathering, education, and lobbying to persuade Congress to impose a literacy test for admission to the country. Enacted in 1917, the literacy requirement was followed during the 1920s by truly exclusionary quotas on immigration. Not all Progressives favored these measures. Like the parallel movement to prohibit the use of alcoholic beverages, immigration restriction was one of the most controversial reforms of the era. But its connection to Progressivism is hard to deny.

Businessmen, too, took an important part in Progressive reform by experimenting, sometimes successfully and sometimes not, with new applications of government. Corporate leaders found that governmental agencies could be of great use in placing an official imprimatur on their products and that policies of economic regulation by no means always harmed, and sometimes greatly helped, the businesses they were designed to supervise. Middle-class reformers frequently assisted the corporations by encouraging the adoption of measures that stabilized the economic and social environment in which business operated. Progressive reforms did not always benefit corporate America, and sometimes the results were truly unexpected. Still, in experimenting with successively more vigorous applications of government, capitalists gained experience in making the modern state their own, just as they had turned the nineteenth-century state to the purposes of economic development. As twentieth-century governmental machinery grew, businessmen learned better than anyone else how to work its levers.

The formation of settlement houses, the fight for woman suffrage, the physicians' campaign for public health, the legal establishment of racial segregation, the restriction of immigration, and the regulation of business corporations all expressed (however diversely) the drive of native, white, middle-class Americans to improve and control the often frightening conditions of industrial life. In pursuing these and related goals and in using the tactics described above, the Progressives and their allies did more than any other Americans to transform public life in the early 1900s. But they were hardly alone in trying to use public, political means to solve problems. From outside the ranks of Progressivism, other men and women also presented programs for shaping social choices in industrial America. Sometimes they joined forces with the Progressives and adopted similar methods, but this should not blind us to the distinctive forms of action that industrial workers, socialists, and immigrants brought to public life.

Compared to middle-class Progressives, industrial workers suffered greater divisions among themselves and possessed less power over others. Not surprisingly, workers experienced unremitting and sometimes bitter disagreements over organizational strategy, political action, and ideological goals. How inclusive should trade unions be? Ought workers to cooperate with the political parties? Should capitalism be accommodated or resisted? Some workers, of course, were better positioned than others to find satisfactory answers, none more favorably than those who belonged to the skilled, white-only craft unions of the AFL. As David Montgomery has shown in *The Fall of the House of Labor*, the AFL was scarcely monolithic in the early 1900s. Its diverse unions embraced a variety of working-class ideologies, and many of its members still nurtured the values of mutualism and class solidarity and rejected the competitive individualism of the marketplace. Increasingly, however, the AFL came to be dominated by Samuel Gompers and his conservative allies, who almost always kept control of the federation's national meetings. Under Gompers, the AFL sought stable relations with business leaders. The existing economic system would not be challenged, and material gains would be won at the bargaining table or on the picket lines, not through political reforms. Although in theory this strategy suggested disdain for the political parties, Gompers moved toward cooperation with the Democrats early in the 1900s; by the time of the Wilson administration the AFL was in firm alliance with the national Democratic leadership. Acting as members of a modern interest group, skilled trade unionists carved out a comfortable place for themselves within the public life of the Progressive era. Time would reveal, however, that working in such ready accord with business interests and party politics produced harm to the labor movement as well as gain.

With the AFL unwilling (and unable) to organize the mass of unskilled workers, socialists and radical unionists plunged aggressively into the void. Led by Eugene V. Debs, an indigenous American radical from Terre Haute, Indiana, the Socialist Party of America (SPA) reached a peak of nationwide strength between 1910 and 1912. In 1911 alone, seventy-four towns and cities elected Socialist officials, and the following year Debs won almost 900,000 votes for president (6 percent of the total). Although the Socialists could never realistically expect to win a national election, their leaders understood the educational value of electoral activity. None grasped this better than Debs, a brilliant orator, whose speeches drew on the traditional American image of the manly, independent worker—even as they appealed for collective political action by the laboring class.

Not everyone on the left was persuaded. The SPA found itself constantly at odds not only with the AFL trade unions (which the party alternately denounced and sought to capture) but also with the Industrial Workers of the World (IWW), a revolutionary labor organization representing what David Brody has termed "a homegrown brand of American syndicalism." Propelled into prominence by a series of strikes, especially between 1909 and 1917, the IWW briefly organized millions of workers across the lines of race, gender, and ethnicity. Many of its members were unskilled immigrants from southern and eastern Europe, workers the AFL ignored; others were native-born miners, migrants, and lumbermen, cut off from ties of family and community. When the IWW became involved in a strike, violence nearly always followed, although the workers were more often the victims than the instigators of bloodshed. Unlike the AFL and SPA, the IWW thoroughly frightened middle-class Americans. Government troops and private vigilantes suppressed the organization during World War I.

Socialism and labor radicalism attracted many of the vast numbers of workers who had recently immigrated to the United States, but immigrants also found a need for other means of organized, public action. For many, urban political machines offered one answer. Just as they had done since the 1840s, city bosses looked to the newcomers for support on election day and, in return, provided all kinds of favors, from emergency housing to a bucket of coal. Often such help was essential in easing the strain of assimilation to American life. Historians have recognized, however, that the party organizations of the early 1900s failed to mobilize the "new" immigrants from southern and eastern Europe as fully as they had recruited the Irish and Germans in an earlier day. At a time when voter turnout was decreasing among most social groups, recent immigrants and their children registered conspicuously low rates of participation. Even immigrants who did vote never placed their full faith in party machines to represent them in public life. More important were their own community organizations: churches, parochial schools, ethnic newspapers, benevolent aid societies, and a host of associations through which immigrants organized for the solution of their problems and protected themselves from an often hostile society.

As new groups and associations proliferated in the public sphere, they drained money, manpower, and organizational muscle from the already beleaguered political parties. Even worse for the Democrats and Republicans, men and women promoting reform causes and special interests soon discovered the unwillingness of the major parties to support measures that divided their large and heterogeneous coalitions. Although some organizations (such as the AFL) formed alliances with the political parties, many others found independence more rewarding. Nonpartisanship, in fact, became a hallmark of the Progressive era. The reformers' democratic rhetoric and their attacks on political corruption inspired the passage of laws regulating the parties and converting them from private into public bodies. Where nominating methods, campaign practices, and appointment powers had remained largely unsupervised throughout the 1800s, they were now encased within a web of law. At the same time, the parties lost some of their control over government. As the states and the nation stepped up their efforts to regulate the economy and insure social welfare, the new tasks of government usually fell not to partisan legislators but to independent boards and commissions.

The decline of the parties should not be exaggerated. Led by Theodore Roosevelt and Woodrow Wilson, the Republicans and Democrats of the early 1900s exhibited a degree of flexibility and responsiveness, mixed with self-interestedness, that surprised their critics. In the states and the cities, too, party leaders demonstrated a remarkable eagerness to try new programs and sometimes enjoyed striking success in adapting to the changed political and governmental environment. Most important, the major parties retained their virtual monopoly over the election of candidates to public office. Even these strengths, however, could not enable the parties to dominate the nation's public life as they had in an earlier era. Innumerable groups and organizations now competed with them for membership and loyalty; government agencies responded to client interest groups, not merely to party bosses; and independent public opinion had come to count for as much as or more than party opinion. American political life was being transformed.

UNEXPECTED CONSEQUENCES AND UNEQUAL POWERS

In any reflection on the changed public life of industrial America, two themes warrant special emphasis. First, men and women were commonly surprised by the results of the reforms they so fervently sought. Woman suffrage, for example, brought little change to American politics, either to the sorts of people elected or to the measures they enacted. Until the 1980s fewer women than men bothered to vote, and women tended to divide between the major parties in more or less the same way as men. The high expectations of many suffragists thus went unfulfilled. So did the vast hopes of those who believed that the social sciences and activist government could erase the class conflicts of an industrial society. What many reformers had failed to anticipate was that scientific experts were not necessarily impartial and that powerful interest groups were capable of dominating administrative agencies. In a very different vein, the southern racists' expectation that blacks would remain forever quiescent under the crushing weight of violence, poverty, and discrimination proved utterly unfounded. Within a half-century after Jim Crow became law, another generation of southern blacks led the whole nation toward a Second Reconstruction. It seems likely that as historical research proceeds, so will our appreciation of the unexpected consequences of reform.

Second, the power to influence public decisions remained unequally distributed on the eve of World War I, just as it had been at the end of Reconstruction. Forty years had brought changes, to be sure. Middle-class women had made great gains, and blacks had suffered crushing losses. A new class of experts in medicine, engineering, and statistics (to name but three fields) had achieved considerable influence; skilled workers had perhaps neither gained nor lost; and the unskilled were probably further removed from power than ever. The new immigrants of the 1890s and early 1900s commanded less political clout than had their counterparts of the 1840s and 1850s. Despite its democratic claims, Progressivism had not come close to equalizing influence within American public life. The decline of the parties had expanded access to government for the well-organized and the unpoor, but not for others. These are scarcely surprising conclusions, but they are sobering.

BIBLIOGRAPHY

Addams, Jane. "The Subjective Necessity for Social Settlements" (1892). In *Twenty Years at Hull-House, with Autobiographical Notes.* New York: Macmillan, 1910.

Baker, Paula. "The Domestication of Politics: Women and American Political Society." *American Historical Review* 89 (June 1984): 620–47.

Berry, Mary Francis, and John W. Blassingame. *Long Memory: The Black Experience in America.* New York: Oxford University Press, 1982.

Bordin, Ruth. *Woman and Temperance: The Quest for Power and Liberty, 1873–1900.* Philadelphia: Temple University Press, 1981.

Boyer, Paul. *Urban Masses and Moral Order in America, 1820–1920.* Cambridge, Mass.: Harvard University Press, 1978.

Brody, David. *Workers in Industrial America: Essays on the Twentieth-Century Struggle.* New York: Oxford University Press, 1980. (See esp. chap. 1.)

Buechler, Steven M. *The Transformation of the Woman Suffrage Movement: The Case of Illinois, 1850–1920.* New Brunswick, N.J.: Rutgers University Press, 1986.

Buhle, Mari Jo. *Women and American Socialism, 1870–1920.* Urbana: University of Illinois Press, 1981.

Buhle, Paul, and Alan Dawley, eds. *Working for Democracy: American Workers from the Revolution to the Present.* Urbana: University of Illinois Press, 1985.

Burnham, Walter Dean. "The Changing Shape of the American Political Universe." *American Political Science Review* 59 (March 1965): 7–28.

Couvares, Francis G. *The Remaking of Pittsburgh: Class and Culture in an Industrializing City, 1877–1919.* Albany: State University of New York Press, 1984.

Dawley, Alan. *Class and Community: The Industrial Revolution in Lynn.* Cambridge, Mass.: Harvard University Press, 1976.

Dubofsky, Melvyn. *Industrialism and the American Worker, 1865–1920.* 2d ed. Arlington Heights, Ill.: AHM, 1975.

DuBois, Ellen Carol. *Feminism and Suffrage: The Emergence of an Independent Women's Movement in America, 1848–1869.* Ithaca, N.Y.: Cornell University Press, 1978.

———. "Working Women, Class Relations, and Suffrage Militance: Harriot Stanton Blatch and the New York Woman Suffrage Movement, 1894–1909." *Journal of American History* 74 (June 1987): 34–58.

Filene, Peter G. "An Obituary for 'The Progressive Movement.'" *American Quarterly* 22 (spring 1970): 20–34.

Fink, Leon. *Workingmen's Democracy: The Knights of Labor and American Politics.* Urbana: University of Illinois Press, 1983.

Goodwyn, Lawrence. *The Populist Moment: A Short History of the Agrarian Revolt in America.* New York: Oxford University Press, 1978.

Gutman, Herbert G. *Work, Culture, and Society in Industrializing America: Essays in American Working-Class History.* New York: Vintage, 1977.

Hahn, Steven. *The Roots of Southern Populism: Yeoman Farmers and the Transformation of the Georgia Upcountry, 1850–1890.* New York: Oxford University Press, 1983.

Hays, Samuel P. "The Politics of Reform in Municipal Government in the Progressive Era." *Pacific Northwest Quarterly* 55 (October 1964): 157–69.

———. *The Response to Industrialism, 1885–1914.* Chicago: University of Chicago Press, 1957.

Hofstadter, Richard. *The Age of Reform: From Bryan to F.D.R.* New York: Knopf, 1955.

Jensen, Richard. *The Winning of the Midwest: Social and Political Conflict, 1888–1896.* Chicago: University of Chicago Press, 1971.

Keller, Morton. *Affairs of State: Public Life in Late Nineteenth-Century America.* Cambridge, Mass.: Harvard University Press, 1977.

Kleppner, Paul. *Continuity and Change in Electoral Politics, 1893–1928.* New York: Greenwood Press, 1987.

———. *The Third Electoral System, 1853–1892: Parties, Voters, and Political Cultures.* Chapel Hill: University of North Carolina Press, 1979.

Kousser, J. Morgan. *The Shaping of Southern Politics: Suffrage Restriction and the Establishment of the One-Party South, 1880–1910.* New Haven, Conn.: Yale University Press, 1974.

Kraditor, Aileen S. *The Ideas of the Woman Suffrage Movement, 1890–1920.* New York: Columbia University Press, 1965.

Kraut, Alan M. *The Huddled Masses: The Immigrant in American Society, 1880–1921.* Arlington Heights, Ill.: Harlan Davidson, 1982.

Link, Arthur S., and Richard L. McCormick. *Progressivism.* Arlington Heights, Ill.: Harlan Davidson, 1983.

McCormick, Richard L. *The Party Period and Public Policy: American Politics from the Age of Jackson to the Progressive Era.* New York: Oxford University Press, 1986.

McGerr, Michael E. *The Decline of Popular Politics: The American North, 1865–1928.* New York: Oxford University Press, 1986.

Montgomery, David. *The Fall of the House of Labor: The Workplace, the State, and American Labor Activism, 1865–1925.* Cambridge: Cambridge University Press, 1987.

O'Neill, William L. *The Progressive Years: America Comes of Age.* New York: Dodd, Mead, 1975.

Ostreicher, Richard. "Urban Working-Class Political Behavior and Theories of American Electoral Politics, 1870–1940." *Journal of American History* 74 (March 1988): 1257–86.

Painter, Nell Irvin. *Standing at Armageddon: The United States, 1877–1919.* New York: Norton, 1987.

Porter, Glenn. *The Rise of Big Business, 1860–1910.* Arlington Heights, Ill.: AHM, 1973.

Rodgers, Daniel T. "In Search of Progressivism." *Reviews in American History* 10 (December 1982): 113–32.

Salvatore, Nick. *Eugene V. Debs: Citizen and Socialist.* Urbana: University of Illinois Press, 1982.

Skowronek, Stephen. *Building a New American State: The Expansion of National Administrative Capacities, 1877–1920.* Cambridge: Cambridge University Press, 1982.

Thelen, David P. *The New Citizenship: Origins of Progressivism in Wisconsin, 1885–1900.* Columbia: University of Missouri Press, 1972.

———. *Paths of Resistance: Tradition and Dignity in Industrializing Missouri.* New York: Oxford University Press, 1986.

Tomlins, Christopher L. *The State and the Unions: Labor Relations, Law, and the Organized Labor Movement in America, 1880–1960.* New York: Cambridge University Press, 1985.

Turner, James. "Understanding the Populists." *Journal of American History* 67 (September 1980): 354–73.

Wiebe, Robert H. *The Search for Order, 1877–1920.* New York: Hill & Wang, 1967.

Williamson, Joel. *A Rage for Order: Black-White Relations in the American South since Emancipation.* New York: Oxford University Press, 1986.

Woloch, Nancy. *Women and the American Experience.* New York: Knopf, 1984.

Woodward, C. Vann. *The Strange Career of Jim Crow.* 3d ed. New York: Oxford University Press, 1974.

6

▪ PROSPERITY, DEPRESSION, AND WAR, 1920–1945

Alan Brinkley

MOST AMERICANS WHO LIVED THROUGH THE PERIOD FROM THE END OF WORLD War I to the end of World War II believed they were experiencing events of special historical importance: an unprecedented capitalist expansion, the greatest economic crisis in the nation's history, a dramatic experiment in political reform, a cataclysmic world conflict, the rise of the United States to unchallenged global preeminence. Contemporaries tried constantly to make sense of their turbulent times, and they produced histories of the era even as it continued. Professional historians were scarcely less eager. Less than a decade after the end of the war, a significant body of scholarship on the interwar years had already begun to emerge.

The initial volume of Frank Freidel's monumental biography of Franklin Roosevelt appeared in 1952, as did Eric Goldman's sweeping (and highly approving) history of twentieth-century liberalism.[1] Three years later, Richard Hofstadter published *The Age of Reform*, which (among other things) attempted to situate the New Deal within a broader reform tradition. In 1956, James MacGregor Burns produced *Roosevelt: The Lion and the Fox*, an important biography of Roosevelt as president. And in 1957, the first of the three volumes of Arthur Schlesinger Jr.'s *The Age of Roosevelt* appeared, an event that, more than any

133

other, defined the directions in which future scholarship on the era would move.[2] Schlesinger's study was notable for its remarkable breadth (it proposed to chronicle the entire interwar period) and its exceptional literary grace. But it was notable, too, for its powerful interpretive stance, a stance that helped shape both popular and scholarly views of the era for at least a generation and that became the basis of much subsequent historiographical debate.

PATTERNS OF HISTORICAL EXPLANATION

Central to Schlesinger's interpretation was his belief that American history moves in a discernible cyclical pattern, what he later called "a continuing shift in national involvement, between public purpose and private interest." Periods of energetic public reform occur every twenty to thirty years, run their course, and give way to periods of retrenchment and preoccupation with private goals. During conservative eras, progressive forces slowly regain momentum and in time again prevail. Hence the reform energies of the Progressive Era gave way to the retrenchment and self-interest of the 1920s, which gave way in turn to the renewal of liberal energies in the 1930s. By the beginning of World War II, the New Deal had largely run its course, and the nation had entered another period of public stasis, which continued until reform energies revived again after 1960.[3]

Schlesinger's cycle theory contained several assumptions beyond the obvious one that swings in the political climate occur in predictable patterns. It reflected the belief that political phenomena are the defining events of historical development. Hence the interwar period was, as the title of Schlesinger's series proclaims, "the age of Roosevelt." Cycle theory also portrayed American history in general (and the interwar years in particular) as a series of sharply discontinuous experiences. The coming of the Great Depression and the advent of the New Deal, for example, marked a sharp break with the 1920s. Similarly, the "New Deal era" was strikingly different from the much more conservative period that followed it. Finally, Schlesinger's interpretation was a highly progressive one. Reform might move in fits and starts, but move it did, pushing the nation inexorably out of an inferior past and toward an improving future. The New Deal, therefore, was part of a long tradition of reform—of popular democratic movements battling successfully against selfish private interests—that stretched back to the early days of the republic.[4]

The three decades since publication of *The Age of Roosevelt* have been marked by dramatic changes in the nature of American historical scholarship. And while Schlesinger's interpretive premises continue to attract significant attention and respect, they have also encountered vigorous challenges from several alternative historiographical stances.

One such challenge emerged from what has come to be known as "the organizational synthesis," an approach to twentieth-century American history that reflects several distinct influences: the ideas of Max Weber, more recent theories of modernization, and, most immediately, several important works of scholarship that appeared in the 1960s. Alfred Chandler Jr.'s *Strategy and Structure* (1962), the first of his path-breaking studies of the development of modern business organizations, was a major event in attracting attention to the nature of modern bureaucracies. Robert Wiebe's *The Search for Order* (1967), an influential interpretation of the late-nineteenth and early-twentieth centuries, emphasizes the rise of large-scale national institutions and the demise of localism, shifting attention away from immediate political events and toward large patterns of social and economic change running beneath them. Neither Wiebe nor Chandler themselves provided an explicit interpretive framework for the interwar years, but their work helped form the basis for a substantial scholarly redefinition of those years in organizational terms.

The "organizational synthesis" is, in fact, a broad rubric that has been used to embrace widely disparate work. But while its central premises are flexible, they are also distinctive. At its core is the assumption (in the words of Louis Galambos, one of its principal spokesmen) that

> some of the most (if not the single most) important changes which have taken place in modern America have centered about a shift from small-scale, informal, locally or regionally oriented groups to large-scale, national, formal organizations. The new organizations are characterized by a bureaucratic structure of authority. The shift in organization cuts across the traditional boundaries of political, economic, and social history. Businesses, reform groups, professional and labor organizations—all developed along somewhat similar lines.

Organizational historians posed a challenge, therefore, both to Schlesinger's notion of "cycles" and discontinuity and to the general belief among historians in the primacy of political events. Momentary fluctuations in the political and cultural climate (such as the contrast between the "stagnant" politics of the 1920s and the "progressive" nature of the New Deal) have seemed less important to them than the broad adaptations imposed on society by the economic and bureaucratic revolution.

The organizational synthesis did not, however, necessarily contest the fundamentally progressive view of history that Schlesinger shared with most other historians until the 1950s. Organizational historians identified a different engine driving society forward (bureaucratic development, not political reform), but they could still portray history as a continually ameliorative process. The challenge to progressive assumptions came from other directions: from the so-called consensus scholars of the 1950s and early 1960s; from historians influenced by the New Left; and from more recent interpretations shaped by (among other things) the sober political realities of the 1970s and 1980s.

Consensus scholarship, which emerged shortly after World War II and flourished in the 1950s and 1960s, has been widely derided by the left as a Cold War effort to celebrate capitalism and delegitimize challenges to it. But the most important consensus historians considered their work highly critical of American values and institutions. At the heart of the American experience, they contended, was what Richard Hofstadter called the "common climate of opinion" that had pervaded most of the nation's history, a climate resting on an almost universal commitment to economic self-aggrandizement through competitive capitalism. Consensus scholars tended to discount the importance (and question the value) of conflict, even as they lamented what they considered the harsh and barren nature of the American political tradition; and they emphasized the limits more than the extent of reform. Hofstadter and others were generally well disposed toward the New Deal, for example, but were more dubious than Schlesinger of its epochal importance.

A less ambiguous assault on progressive assumptions came from historians influenced by the ideas of the New Left, who began in the 1960s to attack the notion, central to Schlesinger's thesis, that liberal reform had been responsible for an increase in democracy and social justice in American life. On the contrary, claimed scholars such as Gabriel Kolko, James Weinstein, and (later) Jeffrey Lustig, the real story of modern America was the decline of genuine democracy: the steady increase in the power of private, corporate institutions, the growing influence of those institutions over the workings of government, and hence the declining ability of the people to control the circumstances of their work and their lives.[5] Reform crusades, some leftist scholars contended, served not to limit the power of "interests" and increase the power of the people, as Schlesinger and his progressive forebears had argued. They were, instead, the products of a "corporate liberalism," through which powerful capitalist institutions expanded and solidified their influence at the expense of the people.

Still another challenge to progressive assumptions has come from scholars who question not so much the benefits of consolidation and "modernization" as the extent to which they have occurred at all. One of the first explicit efforts to base an interpretive model on the existence of such limits is Barry Karl's *The Uneasy State*, published in 1983. Impressed by the persistence of localistic and "anti-modern" forces in late-twentieth-century America, Karl suggests that progress toward national unity has not been the hallmark of modern American development. On the contrary, he claims, twentieth-century society is at least as notable for the degree to which it has *failed* to nationalize, for the extent to which it has *resisted* unity, for the ways in which localism and traditionalism have not only survived, but flourished. Such an argument, he concedes, is a challenge to the essentially "nationalist" assumptions that have characterized virtually all previous interpretations of the twentieth century: Schlesinger's progressive view, the interpretations of the "consensus" historians and the "organizational" scholars, even the more acerbic arguments of historians of the left. Americans' fervent commitment to the preservation of individual liberties has consistently prevented them from defining themselves clearly as a nation.

Karl's contentions are a reflection (even if perhaps an unintended one) of a larger development in American historical scholarship as a whole: an emphasis on diversity; a sense that the history of the nation is many different stories, no one of which can be considered the "main" story; a skepticism about finding common definitions of American nationalism or discovering common values among its people. The growing centrality of the concepts of race, ethnicity, gender, and class within historical scholarship—and the highly varied experiences and values that historians have discovered while exploring those categories—has called into question the viability of any effort to define a "central theme" in the nation's past. Even the most fundamental (and presumably unifying) concepts in political language—the ideas of rights, liberty, citizenship, and "Americanism"—have (as Daniel Rodgers, Roy Rosenzweig, Gary Gerstle, and others demonstrate) had very different meanings for different groups and have been the objects of continual contests for definition. Such arguments are part of what some describe as an overdue amplification of historical scholarship and what others describe as its "deconstruction." In seeking to explain the experiences of groups and subcultures previously consigned to the margins of historical experience, scholars have called into question many of the unifying explanations that once made American history seem whole.

All these broad approaches continue to influence interpretations of the interwar years, even if many individual works do not fit neatly into one or another "school." The result is a scholarly landscape far more varied and conflicted than that of a generation ago.

CULTURAL CONFLICT

Historians examining the twentieth century have moved more slowly than scholars of earlier eras to embrace the movement of modern scholarship away from its concern with politics and toward an increased attention to social and cultural events, but they have moved nonetheless.[6] In particular, scholars have taken an increasing interest in patterns of social and cultural conflict in the 1920s and 1930s.

The first studies of the social and cultural landscape of the interwar years reflected the assumption that the era was a period of sharp discontinuity. The 1920s, according to this view, were a time less of conflict than of stultifying middle-class conformity and bigotry, an interpretation that echoed the assumptions of such contemporary social critics as Sinclair Lewis and H. L. Mencken and of Frederick Lewis Allen's influential popular history of the decade, *Only Yesterday* (1931). Mencken, Lewis, Allen, and others portrayed American culture in the 1920s as the product of a narrow-minded, materialistic middle class (what Mencken liked to call the "booboisie"); and they tended to link such phenomena as racism, nativism, and fundamentalism with conservative Republican politics and the spread of reactionary bourgeois values. Hence Lewis's character George F. Babbitt could be the epitome of the modern middle-class consumer, celebrating the new business culture, and simultaneously a member of a nativist organization clearly modeled on the Ku Klux Klan. Schlesinger's *The Crisis of the Old Order* accepted the broad outlines of this interpretation.

Even before Schlesinger's study appeared, however, alternative interpretations had emerged. Some consensus scholars, for example, linked the resurgence of the Klan, the prohibition crusade, and the growth of fundamentalism to such earlier protest movements as Greenbackism and Populism. All were examples of "symbolic" or "status" politics, which appealed not to the middle class in general but to troubled, usually marginal people who expressed their inchoate anxieties in largely symbolic terms—through a nostalgic call for restoration of a "golden" past or through an embittered attack on symbolic "scapegoats." William Leuchtenburg offers a related, but less pejorative, explanation in his influential history of the 1920s, *The Perils of Prosperity* (1958). He argues that the intense cultural upheavals of the decade were part of a broad conflict between a new, secular urban culture, committed to cultural pluralism and modernist ideas, and an older, rural America, still wedded to traditional values, largely unconnected to the economic advances of the New Era, and feeling threatened by the changes. These interpretations, unlike earlier views, drew a sharp distinction between members of the "new" middle class and those who gravitated to such movements as fundamentalism and the Klan.

Other scholars have revised such explanations in several ways. Some (following the lead of Lawrence Goodwyn, Steven Hahn, and other historians of Populism) have challenged the sharp distinction consensus scholars made between "economic" and "cultural" (or between "rational" and "symbolic") interests. Seemingly rearguard battles to defend "cultural" norms are often, they suggest, democratic efforts to defend rational economic and social interests and to preserve individual and community autonomy. Even some of the unsavory cultural protests of the 1920s, while seldom "democratic" in form, can be seen as an effort to preserve threatened social orders that conferred upon their members not simply "symbolic" rewards but real powers and economic advantages. Kathleen Blee, in examining the women's branch of the Ku Klux Klan, has argued that the women found in the Klan a source of community that was becoming increasingly difficult to create in ordinary social interaction; and that many women found the women's branch a valuable defender of female rights (including suffrage), in addition to being a defender of white supremacy. Leonard Moore's study of the Klan in Indiana suggests, similarly, that members were driven at least as much by resentments of powerful elites as by racial or ethnic prejudice, that a broad cross-section of middle-class white society rallied to the Klan to defend the values of their community against what they considered menacing outside forces. The Klan, in short, was part of a broader effort by individuals to fight their perception of powerlessness in an increasingly bureaucratized world.

Similarly, many historians have seen Leuchtenburg's rural/urban dichotomy as too simple a description of the pattern of conflict. The new, bureaucratic order, they argue, was threatening not just to isolated, provincial people but to everyone whose livelihood or values depended on the survival of localistic, decentralized institutions. Such people could be either urban or rural; working class or middle class; Protestant or Catholic. The Ku Klux Klan, for example, was not simply an organization of rural southerners lashing out against changing racial and ethnic norms. As Kenneth Jackson and Leonard Moore have both demonstrated, the Klan had its greatest support in northern and midwestern cities; and it was concerned not just with suppressing blacks, Jews, and immigrants (although racism, anti-Semitism, and nativism were, of course, rife throughout the organization) but also with combating what it considered the moral laxness of modern life. Its members often lashed out at such violations of traditional norms as adultery and divorce. Protestant fundamentalists, George Marsden has argued, were not just the rural "hicks" satirized in popular portrayals of the Scopes trial; they were also intelligent, educated, urban men and women struggling to preserve a traditional faith that was under assault from a newly aggressive secularism (or what David Hollinger, Terry Cooney, and others have called "cosmopolitanism").

By revising the traditional view of conflict in the 1920s, historians have raised new questions about the turbulence of the 1930s. Rather than contrasting the "cultural" protests of the 1920s with the "economic" dissent of the 1930s, scholars have seen both cultural and economic concerns at work in both periods. One example is the popular dissident movements of the era, such as those associated with Huey Long, Father Charles Coughlin, Francis Townsend, and others, long dismissed as a demagogic aberration from the generally progressive course of the politics of the era. Alan Brinkley and, more recently, Michael Kazin have argued that these phenomena in fact represented an alternative political vision, often at odds with the ideas of the New Deal. As such, they were part of the broad pattern of protest by which "localistic" people were struggling to preserve control of both the economic and the cultural institutions that governed their lives in the face of encroachments from the modern, bureaucratic order—a pattern that reflected some of the impulses that scholars of earlier eras have described as "republicanism." Leo Ribuffo has suggested that even movements of the far right in the 1930s should not be dismissed simply as extremism but should be seen as clues to economic and cultural anxieties that affected much of the mainstream. The turmoil of the 1930s, in short, reflected not just the search for economic advancement but the continuing ambivalence of many Americans about the costs of modernization.

Not all historians have emphasized conflict in examining the cultural history of the interwar years. To one important group of scholars, what needs explanation in this period is not the extent of conflict but its relative absence. A question that has intrigued Marxist scholars and others on the left for many years is, why, given the important inequalities and injustices in modern society, have there been so few class-based challenges to the status quo? Some scholars deny the existence of that anomaly by insisting that there were, in fact, many more such challenges than historians have traditionally been willing to admit. But others have accepted the view that it is the lack of greater conflict that is most in need of explanation. Out of their efforts has come a portrait of modern American culture that is in certain ways similar to the critique first advanced by Mencken, Lewis, and other "debunkers" in the 1920s: a portrait that emphasizes the rising importance of material consumption, not just to the economy, but to the culture.

Warren Susman was among the first to draw attention to the importance of the "consumer culture" in a series of important essays published in the 1960s and 1970s and finally collected in *Culture as History* (1984). Other scholars—among them Christopher Lasch, Jackson Lears, Stuart Ewen, and Roland Marchand—have produced a broad (and highly diverse) literature emphasizing the ways in which material abundance, the pervasiveness of advertising, the homogenization of mass culture, and the increasing availability of consumer goods have defined the nation's social and political values. Most such scholars are highly critical of the hegemonic effects of the consumer culture. Ewen, for example, argues that the consumption ethos served the economic needs of industrial capitalists while undermining efforts to address the human needs of the larger society. Lasch and Lears portray consumerism as a force that erodes traditional moral or spiritual values in favor of material pleasures and personal fulfillment, as the source of a "therapeutic" culture (a culture that serves as therapy for the self). But others (Susman among them) have argued that consumption has the potential to serve as a force for liberation and human fulfillment.

For scholars interested in the questions that have traditionally dominated discussion of the 1920s and 1930s, the consumer culture argument helps to explain why so many people seemed to acquiesce in social and economic changes that appeared in many ways averse to their interests. Although the rise of a new, bureaucratic order was eroding the abilities of individuals and small communities to control their lives and livelihoods, consumption and mass culture were opening up new (if, some argue, superficial) vistas that distracted them from their losses.[7]

THE "NEW ERA"

The political history of the interwar years has undergone substantial revision as well, often as a result of the same impulses that have reshaped interpretations of social and cultural phenomena. In perhaps no area has the traditional view changed more dramatically than in relation to the politics of the 1920s. Until at least the mid-1960s, virtually all scholars accepted the characterization of those years first advanced by Frederick Lewis Allen, then reinforced by several generations of New Deal politicians, and most energetically expressed in Schlesinger's *The Crisis of the Old Order:* that the 1920s were years of political retreat, reaction, and stagnation, a passive interlude between Progressivism and the New Deal. Beginning in the 1960s, however, historians began slowly to revise this essentially negative picture and to see in the politics of those years previously unnoticed progressive impulses. Arthur Link, in an influential 1959 article, made a persuasive case that despite the successes of conservative figures such as Warren Harding and Calvin Coolidge, important elements of the pre–World War I progressive movement survived into the 1920s and displayed significant strength in Congress and in state and local government. But the strongest challenge to the old stereotypes has come from scholars contending that the policies of the Republican administrations themselves were far more active and innovative than previously suspected. According to this view, federal public policy in the 1920s represented an important and active effort to bring a measure of rational organization and scientific planning to economic affairs.

"Organizational" historians (Robert Himmelberg, Louis Galambos, and above all Ellis Hawley) have devoted much attention to what they call the "associational" (and what Donald Brand and others call the "corporatist") ideal, the belief that economic order and scientific management could be achieved by creating a cooperative relationship among labor, capital, and the state. Associationalists shared with many progressive reformers a belief in the need for planning and order in the economy. But their real model was the economic mobilization during World War I, when government had worked closely with business to facilitate cooperation and efficiency within the industrial world. The trade association movement of the 1920s, they argue, was an effort to recreate that "ordered economic world" they believed the wartime experiments had produced.[8]

The central figure of the "progressive" 1920s, such scholars have long argued, was Secretary of Commerce and later President Herbert Hoover, whose historical reputation has been more thoroughly revised in recent years than that of any public figure of his time. Liberal critics of the New Deal era (and after) liked to portray Hoover as a hardened, embittered reactionary, the embodiment of the static old order that the New Deal had triumphantly displaced. Hoover himself, in his later years, did much to support that image. But as Hawley, David Burner, Joan Hoff Wilson, James Stuart Olson, and others have argued, Hoover in the 1920s (and indeed throughout much of his troubled presidency) was far from reactionary. He was, instead (to use Wilson's term), a "forgotten progressive," one of the most active and innovative figures in government and the leading advocate of a more forceful federal role in the management of the economy.

Hoover was the champion of the trade association movement in the 1920s and made extensive use of his powers as secretary of commerce and of his influence with other arms of the federal government to promote economic rationalization and limit "destructive competition." As president, Hoover constructed a program of unprecedented federal activism to deal with the Great Depression—price supports for farmers, federal assistance to public works and relief efforts, direct government loans to banks, railroads, and other troubled businesses—and laid the groundwork for many of the achievements of the New Deal. The New Deal, according to this view, was not a sharp and decisive break with a conservative past. It was the culmination of political forces that had been gathering strength for at least a decade.

THE NEW DEAL

The administration of Franklin D. Roosevelt has long been so central to scholarly views of the interwar years that the slogan "the New Deal" has come to represent not simply a particular set of policies and institutions but, for many historians, the era as a whole. Even those who reject Schlesinger's characterization of the period as the "age of Roosevelt"— even some who doubt the centrality of political history in general— concede that the New Deal was a phenomenon of particular historical importance. As a result, it has generated a larger literature than any other topic in twentieth-century American history. Yet even as studies of the New Deal proliferate, the broad interpretation of the Roosevelt years—as the central event in the progress of the modern United States toward greater unity and democracy—has remained surprisingly impervious to change since Schlesinger and others presented it in the 1950s.

But if there have been relatively few radical revisions in interpretations of the New Deal, there have been significant evolutionary changes. A particularly important moment in that evolution was the appearance in 1963 of William Leuchtenburg's influential synthesis *Franklin D. Roosevelt and the New Deal*, a book that remains the most important single-volume study of the 1930s even three decades later. Although Leuchtenburg was generally sympathetic to the New Deal, he was more sensitive than earlier scholars to its limits and its failures and assessed its results as no more than a "half-way revolution" that left many problems unresolved and created some new problems of its own. He pointed in particular to the Roosevelt administration's failure to end the depression before 1940, the absence of significant structural reform in the industrial economy, the limits of the new welfare state, the failure of government relief measures to help those groups most in need of assistance, and the New Deal's modest record on racial issues.

Leuchtenburg's study anticipated many of the arguments that emerged from the left in the late 1960s and was perhaps one reason why the revisionist interpretation of the New Deal failed for many years to develop very far beyond a few important essays. Articles by such leftist scholars as Barton Bernstein, Ronald Radosh, and Howard Zinn gave considerably greater emphasis to flaws, limits, and conservative impulses than liberal historians such as Leuchtenburg did; but they failed to make more than vague suggestions of a new theoretical framework for understanding the New Deal. More recently, however, scholars influenced by the left have produced more sophisticated critiques of the New Deal. Thomas Ferguson argued in several important articles that a rising group of internationalist capitalists shaped and controlled much of the New Deal agenda. Colin Gordon, whose 1994 book *New Deals* was the first full-scale revisionist interpretation of the New Deal in many decades, argued similarly for the direct influence of corporate forces in the construction and management of New Deal programs.

Despite continuing scholarly critiques from the left (and, occasionally, the right), most historians in the last two decades have accepted some variation of Leuchtenburg's stance of muted praise. At the same time, however, they have begun to ask some different questions about the New Deal, questions that are less concerned with establishing whether it was a good or bad thing than with explaining how it took the form it did, what effects it had, and how it helps illuminate larger patterns of political change in the twentieth century.

Historians have paid most attention, perhaps, to the question of constraints, to defining the limits imposed on New Deal reform by the social, economic, and political realities of the 1930s and by the ideological preconceptions of the New Dealers themselves. The first scholars to consider this question focused primarily on political constraints and argued that Franklin Roosevelt, despite his enormous personal popularity, was never able to ignore powerful opposition to his policies both within the government and in the electorate at large. James MacGregor Burns had criticized Roosevelt for his unwillingness to make full use of his popularity to challenge his opposition and for his failure genuinely to reshape the party system and provide a secure home for Progressives within it. Other scholars, however, have suggested that such a reshaping was never within Roosevelt's power. James Patterson, for example, argued that conservative opposition to the New Deal in Congress was an important factor in the administration's calculations almost from the beginning and became more powerful as time went on. Frank Freidel, Harvard Sitkoff, Nancy Weiss, John Kirby, and others have cited the political importance of the South to the New Deal coalition—in Congress and in the electorate—as an explanation for the failure of the administration to take more active measures on behalf of racial equality; while other scholars (Alan Brinkley and Bruce Schulman, among them) have chronicled the failure of New Deal liberalism to take root in the distinctive political environment of the South.

Many scholars have also emphasized ideological constraints: the degree to which Roosevelt and those around him operated in response to the economic and political orthodoxies of their time. Although the New Deal proved more flexible and less ideological than the administrations that preceded it, it too was constrained by powerful conservative assumptions: the belief in a balanced budget, the mistrust of the "dole," the reluctance to intrude the federal government too deeply into the field of microeconomic management, and others. Frank Freidel argued that Roosevelt was an essentially conservative man, whose innovations were a result of pragmatic political calculation and instinctive sympathies, not of a genuinely radical temperament. Barry Karl and Otis Graham have pointed to the absence of widespread support within the administration for the advanced forms of planning and organization that some 1930s liberals were promoting. Mark Leff has noted the reluctance of New Dealers to promote a genuinely (as opposed to symbolically) progressive tax system and their reliance instead on a series of highly regressive taxes to finance their programs. Herbert Stein, Robert Lekachman, Margaret Weir, and others have noted the economic conservatism that pervaded New Deal thought at least until 1938 and in particular the unwillingness of the administration to make effective use of federal spending as a tool for fighting the depression. (They have also pointed out that the economic assumptions that support such criticisms—the principles of Keynesian economics—were largely unknown to economists and policy-makers alike until the late 1930s.)[9]

Similarly, as James Patterson and others have shown, the clumsy, jerry-built welfare state that emerged from the New Deal (of which the expensive and inefficient Social Security System remains the centerpiece) was in large part a product of the strong ideological opposition, even among many of the most committed liberals, to an overt system of government welfare; and as Jill Quadagno has noted, it reflected too the racist assumptions of much of the political world through its careful initial exclusion from coverage of those occupations in which African Americans (and women) were most heavily represented. Institutional constraints—the absence of sufficient bureaucratic capacity or political experience in the running of a national welfare system—also helped shape Social Security, as Theda Skocpol, among others, has suggested. Social Security was also, Linda Gordon has argued, a product of highly gendered assumptions about the proper distribution of benefits. Both men and women involved in the creation of Social Security retained a strong belief in the centrality of the family wage and offered the most secure and generous benefits of the system to men. Women were left with the frail Aid to Dependent Children (later Aid to Families with Dependent Children) program, which was based on an assumption of female vulnerability and incapacity.

Nowhere has the argument for the New Deal's ideological conservatism been more forcefully advanced than in the field of labor history. New Deal labor laws and the growth of trade unionism they helped to promote—phenomena liberals have long considered among the most important progressive triumphs of the 1930s—have received withering reassessments by a host of recent scholars: James Atleson, David Brody, Sanford Jacoby, Karl Klare, David Montgomery, Bruce Nelson, Ronald Schatz, Katherine Stone, Christopher Tomlins, Stanley Vittoz, and others. These scholars differ from one another on many points, but they generally agree that the events of the 1930s mark a highly limited victory (if not an actual defeat) for labor; that the large hopes for creating a lasting basis for genuine industrial democracy were not achieved; that the New Deal was never fully committed to seeing it achieved. And yet other labor historians have seen in the great working-class struggles of the 1930s a striking (if short-lived) effort to redefine democracy and create a central place in it for labor. Gary Gerstle illustrates how immigrant textile workers in Rhode Island found through their organizing efforts a new way to define Americanism that included them and legitimized their commitment to the union. Lizabeth Cohen, in her study of steelworkers in Chicago, argues that the organizing battles of the 1930s forged a new identity for workers—less ethnically insular, more conscious of class-based grievances—that at least for a time opened up important new democratic possibilities.

Starting in the 1980s, a new body of scholarship began to identify some previously lightly examined constraints imposed on the New Deal by the nature of American governmental and political institutions. In doing so, it has made a case for considering the structure of the state itself as a crucial factor in the actions of government (as opposed to models of state behavior that emphasize the influence of party systems or social forces or constellations of interest groups). Kenneth Finegold, Anna Shola Orloff, Karen Orren, Theda Skocpol, and Margaret Weir (all of them sociologists or political scientists) have been among the many scholars who have shown the importance of political institutions themselves in shaping the results of political battles.[10]

These "state-centered" scholars argue that one reason the New Deal did not do more was because of the absence of sufficient "state capacity"; most of the federal bureaucracy in the 1930s was too small and inexperienced to be able to undertake large tasks. The failure of the National Recovery Administration, for example, according to Finegold and Skocpol, was in large part a result of the absence within the government of institutions capable of supervising the industrial economy; that absence made it almost inevitable that control of the experiment would fall into the hands of businessmen themselves. The relative success of the Agriculture Adjustment Administration, in contrast, is attributable to the far more highly developed bureaucratic capacity of the Agriculture Department: its close relationship to powerful farm organizations, its several generations of experience in attempting to manage the farm economy.

Even before the emergence of the state-capacity argument, several historians were examining other aspects of New Deal history that reveal many of the same constraints. As long ago as 1953, Grant McConnell demonstrated the powerlessness of federal agencies to maintain control over agricultural policies in the face of the power of private farm organizations. In 1969, James Patterson revealed the importance of state governments in administering (and hence shaping) programs designed and at least partially funded by the federal government. Lyle Dorsett, Bruce Stave, Charles Trout, and others writing in the 1960s and 1970s challenged what had come to be known as the "Last Hurrah" thesis (after the novel by Edwin O'Connor); they revealed the degree to which the New Deal, far from destroying the power of traditional urban political machines, in fact strengthened many of them by giving them administrative control of new federal programs. That was in part a result of political choice (the kind of choice Burns criticizes Roosevelt for making); but it was also a result of the absence of federal bureaucratic capacity to provide an alternative administrative structure. The state capacity literature of recent years, which has slowly found an important audience among historians, suggests some important new directions for these arguments.

Another reflection of this growing interest in bureaucracies is the increasing scholarly attention to the way the consequences of policy initiatives often depart from the intentions behind them. New Deal scholars have only occasionally asked such questions about the programs of the 1930s; but they have made clear nevertheless that some of the New Deal's most important accomplishments were ones that Roosevelt and his associates neither anticipated nor desired. In the broadest sense, the unexpected outcomes of New Deal efforts can be seen in the emergence in the 1930s of the "broker state." As Ellis Hawley has shown in *The New Deal and the Problem of Monopoly*, his landmark history of economic policy in the 1930s, by the end of the depression, important new groups—workers, farmers, and others—were beginning for the first time to exercise meaningful political and economic power. The federal government, in the meantime, had largely rejected the idea of trying to impose any central design on the economy or promote a transcendent national goal. Its policies worked, instead, to guarantee the rights of particular interest groups and oversee pluralistic competition in the national marketplace. It had become a broker state.

The rise of the broker state is arguably one of the most significant political developments of the New Deal era, and some historians—in talking about the "second New Deal" that emerged in 1935–36—have argued that it was the result of a deliberate ideological choice by Roosevelt and those around them. But Hawley makes clear that the broker state was in many respects an unintended result of government policies designed to advance other ends. The National Recovery Administration, for example, failed in its avowed goal of stabilizing prices and markets and harmonizing industrial relations (which Donald Brand and others have described as part of a broad corporatist impulse powerful within at least the early New Deal). Its most important legacy may have been a partially unintended one: the organization of the industrial work force into an important competitive actor in the marketplace (which section 7a of the National Industrial Recovery Act—precursor to the 1935 Wagner Act—did much to promote). Other initiatives designed to promote a planned, harmonious economic world failed in their larger goals but similarly left behind newly organized groups capable for the first time of effectively defending their claims. (Hawley termed this process "counterorganization," the mobilization of weaker groups to allow them to confront stronger ones—an alternative New Dealers gradually came to prefer to the more politically difficult effort to curb the influence of existing centers of power directly.)

Another important shift in the scholarly approach to the New Deal is the tendency to see its achievements less as the result of the political and intellectual impulses of the moment and more as the product of long-term social transformations. This has long been a contention of organizational historians, who see the New Deal as a reflection of the broad evolution of managerial systems in both private and public life. A related argument sees many New Deal achievements as the result of the emergence in the twentieth century of coherent interest groups, who were steadily gaining influence at the expense of political parties. Richard McCormick has chronicled the beginnings of that shift in the late nineteenth and early twentieth centuries; Samuel Hays, Louis Galambos, Anthony Badger, and Bernard Bellush are among the many historians whose work suggests the impact of that change on the policies of the 1930s. Other historians (among them Joseph Huthmacher, Mark Gelfand, William Bremer, Charles Trout, and Bruce Stave) have suggested that urbanization, and the growing political power of the city, shaped New Deal programs far more than the ideological inclinations of its leaders; the gradual shift in political attention in the 1930s from rural issues toward such matters as public housing, fair labor standards, and public health is evidence of the mobilization of powerful urban forces. Jordan Schwarz has suggested that one of the principal legacies of the New Deal was its embrace of an effort, spanning several decades, to use the power of government (what Schwarz calls "state capitalism") to develop previously underdeveloped areas of the country; vast public works projects in the South and the West, he claims, were the fulfillment of a dream stretching back at least to World War I, of using public investment to create a basic infrastructure for those regions.

Still other scholars argue that the New Deal was a reflection of the rising emphasis on consumption in American culture and the American economy alike, and that both the economic and the welfare policies of the Roosevelt administration were part of a broad political adaptation to that shift. That transformation found reflection in the policy evolution of the late 1930s and beyond (described by, among others, Herbert Stein, Dean May, Theodore Rosenof, and Alan Brinkley), which introduced Keynesianism to American government.

This emphasis on longer-term transformations invites historians to look to earlier eras to find the foundations of many New Deal policies. It also encourages them to look beyond the 1930s for explanations of trends in public policy that have traditionally been attributed to the New Deal. Partly as a result, scholars have begun to show a heightened interest in the domestic impact of World War II.

POLITICS AND SOCIETY IN WORLD WAR II

For many years, historians had a simple explanation of the domestic impact of World War II: it ended the Great Depression and launched an era of sustained economic growth; it weakened the liberal coalition and ushered in a period of conservative politics. More recent scholarship has not often challenged those conclusions, but it has begun to amplify and augment them.

Several historians have argued that wartime economic arrangements to promote war production formed the basis of more lasting accommodations between the government and business: a powerful "corporate liberalism" that would survive to dominate public life in the postwar years. John Morton Blum and Richard Polenberg, authors of two valuable overviews of the impact of the war on American society and politics, both chronicle the muting of liberal animus toward the corporate world in the 1940s but stop short of embracing the corporate-liberal argument. Kim McQuaid and Robert Collins, however, have suggested the outlines of a more explicitly "corporatist" interpretation of the results of wartime mobilization.

Alan Brinkley has argued that the war did not increase federal control of corporate behavior but contributed instead to a government commitment to indirect management of the economy, through Keynesian tools; in the process liberals in effect repudiated their long battle against monopoly power and began instead to construct a compensatory state. Rather than challenging capitalist institutions, it worked to insure high levels of growth, "full employment," and a broader distribution of purchasing power among consumers.

Nelson Lichtenstein, Steve Fraser, Howell John Harris, and others suggest that the war did not enhance the long-term position of labor but undermined the possibility of achieving anything like genuine industrial democracy. Lichtenstein, in describing the experiences of the CIO during World War II, recounts the failure of efforts by some labor leaders to create power-sharing arrangements, by which unions would have won a voice in making basic production decisions. Instead, the unions settled for guarantees of their own institutional survival and higher wages for their members. Harris, similarly, describes ways in which business leaders used the war years to reassert managerial prerogatives they had lost to the unions in the 1930s and to pave the way toward passage of the anti-union Taft-Hartley Act in 1947. Others have portrayed the political alliance between organized labor and the Democratic party (symbolized by the formation of the CIO's Political Action Committee) as what Mike Davis has called a "barren marriage," by which workers sacrificed any hopes for independent political power in exchange for immediate material gains.

The war years also had important, if still imperfectly understood, effects on many other areas of American society. Historians of black America generally agree that the war made an important contribution to the rise of black consciousness and to the mobilization of dissent that would culminate in the civil rights movement. John Blum and Harvard Sitkoff (among many others) emphasize the participation of blacks in the war (and the rising demands for racial justice that participation inspired) as the most important phenomenon. Arnold Hirsch attributes greater importance to demographic changes. The enormous migration in the 1940s of rural blacks to the cities of both the North and the South greatly increased the size of black urban communities, the principal source of the civil rights movement and black protest. The expanded economic opportunities the war years produced helped enlarge and strengthen the black middle class and made its members less willing to tolerate the barriers that blocked further advances. But the war also helped reinforce the commitment of many southern whites and northern ethnic workers to restore the world they had known before Pearl Harbor. The racial battles of the 1950s and 1960s were in part a result of African American hopes and white fears, both reinforced by the war.

Scholars working in women's history disagree in some respects about the impact of the war on American women. William Chafe has argued that the war greatly expanded economic opportunities for women, while Leila Rupp contends that such gains were only temporary. Yet the work of Karen Anderson, Mary Schweitzer, Sara Evans, and others suggests that whatever the immediate impact of the war on women's work, its long-range impact was profound. The war propelled unprecedented numbers of women into the work force, giving them an experience of independence and self-reliance that many carried with them into the postwar era. (Alice Kessler-Harris has maintained that this movement would have occurred even without the conflict.) And yet among men, as Robert Westbrook and others have suggested, the war strengthened more traditional views of gender roles. Men serving overseas romanticized women in both sexual and domestic terms and dreamed of returning to a world in which gender relationships matched their dreams. Many men (and some women) in the United States during the war looked with alarm at the independence of the single women entering the work force and began efforts to limit their autonomy. On issues of gender, as with issues of race, the war created sharply different expectations: a vision of a more independent future among many women; a dream of returning to a traditional male-dominated world among men.

The important social, cultural, and economic transformations that recent scholarship has begun to reveal in the years between 1920 and 1945 have only slowly informed the ways in which historians have explained the public, political life of the era. But it is clear that exploring the connections between great public events and the less visible social phenomena that form their context is emerging as the next important frontier for historians of twentieth-century America.

N O T E S

1. Freidel, *Franklin D. Roosevelt: The Apprenticeship.* Subsequent volumes were *The Ordeal* (1954), *The Triumph* (1956), and *Launching the New Deal* (1973). A major one-volume biography, *Franklin D. Roosevelt: A Rendezvous with Destiny,* was published in 1990. A full citation for Goldman's book, and for all others mentioned in this essay, appears in the bibliography.

2. Schlesinger, *The Crisis of the Old Order* (1957), *The Coming of the New Deal* (1959), and *The Politics of Upheaval* (1960).

3. Schlesinger derived the "cycle theory" in part from the work of his father, the historian Arthur M. Schlesinger Sr. Schlesinger Jr.'s *The Cycles of American History* (1986) contains his most explicit statement of the theory.

4. An important recent study of the "progressive" approach to American history (and of other approaches discussed below) is Peter Novick, *That Noble Dream: The "Objectivity Question" and the American Historical Profession* (New York: Columbia University Press, 1988).

5. As Galambos has noted, the corporate-liberal synthesis is in most respects compatible with the organizational synthesis, although it contains a normative element that the organizational historians do not generally embrace.

6. Scholarship shaped by the premises of the "new" history has been particularly plentiful for the interwar years in the areas of labor and gender history. Other essays in this collection are devoted specifically to those fields, so I have given less attention to them in this essay than they would otherwise deserve.

7. The sociologists Robert and Helen Merrell Lynd had made similar observations in the 1920s about life in the city of Muncie, Indiana, in their famous study *Middletown* (1929).

8. A useful overview of the 1920s from the organizational perspective is Hawley, *The Great War and the Search for a Modern Order* (1979).

9. Thomas Ferguson and Colin Gordon have gone considerably further and portrayed New Deal economic policy as the product of the influence of powerful corporate interests with close ties to the administration.

10. Two collections of essays represent much of this new literature: Evans, Rueschemeyer, and Skocpol, *Bringing the State Back In* (1985); and Weir, Orloff, and Skocpol, *The Politics of Social Policy in the United States* (1988).

BIBLIOGRAPHY

Allen, Frederick Lewis. *Only Yesterday: An Informal History of the 1920s.* New York: Harper & Row, 1931.

Anderson, Karen. *Wartime Women: Sex Roles, Family Relations, and the Status of Women during World War II.* Westport, Conn.: Greenwood Press, 1981.

Atleson, James. *Values and Assumptions in American Labor Law.* Amherst: University of Massachusetts Press, 1983.

Badger, Anthony J. *The New Deal: The Depression Years, 1933–1940.* New York: Hill & Wang, 1988.

———. *Prosperity Road: The New Deal, Tobacco, and North Carolina.* Chapel Hill: University of North Carolina Press, 1980.

Balogh, Brian. "Reorganizing the Organizational Synthesis." *Studies in American Political Development* 5 (1991): 119–72.

Bellush, Bernard. *The Failure of the NRA.* New York: Norton, 1975.

Bernstein, Barton J. "The New Deal: The Conservative Achievements of Liberal Reform." In Barton J. Bernstein, ed., *Towards a New Past: Dissenting Essays in American History,* 263–88. New York: Knopf, 1968.

Blee, Kathleen M. *Women of the Klan: Racism and Gender in the 1920s.* Berkeley: University of California Press, 1991.

Blum, John Morton. *V Was for Victory: Politics and American Culture during World War II.* New York: Harcourt Brace Jovanovich, 1976.

Brand, Donald R. *Corporatism and the Rule of Law: A Study of the National Recovery Administration.* Ithaca, N.Y.: Cornell University Press, 1988.

Bremer, William W. *Depression Winters: New York Social Workers and the New Deal.* Philadelphia: Temple University Press, 1984.

Brinkley, Alan. *The End of Reform: New Deal Liberalism in Recession and War.* New York: Knopf, 1995.

————. "The New Deal and the Idea of the State." In Steve Fraser and Gary Gerstle, eds., *The Rise and Fall of the New Deal Order*, 85–121. Princeton, N.J.: Princeton University Press, 1989.

————. "The New Deal and Southern Politics." In James C. Cobb and Michael V. Namarato, eds., *The New Deal and the South*, 97–116. Oxford: University of Mississippi Press, 1984.

————. *Voices of Protest: Huey Long, Father Coughlin, and the Great Depression*. New York: Knopf, 1982.

Brody, David. *Workers in Industrial America: Essays on the Twentieth-Century Struggle*. New York: Oxford University Press, 1980.

Burner, David. *Herbert Hoover: A Public Life*. New York: Knopf, 1979.

Burns, James MacGregor. *Roosevelt: The Lion and the Fox*. New York: Harcourt Brace, 1956.

————. *Roosevelt: The Soldier of Freedom*. New York: Harcourt Brace Jovanovich, 1970.

Chafe, William H. *The American Woman: Her Changing Social, Economic, and Political Roles, 1920–1970*. New York: Oxford University Press, 1972.

Chandler, Alfred D., Jr. *Strategy and Structure: Chapters in the History of the American Industrial Enterprise*. Cambridge, Mass.: MIT Press, 1962.

————. *The Visible Hand: The Managerial Revolution in American Business*. Cambridge, Mass.: Harvard University Press, 1977.

Chauncey, George, Jr. *Gay New York: Gender, Urban Culture, and the Making of the Gay Male World, 1890–1940*. New York: Basic Books, 1994.

Cohen, Lizabeth. *Making a New Deal: Industrial Workers in Chicago, 1919–1939*. New York: Cambridge University Press, 1990.

Collins, Robert M. *The Business Response to Keynes, 1929–1964*. New York: Columbia University Press, 1981.

————. "Positive Business Responses to the New Deal: The Roots of the Committee for Economic Development, 1933–1942." *Business History Review* 52 (1978): 369–91.

Conkin, Paul K. *The New Deal*. Arlington Heights, Ill.: AHM, 1967.

Cooney, Terry A. "Cosmopolitan Values and the Identification of Reaction: *Partisan Review* in the 1930s." *Journal of American History* 68 (1981): 580–98.

Davis, Mike. "The Barren Marriage of American Labour and the Democratic Party." *New Left Review* 124 (1980): 43–84.

Dawley, Alan. *Struggles for Justice: Moral Responsibility and the Liberal State*. Cambridge, Mass.: Harvard University Press, 1991.

Dorsett, Lyle W. *Franklin D. Roosevelt and the City Bosses*. Port Washington, N.Y.: Kennikat Press, 1977.

Douglas, Ann. *Terrible Honesty: Mongrel Manhattan in the 1920s*. New York: Farrar Straus Giroux, 1995.

Evans, Peter B., Dietrich Rueschemeyer, and Theda Skocpol, eds. *Bringing the State Back In*. Cambridge: Cambridge University Press, 1985.

Evans, Sara M. *Born for Liberty: A History of Women in America*. New York: Free Press, 1989.

Ewen, Stuart. *Captains of Consciousness: Advertising and the Social Roots of the Consumer Culture*. New York: McGraw-Hill, 1976.

Fausold, Martin L., and George T. Mazuzan, eds. *The Hoover Presidency: A Reappraisal.* Albany: State University of New York Press, 1974.

Ferguson, Thomas. "From Normalcy to New Deal: Industrial Structure, Party Competition, and American Public Policy in the Great Depression." *International Organization* 38 (1984): 41–94.

Finegold, Kenneth, and Theda Skocpol. *State and Party in America's New Deal.* Madison: University of Wisconsin Press, 1995.

Fox, Richard Wightman, and T. J. Jackson Lears, eds. *The Culture of Consumption: Critical Essays in American History, 1880–1980.* New York: Pantheon, 1983.

Freidel, Frank. *F.D.R. and the South.* Baton Rouge: Louisiana State University Press, 1965.

———. *Franklin D. Roosevelt.* 4 vols. Boston: Little, Brown, 1952–73.

———. *Franklin D. Roosevelt: A Rendezvous with Destiny.* Boston: Little, Brown, 1990.

Galambos, Louis. *Competition and Cooperation: The Emergence of a National Trade Association.* Baltimore, Md.: Johns Hopkins University Press, 1966.

———. "The Emerging Organizational Synthesis in Modern American History." *Business History Review* 44 (1970): 279–90.

———. *The Rise of the Corporate Commonwealth: United States Business and Public Policy in the Twentieth Century.* New York: Basic Books, 1988.

———. "Technology, Political Economy, and Professionalization: Central Themes of the Organizational Synthesis." *Business History Review* 57 (1983): 471–93.

Gelfand, Mark I. *A Nation of Cities: The Federal Government and Urban America, 1933–1965.* New York: Oxford University Press, 1975.

Gerstle, Gary. *Working-Class Americanism: The Politics of Labor in a Textile City, 1914–1960.* New York: Cambridge University Press, 1989.

Goldman, Eric. *Rendezvous with Destiny: A History of Modern American Reform.* New York: Knopf, 1952.

Goodwyn, Lawrence. *Democratic Promise: The Populist Movement in America.* New York: Oxford University Press, 1976.

Gordon, Colin. *New Deals: Business, Labor, and Politics in America, 1920–1935.* New York: Cambridge University Press, 1994.

Gordon, Linda. *Pitied but Not Entitled: Single Mothers and the History of Welfare.* New York: Free Press, 1994.

Graham, Otis. "Franklin Roosevelt and the Intended New Deal." In Thomas E. Cronin and Michael Beschloss, eds., *Essays in Honor of James MacGregor Burns.* Englewood Cliffs, N.J.: Prentice-Hall, 1989.

Gusfield, Joseph R. *Symbolic Crusade: Status Politics and the American Temperance Movement.* Urbana: University of Illinois Press, 1963.

Hahn, Steven. *The Roots of Southern Populism: Yeoman Farmers and the Transformation of the Georgia Upcountry, 1850–1890.* New York: Oxford University Press, 1983.

Harris, Howell John. *The Right to Manage: Industrial Relations Policies of American Business in the 1940s.* Madison: University of Wisconsin Press, 1982.

Hawley, Ellis W. *The Great War and the Search for a Modern Order: A History of the*

American People and Their Institutions, 1917–1933. New York: St. Martin's Press, 1979.

————. *The New Deal and the Problem of Monopoly: A Study in Economic Ambivalence.* Princeton, N.J.: Princeton University Press, 1966.

————, ed. *Herbert Hoover as Secretary of Commerce: Studies in New Era Thought and Practice*. West Branch, Iowa: Herbert Hoover Presidential Library Association, 1974.

Hays, Samuel P. "Politics and Society: Beyond the Political Party." In Paul Kleppner, ed., *The Evolution of American Electoral Systems*, 243–67. Westport, Conn.: Greenwood Press, 1981.

Himmelberg, Robert F. *The Origins of the National Recovery Administration: Business, Government, and the Trade Association Issue, 1921–1933*. New York: Fordham University Press, 1976.

Hirsch, Arnold R. *Making the Second Ghetto: Race and Housing in Chicago, 1940–1960*. New York: Cambridge University Press, 1983.

Hofstadter, Richard. *The Age of Reform: From Bryan to FDR*. New York: Knopf, 1955.

————. *The American Political Tradition and the Men Who Made It*. New York: Knopf, 1948.

Hollinger, David A. "Ethnic Diversity, Cosmopolitanism, and the Emergence of the American Liberal Intelligentsia." *American Quarterly* 27 (1975): 133–51.

Huthmacher, J. Joseph. *Senator Robert F. Wagner and the Rise of Urban Liberalism*. Cambridge, Mass.: Harvard University Press, 1968.

Jackson, Kenneth T. *The Ku Klux Klan in the City, 1915–1930*. New York: Oxford University Press, 1967.

Jacoby, Sanford. *Employing Bureaucracy: Managers, Unions, and the Transformation of Work in American Industry, 1900–1945*. New York: Columbia University Press, 1985.

Karl, Barry D. *Executive Reorganization and Reform in the New Deal: The Genesis of Administrative Management, 1900–1939*. Chicago: University of Chicago Press, 1963.

————. *The Uneasy State: The United States from 1915 to 1945*. Chicago: University of Chicago Press, 1983.

Kazin, Michael. *The Populist Persuasion: An American History*. New York: Basic Books, 1994.

Keller, Morton. *Regulating a New Economy: Public Policy and Economic Change in America, 1900–1933*. Cambridge, Mass.: Harvard University Press, 1990.

————. *Regulating a New Society: Public Policy and Social Change in America, 1900–1933*. Cambridge, Mass.: Harvard University Press, 1994.

Kelley, Robin. *Hammer and Hoe: Alabama Communists during the Great Depression*. Chapel Hill: University of North Carolina Press, 1990.

Kessler-Harris, Alice. *Out to Work: A History of Wage-Earning Women in the United States*. New York: Oxford University Press, 1992.

Kirby, John B. *Black Americans in the Roosevelt Era: Liberalism and Race*. Knoxville: University of Tennessee Press, 1980.

Klare, Karl E. "Judicial Deradicalization of the Wagner Act and the Origins of

Modern Legal Consciousness, 1937–1941." *Minnesota Law Review* 65 (1978): 265–39.

Kolko, Gabriel. *Main Currents in Modern American History*. New York: Harper & Row, 1976.

Lasch, Christopher. *The Culture of Narcissism: American Life in an Age of Diminishing Expectations*. New York: Norton, 1978.

———. *The True and Only Heaven: Progress and Its Critics*. New York: Norton, 1991.

Lears, Jackson. *Fables of Abundance: A Cultural History of Advertising in America*. New York: Basic Books, 1994.

Leff, Mark. *The Limits of Symbolic Reform: The New Deal and Taxation, 1933–1939*. New York: Cambridge University Press, 1984.

Lekachman, Robert. *The Age of Keynes*. New York: Random House, 1966.

Leuchtenburg, William E. *The FDR Years: On Roosevelt and His Legacy*. New York: Columbia University Press, 1995.

———. *Franklin D. Roosevelt and the New Deal, 1932–1940*. New York: Harper & Row, 1963.

———. *The Perils of Prosperity, 1914–1932*. Chicago: University of Chicago Press, 1958.

Lichtenstein, Nelson. *Labor's War at Home: The CIO and World War II*. New York: Cambridge University Press, 1982.

Link, Arthur S. "What Happened to the Progressive Movement in the 1920s?" *American Historical Review* 64 (1959): 833–51.

Lustig, R. Jeffrey. *Corporate Liberalism: The Origins of Modern American Political Theory, 1890–1920*. Berkeley: University of California Press, 1982.

Marchand, Roland. *Advertising the American Dream: Making Way for Modernity, 1920–1940*. Berkeley: University of California Press, 1985.

Marsden, George M. *Fundamentalism and American Culture: The Shaping of Twentieth-Century Evangelicalism, 1870–1925*. New York: Oxford University Press, 1980.

May, Dean L. *From New Deal to New Economics: The American Liberal Response to the Recession of 1937*. New York: Garland, 1981.

McConnell, Grant. *The Decline of Agrarian Democracy*. Berkeley: University of California Press, 1953.

McCormick, Richard L. *From Realignment to Reform: Political Change in New York State, 1893–1910*. Ithaca, N.Y.: Cornell University Press, 1981.

McQuaid, Kim. *Big Business and Presidential Power: From FDR to Reagan*. New York: Morrow, 1982.

Melosh, Barbara. *Engendering Culture: Manhood and Womanhood in New Deal Public Art and Theater*. Washington, D.C.: Smithsonian Institution Press, 1991.

Milkis, Sidney M. *The President and the Parties: The Transformation of the American Party System since the New Deal*. New York: Oxford University Press, 1993.

Montgomery, David. *Workers' Control in America: Studies in the History of Work, Technology, and Labor Struggles*. Cambridge: Cambridge University Press, 1979.

Moore, Leonard J. *Citizen Klansmen: The Ku Klux Klan in Indiana, 1921–1928*. Chapel Hill: University of North Carolina Press, 1991.

Nash, Gerald D. *The Great Depression and World War II: Organizing America, 1933–1945.* New York: St. Martin's Press, 1979.

Nelson, Bruce. *Workers on the Waterfront: Seamen, Longshoremen, and Unionism in the 1930s.* Urbana: University of Illinois Press, 1988.

Olson, James Stuart. *Herbert Hoover and the Reconstruction Finance Corporation, 1931–1933.* Ames, Iowa: Iowa State University Press, 1977.

Patterson, James T. *America's Struggle against Poverty, 1900–1980.* Cambridge, Mass.: Harvard University Press, 1981.

————. *Congressional Conservatism and the New Deal: The Growth of the Conservative Coalition in Congress, 1933–1939.* Lexington: University Press of Kentucky, 1967.

————. *The New Deal and the States: Federalism in Transition.* Princeton, N.J.: Princeton University Press, 1969.

Polenberg, Richard. *Reorganizing Roosevelt's Government, 1936–1939: The Controversy over Executive Reorganization.* Cambridge, Mass.: Harvard University Press, 1966.

————. *War and Society: The United States, 1941–1945.* Philadelphia: Lippincott, 1972.

Quadagno, Jill S. *The Transformation of Old Age Security: Class and Politics in the American Welfare State.* Chicago: University of Chicago Press, 1988.

Radosh, Ronald. "The Myth of the New Deal." In Ronald Radosh and Murray Rothbard, eds., *A New History of the Leviathan,* 146–87. New York: Dutton, 1972.

Ribuffo, Leo P. *The Old Christian Right: The Protestant Far Right from the Great Depression to the Cold War.* Philadelphia: Temple University Press, 1983.

Rodgers, Daniel T. *Contested Truths: Key Words in American Politics since Independence.* New York: Basic Books, 1987.

Rosenof, Theodore. *Patterns of Political Economy in America: The Failure to Develop a Democratic Left Synthesis, 1933–1950.* New York: Garland, 1983.

Rosenzweig, Roy. *Eight Hours for What We Will: Workers and Leisure in an Industrial City, 1870–1920.* New York: Cambridge University Press, 1983.

Rupp, Leila J. *Mobilizing Women for War: German and American Propaganda, 1939–1945.* Princeton, N.J.: Princeton University Press, 1978.

Schatz, Ronald W. *The Electrical Workers: A History of Labor at General Electric and Westinghouse, 1923–60.* Urbana: University of Illinois Press, 1983.

Schlesinger, Arthur M., Jr. *The Age of Roosevelt.* 3 vols. Boston: Houghton Mifflin, 1957–60.

————. *The Cycles of American History.* Boston: Houghton Mifflin, 1986.

Schulman, Bruce. *From Cotton Belt to Sunbelt: Federal Policy, Economic Development, and the Transformation of the South, 1938–1980.* New York: Oxford University Press, 1991.

Schwartz, Bonnie Fox. *The Civil Works Administration, 1933–1934: The Business of Emergency Employment in the New Deal.* Princeton, N.J.: Princeton University Press, 1984.

Schwarz, Jordan. *The New Dealers: Power Politics in the Age of Roosevelt.* New York: Knopf, 1993.

Schweitzer, Mary. "World War II and Female Labor Participation Rates." *Journal of Economic History* 40 (March 1980).

Sitkoff, Harvard. *Fifty Years Later: The New Deal Evaluated.* New York: Knopf, 1985.

————. *A New Deal for Blacks: The Emergence of Civil Rights as a National Issue—The Depression Decade.* New York: Oxford University Press, 1978.

Skocpol, Theda. *Protecting Soldiers and Mothers: The Political Origins of Social Policy in the United States.* Cambridge, Mass.: Harvard University Press, 1992.

Stave, Bruce. *The New Deal and the Last Hurrah: Pittsburgh Machine Politics.* Pittsburgh, Pa.: University of Pittsburgh Press, 1970.

Stein, Herbert. *The Fiscal Revolution in America.* Chicago: University of Chicago Press, 1969.

Stone, Katherine Van Wezel. "The Post-War Paradigm in American Labor Law." *Yale Law Journal* 4 (1981): 1509–80.

Susman, Warren I. *Culture as History: The Transformation of American Society in the Twentieth Century.* New York: Pantheon, 1984.

Tomlins, Christopher. *The State and the Unions: Labor Relations, Law, and the Organized Labor Movement in America, 1880–1960.* Cambridge: Cambridge University Press, 1985.

Trout, Charles H. *Boston: The Great Depression and the New Deal.* New York: Oxford University Press, 1977.

Vittoz, Stanley. *New Deal Labor Policy and the American Industrial Economy.* Chapel Hill: University of North Carolina Press, 1987.

Weinstein, James. *The Corporate Ideal in the Liberal State, 1900–1918.* Boston: Beacon Press, 1968.

Weir, Margaret, Ann Shola Orloff, and Theda Skocpol, eds. *The Politics of Social Policy in the United States.* Princeton, N.J.: Princeton University Press, 1988.

Weiss, Nancy J. *Farewell to the Party of Lincoln: Black Politics in the Age of FDR.* Princeton, N.J.: Princeton University Press, 1983.

Westbrook, Robert. "Fighting for the American Family: Private Interests and Political Obligations in World War II." In Richard Wightman Fox and Jackson Lears, eds., *The Power of Culture*, 195–221. Chicago: University of Chicago Press, 1993.

Wiebe, Robert H. *The Search for Order, 1877–1920.* New York: Hill & Wang, 1967.

Wilson, Joan Hoff. *Herbert Hoover: Forgotten Progressive.* Boston: Little, Brown, 1975.

Zinn, Howard, ed. *New Deal Thought.* Indianapolis, Ind.: Bobbs-Merrill, 1966.

7

■■ AMERICA SINCE 1945

William H. Chafe

FEW PERIODS OF HISTORY HAVE WITNESSED AS MUCH PROFOUND CHANGE AS HAS occurred in America since World War II. The economy grew faster than at any time in the twentieth century, with millions of families experiencing for the first time opportunities for home ownership and higher education. The civil rights movement, arguably the most important grassroots insurgency in American history, challenged deeply entrenched patterns of segregation, thereby freeing countless black Americans to seek rewards based on their individual talent and ability. Gender roles altered dramatically as well, partly as a result of skyrocketing employment rates for women and changes in the family but also because of a revitalized feminist movement that sought to free women from traditional assumptions about their "proper place." Yet in the midst of these positive changes, poverty remained an abiding national disgrace, with millions of women, blacks, and young people among the chief victims. Conflict over social and cultural values reached fever pitch in the late 1960s, as student, antiwar, and Black Power protesters challenged an "establishment" they viewed with contempt. And the foreign policy of anti-Communism that had dominated the country since 1947 suddenly came under attack. Even though a new conservative consensus seemed ascendant during the 1970s and 1980s, its roots went back to a period of extraordinary tumult and confusion.

159

How then to make sense of this period, especially when it is still so close to us? Some historians have emphasized particular themes from the postwar era as a means of giving order to these years. Lawrence Wittner, for example, sees the Cold War as decisive to understanding domestic as well as foreign policy developments. William E. Leuchtenburg focuses on the emergence of a consumer culture as a central organizing principle. Alonzo Hamby and Frederick Siegel use politics as their departure point, the former viewing the period from the perspective of liberalism and its challengers, the latter using the issue of conservatism in its "old right" and "new right" forms as an analytical framework. Godfrey Hodgson joins some of these perspectives in his assertion that a "liberal consensus" (in fact, quite conservative) shaped American history in the postwar years, ruling out of bounds any "leftist" or social democratic alternatives to middle-of-the-road politics and using anti-Communism as a rallying point to maintain conformity.

This essay draws on all these contributions but seeks a synthesis as well. No comparable period of history offers so rich a possibility for integrating social and political history, for examining the significance of region and demography on historical patterns, or for exploring the traditional division between those who see consensus among the American people and those who perceive conflict as basic to our national experience. By breaking down the years since 1945 into three distinct periods—the end of World War II to the early 1950s, the years of the civil rights revolution and its aftermath, and the rise of cultural and political conservatism in the 1970s and 1980s—I hope to trace the intersection of social, political, and cultural history in postwar America and, in the process, create a basis for measuring the extent of the change and continuity that have characterized our recent history.

THE IMMEDIATE POSTWAR YEARS

The customary organization of U.S. history by presidential administrations might picture the years from 1945 through 1963 as a roller coaster: beginning with the progressive presidency of Harry Truman, followed by a period of consolidation and conservatism under Dwight Eisenhower, concluding with the advent of vigorous reform under John F. Kennedy. Such a political perspective would focus on 1952 and 1960 as turning points, using the rhetoric of campaign speeches and party platforms as one index of the substantial departures marked by the election of new presidents. I argue, however, that there was more consistency than discontinuity in the policies of Truman, Eisenhower, and Kennedy and that the turning point in the postwar years occurred between 1946 and

1948, when a combination of the Cold War abroad and a politics of virulent anti-Communism at home helped to determine boundaries of political discourse that lasted at least until the mid-1960s. In this context the emergence of a new Red scare severely diminished prospects for significant progress toward social reform, postponing until the explosion of the civil rights movement in the 1960s any possibility for making issues of social justice a primary item on the political agenda.

The potential for political action on these issues after World War II lay largely in the progress that previously disadvantaged groups had been able to achieve during the war itself. Black Americans, for example, had taken advantage of a shortage of labor to migrate to cities in the North and West in quest of industrial jobs. Black civil rights organizations used the leverage of wartime rhetoric against Nazi racism to mobilize domestic support for their double-V campaign: victory for racial equality at home, as well as victory against Fascism abroad. The membership of protest groups such as the National Association for the Advancement of Colored People (NAACP) increased 900 percent during the war years, and a coalition of white liberal and labor groups from the Northeast and civil rights forces in the South and North began to plan for political action, such as a permanent Fair Employment Practices Committee (FECP) to battle racism and begin the war against segregation.

American women also experienced substantial change, especially in their economic status. More than six million took jobs during the war, increasing the female labor force by nearly 60 percent; their wages rose dramatically; and for at least some, a continued life of achievement outside the home became for the first time a viable possibility. At war's end nearly 80 percent of those who had taken jobs declared their determination to stay in their newly won positions.

American male workers as well benefited substantially during the war. Real income grew 50 percent; for the first time in the twentieth century the bottom fifth of the population increased its share of total national income; and the number of workers who were unionized increased nearly 50 percent. In 1945 organized labor boasted fifteen million members; in 1930 the figure had been only three million. Never before had such a large proportion of the work force been unionized.

For each of these groups, of course, there was bad news as well as good. Racial discrimination and violence remained rife, and blacks were still disfranchised throughout the South. Women in the work force were never treated as equals with men, in either wages or opportunities. Workers' gains reflected the benefits of a full-employment war economy as well as the strength of collective bargaining and union representation. Furthermore, many Americans were concerned about the "progressive" character of the changes associated with these groups. If women stayed in the job market, some argued, the family would fall apart, returning soldiers would have no jobs, and the moral foundation of the society would collapse. White southerners worried that "uppity" Negroes returning from the war would destroy their way of life. And big business found the demands of some CIO unions for a share of management's authority positively subversive.

Nevertheless, there was a sense of possibility, as well as uneasiness, in the air as the war drew to a close, and in this context the actions of Harry Truman took on decisive significance. Facing a rapid-fire series of crises at home and abroad, Truman charted a political course that, behind an exterior "tough" and "no-nonsense" style, actually fixed on moderation as a goal. When organized labor sought to protect and build on the gains of the war years by making 1946 the largest year of strikes since 1919, Truman adopted a hard-line stance, threatening to draft striking railroad engineers and to seize control of steel mills. Although his proposed Fair Deal promised full employment, higher minimum wages, national health insurance, and greater federal involvement in housing and welfare, Truman proved relatively ineffective as a legislative leader. When black veterans returned home demanding the right to vote and federal protection to exercise that right, the president refused to intervene, although his Committee on Civil Rights did provide more support for the *idea* of racial justice than had been seen in any previous presidency.

In all of this, the central political event was the Cold War. Convinced that the Soviet Union directly threatened American interests in Europe, Truman determined that he could mobilize congressional and public opinion behind a program of military and economic aid to Europe only through defining the issues as universal and moralistic. Hence, in his Truman Doctrine speech of March 1947, the president insisted that freedom was at war with tyranny, democracy with totalitarianism, God-fearing citizens with atheism. The Cold War abroad soon translated into a cold war at home as well. Just nine days after his Truman Doctrine speech to Congress, the president issued an executive order for interrogations to verify the patriotism and loyalty of federal employees. The same spring the House Committee on Un-American Activities commenced hearings to investigate Communist influence on the entertainment industry.

As a result, there developed a growing tendency to identify any political demands of a radical or progressive nature with subversion and Communism. The purging of many of the most radical unions in the CIO, for example, on the grounds that they were too close to Communists and "fellow travelers" of Communists, rendered powerless a segment of the labor movement that was most committed to economic equality and the organization of workers without regard to their race or sex. Civil rights groups critical of the government were also charged with being Communist inspired. Even the demands of some women's groups for publicly supported day-care centers were ridiculed as products of a socialist and collectivist mentality. Though Truman often denounced anti-Communist hysteria, he had in fact helped to legitimate it. As Godfrey Hodgson has argued, the Red scare, by becoming a weapon for attacking any political program that was left of center, helped to create a politics of moderation and consensus that prevailed until 1963.

In the meantime, a series of positive economic developments, facilitated by government policies, generated the "consumer culture," which William E. Leuchtenburg has discussed, and the massive spread of material comforts among middle-class Americans. Wartime savings (bank deposits had increased 150 percent during the war) fueled postwar purchases of household appliances, automobiles, and other consumer goods. Government policies such as the GI bill helped to guarantee that a healthy foundation would exist for sustained economic growth. With the government paying for veterans' college educations, a new generation of technologically skilled graduates emerged to take their place in the rapidly growing electronics, automobile, and chemical industries. Government loans also encouraged the construction and purchase of new housing. A two-thousand-dollar loan from the Veterans Administration was enough to make a down payment on one of the new houses that sprang up like mushrooms in the suburbs. As a result, between 1940 and 1960 the proportion of Americans owning their own homes increased from 42 to 62 percent. In this booming economy, meanwhile, real income grew as much from 1947 to 1960 as it had grown from 1900 to 1947. With education, jobs, and consumer goods proliferating, millions of Americans understandably turned their attention to the "good life" that had suddenly become a possibility.

Against this background the presidential administrations and policies of Harry Truman and Dwight Eisenhower appear more similar than dissimilar, notwithstanding the rhetoric of the 1952 political campaign. To be sure, there were significant differences between the two, and historians such as Alonzo Hamby have emphasized their importance. But as Godfrey Hodgson has noted, the differences occurred within a broad consensus that American capitalism was healthy and dynamic and that it contained ample room for growth and prosperity, with no need for structural change. Robert Griffith has shown that Eisenhower carried forward to a new level of sophistication the politics of partnership with corporate America, but this was not a partnership that Truman had opposed. Ironically, the man usually associated in the public mind with a rejection of 1950s quietism, John F. Kennedy, was as much a part of this "liberal consensus" as anyone. Kennedy believed fully in the organic health of the American social and economic system; his major criticism of Eisenhower was that he had not let the economy grow fast enough. Instead of far-reaching reform, Kennedy embraced economic growth as the solution to most social problems ("a rising tide lifts all boats," he said) and committed his administration to the task of fine-tuning the economy so that it could perform better. With some exceptions, such as Theodore Sorenson and Arthur Schlesinger Jr., most historians see at least the early Kennedy presidency as more moderate than liberal, and as more concerned with the Cold War and foreign policy than with social reform.

The politics of the years between 1948 and 1963, then, seem characterized more by continuity than by change. The potential insurgent movements growing out of the wartime period were set aside: anti-Communism was an effective barrier to any movement from the left, despite the glaring economic and social inequities that remained. The basic social-welfare legacy of the New Deal remained intact (even Eisenhower did not try to dismantle that), but it did not move to the next stage of social democracy, which characterized most of the states of western Europe. Instead, America appeared anchored in midstream, with observers such as Daniel Bell writing that ideology had no part to play any longer in American politics, because we had reached a position of maturity and affluence where political factions were no longer necessary. Only when a social movement developed around America's oldest inequality would a new political and social era develop.

THE CIVIL RIGHTS MOVEMENT AND THE POLITICS OF THE 1960S

The civil rights movement offers both a central theme through which to understand American history in the postwar years and a pivotal example of how social history informs and shapes political history. Although many Americans still identify the civil rights movement with such national figures as Martin Luther King Jr., and some historians see the presidency as the critical reference point for civil rights activism, a strong case can be made that the movement reflected the strength, persistence, and vitality of grassroots black institutions and that it determined the agenda of presidential activism rather than vice versa. Throughout the late 1940s blacks organized throughout the South around issues of voter registration and school desegregation. When their efforts were repelled by local law enforcement agencies and vigilantes, they turned to the litigation process championed by the NAACP. Even then, however, it was small-town ministers, teachers, and workers who put their lives on the line so that their cases could reach the federal courts. And when court action failed to result in change on a local level, it was average citizens again who stepped into the breach and insisted on progress toward racial equality.

This struggle highlights both the "hidden" history of the quiet and affluent 1950s and the extent to which established political processes, by themselves, offered little basis for optimism about social change. Despite the Supreme Court's unanimous decision in *Brown v. Board of Education* (1954) declaring that integration must occur, little progress in school desegregation actually took place. President Eisenhower refused to implement the court's decision with any vigor, and southern politicians took that indifference as a cue to mount their own campaigns of massive resistance. When it became clear that strong governmental action would not be forthcoming from Washington, the civil rights movement entered a new phase of direct action protest, with local citizens again taking the lead. In Montgomery, Alabama, in 1955 a middle-aged seamstress named Rosa Parks joined with a union leader named E. D. Nixon to spark a boycott of the city's segregated buses that would seize international attention and bring to prominence a young leader named Martin Luther King Jr. A few years later four young black students at North Carolina A & T State University in Greensboro sat in at the Woolworth lunch counter to demand that they be served coffee just as whites were served. Having come of age politically in the years following the *Brown* decision, they determined to take into their own hands the battle to fight continued racism. No one told them what to do. The second day there were twenty-three demonstrators; the third, sixty-six; the fourth, one hundred; and the fifth, a thousand. Within two months similar demonstrations had developed in fifty-four cities in nine different states.

The student-led civil rights movement quickly established racial equality as an issue that could not be ignored. The Student Non-Violent Coordinating Committee (SNCC) carried civil rights protests into the most racist counties of Alabama, Georgia, and Mississippi. King and his Southern Christian Leadership Conference (SCLC) seized national attention through their effective use of the media. Although some students resented the publicity that King garnered, his activity proved crucial to the movement's national visibility. By 1962 and 1963, the *New York Times* was devoting an entire pull-out section each day to coverage of civil rights protests, and network television was bringing the message of these protests to millions of people each night.

Through such effective activity the civil rights movement dramatically transformed the political agendas of the Kennedy and Johnson administrations. Prior to 1963 John F. Kennedy had given lip service to support for civil rights, and during the Freedom Rides of 1961 he had played a somewhat active role in seeking the acceptance of integration on interstate buses. But during the early part of his administration Kennedy failed to pursue the initiatives suggested by his 1960 campaign rhetoric. Partly because of a conservative Congress and partly as a result of his own conviction that American society was basically sound, Kennedy turned out to be a conservative president on most domestic issues. His major legislative initiative in 1962, for example, was tariff reform. It took him twenty-two months to sign an executive order prohibiting racial discrimination in federally financed housing—the order, he had said in his campaign, that would become a reality simply by a "stroke of the pen." Thus, despite a consciously projected image of activism, the Kennedy administration largely accepted the status quo in domestic policy, at least through the middle of 1963.

The civil rights movement helped to liberate the Kennedy presidency, forcing Kennedy for the first time to risk political capital by coming to grips with the moral thrust of the black struggle for equality. By spring 1963, civil rights demonstrations had reached an intensity that compelled a response from Washington. Recognizing that the time had come for action, Kennedy went on national television and in a largely impromptu speech, eloquent in its moral passion, called for the substantial civil rights legislation that eventually became the Civil Rights Act of 1964. Significantly, in the same month he instructed his aides to draw up legislative plans for the war on poverty, an action reflecting the connection between racial and economic equality that had emerged from the civil rights struggle. Indeed, the initial impetus for the war on poverty was a consequence of a survey of black economic conditions that the president had ordered in a search for more information on racial equality.

The civil rights movement, then, together with the major changes in foreign policy attitudes reflected in his June 1963 American University speech calling for detente, created a new presidency for John F. Kennedy. Now willing to take the initiative and aggressively seek action on a political agenda of domestic reform, he seemed suddenly to have found a different voice. The new agenda of civil rights reform and antipoverty legislation, a tax cut, and acceleration of international detente suggested a very different politics than that of just two years earlier—a politics that would have been unimaginable without the pressure from below created by the civil rights movement. Although historians still debate the extent to which these changes represented a permanent departure for Kennedy, virtually all scholars see them as significant.

When Lyndon Johnson took office after Kennedy's assassination, he continued the new movement toward social and economic equality that had been prompted by the civil rights struggle. With skill and political genius, Johnson identified himself with his martyred predecessor, building on that identification to establish his own Great Society program. At no time since the New Deal had any American president been so successful at cajoling legislation from Congress. Model Cities, Medicare, Operation Headstart, the Job Corps, mental health centers—Johnson seized the moment to fulfill his public promise to help feed the hungry, clothe the poor, and bring a better life to all who were disadvantaged. His resounding electoral victory over Barry Goldwater in 1964 suggested that he might even be able to accomplish his goals within a society characterized by consensus.

But Johnson's hopes did not take into account American involvement in Vietnam, a policy initiated by Truman, carried forward by Eisenhower, expanded by Kennedy, and now at a critical stage. Whatever his domestic political expertise, Johnson had had little experience in foreign affairs. Against the background of McCarthyism, he feared being attacked as "soft on Communism" if he failed to expand America's commitment to South Vietnam.

Foreign policy and domestic policy have always been closely related in American politics. As we have seen, the Cold War and its impact at home helped to stifle the insurgent movements that grew out of World War II, and it was no accident that Kennedy's new commitment to domestic social reform coincided with a movement toward detente in foreign policy. Now, Johnson sought to pursue a strong policy against Communism abroad and to achieve his social reforms at home, all the while maintaining his cherished consensus. But as victory in Vietnam proved elusive, protest developed, and it became increasingly evident that the money needed to fight poverty at home was instead being diverted to fight a war nine thousand miles away.

Even before antiwar protests crippled the Johnson presidency, consensus at home had begun to shatter under the impact of insurgent challenges from the civil rights movement and its successors. When the sit-ins began in 1960, civil rights advocates were moderate in their objectives. They sought "freedom now" and believed that with the abolition of discriminatory laws, blacks could achieve their goals of equal opportunity. But as time passed, a new awareness developed that racial discrimination was inextricably tied to economic inequality and that the sources of the problem were systemic, requiring a substantial redistribution of power and wealth in the society as a whole. As Martin Luther King Jr. observed in 1967, class was as much a part of the problem as race. During these same years other black activists, particularly the members of SNCC and the followers of black nationalist Malcolm X, challenged the good faith and integrity of white leaders who, whatever their liberal credentials, often did nothing when blacks were brutalized by southern law enforcement agencies. A growing skepticism developed about the value of pursuing assimilation. Why should blacks seek integration, demanded Stokeley Carmichael and other Black Power advocates, when white society was dominated by values and institutions that were profoundly alien to black interests?

The same kind of radicalization occurred in the women's movement, the student movement, and the antipoverty movement, all of which emerged directly as a consequence of the civil rights struggle. The women's liberation movement, for example, began when white and black women protested being treated by men as second-class citizens within the struggle. But by the time the women's movement became an independent and separatist force in its own right, it had started to raise questions about the entire structure of society; the more radical women at least—like the Black Power advocates—were asking whether they really wished to be part of a mainstream dominated by values of competition, aggression, and hierarchy.

The student movement as well moved from a reformist demand for open debate to an increasingly confrontational stance. Because of the Baby Boom of the postwar years and the technological demands of a growing economy, college enrollments had skyrocketed in the postwar years. In 1940 only 15 percent of nineteen-year-olds were in college; by the 1960s the proportion had increased to 45 percent. A growing minority of these students, schooled in their experience with the civil rights movement, began to challenge the very structure and values of their universities, accusing them of being servants of capitalism and partners in a vicious and inhuman war in southeast Asia through their defense contracts and research. Many of these students became part of what was known as the "counterculture," a vague label for young people who seemed to believe in greater sexual liberation, acid rock music, indulgence in mind-altering drugs, and attitudes of contempt for bourgeois manners and morals. For millions of people who had grown up believing in the traditional values of hard work, monogamy, patriotism, and respect for law and order, these new tendencies among the "liberated" young represented a frontal assault on the morals and institutions of middle-class life.

This confrontation along social and cultural lines eventually helped to define the politics of the 1970s and 1980s. If Lyndon Johnson had been able to maintain a broad base of support for his Great Society while avoiding schisms over Vietnam and issues such as Black Power, it is conceivable that at least some of these social and cultural conflicts could have been avoided. Instead, they were fueled by the war and by the government's failure to address fundamental issues of structural inequality at home. Divisions widened, and by 1968 the society was almost at a point of cultural and social civil war. As that year unfolded, virtually every conceivable conflict exploded into public view. First came the Tet offensive, highlighting the vulnerability of American forces in Vietnam and the American government's lack of credibility when it claimed that the war was almost over. Then came the political turmoil of the "Dump Johnson" movement, the assassinations of Martin Luther King Jr. and Robert Kennedy, the trauma of the Chicago Democratic Convention, and the riots in the streets. Everything seemed to be falling apart.

Significantly, the critical issue of the 1968 presidential campaign was Richard Nixon's determination to stand behind the "silent majority" of Americans who, he said, opposed chaos in the streets and believed in traditional values and morality. In a clash of cultural agendas reflecting vastly different visions of what American society should look like, those who defended traditionalism and the importance of standing fast for law and order prevailed, and the reform era of the postwar years ended with the triumph of a new conservatism.

THE 1970S AND 1980S

Not surprisingly, the political history of more recent times has also revealed the intersection of economic, social, and political developments. In 1969 Kevin Phillips wrote *The Emerging Republican Majority*, which argued persuasively that the old South and the Sunbelt represented the cornerstones of a new conservative coalition in America. More and more middle-class Americans were moving to these areas, Phillips suggested. They were people "on the make," more committed than most to values of religious fundamentalism, and conservative social and economic attitudes. In 1968 George Wallace appealed to many of these voters with his argument against the Washington "establishment," but if Nixon could win that Wallace constituency while holding onto his own "silent majority," he could insure the triumph of the Republican party.

In effect, that is what happened. Nixon won election two times by campaigning on social issues: law and order, the question of busing, and opposition to permissiveness. Although public spending for entitlement programs reached new heights during his presidency, most of Nixon's own political energy went to targeting for destruction those specific policies of the 1960s that had focused on eliminating racism and poverty. He sought to abolish the Office of Economic Opportunity, headquarters of the antipoverty effort; he attacked busing, even asking for congressional action to countermand Supreme Court decisions; and he made the Court's activism on behalf of civil liberties and civil rights a major rallying point for his own attacks on the northeastern establishment. By pursuing a southern strategy of appointing conservative Supreme Court justices, opposing civil rights, and denouncing the permissive values of the radical young, Nixon made giant strides toward developing a new Solid South—no longer the 100 percent Democratic South that had helped elect Franklin Roosevelt and his Democratic successors but a 100 percent Republican South that buttressed a conservative regime.

Despite the setbacks to Nixon's personal political fortunes caused by his abuse of power during the Watergate era, the new conservative coalition remained a dominant force in national politics. Even Jimmy Carter, the only Democratic president since 1968, was elected on a platform of personal morality, arguing that the American people deserved and should receive a government as compassionate, as decent, and as moral as they themselves were. Carter boasted of being a "born-again Christian," a description that as many as fifty million Americans were applying to themselves by 1980. Defense of traditional family and moral values became the centerpiece of evangelical Christianity, with a new generation of television preachers such as Jerry Falwell exhorting the American people to reject the license and permissiveness associated with the Supreme Court and the counterculture.

The emergence of such political/religious groups as the Moral Majority highlighted the ascendancy of cultural politics. Organizing primarily around issues of traditional family morality, they waged war against the "new rules" associated with feminism, gay rights, sexual freedom, and legalized abortion. At the core of almost all these conservative groups was a commitment to the old-fashioned family where men ruled, women were helpmates, and children obeyed their parents. The Moral Majority, the Eagle Forum, and various right-to-life organizations helped to entrench a pattern of political appeal based on clusters of cultural values rather than economic interests. In the past, political parties had rallied support around the horizontal dimension of economic status: middle-class and working-class people usually voted Democratic; upper-middle-class and upper-class people voted Republican. Now, conservatives used the vertical axis of devotion to such traditional cultural values as family and patriotism to attract working-class white ethnics, Catholics, and born-again Christians to vote for the Republican party.

The ultimate practitioner of conservative politics, of course, was Ronald Reagan. By 1984 Reagan had so succeeded in identifying himself with all the traditional virtues of American life that any attack against him became almost an attack on America itself. Significantly, Reagan put together an appeal based on economic, cultural, and political issues.

During the 1970s, rampant inflation—originally caused by Vietnam War spending—had besieged the average citizen. At the same time, an energy crisis caused by the Organization of Petroleum Exporting Countries (OPEC) oil embargo of 1973 created the realization among millions of Americans that they were no longer totally in control of their own destiny—or of the world economy. With the added humiliation of the Iranian hostage crisis, there developed an almost palpable sense of helplessness and powerlessness in the American people.

It was this sense of lost direction and wounded pride that Reagan used as his organizing theme in 1980 and 1984. Although he too waged a moralistic campaign, Reagan differed from Carter in promising America's return to greatness. The United States would "stand tall" once more, refuse to accept limits, resume its authority in the world, and not permit any foreign power to dictate to it. If only the American people would trust him and his policies, Reagan declared, the country would achieve total international dominance while reclaiming the values of personal morality, individualism, and family loyalty. Reagan was even able to secure enactment of a massive economic program that, for conservative ends, used deficits never even envisioned by Keynesian liberals, more than doubling in just six years the total national debt accumulated prior to 1980.

In the midst of this conservative ascendancy, at least some of the gains achieved by women and blacks during the 1960s remained. Those individuals who were economically well off and well educated found it easier to transcend barriers of race and gender. The new opportunities made possible by civil rights legislation and court decisions led to better jobs, more opportunities, and greater fulfillment for many. The number of black Americans attending college, for example, increased from 250,000 in 1960 to 1.2 million by the mid-1970s. Similarly, the number of women attending law schools increased from 5 percent of entering classes in the mid-1960s to nearly 40 percent by 1980. For these individuals, the advances achieved during the era of civil rights reform proved remarkable.

But one of the consequences of the conservative ascendancy was to cut off opportunities for those who had not yet become economically well situated or educationally prepared to take advantage of the new freedom. Class became an increasingly central reality for millions of women, blacks, and other minorities who were condemned to low-income housing, dead-end or nonexistent jobs, and a welfare system that offered little if any opportunity for escape. Indeed, many observers saw as the most critical development of these years the growing significance of class divisions *within* groups such as blacks and women, with upward mobility for some creating a new two-tiered social system in which the less fortunate group members were left behind and forgotten by their more fortunate brothers and sisters. Such social trends went hand in hand with a high-tech economy requiring higher education for decent jobs; and with the increasing "feminization of poverty," which makes it likely that female heads of household and their children, disproportionately black and Hispanic, will constitute the overwhelming majority of poor people by the twenty-first century.

Thus, improvement for some did not bring improvement for all: though discrimination based on gender and race became less significant for those well positioned to take advantage of progress, the triple burdens of class, gender, and race became even more oppressive for millions of others. In a new economy, more dependent on foreign production of such basic commodities as clothing and even automobiles, there were fewer and fewer economic opportunities for those without a college education. As class differences became more entrenched and extreme, there also seemed less likelihood of mobilizing a political constituency able to chart a new politics to address such issues. Indeed, voter participation rates reflected these class divisions, with the lowest percentage of voting occurring in those congressional districts where the poorest people live and the highest percentage in affluent suburbs.

The end of the Cold War and the demise of the Soviet Union highlighted these political dilemmas. Ever since 1947, there had been an inextricable connection between foreign and domestic policy in America. The Cold War not only anchored America's response to virtually every foreign policy issue (Was Egypt sufficiently anti-Communist for us to provide financial aid for building the Aswan Dam?); it also shaped and controlled domestic debate (How could we seriously consider national health insurance under Harry Truman when supporters of the concept were being accused of promoting "socialized medicine"?).

Now suddenly at the end of the 1980s, *perestroika* swept the Soviet Union, a new government led by Mikhail Gorbachev accepted American proposals for arms reduction, and the seeds of democracy burst into bloom throughout Eastern Europe. First came the Solidarity movement in Poland, then the students and workers of Prague, and finally the swelling democratic movement of East Germany that helped topple the Berlin Wall in November 1989. Within two years, Ronald Reagan's "evil empire" itself had collapsed, democratically elected governments sprouted up all over the former Eastern bloc, and Western banks and businesses prepared to establish new branches in Moscow, Saint Petersburg (no longer Leningrad) and Warsaw.

The end of the Cold War had begun under Ronald Reagan and was completed under George Bush. Presumably, this "victory" and the ensuing foreign policy triumphs that accompanied it—especially the U.S.-led alliance against Saddam Hussein in the Iraq war of 1991—virtually guaranteed a continued conservative Republican dominance of American presidential politics. But in fact, the end of the Cold War had the opposite effect. It reopened a whole series of issues that had been presumed closed and led to a political debate liberated by the degree to which the Cold War could no longer be counted upon as the controlling axiom that shaped every other equation.

In effect, the history of American politics from 1988 to 1996 reflected the volatility and instability created by the end of the Cold War and the loss of America's political anchor. Counting on his foreign policy victories, Bush ignored the decline of the economy and the continued worries among working and middle-class Americans about shrinking job security and real income. But a young Bill Clinton, the multi-term governor of Arkansas, zeroed in on these issues, offering the prospect of reform in the economy and progress on such persistent but previously ignored issues as health insurance. In some ways the election of 1992 boiled down to a referendum on whose version of the 1960s Americans wished to endorse—Clinton's, with his ebullient optimism and faith in reform, or Bush's, with his rejection of activism and government responsibility for improving the lot of those least well off.

Clinton's victory in the election seemed to signal a new era of government activism. But Clinton's first two years in office became a frustrating and ultimately self-defeating struggle to put together a coalition behind national health insurance. So angry did many Americans become at the apparent incompetence and divisiveness of their government in Washington that they voted in 1994 for a massive change in Congress, electing a conservative Republican majority more radical in its determination to eliminate government programs than anything even entertained by Ronald Reagan. But the same Americans then became equally disillusioned by Republican efforts to abandon and abolish programs that seemed fundamental to the gains of the past fifty years, such as aid to dependent children and protection of the environment.

In effect, the termination of the Cold War disclosed the degree to which American politics and society were without a clear direction. No longer possessing an automatic compass, politicians and citizens alike scrambled about trying to decide what was and was not necessary for government to provide, how much responsibility the more well off had toward the less well off, and what constituted the definition of rights that America wished to guarantee its diverse citizenry.

CONCLUSION

Thus, as the nation approaches a new millenium, it is unclear what course the country will pursue. Change has been a dominant theme of the past half-century. For millions of Americans the postwar era brought new prosperity, a better life-style, and developments in social and economic life that would have been inconceivable in 1945. Few people then would have believed that by 1995 two-thirds of all married women would be employed, that half of all law school graduates would be female, that black Americans would be voting in equal numbers with whites in the Old Confederacy, and that segregation of public facilities would have totally disappeared.

Equally striking, however, is the persistence of traditional values. Despite the protests of the 1960s, there remains an enormous commitment among most Americans to religion, the nuclear family, and powerful, old-fashioned ideas such as individualism, upward mobility, and middle-class propriety. The persistence of these views, in turn, goes hand in hand with a relatively static—and continuingly unequal—distribution of political and economic resources. Notwithstanding changes in matters of race and gender, the basic alignment of classes in the United States at the end of the century is much as it was in 1940, the gap becoming, if anything, even greater in recent years.

Whither then the nation? The "liberal consensus" of postwar politics appears to have ended with the Cold War. No longer is it clear that Americans agree on the need for a social welfare state. Equally unclear, however, is whether the society can survive without some sense of common purpose and responsibility. The beginnings of a new century could hardly be accompanied by more exciting or challenging questions.

BIBLIOGRAPHY

Overviews

Chafe, William. *The Unfinished Journey: America since World War II*. New York: Oxford University Press, 1986.

Gerstle, Gary, and Steve Fraser, eds. *The Rise and Fall of the New Deal Order*. Princeton, N.J.: Princeton University Press, 1989.

Hodgson, Godfrey. *America in Our Time*. Garden City, N.Y.: Doubleday, 1976.

Leuchtenburg, William E. *A Troubled Feast: American Society since 1945*. Glenview, Ill.: Scott Foresman, 1982.

Patterson, James. *Grand Expectations: The United States, 1945–74*. New York: Oxford University Press, 1996.

Polenberg, Richard. *One National Divisible: Class, Race, and Ethnicity in the U.S. since 1938*. New York: Penguin, 1980.

Siegel, Frederick. *Troubled Journey: From Pearl Harbor to Ronald Reagan*. New York: Hill & Wang, 1984.

Wittner, Lawrence S. *Cold War America: From Hiroshima to Watergate*. New York: Praeger, 1974.

Zinn, Howard. *Post-War America: 1945–1971*. Indianapolis, Ind.: Bobbs-Merrill, 1973.

Civil Rights

Branch, Taylor. *Parting the Waters: America during the King Years*. New York: Simon and Schuster, 1990.

Carson, Clayborne. *In Struggle: SNCC and the Black Awakening of the 1960s*. Cambridge, Mass.: Harvard University Press, 1981.

Chafe, William H. *Civilities and Civil Rights: Greensboro, North Carolina, and the Black Struggle for Freedom*. New York: Oxford University Press, 1980.

Dalfiume, Richard. *Desegregation of the United States Armed Forces: Fighting on Two Fronts, 1939–1945*. Columbia: University of Missouri Press, 1969.

Forman, James. *The Making of Black Revolutionaries: A Personal Account*. New York: Macmillan, 1972.

Garrow, David. *Bearing the Cross: Martin Luther King and the Southern Christian Leadership Conference, 1955–1968*. New York: Morrow, 1986.

Kluger, Richard. *Simple Justice: The History of Brown v. Board of Education and Black America's Struggle for Equality*. New York: Knopf, 1976.

Lawson, Steven. *Black Politics: Voting Rights in the South, 1944–1969*. New York: Columbia University Press, 1976.

Marable, Manning. *Race, Reform, and Rebellion: The Second Reconstruction in Black America, 1945–1982*. Jackson: University Press of Mississippi, 1984.

Meier, August, and Elliot Rudwick. *CORE: A Study of the Civil Rights Movement, 1942–1968*. New York: Oxford University Press, 1973.

Sitkoff, Harvard. *The Struggle for Black Equality, 1954–1980*. New York: Hill & Wang, 1981.

Women's History

Anderson, Karen. *Wartime Women: Sex Roles, Family Relations, and the Status of Women during World War II*. Westport, Conn.: Greenwood Press, 1981.

Chafe, William H. *The American Woman: Her Changing Social, Economic, and Political Roles, 1920–1970*. New York: Oxford University Press, 1972.

Evans, Sara. *Personal Politics: The Roots of Women's Liberation in the Civil Rights Movement and the New Left*. New York: Knopf, 1979.

Freeman, Jo. *The Politics of Women's Liberation: A Case Study of an Emerging Social Movement and Its Relation to the Policy Process*. New York: Longman, 1975.

Hartmann, Susan M. *The Home Front and Beyond: American Women in the 1940s*. Boston: Twayne, 1982.

Wandersee, Winifred. *On the Move: American Women in the 1970s*. Boston: G. K. Hall, 1988.

Politics

Alexander, Charles. *Holding the Line: The Eisenhower Era 1952–1961*. Bloomington: Indiana University Press, 1975.

Ambrose, Stephen. *Eisenhower: The President*. Vol. 2. New York: Simon & Schuster, 1984.

Bernstein, Carl, and Robert Woodward. *All the President's Men*. New York: Simon & Schuster, 1974.

Burnham, Walter. *The Current Crisis in American Politics*. New York: Oxford University Press, 1982.

Caro, Robert. *The Path to Power: The Years of Lyndon Johnson*. Vol. 1. New York: Knopf, 1982.

Crawford, Allan. *Thunder on the Right: The "New Right" and the Politics of Resentment*. New York: Pantheon, 1980.

Donovan, Robert. *Conflict and Crisis: The Presidency of Harry S Truman, 1945–1948*. New York: Norton, 1977.

Edsall, Thomas, with Mary Edsall. *Chain Reaction: The Impact of Race, Rights, and Taxes on American Politics*. New York: Harper & Row, 1992.

Griffith, Robert. *The Politics of Fear: Joseph R. McCarthy and the Senate*. Lexington: University Press of Kentucky, 1970.

Haldeman, H. R., with Joseph DiMona. *The Ends of Power*. New York: Times Books, 1978.

Hamby, Alonzo. *Beyond the New Deal: Harry S Truman and American Liberalism*. New York: Columbia University Press, 1973.

Heath, Jim F. *John F. Kennedy and the Business Community*. Chicago: University of Chicago Press, 1969.

Hersh, Seymour. *The Price of Power: Kissinger in the Nixon White House*. New York: Summit Books, 1983.

Kearns, Doris. *Lyndon Johnson and the American Dream*. New York: New American Library, 1977.

Ladd, Everett, Jr., with Charles D. Hadley. *Transformations of the American Party System: Political Coalitions from the New Deal to the 1970s*. 2d ed. New York: Norton, 1978.

Lubell, Samuel. *The Future of American Politics*. New York: Harper, 1952.

Lyons, Peter. *Eisenhower: Portrait of the Hero*. Boston: Little, Brown, 1974.

Matusow, Allen. *The Unraveling of America: A History of Liberalism in the 1960s*. New York: Harper & Row, 1984.

Nixon, Richard. *Six Crises*. Garden City, N.Y.: Doubleday, 1962.

Parmet, Herbert S. *Jack: The Struggles of John F. Kennedy*. New York: Dial Press, 1980.

Patterson, James T. *Mr. Republican: A Biography of Robert A. Taft*. Boston: Houghton Mifflin, 1972.

Phillips, Kevin P. *The Emerging Republican Majority*. New Rochelle, N.Y.: Arlington House, 1969.

Schlesinger, Arthur, Jr. *A Thousand Days: John F. Kennedy in the White House*. Boston: Houghton Mifflin, 1965.

Steinfels, Peter. *The Neo-Conservatives: The Men Who Are Changing America's Politics*. New York: Simon & Schuster, 1979.

Sundquist, James. *Politics and Policy: The Eisenhower, Kennedy, and Johnson Years*. Washington, D.C.: Brookings Institution, 1968.

Weinstein, Allen. *Perjury: The Hiss-Chambers Case.* New York: Knopf, 1978.

Wills, Gary. *The Kennedy Imprisonment: A Meditation on Power.* Boston: Little, Brown, 1982.

———. *Nixon Agonistes: The Crisis of the Self-Made Man.* New York: New American Library, 1971.

Miscellaneous

Anderson, Terry. *The Movement and the Sixties: Protest in America from Greensboro to Wounded Knee.* New York: Oxford University Press, 1995.

Barnouw, Erik. *Tube of Plenty: The Evolution of American Television.* Rev. ed. New York: Oxford University Press, 1982.

Brody, David. *Workers in Industrial America: Essays on the Twentieth-Century Struggle.* New York: Oxford University Press, 1980.

Clecak, Peter. *America's Quest for the Ideal Self: Dissent and Fulfillment in the Sixties and Seventies.* New York: Oxford University Press, 1983.

D'Emilio, John. *Sexual Politics, Sexual Communities: The Making of a Homosexual Minority in the United States, 1940–1970.* Chicago: University of Chicago Press, 1983.

Donaldson, Scott. *The Suburban Myth.* New York: Columbia University Press, 1969.

Jackson, Kenneth T. *Crabgrass Frontier: The Suburbanization of America.* New York: Oxford University Press, 1985.

Leffler, Melvyn. *A Preponderance of Power: National Security, the Truman Administration, and the Cold War.* Stanford, Calif.: Stanford University Press, 1992.

Lemon, Richard. *The Troubled American.* New York: Simon & Schuster, 1971.

Pells, Richard. *The Liberal Mind in a Conservative Age: American Intellectuals in the 1940s and 1950s.* New York: Harper & Row, 1984.

Reich, Robert. *The Next American Frontier.* New York: Times Books, 1983.

Sale, Kirkpatrick. *Power Shift: The Rise of the Southern Rim and Its Challenge to the Eastern Establishment.* New York: Random House, 1975.

Slater, Philip. *The Pursuit of Loneliness: American Culture at the Breaking Point.* Boston: Beacon Press, 1970.

Thurow, Lester. *The Zero-Sum Society: The Distribution and the Possibilities for Economic Change.* New York: Basic Books, 1980.

Wilson, William J. *The Declining Significance of Race: Blacks and Changing American Institutions.* Chicago: University of Chicago Press, 1978.

Wood, Michael. *America in Movies; or, "Santa Maria, It Has Slipped My Mind."* New York: Basic Books, 1975.

Part II
Major
Themes
in the
American
Experience

8

■■ INTELLECTUAL AND CULTURAL HISTORY

Thomas Bender

A GENERATION AGO INTELLECTUAL HISTORY WAS DEFINED BY THE STUDY OF A group of thinkers and texts constituting a "national tradition," but today neither substantive nor methodological concerns unify the field. If intellectual history has always been eclectic in method, diverse in topics, and various in its definitions, the issue today is less fragmentation than that the boundaries of the field, especially if cultural history is included, have nearly vanished. A field that in the 1970s feared being swept aside by social history now finds itself insinuated into nearly every corner of the discipline, mostly under the aegis of the protean concept of culture.

It has even been suggested by William Bouwsma that the project of intellectual history has realized itself so completely that its independent existence is no longer necessary. And its domain, he further notes, is being broadened from the history of ideas to the history of meaning, a much wider term. Intellectual history thus becomes cultural history, no longer a specialized discourse but an integrative or synthetic mode of inquiry that heals the schism between intellectual history and social history, which in recent years has redefined itself as socio-cultural history. Either we are all becoming intellectual/cultural historians however we identify ourselves, or, put another way, the field is disappearing into general historical practice that has absorbed a considerable portion of its intellectual agenda.

Such speculation exaggerates the present circumstance, even as it captures an important tendency that is today bringing intellectual/cultural history and general historical practice into a very close and fruitful relation. I argue, however, that there are good reasons for attending to intellectual history in a self-conscious way. First, and least important, we need to maintain intellectual history as a specialization that examines a significant social group—intellectuals—as a social type and as active and self-conscious participants in a continuous and ever-changing public discourse on the human condition. Second, and more important, we need to preserve intellectual history as an established way of training historians to read texts closely and rigorously, a skill increasingly important to the degree that in much contemporary social theory language becomes the focus of historical work and experience itself becomes textualized.

THE CULTURAL WORK OF INTELLECTUAL HISTORY

Intellectual and cultural histories become a preoccupation of scholars and intellectuals at particular historical moments. Such moments are not, interestingly enough, eras of great confidence in the power of ideas. On the contrary, historians turn to the study of intellectuals, ideas, and culture in periods defined by uncertainty about the role and power of ideas, about the agency of human thinkers.[1]

Intellectual history as a distinct mode of inquiry can be traced back to the Enlightenment, when grand hopes for the power of ideas were intermingled with serious worries about traditional alternatives to reason. In this spirit Voltaire "invented" the history of civilization, intending to demonstrate the creative power of mind to transcend the habits and superstitions that had so limited human possibility.[2]

The ambitions of the Enlightenment also inspired the first intellectual history written by an American, Samuel Miller's two-volume study of European and American civilization.[3] At once a Jeffersonian political leader and a Presbyterian clergyman, Miller was committed to reason and civilized progress, yet haunted by Calvinism. He eventually resolved this inner conflict by leaving the cosmopolitan and secular world of New York for the smaller and denominational intellectual culture of Princeton Theological Seminary. For a brief time, however, this tension within impelled him to undertake the project of inquiring into contemporary intellectual and cultural history. His conclusion, perhaps predictable, was that the achievements of civilization were commendable, but they did not insure moral progress. It is instructive to compare the conflicted Miller with the confident, almost blithe, George Bancroft, who in post-Enlightenment America was certain that ideas deriving directly from God drove American history. He had no reason to inquire into them, for they were not problematic for him. There is, therefore, very little consideration of ideas in his great history of the United States.

In the second half of the nineteenth century and into the twentieth, when the role of trained intellect in a democratic society had become a matter of increasing concern, American scholars turned to the history of ideas and to the history of the educated classes to authorize their own ambitions. The earliest of these inquiries came from a scientist of remarkably diverse talents and interests, New York University's John W. Draper. Draper was a chemist and founder of the American Chemical Society, a key figure in the founding of the NYU Medical School, and a pioneer in American photography. His bulky portfolio included history as well. The purpose of his intellectual histories of Europe, first published in 1861 and 1874, was, among other things, to justify a public voice for the modern, scientific outlook against the pretense of Victorian America, with its anti-intellectual religious moralism and parochialism.[4]

The promotion of the "New History" by James Harvey Robinson and Charles A. Beard at the turn of the century coincided with the emergence of the "intellectual," newly so named and recognized as a novel social type in Europe and America. The inauguration in 1904 of Robinson's famous course at Columbia University, "The History of the Intellectual Classes of Europe," was an important phase in the creation and legitimation of the category of the intellectual in the United States. In a neo-Enlightenment mode, Beard and Robinson embraced reason but worried about the distortions introduced by interest, irrationality, and corruption. Intellectuals, they claimed, ought to enter the public sphere as custodians of reasoned discourse, unfettered by class interest, the claims of tradition, or established institutions. When Columbia restricted academic freedom during World War I and thus challenged these principles of the intellectuals, Beard resigned to defend them.[5]

During the interwar years, the field of intellectual history emerged as the core of the undergraduate curriculum at Columbia, and a number of distinguished works by historians, philosophers, and literary scholars appeared. In the disillusionment following World War I, there was an anxious search for some basis for belief in the power of reason—and good cause to be skeptical. Intellectual history became one of the ways to address this cultural crisis. There was at the same time—and for some of the same reasons—a desire to identify a "usable" American past that would carry the United States through these years of moral disillusionment and, then, economic depression. Such was the context for major intellectual histories by Carl Becker, Charles and Mary Beard, Vernon L. Parrington, Constance Rourke, Perry Miller, Ralph Gabriel, and Herbert W. Schneider.

By the 1940s intellectual history had taken definition as a field, and it was divided between two camps, each identified with a major figure. Arthur O. Lovejoy, founder of the *Journal of the History of Ideas* (1940), was trained as a philosopher; in his major historical work, *The Great Chain of Being* (1936), he examines the *internal* history, logic, and affinities of that idea over several centuries and in various domains of culture, from science to poetry. Lovejoy pays no heed to political or social causation, nor does he explore the political implications of the ideas he traces. His is a "pure" history of ideas, dealing with the internal development and relations of ideas. In 1943, Merle E. Curti, a pioneer in both intellectual and social history, published *The Growth of American Thought*. Awarded the Pulitzer Prize in that year, the book is extraordinarily wide-ranging in its erudition, examining both elite and popular writings. Curti's intense interest in social and political causation and implications, distinctively different from Lovejoy's approach, was characterized as an *external* approach.

Within the field of history, there was a tendency to identify the internal history of ideas with European history, where, it was often assumed, more significant and richer ideas were available for analysis. Students of American history were expected to resort to external analysis, or to a social history of ideas, since, according to the same prejudices, the American ideas were not so important or so interesting, though the social context and progressive applications of ideas often were. The work of Perry Miller, however, challenged these assumptions or prejudices. It also undermined the impractical division between these two approaches. Miller is often thought to have worked in the internalist mode, but in fact his histories combine the subtle analysis of ideas and their social causation and implications, particularly in *The New England Mind: From Colony to Province* (1953).[6]

At the same time, the American Studies movement was founded on the common ground that intellectual history provided for historians and literary scholars. Historians in the movement—Richard Hofstadter, Louis Hartz, Arthur M. Schlesinger Jr., and C. Vann Woodward—tended to combine intellectual and political history, while the literary scholars—Henry Nash Smith and Leo Marx—combined literature and ideas. Both groups used intellectual history to construct sweeping interpretations of the American experience.

For Richard Hofstadter, who called his work the study of "political culture," the way to political understanding passed through the study of ideas, both specifically political and more general ones (e.g., the "agrarian myth"). Such study, at least for Hofstadter, was not confined to elite thinkers; besides Jefferson, Lincoln, and Thurman Arnold, he examined the thought of marginal, even eccentric thinkers such as William "Coin" Harvey, about whom he wrote so brilliantly and wickedly. Such broad and global histories are no longer written by intellectual historians, and the connection between political and intellectual history has been weakened, though the recent work of James T. Kloppenberg and Daniel T. Rodgers reveals how much potential remains in that vein.[7]

Since the study of intellectual history has always been intertwined with the history of intellectuals in the United States, it should not be surprising that intellectual history flourished as never before in the postwar years, the era when American academics and intellectuals were, in the words of the sociologist Edward Shils, incorporated into the center of American society. In the 1950s intellectuals were both delighted with and worried about their ascent; it was a period of self-conscious exploration of the nature and fate of the American intellectual. The single most important work was Richard Hofstadter's enormously influential *Anti-Intellectualism in American Life* (1963), which became the basic text for intellectuals in the United States, enabling them to understand themselves as alienated victims in a society characterized by the crudest forms of anti-intellectualism.

This self-identity very much affected the way they interpreted the history of intellectuals and approached American ideas. The best minds grasped and spoke the awful truth, but the consequence was isolation and obscurity. Herman Melville's genius, for example, was unrecognized by the democracy in whose interest he wrote. The legitimate aspirations of American intellectuals were continually thwarted by parochial small-mindedness, by business values, by religious bigotry, by the democratic masses. The consequence was a historiography that revealed a profound ambivalence toward democracy: while celebrated, democracy was a problem for the educated and creative. Historians of intellectuals absorbed what Robert Davidoff characterizes as an ironic or Tocquevillian, rather than a Jeffersonian or Deweyan, democratic attitude toward American politics and culture. Projecting their self-perceptions into the past, they portrayed alienated intellectuals who accepted a democratic politics that had no place for them. Historians, wavering between detachment and engagement, typically regretted the political isolation of intellectuals, but they tended to commend, though again not without some ambivalence, the popular politics and culture that seemed to demand this withdrawal.[8]

Between 1960 and 1980, intellectual history fell from its privileged position within American historiography. The challenge of the politics of the 1960s undermined intellectual history in four ways. The left's celebration of experience and participatory democracy was so profoundly at odds with the premises of intellectual history as it was being practiced that the field seemed irrelevant to all concerned. The failed policies of the "best and the brightest" at home and abroad—the catastrophe in Vietnam and the failures of domestic reform—also undermined faith in trained intellect and in elites generally. At the same time—and this was not unrelated—a new generation of historians attached themselves to social history, to the history of ordinary people, sometimes called "history from the bottom up" or the history of the "inarticulate." Most fundamental and troublesome of all for the future of the field, the intellectual and cultural histories of the 1950s had been premised upon a model of consensual pluralism. The social conflicts of the 1960s rendered this premise implausible. Compared with intellectual history, social history was much more attentive to division and conflict. The next generation of historians did not rewrite American intellectual history; they largely ignored it. Many intellectual historians feared that the field might soon disappear.[9]

Making matters worse, some social historians boldly disavowed interest in the subjective or interior experience of historical actors. Implicitly accepting elitist premises, these historians assumed that the mass of ordinary people had no thought to study; only their actions deserved the attention of historians. An outward, behavioral, quantitatively measured history promised to make history a social science. In the end, the dream of such a social science history collapsed on technical methodological issues and massive interpretive problems. But for a decade, it looked like the future; a distinguished French historian even remarked that the historian will become a computer programmer or nothing.

More significantly, other social historians, following the lead of the American historian Herbert G. Gutman and the English historian E. P. Thompson, biographer of the artist William Morris as well as historian of the working class, began to explore the culture and subjective meaning of working-class experience. These histories of the working classes, which evolved into a socio-cultural history of various American groups, provided the basis for a later rapprochement of intellectual and social history as a broadly defined cultural history.

CRISIS AND REFIGURATION

In 1980, when intellectual history seemed to have touched bottom, almost no dissertations were being written in the field, and social history was flourishing. But if one looked more closely, signs of revival, prompted by the challenge of social history, were evident. The bagginess of intellectual history, the lack of any clear definition of the basis for generalization about American thought or the American mind, was being questioned by intellectual historians increasingly attentive to social division and to the group boundaries so significant in social history. New questions, often explicitly informed by social history, now came to the fore. Can one be sure how the writings of intellectuals are read? Do different groups or audiences read them differently? Can they be read by historians in a manner that is sufficiently contextual to grasp their intended and received meanings? What is the role of institutions in the shaping of both the production and reception of knowledge? For whom, in fact, do intellectuals speak? What are the bounds of intellectual discourse? All Americans? Transnational networks? Or identifiable subgroups?

Such questions, raised mainly by the younger participants, infiltrated the discussions at a conference that resulted in the volume *New Directions in American Intellectual History*, edited by John Higham and Paul K. Conkin (1979). And in this period many of the same historians established the *Intellectual History Newsletter*. Its purpose was to provide a serious but informal forum for rethinking these, and other issues, including questions about the relevance for American intellectual and cultural history of the "theory" that was increasingly being taken up by European intellectual historians.[10] During the 1980s and early 1990s, when David Ransell was editor of the *American Historical Review*, the field benefited from his commitment to "move intellectual history and historiography to center stage" as they reemerged "with renewed vitality and excitement."

In the past decade, intellectual history and cultural history, insofar as they have remained distinct, have retreated from the global and largely ungrounded generalizations of the postwar years. Focus has been on the ethnography of groups and their expressive cultures, the development of more precise understandings of contexts, and the delineation of intellectual discourses. Although American historians have been less willing to dissolve the author or to seriously compromise human agency, context and discourse (or language) loom larger in current practice than in the 1950s, when Perry Miller wrote of "man thinking," self-consciously following Emerson's charge in "The American Scholar" to escape history and break forms. Today, emphasis is more clearly on the various ways humans find and explicate meaning within a context of languages and institutions. The intellectual and cultural historian is more likely to move back and forth between written and other forms of cultural expression (images, ritual, material culture), as well as between elite and popular forms.

In the 1990s intellectual and cultural histories have broadened the domain of the field, making it more inclusive and aware of difference, more curious about the relations of intellect and democracy, commerce, and mass culture. The emphasis on reading and extracting meaning, almost an ethnographic impulse, has produced brilliant and evocative historical analysis, but there is a worrisome implication attached to this work: a weakening of the historian's traditional concern for causal explanation. Instead of bringing meaning to bear on explanation, as Max Weber would have it, current practice in intellectual and cultural history focuses more on the act of reading itself, rewarding cleverness and imagination, explication of meaning over explanation of cause.

The most exemplary intellectual history being written today tends to fall into three broad categories, with cultural history, rather loosely defined, constituting a fourth. I am categorizing these approaches by angle of access, whether one begins with a person, with a text, or with community of discourse, whether identified by a shared question, a group, an institutional setting, or a place. In their different ways, these variations all seek greater precision, surer grounding, and more definition of the limits of interpretive claims.

Several recent deeply contextualized biographies exemplify the value of that genre for writing intellectual history. Drew Faust's study of James Henry Hammond examines one man's political and social thought with great care, relating it both to his experience as a planter and to his political career, showing at the same time the ways in which he is and is not typical of the intellectual and political elite of the antebellum South. The relation of Walt Whitman to his time and place and the quality of his poetry are both illuminated by the richly contextual account of his life recently published by David Reynolds. The book's peculiar and effective conceptualization is manifest in the complex title: *Walt Whitman's America: A Cultural Biography* (1995). Almost identical tactics and virtues can be found in the first volume of a projected two-volume biography of W.E.B. Du Bois, by David Levering Lewis. Here, too, the title is revealing: *W.E.B. Du Bois, 1868–1919: Biography of a Race* (1993). Kathryn Kish Sklar, in the first volume of her new biography of Florence Kelley, effectively combines biography with the study of ideas and the ways in which these ideas were forged out of the complex interplay of available intellectual traditions, women's place in political culture, social issues, and the dynamics of public life.

Other historians have begun with a text or a series of texts. David Hall, for example, has used the diary of Samuel Sewell to explore the world of belief in Puritan culture, and Gary Wills has entered late eighteenth- and mid-nineteenth-century American intellectual history with contextual readings of the Declaration of Independence, portraits and sculptures of Washington, and the Gettysburg Address. A series of related texts, whether officially an archive or not, invite inquiry by intellectual historians seeking a bounded topic that will reveal conceptual change, persistence, or the cultural dynamics of public or private life.[11] Beginning with an image or object as a text to be read has been especially appealing to students of visual texts and material culture, from colonial furniture and decorative art objects to Matthew Brady's Civil War photographs to Thomas Eakins's portraits of craft and professional accomplishment to William Sidney Mount's genre scenes to the World War II photographs examined by George H. Roeder Jr.[12]

Almost two decades ago David A. Hollinger proposed the discourse of intellectuals as the domain of intellectual history. Although his argument was in a sense prescriptive, he offered it, accurately, as descriptive of current practice. Much of the distinctive work in intellectual history was in fact the tracking and analysis of the discourse of intellectuals. He explained that such discourse was unified by the questions participants held in common, rather than by their answers. This approach allows for a wide-ranging investigation of the work of intellectuals freed from any search for a single mind or consensus—yet it is not so loose a structure for inquiry that it loses focus and definition. This community of discourse might be socially connected or not. For a proximate or associated community, one might cite the example of books on the New York Intellectuals of the 1930s and Cold War era by Terry A. Cooney and Alexander Bloom. J.G.A. Pocock's delineation of a republican tradition of political thought and James Kloppenberg's study of an international community of social democratic thinkers at the turn of the century provide examples of communities of discourse separated by time and space that confronted a common question. Hazel V. Carby's examination of the developing discourse of black women intellectuals about their identity and place in a racialized, gendered, and class-divided society investigates a less distended discourse.[13] But Hollinger indicated that "discourse is a social as well as an intellectual activity," and various historians have gained access to a discursive community through a focus on institutions, whether universities, disciplines, professions, magazines, artistic circles, or, even, places.[14]

It is impossible in any comprehensive way to describe the various contemporary versions of cultural history—there are studies of women's, bourgeois, immigrant, working-class, and African-American cultures, among other groups; and there are inquiries into American public culture, economic culture, consumer culture, political culture, religious culture, and intellectual culture. Two preoccupations within the study of American culture, however, invite specific notice. The first concerns the question of hierarchy and exclusivity, the second has to do with reception. Important work has been done in both areas.

Twenty-five years ago, Neil Harris published a brilliant essay on the stages of cultural development in American cities; one of his themes concerned degrees of unity and differentiation, hierarchy and access, in that development. These issues were later formed into a strongly argued thesis by Lawrence W. Levine, who proposed that the story of cultural development from 1830 to World War I is one of sacralization and exclusion. While that interpretation may hold for a few places, particularly Boston, the pattern elsewhere was more complex. At the same time the boundary markings noticed by Levine were being established, social and aesthetic categories (sometimes the same ones) were being broken in the course of making modern culture. Movements in various arts forms were very complex and often ambiguous, a process well captured in other studies, for example, Joseph Horowitz's recent investigation of New York's Gilded Age musical culture.

The question of reception has been imaginatively pursued by a number of scholars. The availability of cultural materials precedes any questions of interpretation, and Ronald Zboray has with diligence and imagination provided a persuasive account of the book trade and the distribution of literary genres and even particular titles to identifiable audiences. Others have examined with equal imagination the content that was absorbed from these books, or from the public lectures so common in nineteenth-century America. Barbara Sicherman has illuminated the whole culture of reading by examining diaries and other personal records of readers, while Mary Kupiec Cayton has compared newspaper accounts of Emerson's lectures with his text. This strategy allowed her to gauge the relation between enunciation and reception, opening a space in which the historical sources of "distortion" and construction of meaning might be examined. Working on a more contemporary period, Janice Radway has interviewed readers of popular romances to understand what they brought to the published text and what they took away from the encounter. It turns out that more can be learned about reception than one might have supposed. Empathetic reading is still important, but imaginative research strategies offer empirical guides to interpretation.

CHRONOLOGICAL AND THEMATIC FOCI

Although fine work is being done in all periods and in a wide variety of topics, since the revival of intellectual and cultural history there has been a distinct concentration on two periods, 1770–1820 and 1870–1920. There is some indication that a significant body of work may soon emerge in the middle period. George Fredrickson pioneered the intellectual history of the Civil War in 1964, while more recently Drew Gilpin Faust has examined Confederate nationalism. David W. Blight has explored the connection between Civil War memories, politics, and ideology in the thought of Frederick Douglass.[15] The middle years of the nineteenth century have also been the focus for an increasingly dense literature on the construction of race and on ways in which the white culture was shaped by racial considerations. Fredrickson began this wide-ranging discussion with his study of American attitudes and theories of race. Since then the discussion has been moved by Henry Louis Gates Jr. and Kwame Anthony Appiah from attitude to the construction and meaning of the category, and that focus has directed attention to the construction and development of whiteness as well, with work by David Roediger especially influential. Toni Morrison further widened the discussion by examining the way race, or the experience of a racialized society, has entered, even become an abiding presence, in the broader literary culture of the United States.[16]

The principal historiographical issue in the intellectual history of the period between the Revolution and the War of 1812 has been the relative importance and implications of the classical tradition of republicanism, which insists on a self-denying commitment to civic good, and liberalism, a more individualistic political theory that acknowledges self-interest in politics. It has been a highly ideological debate, with many historians seeing in republicanism a potential critique of liberal capitalist society, while others have found a liberal birth of the nation a justification for values associated with liberalism.[17] So much energy was devoted to this debate that historians were slow to recognize the important point made first by James Kloppenberg and Forrest McDonald: a number of intellectual traditions or political languages—republicanism, liberalism, Christianity, the common law—were available for addressing the political problems of the era, and various groups assembled them and used them in different combinations. The effort to claim various founding lineages has, predictably enough, raised questions about the differing implications of these political languages for democracy and equality, with some specific concerns about gender and racial equality. Republicanism, whatever its communitarian appeal, seems to offer the least comfort here.[18]

As for work on the half-century following the Civil War, the revival of interest in the history of pragmatism has been at once unexpected and important. Partly, I suspect, its appeal is as an American response to the neo-Nietzchean moment, and it is a response that is more moderate than the current French imports, most notably Derridian theories of deconstruction, which deny any certain ground for knowledge and rather explicitly challenge the Enlightenment hopes for reason. But whatever its contemporary appeal, pragmatism's importance in its own historical moment has been rediscovered, most notably by James Kloppenberg and David Hollinger, but by other scholars as well. At the center of this work has been a major reconsideration of the thought and significance of John Dewey. Not only has Dewey been restored to his place as the preeminent American thinker of this century, but the reinterpretation of his thought and politics by Robert B. Westbrook has made him central to a vigorous rethinking of American liberalism and democratic theory.

Several historians of the social and cultural history of turn-of-the-century America—Warren I. Susman, John Kasson, T. J. Jackson Lears, Kathy Peiss, Ross Posnock, and Philip Ethington, among others—have been developing a substantial body of writing on the emergence of newer identities—class, gender, ethnic, racial—and on the emergence of a consumer culture, which, in some arguments, profoundly altered human subjectivity. This convergence of themes suggests a protean historical moment, and in a recent and important book—bold, full of intellectual risk-taking, and, in consequence, marked by more than a few stumbles—James Livingston has tried to bring into a single narrative much of this change, as well as the concurrent transformations in the economy. He begins by offering two narratives common to the period, each a bit schematic in his presentation. The usual social-economic account of the transition from the nineteenth to the twentieth century describes the rise of corporate capitalism and the depression of workers and the lower middle classes. By contrast, the usual cultural narrative, whether about elite avant gardes or the burgeoning and widely accessible new commercial culture, is one of novel freedoms, even liberations from older aesthetic and social forms. Livingston argues that the first narrative would take on new meaning were it related more directly to the second, and that is what his book offers, with pragmatism at once a product of that transformative experience and a means of achieving intellectual control of it. Put crudely, the emergence of a corporate consumer economy and a pragmatic understanding of experience helps people to break old forms, to construct new identities, to liberate new desires, even, by implication, to create a new politics. So many particulars in Livingston's argument are vulnerable to challenge, including his reading of William James, that it would be incautious to accept the argument wholly. Yet it would be a more serious mistake to allow those vulnerabilities to detract from further inquiry into the possibility of the major reorientation in historiography inherent in this ambitious sketch toward a synthesis.

HISTORY AND THEORY

The "culture wars" have affected American history more than have the "theory wars." Insofar as theory has become an issue in history, intellectual and cultural historians have tended to be the most attentive, particularly those with an interest in the social construction of such categories as race and gender. The "linguistic turn," the close examination of languages as a system of signs, has affected the writing of American intellectual history less than it has the European field, where in some cases language has become the singular focus of analysis and the locale of power. Writing on American thought has become more textual in its analytical concern, more sensitive to the power of language, but it has not separated such study from various forms of institutional power and experience.[19]

In 1989, David Harlan raised the specter of an "epistemological crisis" in history that cannot be ignored, "especially by intellectual historians." Even if Harlan and others are correct in saying "there is only the incessant and unremitting play of signifiers—signifiers freed from the tyranny of the signified," it is quite unclear why this should be a special worry of intellectual historians. All text-based scholarly inquiry would seem to be equally vulnerable. At any event, few historians seem to be persuaded of his worry. The combination of a natural pragmatism bred of the empiricist culture of American historical practice and some strongly argued formal pragmatic responses to the various challenges to historical objectivity by, among others, David Hollinger, James Kloppenberg, Thomas Haskell, and myself, seem to have reassured historians of the capacity of their discipline to describe the past, albeit contingently, incompletely, and from some place, no matter how hard they strive, in the words of the philosopher Thomas Nagel, to achieve a view from nowhere.

Even in literature, the theory wars have been over for nearly a decade. Polemics have subsided; critics are reading and interpreting texts, often in an eclectic fashion, using whatever theories and practices will unlock meanings. In history, which has suffered fewer polemics to begin with, younger scholars are now beginning to publish work deeply and fruitfully informed by theory. Moving beyond highly self-conscious and even righteous commitments to "theory," this new work establishes a very productive conversation between theory and history.

Theory can enrich historical accounts without displacing history itself. The best example of these exciting new directions is Gail Bederman's *Manliness and Civilization: A Cultural History of Gender and Race in the United States, 1880–1917* (1995). The period considered is one for which considerable scholarly energy is transforming older interpretations and ways of framing the historical issues, and she builds upon these new approaches to the period. The themes of Bederman's work, race and gender, clearly reflect touchstones of the emerging portrait of that era. She shows how Victorian notions of manliness and masculinity were transformed, under the sign of "civilization," and she demonstrates how race played an active and central role in this reconfiguration of gender identities and relations.

But I want to speak mostly, in this brief account, about her method of doing intellectual and cultural history, a method that takes much that is both brilliant and useful in the work of Michel Foucault, while leaving behind that which is brilliant, but perverse and unuseful. First, she recognizes that some words, ideas, and concepts may be at a given point in history protean—large in potential but not programmed, leaving room for human agents to put them to various uses. Civilization is one such concept. It is open to variant but not unlimited meanings, depending on the perspectives and purposes of users. Moving beyond conventional notions of cultural hegemony and rejecting the now overworked notion of "contested" concepts, she grasps that such protean words can accommodate multiple (and simultaneous) meanings of different and historically changing valence. No one position is likely to establish meaning. Her concern, in fact, is more focused on rhetoric and justification than on domination.[20] "Thus," she writes, "the interesting thing about 'civilization' is not what was meant by the term, but the multiple ways it was used to legitimize different sorts of claims to power." Hence, while white racists used civilization to justify lynching blacks, Ida Wells used the same concept to challenge lynching.[21] As the historical meanings of collateral terms change—manliness, for instance—a particular use of civilization may become historically impossible, or, at least, it might lose its resonance, which is what happened to Ida Wells's use of civilization by the time of World War I.

Bederman's own gifts, personal style, and training largely account, no doubt, for her particular way of doing intellectual and cultural history, but her self-consciousness in approaching theory helps. She does not *use* or *apply* theory; she enters into dialogue with the ideas that are embodied in serious theory. In a very concise way, she recounts this dialogue with Foucault.[22] She starts with his notion of "discourse," which enables her to "presume that intellectual knowledge and concrete power relations are mutually constitutive." Many have observed that Foucault's notion of discourse implies a form of coercion and a denial of human agency, but she focuses differently. For her, his assumption that "ideas and practices comprising any discourse will be multiple, inconsistent, and contradictory" opens up space for an "emphasis on human agency and the possibility of intentional change." If some historians fear that theory promises to undermine history and to foist an interpretive straitjacket on the historical imagination, Bederman's work instances precisely the opposite: theory enables a supple, contextual, and deeply historical analysis.

Once again, it seems, a much constrained faith among historians that thought and reason ought to have a place in human affairs is stimulating a reinvigoration of the field. Perhaps the challenge of Nietzsche—

and the contemporary theories that claim descent from him—deserve our thanks for inciting this renewed and broader commitment to an intellectual and cultural history no longer at war with social history.

NOTES

1. This point, along with others that influence my shaping of this essay, derives from a very fine essay on the field by John Higham, "Study of American Intellectual History."

2. On Voltaire and the history of civilization, see Weintraub, *Visions of Culture.*

3. On Miller and the context of his work, see Bender, *New York Intellect,* 42–45.

4. See also Draper's *Conflict between Religion and Science.* Andrew Dickson White, a historian and first president of Cornell University, later published a similar study of religion and science. On the religious basis of hostility to a scientific outlook, see Hofstadter and Metzger, *Development of Academic Freedom,* pt. 1.

5. Beard's statement upon resigning is conveniently reprinted in Hofstadter and Smith, *American Higher Education,* 2:883–84.

6. The Europeanist Peter Gay, his study of Puritan histories, *Loss of Mastery,* made the same point about the work of Richard Hofstadter.

7. See also Foner, *Tom Paine;* Howe, *Political Culture of American Whigs;* and Ashworth, *"Agrarians" and Aristocrats.*

8. For an example of an alternative interpretation of the place of creative intellectuals, an interpretation that reveals their continuing connection with society and engagement in politics, see Teichgraeber, *Sublime Thoughts.*

9. See Higham and Conkin, *New Directions;* Darnton, "Intellectual and Cultural History."

10. The first issue was spring 1979; it continues publication, now from Indiana University, where the current editor is Casey Blake.

11. See, for example, Bailyn, *Ideological Origins;* Wright, *Moralism and the Model Home;* and Stowe, *Intimacy and Power.*

12. The references here are to Bushman, *Refinement of America;* Trachtenberg, *Reading American Photographs;* and Johns, *Thomas Eakins.*

13. Other important examples include Cmiel, *Democratic Eloquence;* Lears, *No Place of Grace;* Gurstein, *Repeal of Reticence;* and Hollinger, *Science, Jews, and Secular Culture.*

14. See, for example: Kuklick, *Rise of American Philosophy;* Stevenson, *Scholarly Means to Evangelical Ends;* Haskell, *Emergence of Professional Social Science;* Ross, *Origins of American Social Science;* Blake, *Beloved Community;* Guilbaut, *How New York Stole the Idea;* Lewis, *When Harlem Was in Vogue;* and Bender, *New York Intellect.*

15. Other important recent contributions include Trachtenberg, *Reading American Photographs* (chap. 2); Simpson, *Mind;* Stevenson, *Victorian Homefront;* and Fahs, *Publishing the Civil War.*

16. See also Sundquist, *To Wake the Nations.*

17. Key works, from a huge bibliography, would include Bailyn, *Ideological Origins;* Wood, *Creation of the American Republic* and *Radicalism of the American Revolution;* Pocock, *Machiavellian Moment;* Wills, *Inventing America;* Appleby, *Capitalism;* Banning, "Jeffersonian Ideology Revisited"; Bloch, "Gendered Meaning"; Watts, *Republic Reborn;* and Diggins, *Lost Soul of American Politics.*

18. Kerber, *Women of the Republic;* Davidson, *Revolution and the Word;* Morgan, *American Slavery, American Freedom;* Davis, *Problem of Slavery;* Bloch, "Gendered Meaning"; and Rodgers, "Republicanism."

19. For a good guide to this recent trend in European and American studies, see Toews, "Intellectual History."

20. For some sense in the historiographical differences implied here, compare Lears, "Concept of Cultural Hegemony," and Fisher, "Introduction."

21. Evelyn Brooks Higginbotham (*Righteous Discontent*) examines "respectability" in a similar fashion.

22. For an introduction to Foucault, see his *Power/Knowledge.*

Bibliography

Appiah, Kwame Anthony. *In My Father's House: Africa in the Philosophy of Culture.* New York: Oxford University Press, 1992.

Appleby, Joyce. *Capitalism and the New Social Order: The Republican Vision of the 1790s.* New York: New York University Press, 1984.

Ashworth, John. *"Agrarians" and Aristocrats: Party Political Ideology in the United States.* Cambridge: Cambridge University Press, 1987.

Bailyn, Bernard. *The Ideological Origins of the American Revolution.* Cambridge, Mass.: Harvard University Press, 1967.

Bancroft, George. *History of the United States.* 10 vols. Boston: Little, Brown, 1854–74.

Banning, Lance. "Jeffersonian Ideology Revisited: Liberal and Classical Ideas in the New American Republic." *William and Mary Quarterly* 43 (1986): 3–19.

Beard, Charles A., and Mary R. Beard. *The American Spirit: A Study of the Idea of Civilization in the United States.* New York: Macmillan, 1942.

———. *The Rise of American Civilization.* 2 vols. New York: Macmillan, 1927.

Becker, Carl L. *The Declaration of Independence.* New York: Harcourt, Brace & Company, 1922.

Bederman, Gail. *Manliness and Civilization: A Cultural History of Gender and Race in the United States, 1880–1917.* Chicago: University of Chicago Press, 1995.

Bender, Thomas. *New York Intellect.* New York: Knopf, 1987.

———. "The Social Sciences, Objectivity, and Pragmatism." *Annals of Scholarship* 9 (1992): 183–97.

Blake, Casey N. *Beloved Community: The Cultural Criticism of Randolph Bourne, Van Wyck Brooks, Waldo Frank, and Lewis Mumford.* Chapel Hill: University of North Carolina Press, 1990.

Blight, David W. *Frederick Douglass' Civil War.* Baton Rouge: Louisiana State University Press, 1989.

Bloch, Ruth. "The Gendered Meaning of Virtue in Revolutionary America." *Signs* 13 (1987): 37–58.

Bloom, Alexander. *Prodigal Sons: The New York Intellectuals and Their World*. New York: Oxford University Press, 1986.

Bouwsma, William. "From the History of Ideas to History of Meaning." *Journal of Interdisciplinary History* 12 (1981): 279–91.

Bushman, Richard. *The Refinement of America: Persons, Houses, Cities*. New York: Knopf, 1992.

Carby, Hazel V. *Reconstructing American Womanhood*. New York: Oxford University Press, 1987.

Cayton, Mary Kupiec. "The Making of an American Prophet: Emerson, His Audiences, and the Rise of the Culture Industry in Nineteenth-Century America." *American Historical Review* 92 (1987): 597–620.

Cmiel, Kenneth. *Democratic Eloquence: The Fight over Popular Speech in Nineteenth-Century America*. New York: Morrow, 1990.

Cooney, Terry A. *The Rise of the New York Intellectuals: The Partisan Review and Its Circle, 1934–1945*. Madison: University of Wisconsin Press, 1986.

Curti, Merle E. *The Growth of American Thought*. New York: Harper & Brothers, 1943.

Darnton, Robert. "Intellectual and Cultural History." In Michael Kammen, ed., *The Past before Us: Contemporary Historical Writing in the United States*, 327–54. Ithaca, N.Y.: Cornell University Press, 1980.

Davidoff, Robert. *The Genteel Tradition and the Sacred Rage*. Chapel Hill: University of North Carolina Press, 1992.

Davidson, Cathy N. *The Revolution and the Word: The Rise of the Novel in America*. New York: Oxford University Press, 1986.

Davis, David B. *The Problem of Slavery in the Age of Revolution, 1770–1823*. Ithaca, N.Y.: Cornell University Press, 1975.

Diggins, John P. *The Lost Soul of American Politics*. New York: Basic Books, 1984.

Draper, John W. *History of the Conflict between Religion and Science*. 1874. New York: Appleton, 1876.

———. *History of the Intellectual Development of Europe*. New York: Harper & Brothers, 1863.

Ethington, Philip. *The Public City: The Political Construction of Urban Life in San Francisco, 1850–1900*. New York: Cambridge University Press, 1994.

Fahs, Alice. *Publishing the Civil War: Popular Literature and the Meanings of the Nation, 1861–1865*. Chapel Hill: University of North Carolina Press, forthcoming.

Faust, Drew Gilpin. *The Creation of Confederate Nationalism: Ideology and Identity in the Civil War South*. Baton Rouge: Louisiana State University Press, 1988.

———. *James Henry Hammond and the Old South*. Baton Rouge: Louisiana State University Press, 1982.

Fisher, Phil. "Introduction: The New American Studies." In Phil Fisher, ed., *The New American Studies*, vii-xxii. Berkeley: University of California Press, 1991.

Foner, Eric. *Free Soil, Free Labor, Free Men: The Ideology of the Republican Party before the Civil War*. New York: Oxford University Press, 1970.

———. *Tom Paine and Revolutionary America*. New York: Oxford University Press, 1976.

Foucault, Michel. *Power/Knowledge: Selected Interviews and Other Writings*. New York: Pantheon, 1980.

Fredrickson, George. *The Black Image in the White Mind*. New York: Harper & Row, 1971.

———. *The Inner Civil War*. New York: Harper & Row, 1964.

Gabriel, Ralph H. *The Course of American Democratic Thought*. New York: Ronald, 1940.

Gates, Henry Louis, Jr. *Figures in Black: Words, Signs, and the "Racial" Self*. New York: Oxford University Press, 1987.

Gay, Peter. *A Loss of Mastery*. Berkeley: University of California Press, 1966.

Guilbaut, Serge. *How New York Stole the Idea of Modern Art*. Chicago: University of Chicago Press, 1983.

Gurstein, Rochelle. *The Repeal of Reticence*. New York: Hill & Wang, 1996.

Gutman, Herbert G. *Work, Culture, and Society in Industrializing America: Essays in American Working-Class History*. New York: Knopf, 1976.

Hall, David D. "The Mental World of Samuel Sewell." In *Worlds of Wonder, Days of Judgment: Popular Religious Belief in Early New England*, 213–38. New York: Knopf, 1989.

Harlan, David. "Intellectual History and the Return of Literature." *American Historical Review* 94 (1989): 581–609.

Harris, Neil. *Cultural Excursions*. Chicago: University of Chicago Press, 1990.

Hartz, Louis. *The Liberal Tradition in America*. New York: Harcourt, Brace & World, 1955.

Haskell, Thomas L. *The Emergence of Professional Social Science*. Urbana: University of Illinois Press, 1977.

———. "Objectivity Is Not Neutrality: Rhetoric vs. Practice in Peter Novick's *That Noble Dream*." *History and Theory* 29 (1990): 129–57.

Higginbotham, Evelyn Brooks. *Righteous Discontent: The Women's Movement in the Black Baptist Church, 1880–1920*. Cambridge, Mass.: Harvard University Press, 1993.

Higham, John. "The Study of American Intellectual History." In *Writing American History*, 41–72. Bloomington: Indiana University Press, 1970.

Higham, John, and Paul K. Conkin, eds. *New Directions in American Intellectual History*. Baltimore, Md.: Johns Hopkins University Press, 1979.

Hofstadter, Richard. *The Age of Reform*. New York: Knopf, 1955.

———. *Anti-Intellectualism in American Life*. New York: Knopf, 1963.

Hofstadter, Richard, and Walter P. Metzger. *The Development of Academic Freedom in the United States*. New York: Columbia University Press, 1955.

Hofstadter, Richard, and Wilson Smith, eds. *American Higher Education: A Documentary History*. 2 vols. Chicago: University of Chicago Press, 1961.

Hollinger, David A. "Historians and the Discourse of Intellectuals." In Higham and Conkin, *New Directions*, 42–62.

———. *In the American Province: Studies in the History and Historiography of Ideas*. Bloomington: Indiana University Press, 1985. Chaps. 1–2.

———. "The Return of the Prodigal: The Persistence of Historical Knowing." *American Historical Review* 94 (1989): 610–26.

———. *Science, Jews, and Secular Culture: Studies in Mid-Twentieth-Century American Intellectual History*. Princeton, N.J.: Princeton University Press, 1996.

Horowitz, Joseph. *Wagner Nights: An American History*. Berkeley: University of California Press, 1994.

Howe, Daniel Walker. *The Political Culture of the American Whigs*. Chicago: University of Chicago Press, 1979.

Johns, Elizabeth. *American Genre Painting: The Politics of Everyday Life*. New Haven, Conn.: Yale University Press, 1991.

———. *Thomas Eakins: The Heroism of Modern Life*. Princeton, N.J.: Princeton University Press, 1983.

Kasson, John. *Amusing the Million: Coney Island at the Turn of the Century*. New York: Hill & Wang, 1978.

Berber, Linda. *Women of the Republic: Intellect and Ideology in Revolutionary America*. Chapel Hill: University of North Carolina Press, 1980.

Kloppenberg, James T. "Objectivity and Historicism: A Century of American Historical Writing." *American Historical Review* 94 (1989): 1010–30.

———. "Pragmatism: An Old Name for Some New Ways of Thinking." *Journal of American History* 83 (1996): 100–38.

———. *Uncertain Victory: Social Democracy and Progressivism in European and American Thought, 1870–1920*. New York: Oxford University Press, 1987.

———. "The Virtues of Liberalism: Christianity, Republicanism, and Ethics in Early American Political Discourse." *Journal of American History* 74 (1987): 9–33.

Kuklick, Bruce. *The Rise of American Philosophy: Cambridge, Massachusetts, 1860–1930*. New Haven, Conn.: Yale University Press, 1977.

Lears, T. J. Jackson. "The Concept of Cultural Hegemony: Problems and Possibilities." *American Historical Review* 90 (1985): 567–93.

———. *Fables of Abundance: A Cultural History of Advertising in America*. New York: Basic Books, 1994.

———. *No Place of Grace: Antimodernism and the Transformation of American Culture, 1880–1920*. New York: Pantheon, 1981.

Levine, Lawrence W. *Highbrow/Lowbrow: The Emergence of Cultural Hierarchy in the United States*. Cambridge, Mass.: Harvard University Press, 1988.

Lewis, David Levering. *W.E.B. Du Bois, 1868–1919: Biography of a Race*. New York: Henry Holt, 1993.

———. *When Harlem Was in Vogue*. New York: Knopf, 1981.

Livingston, James. *Pragmatism and the Political Economy of Cultural Revolution, 1850–1940*. Chapel Hill: University of North Carolina Press, 1994.

Lovejoy, Arthur O. *The Great Chain of Being*. Cambridge, Mass.: Harvard University Press, 1936.

Marx, Leo. *The Machine in the Garden*. New York: Oxford University Press, 1964.

McCoy, Drew. *The Elusive Republic: Political Economy in Jeffersonian America*. Chapel Hill: University of North Carolina Press, 1980.

McDonald, Forrest. *Novus Ordo Seculorum: The Intellectual Origins of the Constitution*. Lawrence: University Press of Kansas, 1985.

Miller, Perry. *The New England Mind: From Colony to Province*. Cambridge, Mass.: Harvard University Press, 1953.

————. *The New England Mind: The Seventeenth Century*. Cambridge, Mass.: Harvard University Press, 1939.

————. *Orthodoxy in Massachusetts*. Cambridge, Mass.: Harvard University Press, 1933.

Miller, Samuel Miller. *A Brief Retrospect of the Eighteenth Century . . . containing a Sketch of the Revolutions and Improvements in Science, Arts, and Literature during that Period*. New York: T. & J. Swords, 1803.

Morgan, Edmund S. *American Slavery, American Freedom*. New York: Norton, 1975.

Morrison, Toni. *Playing in the Dark: Whiteness and the Literary Imagination*. Cambridge, Mass.: Harvard University Press, 1990.

Nagel, Thomas. *The View from Nowhere*. New York: Oxford University Press, 1986.

Parrington, Vernon L., Jr. *Main Currents in American History*. 3 vols. New York: Harcourt, Brace & World, 1927–30.

Peiss, Kathy. *Cheap Amusements: Working Women and Leisure in Turn-of-the-Century New York*. Philadelphia: Temple University Press, 1986.

Pocock, J.G.A. *The Machiavellian Moment*. Princeton, N.J.: Princeton University Press, 1975.

Posnock, Ross. *Trial of Curiosity: Henry James, William James, and the Challenge of Modernity*. New York: Oxford University Press, 1991.

Radway, Janice. *Reading the Romance: Women, Patriarchy, and Popular Literature*. Chapel Hill: University of North Carolina Press, 1984.

Ransell, David. "Summing Up." *American Historical Review* 100 (1995): 1009.

Reynolds, David S. *Walt Whitman's America: A Cultural Biography*. New York: Knopf, 1995.

Robinson, James Harvey. *The Mind in the Making*. New York: Harper & Brothers, 1921.

————. *The New History*. New York: Macmillan, 1912.

Rodgers, Daniel T. *Contested Truths: Keywords in American Politics since Independence*. New York: Basic Books, 1987.

————. "In Search of Progressivism" *Reviews in American History* 10 (1982): 113–32.

————. "Republicanism: The Career of a Concept." *Journal of American History* 79 (1992): 11–38.

Roeder, George H., Jr. *The Censored War: American Visual Experience during World War II*. New Haven, Conn.: Yale University Press, 1933.

Roediger, David. *The Wages of Whiteness: Race and the Making of the American Working Class*. New York: Verso, 1991.

Ross, Dorothy. *The Origins of American Social Science*. New York: Cambridge University Press, 1991.

Rourke, Constance. *American Humor*. New York: Harcourt, Brace & Company, 1931.

————. *The Roots of American Culture*. New York: Harcourt, Brace & World, 1942.

Schlesinger, Arthur M., Jr. *The Age of Jackson*. Boston: Little, Brown, 1945.

Schneider, Herbert W. *The History of American Philosophy*. New York: Columbia University Press, 1946.

Shils, Edward. *The Constitution of Society*. Chicago: University of Chicago Press, 1982.

Sicherman, Barbara. "Sense and Sensibility: A Case Study of Women's Reading in Late-Victorian America." In Cathy Davidson, ed., *Reading in America*, 201–25. Baltimore, Md.: Johns Hopkins University Press, 1989.

Simpson, Lewis. *Mind and the American Civil War*. Baton Rouge: Louisiana State University Press, 1989.

Sklar, Kathryn Kish. *Florence Kelley and the Nation's Work: The Rise of Women's Political Culture, 1830–1900*. New Haven, Conn.: Yale University Press, 1995.

Smith, Henry Nash. *Virgin Land*. Cambridge, Mass.: Harvard University Press, 1950.

Stevenson, Louise L. *Scholarly Means to Evangelical Ends: The New Haven Scholars and the Transformation of Higher Learning in America, 1830–1890*. Baltimore, Md.: Johns Hopkins University Press, 1986.

———. *The Victorian Homefront: American Thought and Culture, 1860–1880*. New York: Twayne, 1991.

Stowe, Steven M. *Intimacy and Power in the Old South: Ritual in the Lives of the Planters*. Baltimore, Md.: Johns Hopkins University Press, 1987.

Sundquist, Eric. *To Wake the Nations: Race in the Making of American Literature*. Cambridge, Mass.: Harvard University Press, 1993.

Susman, Warren I. *Culture as History: The Transformation of American Society in the Twentieth Century*. New York: Pantheon, 1984.

Teichgraeber, Richard F., III. *Sublime Thoughts/Penny Wisdom: Situating Emerson and Thoreau in the American Market*. Baltimore, Md.: Johns Hopkins University Press, 1995.

Thompson, E. P. *The Making of the English Working Class*. New York: Pantheon, 1963.

Toews, John. "Intellectual History after the Linguistic Turn: The Autonomy of Meaning and the Irreducibility of Experience." *American Historical Review* 92 (1987): 879–907.

Trachtenberg, Alan. *Reading American Photographs*. New York: Hill & Wang, 1989.

Watts, Steven. *The Republic Reborn: War and the Making of Liberal America, 1790–1820*. Baltimore, Md.: Johns Hopkins University Press, 1987.

Weintraub, Karl. *Visions of Culture*. Chicago: University of Chicago Press, 1966.

Westbrook, Robert B. *John Dewey and American Democracy*. Ithaca, N.Y.: Cornell University Press, 1991.

White, Andrew Dickson. *The Warfare of Science and Religion*. 1876. New York: Appleton, 1896.

Wills, Gary. *Cincinnatus: George Washington and the Enlightenment*. New York: Doubleday, 1984.

———. *Inventing America*. New York: Doubleday, 1978.

———. *Lincoln at Gettysburg*. New York: Simon & Schuster, 1992.

Wood, Gordon S. *The Creation of the American Republic, 1776–1787*. Chapel Hill: University of North Carolina Press, 1969.

———. *The Radicalism of the American Revolution*. New York: Knopf, 1992.

Woodward, C. Vann. *The Burden of Southern History.* Baton Rouge: Louisiana State University Press, 1960.

———. *Tom Watson.* New York: Macmillan, 1938.

Wright, Gwendolyn. *Moralism and the Model Home: Domestic Architecture and Cultural Conflict in Chicago, 1873–1913.* Chicago: University of Chicago Press, 1980.

Zboray, Ronald. *A Fictive People: Antebellum Economic Development and the American Reading Public.* New York: Oxford University Press, 1993.

9

■ WESTERN HISTORY

Richard White

IN THE AMERICAN IMAGINATION THE WEST HAS COME TO STAND FOR AMERICA. Pioneers and cowboys, log cabins and wagon trains are national icons. In popular portrayals of Western history, core American values—democracy, equality, individualism, a belief in progress—are supposedly displayed in their purest form. Such popular portrayals gained intellectual legitimacy from their connection with the Turner thesis, which became academic orthodoxy in the early twentieth century. "The existence," Turner wrote, "of an area of free land, its continuous recession, and the advance of American settlement westward explains American development." This, in a nutshell, was the Turner thesis. Popular histories still conflate the West with Turner's moving frontier where free land acts as the quintessential Americanizing force reproducing American values and Americanizing immigrants.

Such popular histories, along with representations of the West in novels, movies, stories, art, photographs, museums, Wild West shows, and more have themselves become topics of historical interest. Particularly Richard Slotkin in his trilogy of books on the western myth but also scholars such as Brian Dippie, Paul Hutton, Anne Hyde, and L. G. Moses studied how these representations and myths of the West have influenced how people have viewed the West, acted in it, and thus, to some extent, shaped the West. David Wrobel has explored how in the late nineteenth and early twentieth centuries the idea of the "closed frontier" served as cultural sonar bouncing off and revealing some of the deepest American anxieties.

By the 1940s most historians had rejected the frontier thesis; it lived on in Western history largely through Martin Ridge's and Ray Allen Billington's work. During these years, despite some often very sophisticated scholarship, Western and frontier history slipped from the mainstream of academic history into something of a backwater. The popular fascination with the West became but another means of discrediting Western history within the academy. Courses in Western history were derided as "cowboy and Indian" or "buffalo chip" history.

The past twenty years have brought a considerable resurgence in Western history. The rising importance of the West in contemporary America has helped restore Western history to prominence. The respectability that historians of the South gave to regional studies also benefited Western history. The extension of social and cultural history to western topics and increased concern among Western historians with studies of race, class, and gender made the field more mainstream. But the resurgence has also been the result of new work in areas long intimately connected with Western history—environmental history, histories of settlement and community formation, histories of federal activities in the West, and the history of Indian peoples.

THE NEW WESTERN HISTORY: FRONTIER VERSUS REGION

The newer work is hardly homogenous. The so-called New Western history is composed predominantly of regionalists such as Patricia Limerick, Elliott West, William Robbins, Donald Worster, and myself, but the label is often used far more broadly to include neo-Turnerians such as William Cronon, John Mack Faragher, Walter Nugent, and David Weber. Although the two groups regularly cite and praise one another's work, differences among New Western historians have yielded controversies within the field that have pitted regionalists against neo-Turnerians. These debates, now grown rather stale and tired, did for a while prove quite fruitful, forcing each side to examine and refine its own assumptions and formulations. They are thus worth recaptitulating one more time.

The core controversy between regionalists and neo-Turnerians has been phrased as place (region) versus process (frontier) but is perhaps most easily approached through a very simple question: what do historians mean when they say "West"? Do they mean a series of places sharing similar characteristics that began at the Appalachians and ultimately became the Old Northwest, the Old Southwest, the Midwest, and, finally, the West? Or do they mean the history of the modern region that we today refer to as the West, leaving aside for the moment the question of its boundaries? The various positions on this question are far more nuanced than they are often portrayed.

The neo-Turnerians, who emphasize the process of settlement, are not upholders of the frontier thesis. They have discarded much of their Turnerian baggage. They recognize how many people—women, Indian peoples, nonwhites in general—Turner's frontier rendered largely invisible, and they include them in their histories. They willingly admit that prior histories and larger national and international factors such as the market and the state played a far greater role in this history than Turner acknowledged in his zeal to promote the explanatory power of free land.

What they insist on preserving is the linkage between various frontiers that was critical to Turner. In *Women and Men on the Oregon Trail* and *Sugar Creek,* for example, John Mack Faragher wrote nuanced and sophisticated social histories that explore the connections between the frontier communities of the Midwest and the new communities of the West. Particular patterns of kinship and gendered divisions of labor, for example, organized family and community across a series of American migrations. William Cronon's *Nature's Metropolis* links the development of Chicago with the growth of both the rural Midwest and the West and provides the strongest statement of how international markets and environmental conditions interacted to provide a history far more complicated than a Turnerian history of free land. David Weber has demonstrated how a frontier model can be applied to settlement from Mexico as well as the East. Cronon and Faragher, in particular, insist on keeping the basic continuity between successive waves of American settlement moving westward. There were certain commonalties in this frontier process from the displacement of Indian peoples, to the availability of inexpensive land, to the initial organization of migration and communities.

The regionalists have not so much denied this process as changed the emphasis by arguing that other factors played equally significant roles in the creation of the West. They have argued that the frontier obscured these factors and that Turner's influence was so great that the word frontier necessarily carried Turnerian baggage.

What matters most to the regionalists is the space—physical, cultural, economic, social, and political—in which people would create the West. They have taken their narrative stance not with Anglo Americans moving West, whom they had no desire to remove as a critical element in this history, but within the already inhabited area that would become the West.

They argue for regional distinctiveness on several not fully reconcilable grounds. Donald Worster emphasizes environmental factors—particularly aridity—as the key to the environment and history of much of the region. Patricia Limerick emphasizes the West as a site of conquest. Her point is not that other regions of the United States had not been conquered but that in the West large numbers of the conquered—Indian peoples and Mexican Americans—remained in place, creating a distinctive pattern of mixing and interaction. William Robbins emphasizes the West as the American section that was most purely the creation of American capitalism. Much of its history was encompassed by a colonial relation of the West to the centers of capitalist power in the East.

As regionalists are pressed to defend the West as a viable area of study, the definition becomes more and more relational. In my own definition, the West was not a region because it possessed a set of fixed and essential characteristics that were present at its birth and whose disappearance would mark its death. It was instead a product of shifting relationships to other entities: the East and South, Europe and Mexico. Some of these relationships were long-lasting, others were transitory.

In this interpretation the trans-Missouri West was not just another stage in American frontiering. The timing and locale of this stage of American expansion made a difference. It took place under the sponsorship of a growing American state rather than a weak central government; it confronted huge areas of nonarable lands. More than in other parts of the United States, migration flowed in from the west and south as well as the east.

Finally, the American West became the most urban area of the United States. What Carl Abbott has called the metropolitanization of the West produced urban areas characterized by urban sprawl, reliance on the automobile, and eventually—as in Los Angeles, Orange County, Phoenix, and Seattle—multiple rather than single cores. John Findlay has argued that the western metropolitan areas that emerged following World War II were consciously different from eastern cities. Denouncing their failure to conform to "ideal" urban patterns is misguided. What Findlay calls "magic lands"—Disneyland, the Stanford Industrial Park, Sun City—were not bizarre western anomalies but models for alternative ways of conceiving of cities and development.

The Civil War is critically important in this history of western origins. Early American expansion was sectional. The North expanded into the Midwest; the South expanded from the Ohio to the Gulf of Mexico. Both then moved across the Mississippi. This linked expansion yielded the aptly named Old Northwest and Old Southwest. Slavery marked boundaries in the trans-Appalachian West just as it did farther east.

The Civil War, which settled the question of sectional dominance, removed slavery as an issue and helped set the stage for the emergence of a far more powerful central state. It created the conditions in which the West arose. Unlike areas east of the Mississippi, the West was the product of national expansion rather than sectional expansion.

The West did not cause the growing power of the federal government, but the power of the central government met less resistance there simply because there were not well-established states and Anglo American communities in place. In many ways the nineteenth-century West served as the kindergarten of the American state: it was the home of much of the admittedly minuscule American army; it was the site of distinctive regional bureaucracies such as the Bureau of Indian Affairs and the Geological Survey. Later there was the Bureau of Reclamation, the Forest Service, the National Park Service, and the Bureau of Land Management.

One of the factors that cemented this greater federal presence was land and environment. The West was the region where the federal government—because of both environmental factors and the growth of a managerial state—reversed the old policy of alienating the public lands and retained huge portions of them under federal ownership.

Again, none of these things made the region culturally, socially, or environmentally homogeneous. The West has always been a much-divided place: a series of urban enclaves and rural communities, a mixture of peoples whose links have never been based on common culture or mutual affection.

What connects the various parts of the West and its various ethnic and racial groups and classes is a series of interlocking relationships. A history of a common dependent relationship to the federal government and a common economic origin in a largely extractive and service-based economy were formative influences. A dual labor system based on race and the existence of minority groups with distinctive legal relationships to the larger society have helped define the West. There are also particular patterns of party loyalty and political organization, and, with the exception of California and Texas and perhaps Oregon (the earliest western states), weak state governments. The West is an evolving region. New factors may define the West in the future, or it may cease to exist in any meaningful form.

It is within the competing frameworks of frontier and region that the newer scholarship has evolved. Like the West itself, this scholarship breaks down into separate components that exist in sometimes uneasy relationship to each other.

INDIAN HISTORIES

Changes in the study of Indian tribes and Indian policy give some indication of the changes in Western history. Following the lead of colonial historians, Western historians have gradually begun to see the social and political organization and identities of Indian peoples as a product of contact. Diseases that had become part of a common disease pool in Asia, Africa, and Europe found populations in the Americas that possessed no resistance. The results were so-called virgin soil epidemics that devastated many Indian peoples before they ever saw Europeans. Sustained contact that brought slaving, war, and loss of land rendered the diseases even more destructive. Such losses alone have made it hard to conceive how many Indian societies could have moved from the precontact to the contact period without substantial change.

These epidemics were part of what Alfred Crosby has called the Columbian Exchange: the movement of plants, animals, and diseases between the hemispheres. Although by and large this exchange was disastrous for Indian peoples, the consequences were not entirely negative. Navajo sheep herding, Great Plains pastoralism, and other quite Indian ways of life would have been impossible without it.

This ecological exchange has complicated earlier and simpler histories. Dan Flores and Elliott West, for example, now see the decline of bison as a result of epizootic diseases, Indian migrations, and competition from exotic grazers such as horses and cattle, as well as drought. It is this earlier decline that makes bison vulnerable to overhunting following the Civil War.

Population decline, ecological and material change, and the arrival of new peoples formed a cauldron from which many historical Indian peoples emerged. Willard Rolling's study of the Osage, Peter Iverson's work on the Navajos, Alexandra Harmon's study of the peoples of Puget Sound all, to varying degrees, look at the historical construction of Indian nations. Americans sometimes did face Indian peoples who had been in place for centuries and lived much like their ancestors, but more often they faced relatively new peoples whose ways of life and locations had dramatically changed, and was still changing, as a consequence of contact with whites. Disease and American expansion often worked in tandem, destabilizing peoples and forcing social change. Indian Removal pushed new peoples into the West, many of whom carried plow agriculture, Christianity, and American forms of representative government into the region before American settlers had arrived. The treaty-making process and reservation system forced other changes and led to the creation of new political units.

In the newer scholarship the American conquest of the region becomes a more complicated process than the advance of Americans against retreating Indians. Instead, the advancing Americans confronted a mix of Indian peoples: many were already facing a crisis from the impact of epidemics, decline of game, and pressures from European powers, but others such as the Comanches or the Lakotas and their allies were expanding at the expense of their enemies. In the wars of the mid-nineteenth century, groups who felt more immediately threatened by expanding Indian enemies often sided with the Americans. In the American war against the Lakotas, the Americans easily recruited Pawnees, Arikaras, and Crows as allies.

The literature on these Indian wars has remained a staple of Western history. In the work of Paul Hutton, Sherry Smith, Robert Utley, and others, however, there has emerged a much more complicated and nuanced portrait of the military, military attitudes, and military policy in which military leaders sometimes emerge as more sympathetic toward the Indians than other non-Indian westerners.

Governing relations with Indian peoples was one of the primary tasks of the federal government in the West, and a single scholar, Francis Paul Prucha, has dominated studies of Indian policy to an extent probably unequaled by any other single scholar in any other subfield in American history. Prucha has insisted that American policy-making was not dominated by Indian haters—who certainly abounded in the West—but by self-declared "Friends of the Indian" who came from eastern Protestant reform groups. The failures of American Indian policy and the havoc the policy wreaked on Indian peoples were thus not the result of simple racism or hatred; they sprang instead from a Protestant benevolence that imagined integrating and uplift Indian peoples into American society. American policy rested, at least until the early twentieth century, not on claims of Indian racial inferiority but on a belief in Indian equality. Culturally, the reformers regarded the Indians as inferior, just as they regarded Italians, Jews, and other European immigrants as culturally inferior, but they thought of them as potentially equal and thus worthy of uplift. Reformers relentlessly attacked Indian culture, but their goal was to assimilate actual Indians into American society. As Clyde Milner indicates in his aptly titled *With Good Intentions*, American Indian policy raises the question of how philanthropists, convinced that they had the best interest of Indians at heart, could cause such harm to Indians.

Prucha's interpretation has proved a far more devastating critique of American policy than arguments that it was racist or genocidal. Its terrible consequences, he argues, came from what Americans regarded as their best instincts and attributes, not their worst. Their belief in progress, their desire for an inclusive homogenous republican citizenry, their ideological commitment to equality had as much to do with the disasters that befell Indian peoples as American greed, racism, and imperial ambitions, which were all certainly present.

Prucha's themes and work have hardly gone unquestioned or uncriticized. Frederick Hoxie, for example, has shown that racism did play a major role in early twentieth-century Indian policy. Other scholars have insisted that Indian peoples acted as well as were acted upon and this had to be a part of policy studies. James Ronda's work on both the Lewis and Clark expedition and on Astoria makes Indians active and shrewd pursuers of their own interests within a world of sweeping American ambitions.

The newer scholarship stresses Indian agency. David Lewis's, *Neither Wolf nor Dog: American Indians, Environment, and Agrarian Change*, for example, makes no sense within a framework of genocide. Indians appear as agents, actors, and resistors. They are a people who are victimized but they are hardly simple victims. They partially shape their fate under conditions not of their own choosing. Tsianina Lomawaima has extended such interpretations to boarding schools, which in her hands cease to be one-dimensional institutions, and Indian children become complicated actors. Much of the extension of policy studies into the twentieth century has come at the insistence of Indian peoples and native scholars such as Donald Fixico and Steven Crum who demanded study of the important presence of Indians in the contemporary West and the problems they face.

SOCIAL HISTORIES

In social history, as well as in Indian history, there have been clear turns in the road that connects newer and older studies. The older Turnerian history with its deep interest in migration, community formation, and cultural values was certainly receptive to social history. The first Western community and social histories were in part an indigenous growth that rose from earlier work on frontier settlement by James Malin and Merle Curti, and part an imitation of community studies that transformed colonial history in the 1960s and 1970s.

As it did elsewhere, the newer social history in the West focused on ordinary people and the conditions that shaped their lives. Many of these studies were quantitative, concerned with the distribution of wealth and physical and social mobility in the late nineteenth century. Scholars looked for sharp distinctions between West and East, and, on the whole, they did not find them. The people of the three western agricultural communities Dean May surveyed for his *Three Frontiers* all came from the same modern capitalist world as easterners. There were marked variations in the communities people formed, but they were variations on a theme. With a few exceptions, settlers in the West did not come to remake the world as much as to change their own place in it.

Most quantitative studies failed to find evidence that opportunity, social mobility, and economic equality were greater in the West than in the East, but they did turn up a wealth of information on specific communities, ethnic groups, and migrations. Scholars turned toward detailing and describing the wide range of social experiences in western communities. They produced studies of settlement in the Willamette Valley, middle-class Jews in Portland, Oregon, and Scandinavian women in Seattle. There are studies of cattle towns, Mexican immigrants in El Paso, African American Exodusters in Kansas, and Italian immigrants in San Francisco. Ralph Mann followed the fate of miners and their families after the Gold Rush, Jon Gjerde followed immigrants from Balestrand, Norway, to the Midwest and West, Albert Hurtado looked at the Indians of California.

Some of the most searching of these histories describe the communities from which early Anglo-American migrants into the West originated as well as their journeys farther West. John Faragher and John Unruh have both given accounts and analyses of the iconic migration: the Oregon Trail. James Gregory has examined the migration and experience of a twentieth-century group—"the Okies"—who achieved an equally iconic status during a period of capitalist crisis. Gregory's social history reveals a much broader and complicated migration than the usual *Grapes of Wrath* image, and he produced a compelling cultural history of the creation of "plain folks Americanism."

Taken as a whole, Western social history has provided an admirable corrective to the popular idea that, once Indians and Mexicans had been dispossessed, the West became a relatively homogenous region occupied by Anglo-American settlers. Studies of ethnicity, western cities, and immigration provided the foundation for newer descriptions of the West as an ethnically diverse, urban, and internally segmented region. Both Gold Rush California, the subject of a new study by Malcolm Rohrbough, and the late-nineteenth-century Great Plains, for example, had been among the most ethnically diverse sections of the United States. Indeed, California in 1850 and North Dakota in 1890 were the states with the highest percentage of foreign-born residents.

After the Gold Rush, a basic social division persisted in this diverse West until well into the twentieth century. There was one West of farms and middle-class small towns. This was a West of family, children, and kinship and community networks that John Faragher, Elliott West, and

others have explored. There was also a second West of extractive industry, cattle raising, military posts, and cities. In this second West young,
single male workers, often only seasonally employed and enduring dangerous working conditions, long predominated.

Neither of these Wests was a simple place. The newer scholarship
has found what seems an anomalous pattern of great mobility—large
portions of the population moved on every decade—and a stable local
elite. The two patterns are reconcilable. Those who stayed tended to find
friends or relatives to aid them; their families intermarried; they achieved
success and property. Those who did not possess or failed to obtain kin
or connections within a community moved on relatively quickly. Most,
but not all, of those who moved were young, single, and relatively poor.

The second West of extractive industries and largely migrant labor
acquired a reputation for violence that became an enduring part of the
popular image of the region. This violence was real but not undifferentiated. When young men consumed large amounts of alcohol, they often
fought. When drunken young men had guns available, they used them
to deadly effect. In towns with rudimentary gun control—the confisca-
tion of guns from those entering the town—young men still drank and
fought, but they much more rarely killed one another.

But there was a second level of more organized violence beyond
the results of drunks with guns. This violence was not the individual
violence of two armed men in a dusty street; instead it was the violence
of organized but nonmilitary killings of Indians or the expulsion of nonwhite miners. It was the social violence middle-class vigilante movements directed against criminals and, more significantly, against those
thought of as socially undesirable. It was the economic violence between
capitalists and workers. Richard Maxwell Brown has characterized these
diverse conflicts and more as a western civil war of incorporation in
which the "conservative, consolidating authority of capital" overcame
local, often violent, resistance.

An apparent danger of the new social history of the West has been
the incremental creation of a portrait of a region so subdivided by ethnicity, race, class, gender, and culture as to make the West itself seem
less a region than a sort of social aquarium in which separate social
species came into accidental proximity with one another. Many social
historians have been much more concerned with their specific subject—
Mexican Americans, workers, women—than with the West itself. The
West itself seemed an afterthought; it took shape, if it did at all, as the
cumulative result of these separate social histories.

As in American history as a whole, some Western historians have
complained that social history has fragmented the history of the region

into smaller and smaller pieces so that scholars knew more and more about less and less. Until recently, relatively few historians or historical sociologists attempted to synthesize this sprawling literature. Martin Ridge continued to synthesize the literature in *Westward Expansion,* but its history ended in 1890. In 1980 Robert Hine made an early attempt to pull some of this literature together in his *Community on the American Frontier.* Carlos Schwantes produced a history of the Pacific Northwest, and Thomas Hall in *Social Change in the Southwest* produced a nuanced and sophisticated account of the incorporation of the Southwest in the European world-system. More recently Patricia Limerick, Richard Etulain and Michael Malone, Clyde Milner and Carol O'Connor, and I have all attempted to synthesize the literature.

Complaints about fragmentation have ignored the way mid-range generalizations began to emerge as scholars focused on questions of race, class, and gender. Like region itself, race, class, and gender are comparative categories. They are markers of difference; they make only comparative sense; they need other categories. "Workers" demand the "middle class" and "capitalists"; "blacks" make sense only if there are "whites"; if some qualities are gendered female, others must be gendered male. Asking how such categories arose and were maintained forced attention to social and cultural power as well as economic and political power.

In practice this emphasis has often pushed toward integration rather than fragmentation. Peggy Pascoe's *Relations of Rescue* with its emphasis on Christian middle-class women who became reformers in the West might seem precisely the type of narrow study for which social history is criticized. But the book is, in fact, a carefully constructed comparative account that manages to bring race, class, and gender, as well as culture and religion, into play over a wide geographic expanse. Pascoe demonstrates that the attitude of these reformers toward nonwhite women could not be analyzed without considering their attitude toward nonwhite men, which, in turn, depended in part on their own relations with white men in both social and institutional settings. What becomes visible through Peggy Pascoe's analysis is a set of intertwined ties and relationships that knit together seemingly separate and disparate groups.

Similarly, Lisbeth Haas's recent study of two small communities in Orange County is anything but small in its ambitions. Haas has grounded her communities in quite specific material and social relations. She has tried to understand how particular identities, in this instance "Indian" and "Mexican," are constructed and contested, and how the creation of the master categories of "white" and "American" depended on ideas

about "Mexican." She has sought to make prejudice rather than difference the object of historical investigation.

MULTICULTURALISM AND
HISTORICIZING WESTERN SOCIETY

In Western history, as in American history as a whole, social histories
connected with race, class, and gender have become closely linked with
multiculturalism. The two are hardly identical. Both are, however, interested in deconstructing an older view of American history—and Western history. This older view of the United States recognizes difference—
between immigrant and native-born, between North and South, between
black and white, between worker and middle-class—but these differences are ideally being erased and their bearers gradually absorbed into
a common culture. Both multiculturalism and studies of race, class, and
gender stress the persistence of difference.

The impact of multiculturalism on Western history has been particularly pronounced. This is hardly surprising. Western historians' subject
matter makes them sensitive to difference and the way difference constantly shades back into similarities and connections. The West must be
in some way different from the East or historians of the West lose their
subject, just as the West must be attached to the East or it ceases to be a
field of American history. Finally, multiculturalism's emphasis on persisting difference resonates with a western past and present of Indian
peoples and reservations, diverse European ethnic migration from Asia,
Mexico, and Latin American, and the history of particularly strong and
often violent class conflict in the late-nineteenth- and early-twentieth-
century West.

By positing multiple differences within American society, multiculturalism offers an escape from the twinned dualisms that dominate
the master narrative of most recent U.S. history: the divide between
blacks and whites and between North and South and the long struggle
to eradicate them. It is very difficult to understand the West in terms of
these dualisms that dominate much of American historical writing, at
least after the colonial period.

Despite a few classic studies, African American history, a field so
critical to recent American historiography elsewhere in the country, has
a much less striking presence in Western history than does Mexican
American, Indian, and Asian American history. Until after World War II,
African American communities and population was small outside of
Texas and Oklahoma. The African American presence was also occupationally localized: African Americans appeared as cowboys, although not

in the high percentages often cited, as soldiers, domestic workers, as Pullman porters on western railroads, and as miners brought in to break strikes. World War II, which transformed so many aspects of Western society, brought a large African American migration from Texas and elsewhere in the country to work in the war industries of the Pacific Coast.

African Americans confronted distinctive conditions in much of the West. In an important study of Seattle, Quintard Taylor has shown not only how African Americans had to resolve deep divisions within their own communities between longtime residents and recent migrants but how they also had to negotiate relations with other nonwhite groups who competed with them for the bottom-tier jobs that were usually theirs by default. The relations between African Americans and Asian Americans in Seattle or African Americans and Mexican Americans in Los Angeles were critical parts of their history in the West.

Opponents often accuse multiculturalists of celebrating or exaggerating difference for its own sake. But such broad scatter-gun attacks fail to appreciate the ways that various strands of multiculturalism try to reconstruct a history of the nation as relations between disparate and often shifting groups.

Two broad strains of multiculturalism dominate much Western history. The first, and the one with the greatest popular impact, is best seen in the work of Ronald Takaki. Takaki's concerns go beyond the West, but he writes eloquently of key cultural groups in Western history and of western places themselves. The western flavor of Takaki's multiculturalism is readily apparent when it is compared to African American histories that tend to get the most attention when critics talk of multiculturalism east of the Mississippi.

In *A Different Mirror* Takaki asks how "we, the people" should be and has been defined. He recognizes that multiple groups existed within the United States and that gains for some groups involved losses for others. There is no history of undifferentiated progress. Takaki avoided both celebratory history and a history of victimization.

What differentiates Takaki's brand of multiculturalism from a second strain in Western history is the question of ethnic, and to a lesser extent, racial identity. Takaki often grants identity a stability and a cultural purity that other scholars fail to find. He downplays the invented-ness of traditions and culture and makes them largely an inheritance from Europe, Asia, and Africa. Ethnic and racial groups in Takaki act as coherent units. They may change, but it is an internal evolution; their essential identity remains intact.

A second, more complex multiculturalism that has yet to receive as vigorous and united a formulation as Takaki's takes a different approach. In this second multiculturalism, difference—including ethnic difference and cultural difference—is always being created and erased. No American ethnic group can ever recreate in America the complexity of the society from which it came. American ethnic groups are not simple importations; they are partially formed in place, and are better understood as a way of proclaiming an American identity than some separate cultural identity. Such groups are always in the midst of change. Whole new groups can and do appear and old groups lose coherence. Even indigenous cultures, such as those of Indian peoples, can take on new forms and create new identities under the pressure of contact.

This more complicated multiculturalism is thus as much about the breaching of boundaries as their maintenance. It emphasizes the fluidity and intermeshing of cultures in new American or regional combinations rather than the purity of cultures that only members can understand. It understands claims of cultural identity and purity as themselves partially political—a weapon aimed at the larger society to gain political, economic, and social ends.

In this scholarship various western groups—the "cultures" of multiculturalism—are American creations. William Toll's study of Jews in Portland, Dino Cinel's Italians in San Francisco, John Modell's Japanese, and George Sanchez's Mexicans in Los Angeles all show the creation of ethnic cultures that are a response to American conditions and make claims to American identity rather than simply seeking to replicate older identities and cultures.

As my own repeated use of "American" shows, this more complicated multiculturalism does not deny that there is a common core of culture and values in the United States. It does deny, however, that this core is either static—something handed down unchanged from the founding of the republic—or that it is the possession of one group that then leads others to adopt these values. Instead multiculturalists historicize Americanism and show how much of American history has been a battle by competing groups to control and define what it is to be an American. The label "American," in short, is now and has long been contested. Multiculturalists seek to emphasize and understand that contest; opponents of multiculturalism seek to deny that contest.

The Mormons, a group not usually prominent in many multicultural texts, can stand as a leading example of this more complicated process in the West. They were, and to an extent still are, one of the most exotic groups in the West in terms of their religious and social practices. No other western group has created so quickly such elaborate and new religious, family, and church structures. But Mormon history displays a real tension between demarcating differences between Mormons and larger American society and a claim to American identity, values, and privileges. Mormons created difference—in their economy, society, politics, religion, family organization—by working with available native cultural materials. Their origins are very American, and they used the promise of America to recruit members abroad. They show how the creation of difference is just as much a property of Western history as the assimilation and eradication of difference. There is no single process operating in the West.

Nowhere is the eradication and creation of difference more apparent than in Mexican American history. Along with some of the best feminist scholarship on the West—with which it often overlaps—Mexican American history has moved well beyond simplistic identity history typical of a crude multiculturalism. The scholarship on Mexican Americans has disaggregated what once seemed a monolithic and homogenous "Spanish" or "Mexican" experience. Instead, these histories, like the work of David Weber, demonstrated the complexity and diversity of the Spanish and Mexican past, and in later work on the American period how Mexican Americans, as much as Americans as a whole, were cut by numerous social, cultural, regional, class, and gender divisions. The histories of Texas, California, New Mexico, and Arizona had, for example, very different patterns and trajectories. *Nuevo mexicanos, tejanos,* and *californios,* let alone recent immigrants, were not a single people with a single history.

Mexican American history, however, did not dissolve into smaller and smaller fragments. In a brilliant and controversial landmark of recent scholarship in Western and national history, Ramon Gutiérrez shows how existing social and gender divisions can be sources for emerging identities and not something that later appears to divide a once unified people. Historicizing race, religion, and family, and using gender as an analytical tool, Gutiérrez examines "a complex web of interactions between men and women, young and old, slave and free, Spaniard and Indian, all of whom fundamentally depended on the other for their own self-definition."

The construction of identity and culture, rather than their mere preservation as in a simpler multiculturalism, has come more and more to the fore in recent scholarship on Mexican Americans. To Anglos, the old and new residents of Los Angeles, for example, were all "Mexicans," but, as George Sanchez shows, a far more complicated and interesting community resided there. Sanchez used the very divisions within the communities he studies to create a bridge to wider, more encompassing histories. Sanchez not only looked at the diverse origins of Mexican Americans, he looked at why and how they came to the city. His history begins with forces originating in eastern centers and operating not only in the West but in Mexico proper.

David Gutiérrez in his book *Walls and Mirrors* has moved entirely beyond community studies to approach the issues of culture, ethnicity, and immigration from a different angle. Gutiérrez's concern is with the relations between Mexican Americans and Mexican immigrants and what he calls the politics of ethnicity. He attacks critics of multiculturalism whose own happier histories ignore the way that ethnocentricism, racism, and legally enforced segregation themselves played roles in creating ethnic and racial consciousness. In a subtle and detailed analysis he explores how Mexican Americans establish a political presence within the context of segregation and racism within the United States. Mexican American identity is a creation; it is contested; and leaders within the Mexican American community themselves are in conflict about who exactly that represents. Mexican Americans long resident in the United States have clashing attitudes toward recent immigrants who seem at once allies and threats. Culture and identity in Gutiérrez's account are not fixed. While the categories of Mexican and American have a quite important political reality, they do not adequately encompass a more complicated social and cultural reality.

Social history in general, and multiculturalism in particular, can seem to replicate conditions that nineteenth-century union organizers in the West and elsewhere lamented: in emphasizing cultural and ethnic divisions, they downplay class interests and structural positions that cut across ethnic boundaries. This danger is avoided in the best work.

Combining race, ethnicity, and gender with class leads to more nuanced analyses of class struggles in the West. On a structural level, Mario Barrera's idea of a segmented western labor force in which nonwhite workers are confined to bottom-tier jobs has proved immensely useful for understanding the experience of both white and nonwhite workers in the West.

In bad history the abstract categories of race, ethnicity, gender, and class can become reductionist and deterministic. Complicated peoples become simple exhibits of historical categories. But in good history these abstract categories are put to work in tandem in ways that defeat mechanical understandings. In these studies, as in lived experience, the boundaries between various analytic categories blur. Class is not all that defines workers.

A whole series of studies has demonstrated how useful these categories can be when working in tandem. Vicki Ruiz in her study of cannery women emphasized the intersection of class, gender, race, and ethnicity in understanding both the success and failure of union efforts. Devra Weber, focusing on the differences between the response of Mexican and Anglo agricultural workers to unionization in the cotton fields of California, traced the greater Mexican enthusiasm not just to cultural factors but to the condition of many of them as aliens and their structural position in the economy.

Dave Emmons's work on Butte, Gunther Peck's on Bingham, Utah, and David Brundage's on Denver have created a sense of complicated working-class communities where it is counterproductive to try to rank class, ethnicity, and race as competing influences. The critical thing is their intersection. Class divided ethnic groups, but the pull of Irish or Greek nationalism could unite people across class lines; southern Europeans and, sometimes, Mexicans were white in some contexts, nonwhite in others; there was often a fuzzy line between working-class jobs and small-scale entrepreneurial activity. The quite different labor traditions found in the Knights of Labor, the American Federation of Labor, the early industrial unions such as the Western Federation of Miners, and syndicalists like the Industrial Workers of the World unionism could appear to be reconcilable and quite coherent to workers in a city such as Denver.

These studies suggest the relentless change at work in the West as a new and powerful capitalism drove American expansion as well as the complicated results of this change as it interacted with local traditions and other social categories. Detailed local studies of this capitalist penetration such as Carroll Van West's *Capitalism on the Frontier* have begun to appear. At its best this scholarship suggests the contingent and surprising routes of social change. In Sarah Deutsch's work the tightening economic vise in northern New Mexico that accompanies the expansion of capitalism at once deprives *nuevo mexicano* villagers of land and provides other distant opportunities for labor. The response is gendered with men leaving for work while women stay behind, and this, in turn, prompts further changes within the already gendered world of work and family of the villages.

In the largest sense work is at the center of many of these Western histories, even if it is not explicity conceptualized as a central theme. The scholarship on Asian Americans is indicative of the centrality of work and how it, in turn, can be understood only within a larger political, social, and cultural context. Because so many of the early Asian migrants were men without families, their histories have tended to focus on work groups and economic endeavors. These studies have drawn a far more complicated picture of, for example, Chinese labor and commercial activities than earlier portrayals of cheap and submissive contract labor controlled by merchants and tongs. Chinese labor was versatile, often skilled, and in industries like fish processing for a long time indispensable. In mining, agriculture, and urban industrial activities the Chinese were quick to exploit niches that pervasive prejudice and eventually pervasive violence left open to them.

PERSISTING THEMES: CAPITALISM,
THE STATE, AND NATURE

Neither the new social history nor multiculturalism has been able to stand completely on its own. The social and cultural histories they explore have evolved within an expanding capitalist economy and have been heavily influenced by the growing American state. Economic history and political history remain essential parts of Western history, but they have also been influenced by the newer histories.

Western politics has been distinctive in a variety of ways. Because a portion of the inhabitants of the West—Asian Americans, Indians, Mexican immigrants—were either denied citizenship or did not desire it, the electorate was largely white. Suffrage, however, was for reasons that remain debated extended much more quickly to women in the West than in the East. As Paul Kleppner has argued, despite groups like the American Protective Association and the Ku Klux Klan, voters in the West have been more resistant to ethnocultural politics—politics with a religious or cultural appeal that often pit Roman Catholics against Protestants, native-born against immigrants, and so on—and westerners have had less party loyalty than people elsewhere in the country. They have led the way in adopting the Progressive reforms of direct democracy—the initiative and referendum and recall.

Western politics has largely been federal politics. The region, with the exception of Texas, California, and Oregon, has been characterized by weak state governments, comparatively strong federal bureaucracies, and large amounts of public land administered directly by the federal government. Nonetheless, the best political studies in the West are state based. Populism provides a good example.

The importance of the Populist party has tended to shrink considerably in the recent literature. Lawrence Goodwyn has grounded his thesis of Populism as a strong social and cultural movement with a deep potential base and radical ambitions on the South; if anything, the West provided the antithesis in the form of a shadow movement. A series of studies on the state level have made the western agrarian Populists seem much more fragile and limited than in earlier work. The Populists evolved within a basically two-party system and, as Peter Argersinger has argued, never transcended its limits. Jeffrey Ostler in a tightly focused study explains the varied success of populism within the context of state and two-party politics. Where there was real competition between Democrats and Republicans, as in Iowa, reformers could work within the existing party system. Where there was single party dominance, as in Kansas and Nebraska, reformers were forced to form a new party. Argersinger defends the Populists as serious reformers, but tactically, he argues, they needed to fuse with the Democrats in the West to achieve immediate political goals. Their own members, however, still retained enough residual loyalty to their old parties that a tactical movement toward the Democrats threatened to drive former Republicans from the party. Work by Marilyn Watkins on western Washington suggests, however, that in particular settings strongly rooted traditions of rural social radicalism and reform could persist beneath the fluctuations of party politics. Ironically, Populism as a radical force survives more in the literature of Rocky Mountain Populism, where Populists recruited heavily among workers, than in the literature on the Great Plains.

One of the *bete noirs* of the Populists and other western reform movements was the railroad, and William Deverell in a fascinating blend of economic, social, cultural, and political history looks at the railroad as the complicated symbolic center of California politics. The signification of the railroad was multifaceted, and what from a distance looked like a single strand of railroad reform was much more diverse.

Studies of the federal role in the West have had less to do with political parties than with bureaucracies and development. Federal power has not necessarily meant dictation; it can be locally manipulated. Roger Lotchin in *Fortress California* details how city leaders in California used federal military resources and federal spending to create "urban empires." Other studies look at federal spending to create a western infrastructure of dams, electrical systems, irrigation works, highways, universities, and research institutes.

Although federal influence in the region was longstanding, its key moment was, as Gerald Nash has emphasized, World War II. World War II transformed the West economically, demographically, and socially. Federal investment in military bases and factories and federal contracts gave much of the West the industrial base that it had long desired and, except for California, had failed to achieve. It created a massive migration into the West that continued after World War II.

Studies of federal agencies and capitalism provide a bridge to a final area of Western history that has proved particularly influential and has now moved well beyond the West: environmental history. Older Western history had already produced a distinguished literature on the conservation movement, and this had continued in studies on the national parks and federal resource agencies. What environmental history added was both a social and cultural history of these developments and a historicizing of nature itself, although the extent to which nature can or should be historicized is the center of a lively debate within environmental history.

Many of the environmental histories of the West have been local case studies that combine social and environmental histories such as Hal

Rothman's work on Pajarito Plateau around Los Alamos, New Mexico; William deBuys's study of the Sangre de Cristos; Peter Boag's book on the Williamette Valley; and my own study of Island County, Washington. Others have taken critical looks at environmental policies and federal agencies such as Paul Hirt's *Conspiracy of Optimism*, Nancy Langston's examination of Forest Service policy in the Blue Mountains, and Mark Harvey's and Alfred Runte's work on national parks. But the most influential studies have directly addressed the critical link between capitalism, the development of the West, and the environment.

The interlinked themes of capitalist expansion and environmental change come together most compellingly in the work of William Cronon, William Robbins, and Donald Worster. American expansion into the West was capitalist from the outset. William Cronon has elegantly traced the consequences of this commodification of nature in *Nature's Metropolis*. William Robbins has concentrated on the extractive economy of the West and on how capitalist development forced emerging western communities into colonial relationships with the East. Donald Worster has focused his work on agriculture and on the consequences of capitalist exploitation for westerners and the land itself.

Worster has produced two searing, eloquent books and several collections of essays that look at the environmental consequences of what he sees as a culture of capitalism. The West, as Worster puts it in *Rivers of Empire*, is not primarily a place of freedom, it is "more decisively, a land of authority and restraint, of class and exploitation, and ultimately of imperial power." It got to be that way, he contends, because of the desire to control and commodify nature that drove its history. The control and commodification of nature inexorably involved the control of human beings.

Worster's formulation, rooted in the agriculture of the arid West, has sparked a lively debate. Norris Hundley finds contesting interest groups where Worster sees a power elite, and popular consent where Worster sees coercion. Donald Pisani has stressed irrigation as a tool, albeit a failed one, for social reform in California. John Walton, while praising Worster's emphasis on the state, sees local communities as being able to reduce outside domination. It is Worster's work, however, that provides the center around which this debate pivots.

Worster's scholarship provides a good place to close for it is an example of the way Western history, once central to the study of American history as a whole, has begun to reassert itself as critical for understanding both the national history of the United States and broad themes, such as environmental history, that extend across national boundaries.

BIBLIOGRAPHY

Abbott, Carl. *The Metropolitan Frontier: Cities in the Modern American West.* Tucson: University of Arizona Press, 1993.

Alexander, Thomas G. *Mormonism in Transition: A History of the Latter-Day Saints, 1890–1930.* Urbana: University of Illinois Press, 1986.

Anderson, Karen. *Changing Woman: A History of Racial Ethnic Women in Modern America.* New York: Oxford University Press, 1996.

Argersinger, Peter H. *The Limits of Agrarian Radicalism: Western Populism and American Politics.* Lawrence: University Press of Kansas, 1995.

Armitage, Susan, and Elizabeth Jameson, eds. *The Women's West.* Norman: University of Oklahoma Press, 1987.

Barrera, Mario. *Race and Class in the Southwest: A Theory of Racial Inequality.* Notre Dame, Ind.: University of Notre Dame Press, 1979.

Blackwelder, Julia Kirk. *Women of the Depression: Caste and Culture in San Antonio, 1929–1939.* College Station: Texas A&M University Press, 1984.

Boag, Peter. *Environment and Experience: Settlement Culture in Nineteenth-Century Oregon.* Berkeley: University of California Press, 1992.

Bottles, Scott L. *Los Angeles and the Automobile: The Making of the Modern City.* Berkeley: University of California Press, 1987.

Bowen, William. *The Willamette Valley: Migration and Settlement on the Oregon Frontier.* Seattle: University of Washington Press, 1978.

Brown, Richard M. *No Duty to Retreat: Violence and Values in American History and Society.* New York: Oxford University Press, 1991.

Brundage, David. *The Making of Western Labor Radicalism: Denver's Organized Workers, 1878–1905.* Urbana: University of Illinois Press, 1994.

Burchell, Robert A. "Opportunity and the Frontier: Wealth-Holding in Twenty-Six Northern Californian Counties, 1848–1880." *Western Historical Quarterly* 52 (April 1987): 177–96.

Butler, Anne M. *Daughters of Joy, Sisters of Misery: Prostitutes in the American West, 1865–90.* Urbana: University of Illinois Press, 1985.

Camarillo, Albert. *Chicanos in a Changing Society: From Mexican Pueblos to American Barrios in Santa Barbara and Southern California, 1848–1930.* Cambridge, Mass.: Harvard University Press, 1979.

Chan, Sucheng. *The Bittersweet Soil: The Chinese in California Agriculture, 1860–1910.* Berkeley: University of California Press, 1986.

Cinel, Dino. *From Italy to San Francisco: The Immigrant Experience.* Stanford, Calif.: Stanford University Press, 1982.

Clary, David. *Timber and the Forest Service.* Lawrence: University Press of Kansas, 1986.

Cornell, Stephen. *The Return of the Native: American Indian Political Resurgence.* New York: Oxford University Press, 1988.

Crockett, Norman L. *The Black Towns.* Lawrence: Regents Press of Kansas, 1979.

Cronon, William. *Nature's Metropolis: Chicago and the Great West.* New York: Norton, 1991.

Cronon, William, George Miles, and Jay Gitlin, eds. *Rethinking America's Western Past*. New York: Norton, 1991.

Crosby, Alfred W., Jr. *The Columbian Exchange: Biological and Cultural Consequences of 1492*. Westport, Conn.: Greenwood Press, 1972.

Crum, Steven J. "Po'i Pentun Tammen Kimmappeh," *The Road on Which We Came: A History of the Western Shoshone*. Salt Lake City: University of Utah Press, 1994.

Daniel, Cletus E. *Bitter Harvest: A History of California Farmworkers, 1870–1941*. Berkeley: University of California Press, 1981.

Daniels, Roger. *Prisoners Without Trial: Japanese Americans in World War II*. New York: Hill & Wang, 1993.

Davis, Mike. *City of Quartz: Excavating the Future in Los Angeles*. New York: Vintage, 1992.

deBuys, William. *Enchantment and Exploitation: The Life and Hard Times of a New Mexico Mountain Range*. Albuquerque: University of New Mexico Press, 1985.

Decker, Peter, *Fortunes and Failures: White-Collar Mobility in Nineteenth-Century San Francisco*. Cambridge, Mass.: Harvard University Press, 1978.

Derickson, Alan. *Workers' Health, Workers' Democarcy: The Miners' Struggle, 1891–1925*. Ithaca, N.Y.: Cornell University Press, 1988.

Deutsch, Sarah. *No Separate Refuge: Culture, Class, and Gender on an Anglo-Hispanic Frontier in the American Southwest, 1880–1940*. New York: Oxford University Press, 1987.

Deverell, William. *Railroad Crossing: California and the Railroad, 1850–1910*. Berkeley: University of California Press, 1994.

Dinel, Dino. *From Italy to San Francisco: The Immigrant Experience*. Stanford, Calif.: Stanford University Press, 1982.

Dippie, Brian. *Custer's Last Stand: The Anatomy of an American Myth*. 1976. Lincoln: University of Nebraska Press, 1994.

———. *Looking at Russell*. Ft. Worth, Tex.: Amon Carter Museum, 1987.

Dykstra, Robert. *The Cattle Towns*. New York: Atheneum, 1976.

Emmons, David M. *The Butte Irish: Class and Ethnicity in an American Mining Town, 1873–1925*. Urbana: University of Illinois Press, 1989.

Etulain, Richard, and Michael Malone. *American West: A Twentieth-Century History*. Lincoln: University of Nebraska Press, 1989.

Faragher, John Mack. *Sugar Creek: Life on the Illinois Prairie*. New Haven, Conn.: Yale University Press, 1986.

———. *Women and Man on the Oregon Trail*. New Haven, Conn.: Yale University Press, 1979.

Ficken, Robert. *Rufus Woods: The Columbia River and the Building of Modern Washington*. Pullman: Washington State University Press, 1995.

Findlay, John. *Magic Lands: Western Cityscapes and American Culture after 1940*. Berkeley: University of California Press, 1992.

Fixico, Donald L. *Termination and Relocation: Federal Indian Policy, 1945–1960*. Albuquerque: University of New Mexico Press, 1986.

Flores, Dan. "Bison Ecology and Bison Diplomacy: The Southern Plains from 1825 to 1850." *Journal of American History*, September 1991.

Foster, Mark S. *Henry J. Kaiser: Builder in the Modern American West.* Austin: University of Texas Press, 1989.

Fowler, Loretta. *Arapahoe Politics, 1851–1978: Symbols in Crises of Authority.* Lincoln: University of Nebraska Press, 1982.

Friday, Chris. *Organizing Asian American Labor: The Pacific Coast Canned-Salmon Industry, 1870–1942.* Philadelphia: Temple University Press, 1994.

Garcia, Mario. *Desert Immigrants: The Mexicans of El Paso, 1880–1920.* New Haven, Conn.: Yale University Press, 1981.

Gjerde, Jon. *From Peasants to Farmers: The Migration from Balestrand, Norway, to the Upper Midwest.* New York: Cambridge University Press, 1985.

Goetzmann, William. *New Lands, New Men: America and the Second Great Age of Discovery.* New York: Viking, 1986.

Goldberg, Robert A. *Back to the Soil: The Jewish Farmers of Clarion, Utah, and Their World.* Salt Lake City: University of Utah Press, 1986.

Goodwyn, Lawrence. *Democratic Promise: The Populist Movement in America.* New York: Oxford University Press, 1976.

Green, James. *Grass Roots Socialism: Radical Movements in the Southwest, 1895–1943.* Baton Rouge: Louisiana State University Press, 1978.

Gregory, James. *American Exodus: The Dust Bowl Migration and Okie Culture in California.* New York: Oxford University Press, 1989.

Grossman, James, ed. *The Frontier in American Culture.* Berkeley: University of California Press, 1994.

Guerin-Gonzales, Camille. *Mexican Workers and American Dreams: Immigration, Repatriation, and California Farm Labor, 1900–1939.* New Brunswick, N.J.: Rutgers University Press, 1994.

Gutiérrez, David G. *Walls and Mirrors: Mexican Americans, Mexican Immigrants, and the Politics of Ethnicity.* Berkeley: University of California Press, 1995.

Gutiérrez, Ramón A. *When Jesus Came, the Corn Mothers Went Away: Marriage, Sexuality, and Power in New Mexico, 1500–1846.* Stanford, Calif.: Stanford University Press, 1991.

Haas, Lisbeth. *Conquests and Historical Identities in California, 1769–1936.* Berkeley: University of California Press, 1995.

Hall, Thomas. *Social Change in the Southwest, 1350–1880.* Lawrence: University Press of Kansas, 1989.

Harmon, Alexandra. "Lines in Sand: Shifting Boundaries between Indians and Non-Indians in the Puget Sound Region." *Western Historical Quarterly* 26 (winter 1995): 429–54.

Harvey, Mark W. T. *A Symbol of Wilderness: Echo Park and the American Conservation Movement.* Albuquerque: University of New Mexico Press, 1994.

Hietala, Thomas R. *Manifest Design: Anxious Aggrandizement in Late Jacksonian America.* Ithaca, N.Y.: Cornell University Press, 1985.

Hine, Robert V. *Community on the American Frontier: Separate but Not Alone.* Norman: University of Oklahoma Press, 1980.

Hirt, Paul W. *A Conspiracy of Optimism: Management of the National Forests since World War II.* Lincoln: University of Nebraska Press, 1994.

Holliday, J. S. *The World Rushed In: The California Gold Rush Experience*. New York: Simon & Schuster, 1981.

Horsman, Reginald. *Race and Manifest Destiny*. Cambridge, Mass.: Harvard University Press, 1988.

Hoxie, Frederick. *A Final Promise: The Campaign to Assimilate the Indians, 1880–1920*. Lincoln: University of Nebraska Press, 1984.

Hundley, Norris. *The Great Thirst: Californians and Water, 1770s–1790s*. Berkeley: University of California Press, 1992.

Hurtado, Albert. *Indian Survival on the California Frontier*. New Haven, Conn.: Yale University Press, 1988.

Hutton, Paul. *Phil Sheridan and His Army*. Lincoln: University of Nebraska Press, 1985.

———. "From Little Big Horn to Little Big Man: The Changing Image of a Western Hero in Popular Culture." *Western Historical Quarterly* 7, no. 1 (1976): 19–46.

Hyde, Anne F. *An American Vision: Far Western Landscape and National Culture*. New York: New York University Press, 1990.

Ichioka, Yuji. *The Issei: The World of First-Generation Japanese Immigrants, 1885–1924*. New York: Free Press, 1988.

Issel, William, and Robert W. Cherny. *San Francisco, 1865–1932: Politics, Power, and Urban Development*. Berkeley: University of California Press, 1986.

Iverson, Peter. *Carlos Montezuma and the Changing World of American Indians*. Albuquerque: University of New Mexico Press, 1982.

———. *The Navajo Nation*. Albuquerque: University of New Mexico Press, 1981.

———. *When Indians Became Cowboys: Native Peoples and Cattle Ranching in the American West*. Norman: University of Oklahoma Press, 1994.

Jeffrey, Julie Roy. *Frontier Women: The Trans-Mississippi West, 1840–1880*. New York: Hill & Wang, 1979.

John, Elizabeth. *Storms Brewed in Other Men's Worlds: The Confrontation of Indians, Spanish, and French in the Southwest, 1540–1795*. College Station: Texas A&M University Press, 1975.

Josephy, Alvin. *The Civil War in the American West*. New York: Knopf, 1991.

Kahrl, William L. *Water and Power: The Conflict over Los Angeles' Water Supply in the Owens Valley*. Berkeley: University of California Press, 1982.

Kazin, Michael. *Barons of Labor: The San Francisco Building Trades and Union Power in the Progressive Era*. Urbana: University of Illinois Press, 1987.

Kleppner, Paul. "Politics without Parties: The Western States, 1900–84." In Gerald D. Nash and Richard W. Etulain, eds., *In the Twentieth Century West*, 295–398. Albuquerque: University of New Mexico Press, 1989.

Langston, Nancy. *Forest Dreams, Forest Nightmares: The Paradox of Old Growth in the Inland West*. Seattle: University of Washington Press, 1995.

Larson, Robert, *Populism in the Mountain West*. Albuquerque: University of New Mexico Press, 1986.

Lawson, Michael L. *Dammed Indians: The Pick-Sloan Plan and the Missouri River Sioux, 1933–1953*. Norman: University of Oklahoma Press, 1982.

Lewis, David Rich. *Neither Wolf nor Dog: American Indians, Environment, and Agrarian Change.* New York: Oxford University Press, 1994.

Limerick, Patricia Nelson. *The Legacy of Conquest: The Unbroken Past of the American West.* New York: Norton, 1987.

Lomawaima, K. Tsianina. *They Called It Prairie Light: The Story of Chilocco Indian School.* Lincoln: University of Nebraska Press, 1994.

Lotchin, Roger W. *Fortress California, 1910–1961: From Warfare to Welfare.* New York: Oxford University Press, 1992.

Lowitt, Richard. *The New Deal in the West.* Bloomington: Indiana University Press, 1984.

Luebke, Frederick C. *Ethnicity on the Great Plains.* Lincoln: University of Nebraska Press, 1990.

Malone, Michael P. *The Battle for Butte: Mining and Politics on the Northern Frontier, 1864–1906.* Seattle: University of Washington Press, 1981.

Mann, Ralph. *After the Gold Rush: Society in Grass Valley and Nevada City, California, 1849–1870.* Stanford, Calif.: Stanford University Press, 1982.

May, Dean. *Three Frontiers: Family, Land, and Society in the American West, 1850–1900.* New York: Cambridge University Press, 1994.

McEvoy, Arthur. *The Fisherman's Problem: Ecology and Law in the California Fisheries, 1850–1980.* New York: Cambridge University Press, 1986.

McGrath, Roger. *Gunfighters, Highwaymen, and Vigilantes: Violence on the Frontier.* Berkeley: University of California Press, 1984.

McLoughlin, William. *After the Trail of Tears: The Cherokees' Struggle for Sovereignty, 1839–1880.* Chapel Hill: University of North Carolina Press, 1993.

Milner, Clyde. *With Good Intentions: Quaker Work among the Pawnees, Otos, and Omahas in the 1870s.* Lincoln: University of Nebraska Press, 1982.

Milner, Clyde, Carol O'Connor, and Martha Sandweiss, eds. *The Oxford History of the American West.* New York: Oxford University Press, 1994.

Modell, John. *The Economics and Politics of Racial Accommodation: The Japanese of Los Angeles, 1900–1942.* Urbana: University of Illinois Press, 1977.

Montejano, David. *Anglos and Mexicans in the Making of Texas, 1836–1986.* Austin: University of Texas Press, 1987.

Moses, L. G. *Wild West Shows and the Images of American Indians, 1883–1933.* Albuquerque: University of New Mexico Press, 1996.

Myrea, Sandra L. *Westering Women and the Frontier Experience, 1800–1915.* Albuquerque: University of New Mexico Press, 1982.

Nash, Gerald. *The American West Transformed: Impact of the Second World War.* Bloomington: Indiana University Press, 1985.

———. *World War II and the West: Reshaping the Economy.* Lincoln: University of Nebraska Press, 1990.

Nash, Gerald, and Richard W. Etulain. *In the Twentieth-Century West: Historical Interpretations.* Albuquerque: University of New Mexico Press, 1967.

Nelson, Paula M. *Homesteaders and Town Builders in Western South Dakota, 1900–1917.* Iowa City: University of Iowa Press, 1986.

Nugent, Walter. "Frontiers and Empires in the Late Nineteenth Century." *Western Historical Quarterly* 20, no. 4 (November 1989): 393–408.

Ostler, Jeffrey. *Prairie Populists: The Fate of Agrarian Radicalism in Kansas, Nebraska, and Iowa, 1880–1892.* Lawrence: University Press of Kansas, 1992.

Painter, Nell Irvine. *Exodusters: Black Migration to Kansas after Reconstruction.* New York: Norton, 1976.

Pascoe, Peggy. *Relations of Rescue: The Search for Female Moral Authority in the American West, 1874–1939.* New York: Oxford University Press, 1990.

Peck, Gunther. "Padrones and Protest: 'Old' Radicals and 'New' Immigrants in Bingham, Utah, 1905–1912," *Western Historical Quarterly* 24, no. 2 (May 1993): 157–58.

Peterson, Richard. *The Bonanza Kings: The Social Origins and Business Behavior of Western Mining Entrepreneurs, 1870–1900.* Lincoln: University of Nebraska Press, 1977.

Petrik, Paula. *No Step Backward: Women and Family on the Rocky Mountain Mining Frontier.* Helena: Montana Historical Society Press, 1987.

Pisani, Donald. *From the Family Farm to Agribusiness: The Irrigation Crusade in California and the West, 1850–1931.* Berkeley: University of California Press, 1984.

Prucha, Francis Paul. *The Great Father: The United States Government and the American Indians.* Lincoln: University of Nebraska Press, 1984.

Ridge, Martin, and Ray Allen Billington. *Westward Expansion: A History of the American Frontier.* New York: Macmillan, 1982.

Riley, Glenda. *Building and Breaking Families in the American West.* Albuquerque: University of New Mexico Press, 1982.

———. *A Place to Grow: Women in the American West.* Arlington Heights, Ill.: Harlan Davidson, 1992.

Robbins, William G. *Colony and Empire: The Capitalist Transformation of the American West.* Lawrence: University Press of Kansas, 1994.

Rohrbough, Malcolm J. *Aspen: The History of a Silver-Mining Town, 1879–1893.* New York: Oxford University Press, 1986.

———. *Days of Gold: The California Gold Rush and the American Nation.* Berkeley: University of California Press, 1997.

Rollings, Willard. *The Osage: Ethnohistorical Study of Hegemony on the Prairie-Plains.* Columbia: University of Missouri Press, 1992.

Ronda, James. *Astoria and Empire.* Lincoln: University of Nebraska Press, 1991.

———. *Lewis and Clark among the Indians.* Lincoln: University of Nebraska Press, 1984.

Rothman, Hal. *On Rims and Ridges: The Los Alamos Area since 1880.* Lincoln: University of Nebraska Press, 1992.

———. *Preserving Different Pasts: The American National Monuments.* Urbana: University of Illinois Press, 1989.

Rowley, William D. *U.S. Forest Service Grazing and Rangelands: A History.* College Station: Texas A&M University Press, 1985.

Ruiz, Vicki. *Cannery Women, Cannery Lives: Mexican Women, Unionization, and the California Food Processing Industry, 1930–1950.* Albuquerque: University of New Mexico Press, 1987.

Runte, Alfred. *National Parks: The American Experience.* Lincoln: University of Nebraska Press, 1987.

Sanchez, George. *Becoming Mexican American? Ethnicity, Culture, and Identity in Chicano Los Angeles, 1900–45.* New York: Oxford University Press, 1993.

Sandweiss, Martha. *Laura Gilpin: An Enduring Grace.* Fort Worth, Tex.: Amon Carter Museum, 1986.

Scharff, Virginia. "Gender and Western History: Is Anybody Home on the Range?" *Montana* 41, no. 2 (spring 1991): 62–65.

———. "A West of One's Own." *Annals of Wyoming* 66, no. 3 (fall 1994).

Schwantes, Carlos A. *Hard Traveling: A Portrait of Work Life in the New Northwest.* Lincoln: University of Nebraska Press, 1996.

———. *The Pacific Northwest: An Interpretive History.* Lincoln: University of Nebraska Press, 1996.

Sherow, James E. *Watering the Valley: Development along the High Plains Arkansas River, 1870–1950.* Lawrence: University Press of Kansas, 1990.

Shipps, Jan. *Mormonism: The Story of a New Religious Tradition.* Urbana: University of Illinois Press, 1985.

Slotkin, Richard. *The Fatal Environment: The Myth of the Frontier in the Age of Industrialization.* New York: Atheneum, 1985.

———. *Gunfighter Nation: The Myth of the Frontier in Twentieth-Century America.* New York: Atheneum, 1992.

Smith, Michael L. *Pacific Visions: California Scientists and the Environment, 1850–1915.* New Haven, Conn.: Yale University Press, 1987.

Smith, Sherry. *The View from Officer's Row: Army Perceptions of Western Indians.* Tucson: University of Arizona Press, 1990.

Szasz, Ferenc Morton. *The Protestant Clergy in the Great Plains and Mountain West, 1865–1915.* Albuquerque: University of New Mexico Press, 1988.

Szasz, Margaret, ed. *Between Indian and White Worlds: The Cultural Broker.* Norman: University of Oklahoma Press, 1994.

Takaki, Ronald. *A Different Mirror: A History of Multicultural America.* Boston: Little, Brown, 1993.

———. *Strangers from a Different Shore: A History of Asian Americans.* Boston: Little, Brown, 1989.

Tank, Robert M. "Mobility and Occupational Structure on the Late-Nineteenth-Century Urban Frontier: The Case of Denver, Colorado." *Pacific Historical Review* 47 (May 1978): 189–216.

Taylor, Graham D. *The New Deal and American Indian Tribalism: The Administration of the Indian Reorganization Act, 1934–45.* Lincoln: University of Nebraska Press, 1980.

Taylor, Quintard. *The Forging of a Black Community: Seattle's Central District through the Civil Rights Era.* Seattle: University of Washington Press, 1994.

Toll, William. *The Making of an Ethnic Middle Class: Portland's Jewry over Four Generations.* Albany: State University of New York Press, 1982.

Tsai, Shih-Shan Henry. *The Chinese Experience in America.* Bloomington: Indiana University Press, 1988.

Unruh, John D., Jr. *The Plains Across: The Overland Emigrants and the Trans-Mississippi West, 1840–1860.* Urbana: University of Illinois Press, 1979.

Utley, Robert. *The Indian Frontier of the American West.* Albuquerque: University of New Mexico Press, 1984.

Van West, Carroll. *Capitalism on the Frontier: Billings and the Yellowstone Valley in the Nineteenth Century*. Lincoln: University of Nebraska Press, 1993.

Walton, John. *Western Times and Water Wars: State, Culture, and Rebellion in California*. Berkeley: University of California Press, 1992.

Watkins, Marilyn P. *Rural Democracy: Family Farmers and Politics in Western Washington, 1890–1925*. Ithaca, N.Y.: Cornell University Press, 1995.

Weber, David. *The Mexican Frontier, 1821–46: The American Southwest under Mexico*. Albuquerque: University of New Mexico, 1982.

———. *The Spanish Frontier in North America*. New Haven, Conn.: Yale University Press, 1992.

Weber, Devra. *Dark Sweat, White Gold: California Farm Workers, Cotton, and the New Deal*. Berkeley: University of California Press, 1994.

[Webster] Rieff, Janet. "Domestication and Americanization: Scandinavian Women in Seattle, 1880–1900. *Journal of Urban History* 4 (1978): 275–90.

West, Elliott. *Growing Up with the Country: Childhood on the Far Western Frontier*. Albuquerque: University of New Mexico Press, 1989.

———. *The Way to the West: Essays on the Central Plains*. Albuquerque: University of New Mexico Press, 1995.

White, Richard, *"It's Your Misfortune and None of My Own": A New History of the American West*. Norman: University of Oklahoma Press, 1991.

———. *Land Use, Environment, and Social Change: The Shaping of Island County, Washington*. Seattle: University of Washington Press, 1980.

———. *The Organic Machine: The Remaking of the Columbia River*. New York: Hill & Wang, 1995.

———. "The Winning of the West: The Expansion of the Western Sioux in the Eighteenth and Nineteenth Centuries." *Journal of American History* 45 (September 1978): 319–43.

Wishart, David. *The Fur Trade of the American West, 1807–1840: A Geographic Synthesis*. Lincoln: University of Nebraska Press, 1982.

———. *An Unspeakable Sadness: The Dispossession of the Nebraska Indians*. Lincoln: University of Nebraska Press, 1994.

Worster, Donald. *Dust Bowl: The Southern Plains in the 1930s*. New York: Oxford University Press, 1979.

———. *Rivers of Empire: Water, Aridity, and the Growth of the American West*. New York: Pantheon, 1985.

Wrobel, David M. *The End of American Exceptionalism*. Lawrence: University Press of Kansas, 1993.

Wunder, John. *"Retained by the People:" A History of American Indians and the Bill of Rights*. New York: Oxford University Press, 1994.

Wyman, Mark. *Hard Rock Epic: Western Miners and the Industrial Revolution, 1860–1910*. Berkeley: University of California Press, 1979.

Yung, Judy. *Unbound Feet: A Social History of Chinese Women in San Francisco*. Berkeley: University of California Press, 1995.

10

◫ SOCIAL HISTORY

Alice Kessler-Harris

WHAT IS SOCIAL HISTORY? A GENERATION AGO ONE MIGHT HAVE DESCRIBED IT readily: in contrast to other historical subspecialties, its major concern was with the private rather than the public sphere of life. Instead of focusing on political events and the process of social change, it emphasized descriptions of individual and family life. The well-known British historian G. M. Trevelyan, in the introduction to his *Social History of England,* defines the field as "the history of a people with the politics left out." Generations of graduate students affectionately dubbed it "pots and pans" history. The label captured the tenuous relationship of social history to the profession. And its marginality was confirmed by the practice of teaching social and intellectual or economic history together, as if social history lacked the scholarly legitimacy required to stand on its own.

In the 1960s, this changed. Social history moved to the center of the scholarly enterprise as the scope and content of historical studies in America altered dramatically. John Higham, a historian not known for hyperbole, compared the change to an earthquake that "split the dam and released a flood of waters across the entire terrain of scholarship." Like a flood, the new social history shifted the course of the profession's mainstream, carving out new directions for exploration, raising a series of questions about the nature of the craft of history and transforming our understanding of the past. The historian Peter Burke, trying to describe social history in 1980, came up with the most inclusive definition imaginable. Under its rubric, he suggested, could be included the history of social relationships, social structure, everyday life, private life, social solidarities, social conflicts, social classes, and social groups "seen as both separate and mutually dependent units." Other historians have more or less agreed. Eric Hobsbawm called the field nothing less than a "history of society." Peter Stearns declared it "an approach to the entirety of the past." And Geoff Eley commended its "totalizing potential." A new generation of historians asserted that the task of social history was to make political history unimaginable without social analysis.

The flood tide of social history has now receded somewhat, leaving behind a series of yet-to-be explored tributaries as well as a good deal of debris. The subject matter carried with it waves of exciting new knowledge, but coherence, purpose, and direction all floundered in the churning waters. By 1976 some historians were calling attention to the "crisis" of the field, deriding its indifference to theory and its lack of political content. In 1979 the British historian Tony Judt angrily attacked it as merely "a gathering place for the unscholarly, for historians bereft of ideas and subtlety." Yet social history remains indispensable for anyone trying to understand or teach our history today.

What then is social history? Can it create coherence out of our past? Does it hold the key to explaining historical change? What accounts for its rapid transition from the easily dismissible periphery of historical scholarship to its center? Has all of history become social history? This essay will attempt to come to terms with these questions by looking at how the field emerged, the methods on which it relies, and some of the salient issues it raises. Because of its limited scope, much will be omitted. Rather than try to include all of the exciting areas that social history now encompasses, I attempt here to provide a sense of structure within which students and teachers can locate the proliferating subject matter of this rapidly expanding field.

R O O T S

In the United States, early social history is perhaps best exemplified by the thirteen-volume *History of American Life*, edited by Arthur M. Schlesinger Jr. and Dixon Ryan Fox and published between 1927 and 1948. In this series, and in other books written around the same time by scholars such as Alice Morse Earle, Elizabeth Dexter Perkins, and Julia Spruill, social history encompassed a broad subject matter but was rarely related to broader economic and political trends. It described such matters as household living practices and material processes, the daily lives of women and children, and rudimentary work practices. This history was colorful and anecdotal. Yet it lacked explanatory capacity, and it raised serious questions about bias and perspective. Patriotic in nature, it was meant to contribute to a myth of past glory. At its most myopic, it suffered the blindness of Frank Owlsey's *Plain People of the Old South,* which manages to chronicle the history of antebellum Southerners without ever mentioning slavery. Perhaps the old social history could have taken no other shape, for it assumed the role of handmaiden to a purposeful interpretation of the past that purported to chronicle the progress of a nation from infancy to mature development. Because these historians believed national growth and maturity derives from elite, articulate decision-makers, their social history attempted only to embroider the edges of mainstream interpretations.

Yet social history was not to remain on the periphery for long. U.S. history, it may be argued, has gone through three broad waves of interpretation. In its first professional incarnation, from the 1890s to the 1930s, it was primarily the province of those interested in politics and economics; its mandate was to explore national origins and destiny; and its dominant interpreters saw that destiny as unfolding in an on-going struggle between "special interests" and "the people." Its second incarnation, during the 1940s and 1950s, was marked by a search for American character. In contrast to the "progressive" historians, the new generation—led by intellectual historians identified as the "consensus" school—shared a fundamental agreement that the nation's direction had been shaped by a broadly accepted set of values that overrode ethnic and class distinctions. For the most part, consensus historians ignored racial exclusions. The new social history, which emerged in the 1960s, is arguably the third great wave to sweep over the historical profession, challenging both the notion of a single, monolithic national destiny and that of a national character.

In one sense, the ascendancy of social history was inspired by the visible tensions of the 1960s. With society rent asunder by the civil rights movement, antiwar protests, and feminist demands, a new generation of historians had difficulty reconciling myths of national progress and consensus with the tensions around them. Rejecting assumptions of unity, they argued that a history rooted in the ideas of an unrepresentative Protestant elite of ministers, lawyers, and political leaders could hardly speak for all of American society. Instead, they explored the dynamic interaction of a multiracial and multiethnic population in an effort to understand how interest groups and classes compete for power and to develop a sense of how race, sex, and ethnicity mold and inhibit conceptions of common national purpose. The resurgent populist impulse of the 1960s also brought into question the assumption that a study of leaders could adequately reflect the political process, and it heightened interest in the agency of ordinary people. Beginning, then, with the challenge of a divided society, rather than with the assumption of a unified one, social historians took the poor, the black, and the excluded as their special domain and set out to rewrite the history of the United States. As they did so, they discovered how racial, ethnic, and gendered ideas and behavior have been woven into the fabric of American society.

Their early ventures drew on the intellectual traditions of both Europe and America. Some historians turned to their European colleagues and especially to the French "Annales" school. Named for its journal, the *Annales d'histoire, economique et sociale*, the Annales school was guided by the principle that history occurs, in large part, as a result of factors outside of human control, such as climate, biology, and geography. Historians, they believed, should concern themselves not with discrete events but with the long-term evolution of these underlying factors or structures (*longue durée*). Using rigorous quantitative methods and attention to detail, and especially paying attention to the popular fantasies and habits of ordinary folk (their *mentalités*), they hoped to find explanations not only for why particular kinds of economic organization or social structure had prevailed but for political behavior as well. Analysis of such matters as trade patterns, food production, and human demography, according to the Annalistes, would ultimately prove more important than studying even the most critical short-term events such as wars, treaties, or dynastic marriages. In the early 1960s, historians of the United States borrowed from this approach an emphasis on the material realities of existence and on deeply researched local studies. Employing ethnographic and quantitative techniques, they expanded the body of available information, searching for clues to larger issues of structure by means of microscopic examination.

Two opposing intellectual traditions contributed to this effort. The first was the strong pull exerted by the empirical methods of behavioral social scientists. Attracted by the promise of precision and predictability, historians began to challenge as too subjective the humanist literary tradition in which descriptive history had been rooted. They turned to what some felt was the more neutral ground of the social sciences. From the influential sociologist Talcott Parsons they borrowed theories of systematic relations in the world of social reality and began to look for the relationship between social structure and function. Parsons's notions of social equilibrium and of the self-maintaining qualities of social organisms suggested that social institutions could best be understood in terms of the principles that ordered them. Historians began to seek these ordering principles—the factors that encourage stability and stasis—and to separate them from the disruptive circumstances that would account for change within nations and communities and fashion a new equilibrium. Employing new statistical techniques and computer technology that permitted greater precision in the collection of data about how people behave, they investigated a wide range of areas, including job retention, geographic mobility, where people live and how well, mortality rates and voting patterns, the kinds and amounts of food people consumed, and the size and shape of their households and communities.

Mountains of new statistical data lent credence to their discoveries but did little to enhance the explanatory capacity of the field. In Lee Benson's studies of Jacksonian voting patterns, for example, careful research revealed who voted, and when, but could not suggest why people voted as they did except by extrapolating from their behavior. The resulting debate over the relationship between motivation and action still goes on. Quantifiers assumed that behavior and action reflect consciousness and motivation, that answers to why certain behaviors occur will reveal themselves if each case is tested without a theoretical predisposition, and if each hypothesis is tested anew for different circumstances. Opponents objected that people frequently act from invisible motives, that the collection and interpretation of data reflect the values and biases of the researcher, and that quantification leads to an overemphasis on factors for which data happens to be available.

The second intellectual tradition supporting an emphasis on material roots derived from Marxism, newly resurgent by the late 1960s. Sharing the assumption of the Annalistes that history is subject to scientific rules, historians working within a Marxian tradition insisted on the crucial role of production in shaping social relations in modern society. In their view, different "relationships of production" yield conflicting interests among people and manifest themselves in class divisions. Because such divisions are inherently antagonistic, they foster dissent and can, under special circumstances, threaten existing hierarchies of power and the governments they sustain. In short, they can produce rebellion, or even revolution. Marxists had to explain why class conflict, despite its enormous potential for disruption, generally does not undermine social and political institutions. Their answer was ideology. Social divisions and the resulting conflicts are legitimized by a system of ideas that maintain equilibrium. Where the followers of Talcott Parsons saw social equilibrium as a function of social reality, his opponents, including such scholars as Leo Marx and John William Ward, saw it as a product of unspoken rationalizations that legitimize economic inequality. In their view, true historians ought not merely to chronicle the on-going struggle of ordinary people to create satisfying work and family situations but to explore the ideas and symbols that provide the framework within which people understand the meanings of their lives. The continuing interaction between social reality and ideological justification provides the dynamic impetus in a dialectical process that, Marxists argued, explains historical change. The insertion of notions like ideology and consciousness into the historical debate opened the door to the poststructuralist analysis, which would soon influence the field.

If many social historians rejected affiliation with Marxian labels, and particularly objected to the implicit goals of Marxist historiography, they nevertheless learned from and adopted some of the categories of Marxian thought as it emerged in the work of several of its distinguished practitioners. By the mid-1970s, creative elements of these schools of thought had married to produce a search for the culture of working people that became the leading edge of social history. Four elements were particularly important. First, the search for the intricate relationship between social and material reality on one hand and individual and collective consciousness on the other added a new dimension to social history. Most effectively played out by the British historian E. P. Thompson in his influential *Making of the English Working Class*, the effort posited that social change can be understood not by comprehending its structure so much as by exploring the imperatives on which people act. Second, dialectical analysis exposed the consciousness of ordinary people in a variety of ways but primarily through language, religion, and ritualistic and symbolic behavior. Each of these became a fertile analytic tool. Third, the focus on the relationship between social identity and action opened a continuing debate on the nature of "culture," how to locate and identify it, and how to measure its political impact. Finally, questions about how knowledge was produced, by whom and under what circumstances, dogged the discussion. Together these elements inspired social historians to abandon the notion that history can function without theory and encouraged debate about the relationship between individual human agency and historical change. This paved the way for historians to pay close attention to the language that historical actors use to describe themselves and their actions, or to what has been called the "linguistic turn."

METHOD

A new self-consciousness about historical method accompanied the melding of behavior with ideas. Analysis of written sources, left largely by political and intellectual leaders, had encouraged an earlier generation of historians to characterize the elite members of society as representative of the "American mind" or of the belief systems of the nation. But when the origins and legitimacy of that elite became a subject for investigation, the concept of the "mind" of the nation acquired more pluralistic dimensions and encouraged new ways of discovering the collective mentality. Ritual and celebration; close textual analysis of a worker's speech or of a slave's song; wills, oral histories, and changes in dress all opened access to understanding the values of ordinary people. These new sources lent themselves to phenomenological approaches. Massive accumulations of detail were allowed to represent the mind of the worker; the "self-experiences" of historical actors became the filters through which historians viewed and interpreted an issue or problem. They tried to chronicle the behavior of ordinary people by recording how they voted, where they lived, what they ate and drank, what alliances they made, what size families they had, and how they spent and saved their money. The new social science enabled historians to use numbers to make their assumptions more precise, to define their terms more carefully, to refine their research strategies. It also created a dialogue about the uses of and the biases lodged in different techniques for getting at truth. Quantifiers, oral historians, and observers of material culture competed with one another to get closer to what anthropologists might have called the "speaking subject."

The initial and perhaps continuing response was what the colonialist James Henretta called "a new empiricism." As social history moved swiftly into the camp of social science, some historians began to insist that the acquisition of increasing amounts of data would validate their efforts to reconstruct the past. Instead, they produced a negative reaction. In 1975 Herbert Gutman, who had rejuvenated labor history in the United States by relying heavily on manuscript census data to sort out the lives of workers, took issue when the economic historians Robert Fogel and Stanley Engerman relied on numbers to demonstrate that the living standards of some slaves might have exceeded those of Northern white workers. Vigorously objecting to the capacity of this kind of evidence to measure the quality of life, Gutman evoked the symbolic power of such coercive behavior as whipping slaves to reassert the importance of ideas in measuring individual well-being. The questions Gutman raised had never been far from the surface of the new social history and, by the late 1970s, provoked intensive debate. Some social historians argued that scholars' political ideology and belief systems were embedded in the questions they asked, in the kinds of sources they validated, and in their organization and interpretation of data, making the collection of numbers as subjective as the analysis of written sources.

Focusing on ethnographic detail could be equally problematic. The structure of a once-important town, the drama of a protest demonstration, the evolution of a celebratory day, the emergence of an immigrant community—all these might offer the exciting joy of discovery and reveal the intensity of a moment. But if such strategies produced a good story, they also encouraged historians to abandon the analytical narrative in favor of satisfying description. Unavoidably, the new technique favored the particular experiences of unique historical actors, treating each as if it contained an important truth. Sometimes that produced a brilliant effect, as in Laurel Thatcher Ulrich's *Midwife's Tale*, which carefully unravels the clues around a Maine midwife's life to illuminate the structure of social experience in the revolutionary period. But as often the method romanticized ordinary folk experience and treated individual lives as if each could tell us something about larger trajectories of change. By attempting to explain a particular form of behavior in terms of how people understood their own traditions, historians tended to emphasize continuities rather than discontinuities, the stable rather than the changing modes of their lives. The result has been an enormous temptation to avoid explanations of the sources of, and resistances to, change in favor of colorful depictions of behavior. Valiant workers, for example, struggle bravely to maintain humane values against the onslaught of the powerful and evil forces of industrialization. Inquiring into the particular enhanced the threat of fragmentation by producing painstakingly detailed portraits that revealed more and more about less and less. In the search for the speaking subject, each specialized entity—workers, women, city dwellers, farmers, immigrants—came to constitute a field in itself, with its own academic journals, meetings, and historiographical debates.

Convinced by the early 1980s that the writer could not be separated from the process of interpretation, some historians began to raise questions about the core of the historian's task: the nature of truth, the validity of evidence, the possibility of objectivity, the legitimacy of certain kinds of argument, and finally, and most crucially, the relationship between how knowledge is conceived and acquired and how power is distributed. This last led directly to challenges to the plausibility of accessing a "real" or "material" past. A few historians, among them Joan Scott, viewed the past as unstable—a product of the interaction between the interpreter and the event and therefore not a "really existing" moment waiting to be recovered. The best the historian can do, they said, was to use language to uncover how historical actors situate themselves. As the British social historian Patrick Joyce put it, "the events, structures and processes of the past are indistinguishable from the forms of documentary representation, the conceptual and political appropriations, and the historical discourses that construct them." Some practitioners insisted that language (defined to include many forms of public expression and their representations) so effectively mediates between the knower and the known that it is the only proper subject for historical research. From there it is but a small step to asking whether language is not all there is of history, and its interpretation the core of the historian's enterprise.

Most social historians rebelled against what they described as the reduction of context to text, vigorously protesting a revolution in methods and goals that, some felt, would destroy the meaning of history altogether. But many began to use some of the insights and techniques of poststructuralist and literary analysis to reconfigure the questions framed by social historians. For example, Linda Gordon effectively adapted the technique of deconstruction (finding the conflicting meanings embedded in a word or idea) to explore the changing content of dependence. Others, like the French historian Michel Foucault, used poststructuralism's critique of a world divided into opposites (good and evil, male and female) to explore the complexities of hierarchical relationships and to locate power and sexuality in diverse places. The poststructuralist's focus on how knowledge is produced has led historians to think anew about the power inherent in ideas and especially to explore the "structure of ideas" that constitutes the arena (or discourse) within which historical agents act. To the poststructuralist, the language of the body and of space is as important as words, and thus dress, housing, and other forms of material culture have once again emerged into the historian's sphere and become the subjects of close readings.

Between those who eagerly developed new empirical techniques (sometimes called materialists), and those tempted by the relative freedom of interpretation offered by poststructuralism (sometimes called culturalists), a deep chasm has developed. The first group continues to believe that the second threatens history as we knew it; the second that without a continuing search for social meaning, the purposes of social history will founder. To accommodate these factions, social history has developed an eclectic set of methods, a large and capacious umbrella that includes culture and religion, ethnography, and ritual, ideas and *mentalités*. By the middle of the 1990s, the promise of coherence within the field seems to have vanished. And yet its capacity to bring coherence to the American past may well have expanded.

PRACTICE

How then do we make sense of a field that employs culture as a descriptive category but whose practitioners cannot agree on appropriate methods of analysis and sometimes question the feasibility of narrative history? How do we begin to think about a field that encompasses such diverse areas as labor history, women's history, the history of the family, leisure, sexuality, and ethnicity—a field that includes institutions as well as feelings and ideas? Bitter as the theoretical and methodological battles have been, the practice of social history leaves much room for hope, particularly around its capacity to meld old and new methods. Still drawn to empirical data, many quantitative historians find that the range of information they can access is enriched by interpretive material about the location of the subject and the historian and particularly by attention to questions of identity and subjectivity. The resulting flexibility of method and theory may yet yield a new synthesis. To trace these changes in historical practice, I focus on four categories central to the field: culture and values; the structure of everyday life; mobility and migration; and urbanization, industrialization, and postindustrialism.

The first poses a set of questions that revolve around the nature and strength of traditional culture. Did Americans share a set of values that transcended gendered lines as well as those of race, class, religion, and ethnicity? To what extent are norms and behavior peculiar to people of different religions, classes, and ethnic and racial groups? How are they transformed into the occupationally mobile and acquisitive values of the middle class?

Explorations into the texture of daily life and the culture of working people have made it apparent that at least until the end of the nineteenth century and for much of the twentieth, diverse sets of assumptions and goals divided Americans. For example, the meaning of republicanism in the early nineteenth century apparently differed for women, for artisans, and for the rising merchant class. For artisans the ideology of free labor represented the capacity to free themselves from wage labor, which they saw as servitude, and thus to distinguish themselves first from slaves and then from free black men. Merchants translated those ideas into freedom from government restraint; middle-class women saw republicanism as a call to create an educated citizenship; working-class white women clung to the idea of liberty as a way of distinguishing their poverty-stricken and overworked lives from the terrors of slavery. Within these varied meanings of liberty, the defense of the republic could involve language and rituals that ranged from arguments for individual freedom to explicit anticapitalism.

These distinctions beg a series of related questions whose answers remain more speculative. To what value systems do ordinary people respond? Are they the product of race, class, gender, religion, generation, neighborhood, ethnic background, or some combination of these and other factors? Insofar as working people possess a separate culture, how is it reinforced and sustained by other social identities such as those that emerge from family and sexual preference? Answers have come from a variety of directions, many of them rooted in a dispute over the construction of culture itself. Eugene Genovese, historian of the pre–Civil War South, has suggested, for example, that the behavior of slaves (including their capacity to resist slavery) can best be explained by their location in a paternalistic culture with which they partially identified. Herbert Gutman and others have taken exception to this interpretation, proposing instead that strong African and familial roots along with cruel coercion accounted for the values and behavior of black people in slavery. This dispute, like the dispute over how working people accommodated to and resisted oppressive working and living conditions, grows out of a disagreement over how far culture is rooted in dominant and widely influential ideas, and how far it emerges from each individual's experience with conditions of work and life.

Exploring these issues has produced exciting discoveries about how ordinary people understand the meanings of their lives. Lacking letters and diaries, historians turned to behavior as source material. European historians such as E. P. Thompson, George Rude, and Eric Hobsbawm pioneered in interpreting the meaning of crowd activity, of holiday parades, and of riots and protests. More recently, Jürgen Habermas has educated a generation of social historians about the civic and social uses of public space. Adopting the methods of the anthropologists Clifford Geertz and Victor Turner, historians now use artifacts to piece together rich portraits of lost cultures. Turner's insights into the meanings of ritual behavior, and especially his interpretations of symbolic acts, have encouraged historians to try to "read" myths and images as documents. For example, Carroll Smith-Rosenberg suggests that the shifting sexual imagery of early nineteenth-century America tells us something about a society trying to cope with large-scale social change. Seen through the lens of symbolic analysis, irrational as well as rational behavior reveals much about the values and orientations of different people and about the meaning systems of their lives.

From this vantage point it is but a small step to exploring the impact of racialized and gendered identities. Sociologists such as Mary Ann Clawson and historians such as Ramón Gutiérrez and David Roediger describe the political consequences of internalized conceptions of sexuality, masculinity, and constructions of whiteness. In the most influential of these interpretations, Roediger suggests that nineteenth-century white workers whose sense of themselves relied on sharp differentiations from black workers (free and slave) modeled their behavior, including voting preferences, exclusionary behavior at work, and demands for social preferences on their expectations of what was appropriate to their white identities. Ethnic identity fostered a sense of self that could sometimes lead to confrontation. Eliot Gorn, who has chronicled the history of bare-knuckle prizefighting in the nineteenth century, offers a particularly clear example. In Gorn's hands, the funeral of a dead boxer becomes a metaphor for the meanings of masculinity in an immigrant community; it captures as well the complementary functions of ethnic loyalty and patriotism among the nineteenth-century New York Irish.

The structure of everyday life and the textures of the social institutions that regulate it constitute a second nexus around which questions about social history have revolved. The dynamic force behind these investigations is the attempt to discover the nature of demographic transition and migration. Robert Wells's studies of American demographic history manage to draw a picture of how the family has changed its shape since the colonial period and simultaneously to argue that shifts in family size and individual life cycle constitute both source and explanation of changing social patterns. Tamara Hareven has effectively described the shape of the household, its composition, and the texture of relationships within it to develop an argument that intimately relates kinship structures to the experience of wage work. These historians would agree that the context of the family, its ethnic roots, its members' ages, and so on, provide significant clues to understanding how people have played out their roles in broader issues of social change. Joseph Kett's research suggests that while the concept of adolescence in the late nineteenth century emerged from industrial change, its particular form reflected a distinctive view about the malleability of children's morals. In a narrower context, Julia Kirk Blackwelder's study of San Antonio in the depression 1930s suggests a strong relationship between how people coped with economic distress and their racial and ethnic experiences.

These historians tend to use statistics where they are available, but they also search for qualitative sources that provide access to the texture of daily life. Surprising riches have turned up in contemporary records. They include the immigrant press, reports of charitable societies, minutes of trade union meetings, and working-class autobiography as well as evidence gleaned from institutions like schools, taverns, and churches. Together these enable historians to ask how institutions functioned as mediums of cultural transmission and as mechanisms for preserving traditional values. They have led to particularly imaginative and fruitful discussions of questions of social control. According to Roy Rosenzweig, for example, when the working people of Worcester, Massachusetts, were forced by state law to stop drinking in the kitchens of women who brewed beer and ale, the men went instead to licensed taverns. Their new behavior altered the texture of family life, weakening the central place of women within the family. The result seems to have been to strengthen one form of social control at the expense of another. Schools, churches, and public welfare agencies have come under special scrutiny as historians have tried to identify the roles they played in regulating the behavior patterns of poor and working people. Barbara Brenzel's *Daughters of the State,* for example, superbly illustrates the relationship between the fate of juvenile delinquents and a broader shift from optimism to pessimism and from idealism to determinism in the last half of the nineteenth century. It is part of a long literature exploring the origins of compulsory education, the regulation of public schools, and the processes of learning within them. The literature on the origins of the welfare state is rife with analysis of how a growing government bureaucracy in the 1930s and new messages about appropriate and inappropriate behavior changed the shape of family life, most especially for African Americans. So too, new comparative work on immigration, focusing especially on such groups as Mexicans in the Southwest and Germans in Chicago, and on the work experiences of miners and textile workers in Britain and the United States, have revealed more complex relationships between migration patterns and work habits and values than we earlier imagined.

A third set of questions involve the nature, existence, and meaning of social and occupational mobility. These issues assumed importance in the 1960s in the attempt to test the viability of the "American dream." The notion of social mobility had been sustained by a generation of historians who noted the progress made by the children of immigrants. Yet an issue remains: has the promise of upward mobility been largely mythical or does it reflect a reasonable degree of social and economic progress among the generations of immigrants and their children?

As presented in Oscar Handlin's *Boston's Immigrants,* which first sought to systematize the experience of immigrants, upward mobility was a reality. But Handlin's evidence, drawn largely from census manuscript schedules, is based on simple numerical calculations and remains heavily impressionistic. His conclusion that immigrant families broke down in the New World only to reconstitute themselves in its image has been widely challenged. Nevertheless, the book encouraged Stephan Thernstrom to use computerized data to test its hypothesis. First in *Poverty and Progress* and then in *The Other Bostonians,* Thernstrom concluded that the typical child of the late nineteenth-century unskilled immigrant worker might expect to move no more than one slot up the economic ladder. A high degree of transience and downward mobility tempered even this possibility. Thernstrom also discovered that to immigrants property ownership was the most important form of mobility. In the end, he argued that although there is only limited truth to the myth of rapid upward mobility, it contains sufficient reality to sustain belief in an egalitarian society. His conclusions have since been supported by studies of other major cities, including New York and San Francisco.

Mobility studies have lent fuel to both sides of an ongoing argument. Critics suggest that upward mobility is more readily explained by a shifting occupational structure than by individual success. They argue that as new jobs opened up, people tended to move up with their group, not out of it. Since those immigrants who returned home tended to be the least successful, the data reveal more upward mobility than really occurred. Critics also suggest that the implicit value judgments contained in mobility studies (which measure people's lives in terms of movement from one job to another or in terms of property ownership) are not those by which people might have measured their own lives. John Bodnar, for example, who records little occupational mobility among Pittsburgh's Slavic population in the first part of the twentieth century, and who has extensively interviewed other Pennsylvania workers, reports that most workers neither uncritically adopted the American dream of upward mobility nor struggled ceaselessly against collective injustice. Instead they avoided the risks that new jobs or geographic mobility might have entailed, preferring the relative security of poorer jobs and home ownership in known communities. Judith Smith and Donna Gabbaccia, among others, note that intergenerational mobility might be far more dependent on gendered values within the household, and especially on women's work and reproductive choices. African American workers, especially, took advantage of education for their daughters and repeatedly carved out new occupational niches whenever the opportunity presented itself.

The pressures of industrialization and technological change play a major role in structuring opportunity, and historians have long wondered how ordinary people take advantage of powerful and seemingly uncontrollable forces, and sometimes resist them. What then happens to traditional culture? An older history, including the pioneering work of Siegfried Giedion and Rolla Milton Tryon, assumed that technology has its own imperative. More recently, such books as David Noble's *Forces of Production* and Harry Katz's *Shifting Gears* have examined the adoption, applications, and consequences of technology as a product of decisions made by privileged individuals and groups. Histories of highways, medicines, automobiles, refrigerators, and the atomic bomb have all suggested that along the path of development a variety of complex factors have influenced the particular technological routes chosen. These include the needs of investors, the viability of labor markets, and the preconceived notions of influential people. This scholarship suggests that technology is part of a larger social structure within which it grows and which it ultimately sustains. No matter how theoretically attractive, technologies that might undermine the interests of privileged groups or their ways of being (such as homeopathic medicine, the electric automobile, or the gas refrigerator) tend to be squelched and the surviving technology rationalized as all that was possible.

On a broader level, the social impact of technology appears in the location and construction of communities. The growth of northern factory towns and of southern mine and mill communities now appears to be less a result of the accidental meshing of labor surplus with the needs of industry than a product of concerted attempts to structure communities so that they fit the needs of particular industries. Some employers provided houses big enough for boarders, while others built tiny dwellings in which they allowed workers and their families to live only while they remained on the company payroll. They based their choices on the kind of labor force they expected to attract, predictions about its loyalty, the degree of control they hoped to exercise, the turnover they needed, and a sense of whether the labor force would be replaced by new migrants or by births. But questions about why workers move to these places, what they understand by the transition, and how identities are reconstructed remain to be asked. Lizabeth Cohen's *Making of a New Deal* argues that traditional culture changes only slowly as working people, rooted in ethnic patterns, resist the encroachment of an acquisitively oriented society in a variety of ways. Resistance, in her view, takes socially conservative forms.

Insofar as choices exist around technological change, who controls it, and the pace of its adoption, the study of technology calls into question the issue of how ordinary people participate in these changes. Words such as proletarianization, modernization, and industrialization capture not only abstract processes but the abrasive interaction of people with new historical circumstances. They challenge the social historian to find out what happens to traditional cultures when new techniques of production confront traditional values and norms. What changes? For whom? In what ways? In Cohen's view, resistance takes socially conservative forms. But Sean Wilentz offers another perspective from a century earlier. He suggests that New York City's pre–Civil War craft workers clung to their craft traditions, legitimizing their actions by means of republican rhetoric and sustaining them with organizations embedded in the workplace. In contrast, David Montgomery and others use workers' efforts to protect their shop-floor privileges to illustrate wider commitments to preserving humane values. These struggles spill over into the political arena. A major strike or municipal election results might reflect, for example, the family's resistance to social change.

The picture of workers aggressively resisting technology and its concomitants is challenged by portraits of specific groups who, even in the face of some deprivation, perceived technology and industry as liberating and the changes produced as generally beneficial. The mill women of Lowell, Massachusetts, studied by Thomas Dublin, for example, seem to have benefited from the greater economic independence provided by employment in the mills; many of them turned the experience into a source of personal independence as well. Similar statements might apply to female immigrants from Ireland who, according to Hasia Diner, took advantage of the relative freedom of industrialization to emigrate to the New World. Some portion of Jewish women and a core of educated black women as well fall into the ranks of those whose educations in office machinery enabled them to enhance the living standards of their families. John Bodnar and other historians of immigration argue that although incoming groups attempt to retain their identities, they acquiesce to changes that do not threaten such ethnically derived activities as weddings, church functions, and education for the children.

Questions of identity lurk at the edges of many of these issues. However they responded to and attempted to shape technology, ordinary people in the end were changed by it. Nothing illustrates this so well as the dichotomy between those historians who focus on resistance to technology and those who worry about the power and influence of mass culture. In the view of many social historians, in the post–World War II period new and progressively more powerful technology sustained and was sustained by pervasive cultural forms, including film, radio, and television. These tended to encourage the acquisition of material goods, to undermine working-class identity. But its impact on racial and ethnic identity is less clear. In the postmodernist spirit, historians have only recently begun to explore the claims to identity that have resulted from the centripetal effects of mass culture.

Finally, a fourth major concern of social historians involves the process and results of urbanization. Does urbanization necessarily result in the disintegration of social order, in an increase of poverty and crime? Can its impact be differentiated for people of different classes and racial groups? As for studies of social mobility, the quantitative sources that lie at the heart of urban history are detailed local records (manuscript census schedules, city directories, tax rolls, and so on). And like new research in social mobility, research in the "new" urban history seeks to follow the lives of ordinary people and to tell their stories.

Before there was a new social history, urban history concerned itself with the structure, geography, and sometimes government of emergent cities. While it could comfortably encompass such areas as municipal reform, it mainly focused on the changing landscape of the city environment. As molded by the concerns of social history, the geography and mechanisms of a city's growth have taken second place to how the environment influences the lives of its citizens and is conditioned by their goals. Early illustrations of a pattern that integrated structure with human behavior include Gilbert Osofsky's descriptions of the rise of Harlem and Sam Bass Warner's analysis of the influence of streetcars. More recently, Kenneth Jackson's *Crabgrass Frontier* has demonstrated the dynamic interaction between the American dream and the growth of the suburbs. Jackson sweeps through the history of suburbanization to argue that this quintessentially American life-style resulted from government policy as much as from the preferences of Americans for detached dwellings of their own.

These new directions have not stilled skepticism about the necessity for a special field called urban history. Stephan Thernstrom, a pioneer in urban research, put it neatly when he asked whether a proper study of the groups that constitute city dwellers (largely drawn from rural surroundings) should not be "a history of population and social structure." As urban history has made the transition to social history, its boundaries seem to have become increasingly obscure. And yet its strengths lie in its capacity to illuminate (or exploit) social theory more directly than most other forms of social history. Controversial but impressive results have been achieved in two areas. First, urban poverty and family disorganization, which social theorists blame on the urban experience of crowding and the breakdown of community, take on a different shape in the hands of urban historians. They suggest that a number of contiguous neighborhoods made up the city of the past, each of them with its own character and each maintaining continuity between rural or Old World cultures and the new experiences of the city. Christine Stansell's study of working-class women in early nineteenth-century New York beautifully illustrates the point. Stansell found that working-class attitudes toward sexuality were regulated by neighborhood mores far more than by the standards of the Victorian middle class, with whom working-class women had little contact. And studies of Italian immigrants have repeatedly shown that Italians defended their culture by preserving neighborhoods that provided institutional support systems. Second, historians view crime and violence differently from sociologists and others who attribute it to poverty and urban life. Eric Monkkonen, for example, finds no evidence that the rate of either crime or poverty increased with city growth and little to indicate that pauperization led to crime. Roger Lane confirms these conclusions, suggesting little connection between urban growth and violence.

But linking the behavior of urban dwellers to the urban environment is only one aspect of urban studies. The construction of space and the relationship of individual conceptions of self to space have also begun to concern historians who now use increasingly sophisticated theoretical models and techniques. The pioneering methods of the anthropologist Anthony Wallace illustrates the point. His study of early nineteenth-century Rockdale traces the conflicts surrounding the substitution of one life-style for another to reveal how struggles over small issues opened access to the meaning of social ideology. Clyde and Sally Griffen's work on Poughkeepsie demonstrates how attention to occupational differentiation and the relation of family structure to women's work can tell us something about the development of the urban environment. Worcester, Massachusetts, as portrayed by Roy Rosenzweig, has provided the locus for an explanation of workers' leisure. Earl Lewis's work on Richmond, Virginia, has revealed details about how the African American working class adapted to, and constructed, their urban environment. Joe Trotter demonstrates how the growth of Milwaukee framed a tenuous alliance of working-class blacks with the black middle class.

How relations of power appear in and are transformed by space occupy the cutting edge of these endeavors. By using newly developed conceptions of the meaning of space to analyze urban geography, historians have illuminated the dimensions of power and its pervasive reach into the lives of seemingly insulated or excluded groups. George Chauncey's work, for example, effectively interleaves the cultural and geographic spaces occupied by gay men in early twentieth-century New York City. Mary Ryan suggests some of the uses that women made of public space to overcome an insidious political exclusion.

THE PROBLEM OF SYNTHESIS

The sources and methods of the new social history may be less conducive to grand-scale interpretation of the American past than older political and intellectual histories, but they are not hostile to it. Depending on empirical sources that speak to the diversity and particularity of American life, most new social historians have chosen to elaborate the microcosm in the hope that their own tiny contributions to the jigsaw puzzle will help ultimately to construct a new interpretation of our past. If the subfields of social history—such as urban and labor history, the history of women and of African Americans—have not yet brought their creative energy to bear on the formation of a larger synthesis, they have engendered a healthy discontent about the kinds of generalizations produced by more traditional fields. Still, that discontent has not protected the field from harsh external criticisms and incessant self-examination, or from the deeper concern that a conception of history that insists on the importance of the unique event and reifies the diversity of ordinary people necessarily fosters fragmentation. Such techniques, critics argue, do not contribute to understanding the structure of culture, of political life, or of social change.

But a profusion of regional and local studies that focus on small towns and on single industries may disguise an implicit interpretive framework that is beginning to take shape. I want to suggest that the challenges of poststructuralist thought may lend themselves to fruitful debate, especially as they cohere around issues of gender, race, and class. Fundamental to social history is a search for a determinative context, a respect for the cultures of different groups, and a recognition of the power of diversity. Less clearly understood is how and by whom those cultures are transmitted, under what circumstances, and with what resistance. These are at root political questions to the extent that politics is understood as the way in which power is exercised at all levels of society and as the way in which mechanisms of change occur not merely as a function of legislatures and presidents but as expressions of public will, and therefore of a larger conception of the public self.

Everyone who comments on the fragmentation of social history agrees that it somehow lost its path as a result of its disconnection from politics, broadly defined. But while some scholars fear that a social history set in the framework of politics will return us to traditional ways of seeing, the need remains to seek some relationship between everyday life, the values and behavior of ordinary people, and the larger mechanisms of change. Attempts to understand the relationship between political mobilization or action and the values of ordinary people lie at the heart of the new social history. Its new focus reveals something of how a society mediates the "continuing claims of order, authority, freedom and rebellion." The field now directly confronts historians with such questions as How do people exercise power? How is it transmitted? How is it influenced? What is the relation between mechanisms of order and those of protest? The new social history searches in the details of ordinary lives for clues to how discrete groups and individuals see themselves as actors on a larger stage.

How to do this remains in dispute. Elizabeth Fox-Genovese and Eugene Genovese proposed "who rides whom and how" as the central problematic and the core of synthesis. In their view, class constitutes the determinative power relationship, with race and gender functioning to sustain social hierarchy. Holding class as the constant, however, poses problems for those who see ethnicity, race, and gender as more powerful shaping forces in the American past. Herbert Gutman, for example, might have agreed with the abstract formulation but would certainly have disagreed that class, rather than race or ethnicity at certain moments, constitutes the shaping framework of people's lives. Similarly, many historians of women now insist on the centrality of gender and sexuality in the creation and perpetuation of social inequalities.

Thomas Bender suggests integrating political process with social formations by turning the "making of public culture" into the central problematic of a new synthesis of national history. Understood as "the ever-changing always contingent outcome of a continuing contest among social groups and ideas," public culture, he argues, "embraces a wide range of manifestations of power in society—from the institutional power of the state through the more subtle power to assign meaning and significance to various cultural phenomena, including the power to establish categories of social analysis and understanding."

An exploration of public culture that includes questions of how meaning and significance are assigned will require combining strategies of poststructuralist analysis with more traditional forms of social history. Keith Nield and Geoff Eley, two historians of Britain, suggest how this might be done. The key to historical synthesis, they argue, lies in the search for social formations as they are constructed and reconstructed in a continuing process. For them, class is one form of "social formation" but the rubric does not rule out race, gender, and ethnicity as well. Understanding the process of change requires, in their view, a conception of hegemony, which they define as an "institutionally negotiable process in which the social and political forces of contest, breakdown and transformation are constantly in play." Here, the methods of deconstruction are put to use. As Joan Scott suggests, they can help illuminate how political meaning is transmitted through language. To understand politics, she suggests, we need to understand how culture is produced and its meanings circulated—which puts language at the center of the historian's enterprise. Refusing the extremes to which this strategy could take us, many social historians seem nevertheless to make increasingly effective use of them to question old ways of knowing while illuminating the material world from which they emerge.

The best social history attempts to integrate new research in institutional structures with consciousness and ideology in a way that creates understanding of broader political process and of the tensions that ultimately yield changes. In so doing, it has already begun to develop a complex interpretation of American society that rests on neither conflict nor consensus but on a subtle and changing construction of relationships between groups of people and their orientations to social reality, and the actions they take to defend the world that is theirs.

BIBLIOGRAPHY

This highly selective bibliography focuses largely on materials that illustrate the points made in the essay, and that are likely to be widely available.

Appleby, Joyce, Lynn Hunt, and Margaret Jacob. *Telling the Truth about History.* New York: Norton, 1994.

Bender, Thomas. "Wholes and Parts: The Need for Synthesis in American History." *Journal of American History* 73 (June 1986): 120–36.

Benson, Lee. *The Concept of Jacksonian Democracy: New York as a Test Case.* Princeton, N.J.: Princeton University Press, 1961.

Blackmar, Elizabeth. *Manhattan for Rent, 1785–1850.* Ithaca, N.Y.: Cornell University Press, 1989.

Blackwelder, Julia Kirk. *Women of the Depression: Caste and Culture in San Antonio, 1929–39.* College Station: Texas A & M University Press, 1984.

Blassingame, John W. *The Slave Community: Plantation Life in the Ante-Bellum South.* Rev. ed. New York: Oxford University Press, 1972.

Bodnar, John. *Immigration and Industrialization: Ethnicity in an American Mill Town, 1870–1940.* Pittsburgh, Pa.: University of Pittsburgh Press, 1977.

Brenzel, Barbara. *Daughters of the State: A Social Portrait of the First Reform School for Girls in North America, 1856–1905.* Cambridge, Mass.: MIT Press, 1983.

Chauncey, George, Jr. *Gay New York: Gender, Urban Culture, and the Making of the Gay Male World, 1890–1940.* New York: Basic Books, 1994.

Clawson, Mary Ann. *Constructing Brotherhood: Class, Gender, and Fraternalism.* Princeton, N.J.: Princeton University Press, 1989.

Cohen, Lizabeth. *Making of a New Deal: Industrial Workers in Chicago, 1919–1939.* New York: Cambridge University Press, 1990.

Curti, Merle, *The Making of an American County: A Case Study in Democracy in a Frontier County.* Stanford, Calif.: Stanford University Press, 1959.

Davis, Allen F., and Mark Haller. *The Peoples of Philadelphia: A History of Ethnic Groups and Lower-Class Life, 1790–1940.* Philadelphia: Temple University Press, 1973.

Decker, Peter R. *Fortunes and Failures: White-Collar Mobility in Nineteenth-Century San Francisco.* Cambridge, Mass.: Harvard University Press, 1978.

Deutsch, Sarah. *No Separate Refuge: Culture, Class, and Gender on an Anglo-Hispanic Frontier in the American Southwest, 1880–1940.* New York: Oxford University Press, 1987.

Diner, Hasia. *Erin's Daughters in America: Irish Immigrant Women in the Nineteenth Century.* Baltimore, Md.: Johns Hopkins University Press, 1983.

Dublin, Thomas. *Transforming Women's Work: Women's Lives in the Industrial Revolution.* Ithaca, N.Y.: Cornell University Press, 1994.

Earle, Alice Morse. *Colonial Dames and Goodwives.* 1927. Berkshire Trails Press, 1974.

Eley, Geoff. "Some Recent Tendencies in Social History." In Georg G. Iggers and Harold Parker, eds., *International Handbook of Historical Studies,* 55–70. Westport, Conn.: Greenwood Press, 1979.

Eley, Geoff, and Keith Nield. "Why Does Social History Ignore Politics?" *Social History* 5 (May 1980): 249–71.

Fogel, Robert William, and Stanley Engerman. *Time on the Cross: The Economics of American Negro Slavery.* New York: Little, Brown, 1974.

Fox-Genovese, Elizabeth, and Eugene Genovese. "The Political Crisis of Social

History: A Marxian Perspective." *Journal of Social History* 10 (Winter 1976): 205–20.

Friedlander, Peter. *The Emergence of a UAW Local, 1936–1939: A Study in Class and Culture.* Pittsburgh, Pa.: University of Pittsburgh Press, 1975.

Frisch, Michael. *Town into City: Springfield, Massachusetts, and the Meaning of Community, 1840–1880.* Cambridge, Mass.: Harvard University Press, 1972.

Geertz, Clifford. *The Interpretation of Cultures: Selected Essays.* New York: Basic Books, 1973.

Genovese, Eugene D. *Roll, Jordan, Roll: The World the Slaves Made.* New York: Pantheon, 1974.

Giedion, Siegfried. *Mechanization Takes Command: A Contribution to Anonymous History.* New York: Oxford University Press, 1948.

Gordon, Linda. *Pitied but Not Entitled: Single Mothers and the History of Welfare.* New York: Free Press, 1994.

Gorn, Elliott J. *The Manly Art: Bare-Knuckle Prize Fighting in America.* Ithaca, N.Y.: Cornell University Press, 1986.

Griffen, Clyde, and Sally Griffen. *Natives and Newcomers: The Ordering of Opportunity in Mid-Nineteenth Century Poughkeepsie.* Cambridge, Mass.: Harvard University Press, 1978.

Gutman, Herbert G. *The Black Family in Slavery and Freedom: 1750–1925.* New York: Pantheon, 1976.

———. *Slavery and the Numbers Game: A Critique of Time on the Cross.* Urbana: University of Illinois Press, 1975.

———. "Whatever Happened to History?" *The Nation,* November 21, 1981, 553–54.

Habermas, Jürgen. *The Structural Transformation of the Public Sphere: An Inquiry into a Category of Bourgeois Society.* Cambridge, Mass.: MIT Press, 1989.

Handlin, Oscar. *Boston's Immigrants, 1790–1880.* New York: Atheneum, 1971.

Hareven, Tamara, ed. *Anonymous Americans: Explorations in Nineteenth-Century Social History.* Englewood Cliffs, N.J.: Prentice-Hall, 1971.

Hareven, Tamara, and Randolph Langenbach. *Amoskeag: Life and Work in an American Factory City.* New York: Pantheon, 1979.

Henretta, James. "Social History as Lived and Written." *American Historical Review* 84 (December 1979): 1293–322.

Higham, John, and Paul Conkin. *New Directions in American Intellectual History.* Baltimore, Md.: Johns Hopkins University Press, 1979.

Hirschhorn, Larry. *Beyond Mechanization: Work and Technology in a Postindustrial Age.* Cambridge, Mass.: MIT Press, 1984.

Hobsbawm, Eric. "From Social History to the History of Society." *Daedalus* 100 (fall 1971): 20–45.

Hobsbawm, Eric, and George Rude. *Captain Swing.* London: Lawrence & Wishart, 1968.

Hoerder, Dirk. *Struggle a Hard Battle: Essays on Working Class Immigrants.* De Kalb: Northern Illinois University Press, 1986.

Jackson, Kenneth T. *Crabgrass Frontier: The Suburbanization of the United States.* New York: Oxford University Press, 1985.

Johnson, Paul. *A Shopkeeper's Millennium: Society and Revivals in Rochester, New York, 1815–1837.* New York: Hill & Wang, 1978.

Jones, Jacquelyn. *Labor of Love, Labor of Sorrow: Black Women, Work, and the Family from Slavery to the Present.* New York: Basic Books, 1985.

Joyce, Patrick. "History and Post-Modernism." *Past and Present* 133 (November 1991): 204–9.

Judt, Tony. "A Clown in Regal Purple: Social History and the Historians." *History Workshop* 7 (spring 1979): 66–94.

Kammen, Michael, ed. *The Past before Us: Contemporary Historical Writing in the United States.* Ithaca, N.Y.: Cornell University Press, 1982.

Katz, Harry. *Shifting Gears: Changing Labor Relations in the U.S. Automobile Industry.* Cambridge, Mass.: MIT Press, 1985.

Katz, Michael. *The Irony of Early School Reform: Educational Innovation in Mid-Nineteenth-Century Massachusetts.* Boston: Beacon Press, 1968.

———. *Poverty and Policy in American History.* New York: Academic Press, 1983.

Kelley, Robin, ed. *Race Rebels: Culture, Politics, and the Black Working Class.* New York: Free Press, 1994.

Kennedy, Elizabeth Lapovsky, and Madeline D. Davis. *Boots of Leather, Slippers of Gold: The History of a Lesbian Community.* New York: Penguin, 1994.

Kessler-Harris, Alice. *Out to Work: A History of Wage-Earning Women in the United States.* New York: Oxford University Press, 1982.

———. *A Woman's Wage: Social Meanings and Historical Consequences.* Lexington: University Press of Kentucky, 1992.

Kessner, Thomas. *The Golden Door: Italian and Jewish Immigrant Mobility in New York City, 1880–1915.* New York: Oxford University Press, 1977.

Kett, Joseph F. *Rites of Passage: Adolescence in America, 1790 to the Present.* New York: Basic Books, 1977.

Lane, Roger. *Violent Death in the City: Suicide, Accident, and Murder in Nineteenth-Century Philadelphia.* Cambridge, Mass.: Harvard University Press, 1979.

Lewis, Earl. *In Their Own Interests: Race, Class, and Power in Twentieth-Century Norfolk, Virginia.* Berkeley: University of California Press, 1991.

Litwack, Leon. *Been in the Storm So Long: The Aftermath of Slavery.* New York: Knopf, 1979.

Marx, Leo. *The Machine in the Garden: Technology and the Pastoral Idea in America.* New York: Oxford University Press, 1964.

Mayfield, David, and Susan Thorne. "Social History and Its Discontents: Gareth Stedman Jones and the Politics of Language." *Social History* 17 (May 1992): 165–88.

Merrill, Michael, and Sean Wilentz, eds. *The Key of Liberty: The Life and Democratic Writing of William Manning.* Cambridge, Mass.: Harvard University Press, 1993.

Monkkonen, Eric H. *The Dangerous Class: Crime and Poverty in Columbus, Ohio, 1860–1885.* Cambridge, Mass.: Harvard University Press, 1975.

Montgomery, David. *Workers' Control in America: Studies in the History of Work, Technology and Labor Struggles.* New York: Cambridge University Press, 1979.

Noble, David F. *America by Design: Science, Technology, and the Rise of Corporate Capitalism*. New York: Knopf, 1977.

————. *Forces of Production: A Social History of Industrial Automation*. New York: Knopf, 1984.

Osofsky, Gilbert. *Harlem: The Making of a Ghetto—Negro New York, 1890–1930*. New York: Harper & Row, 1966.

Owsley, Frank. *The South: Old and New Frontiers*. Athens: University of Georgia Press, 1969.

Palmer, Bryan. *Descent into Discourse: The Reification of Language and the Writing of Social History*. Philadelphia: Temple University Press, 1990.

Pessen, Edward. *Three Centuries of Social Mobility in America*. Lexington, Mass.: Heath, 1974.

Prude, Jonathan. *The Coming of the Industrial Order: Town and Factory Life in Rural Massachusetts, 1810–1860*. New York: Cambridge University Press, 1983.

Rorabaugh, W. J. *The Alcoholic Republic: An American Tradition*. New York: Oxford University Press, 1979.

Rosenzweig, Roy. *Eight Hours for What We Will: Workers and Leisure in an Industrial City, 1870–1920*. New York: Cambridge University Press, 1983.

Rothman, David. *The Discovery of the Asylum: Social Order and Disorder in the New Republic*. Boston: Little, Brown, 1971.

Ryan, Mary P. *Cradle of the Middle Class: The Family in Oneida County, New York, 1790–1865*. New York: Cambridge University Press, 1981.

————. *Women in Public: Between Banners and Ballots, 1825–1880*. Baltimore, Md.: Johns Hopkins University Press, 1990.

Sanchez, George. *Becoming Mexican-American: Ethnicity, Culture, and Identity in Chicano Los Angeles: 1900–1945*. New York: Oxford University Press, 1993.

Saxton, Alexander. *The Rise and Fall of the White Republic: Class Politics and Mass Culture in Nineteenth-Century America*. London: Verso, 1990.

Scott, Joan. *Gender and the Politics of History*. New York: Columbia University Press, 1988.

Schlesinger, Arthur, Jr. *The Disuniting of America: Reflections on a Multicultural Society*. New York: Norton, 1992.

Shammas, Carole, Marylynn Salmon, and Michel Dahlin. *Inheritance in America: From Colonial Times to the Present*. New Brunswick, N.J.: Rutgers University Press, 1987.

Smith, Judith. *Family Connections: A History of Italian and Jewish Immigrant Lives in Providence, Rhode Island, 1900–1940*. Albany: State University of New York Press, 1985.

Smith-Rosenberg, Carroll. *Disorderly Conduct: Visions of Gender in Victorian America*. New York: Knopf, 1985.

Spruill, Julia Cherry. *Women's Life and Work in the Southern Colonies*. Chapel Hill: University of North Carolina Press, 1938.

Srebnick, Amy Gilman. *The Mysterious Death of Mary Rogers: Sex and Culture in Nineteenth-Century New York*. New York: Oxford University Press, 1995.

Stansell, Christine. *City of Women: Sex and Class in New York, 1789–1860*. New York: Knopf, 1986.

Stearns, Peter. "Coming of Age." *Journal of Social History* 10 (winter 1976): 246–55.

Thernstrom. Stephan. *The Other Bostonians: Poverty and Progress in the American Metropolis, 1880–1970.* Cambridge, Mass.: Harvard University Press, 1973.

———. *Poverty and Progress: Social Mobility in a Nineteenth-Century City.* Cambridge, Mass.: Harvard University Press, 1964.

Thompson, E. P. *The Making of the English Working Class.* New York: Vintage, 1963.

Tilly, Louise. "Gender and Women's History." *Social Science History* 13 (winter 1989): 439–61.

Trotter, Joe William, Jr. *Black Milwaukee: The Making of an Industrial Proletariat, 1915–45.* Urbana: University of Illinois Press, 1985.

Tryon, Rolla Milton. *Household Manufactures in the United States, 1640–1680: A Study in Industrial History.* Chicago: University of Chicago Press, 1917.

Turner, Victor. *The Ritual Process: Structure and Anti-Structure.* Chicago: Aldine, 1969.

Ulrich, Laurel Thatcher. *A Midwife's Tale: The Life of Martha Ballard Based on Her Diary, 1785–1812.* New York: Vintage, 1991.

Veysey, Laurence. "The 'New' Social History in the Context of American Historical Writing." *Reviews in American History* 7, no. 1 (1979): 1–12.

Wallace, Anthony F. C. *Rockdale: The Growth of an American Village in the Early Industrial Revolution.* New York: Knopf, 1978.

Ward, John William. *Andrew Jackson: Symbol for an Age.* New York: Oxford University Press, 1953.

Warner, Sam B. *Streetcar Suburbs: The Process of Growth in Boston, 1870–1900.* Cambridge, Mass.: Harvard University Press, 1962.

Wells, Robert V. *Uncle Sam's Family: Issues in and Perspectives on American Demographic History.* Albany: State University of New York Press, 1985.

White, Deborah Gray. *Ar'n't I a Woman? Female Slaves in the Plantation South.* New York: Norton, 1985.

Wilentz, Sean. *Chants Democratic: New York City and the Rise of the American Working Class, 1788–1850.* New York: Oxford University Press, 1984.

Yans-McLaughlin, Virginia. *Family and Community: Italian Immigrants in Buffalo, 1880–1930.* Ithaca, N.Y.: Cornell University Press, 1977.

Zukin, Sharon. *Landscapes of Power: From Detroit to Disney World.* Berkeley: University of California Press, 1991.

Zunz, Olivier. *Reliving the Past: The Worlds of Social History.* Chapel Hill: University of North Carolina Press, 1985.

11

■ U.S. WOMEN'S HISTORY

Linda Gordon

IN NO OTHER FIELD OF HISTORY HAS THERE BEEN SO MUCH PRODUCTIVITY, INNOVA-
tion, and interest since the 1970s as in U.S. women's history. The revival
of a women's liberation movement in the late 1960s and early 1970s
revealed the neglect of the historical activities of women. Influenced by
the women's movement, important fields of women's studies developed
not only in history but also in education, sociology, art criticism, literature, philosophy, psychology, and political and social theory. History is
outstanding, however, for the volume of new scholarship focused on
women. Hundreds of colleges and universities offer women's history
courses, and many graduate schools are training specialists in women's
history. The impact has been widespread. The materials and ideas of
women's history are particularly vivid for teaching, because they offer
concrete and intimate images of the past as well as challenging new
questions. Women's history often addresses daily-life experience—sex,
courtship, childbirth, child rearing—and illuminates the sources of con-

The author thanks Laura McEnaney for helpful suggestions on this revision and several
other members of the University of Wisconsin women's history community for bibliographical suggestions.

temporary controversies such as abortion, women's employment, and female-headed households.

Women's history scholarship has also changed many other areas of history. It does not simply add women to the pictures we already have of the past, like painting additional figures into the spaces of an already completed canvas. It requires repainting the earlier pictures, because some of what was previously on the canvas was inaccurate and more of it misleading. Two examples may illustrate. First, in the history of American religion, the challenge to Puritan orthodoxy led by Anne Hutchinson was for years described exclusively as the antinomian controversy, an example of the theological tensions between works and faith. In fact, Hutchinson's threat to the social and political order of the seventeenth-century Puritan colonies resulted as much from her defiance of woman's assigned place as from her theology.[1] Second, historians saw the temperance and prohibition movements of the nineteenth and twentieth centuries primarily as a Protestant attack on the different cultural patterns of Roman Catholic immigrants. Women's historians demonstrated, however, that temperance was also a women's movement challenging the male world of the saloon, the wife beating and child abuse associated with drinking, and the mental and physical ill health created by liquor.[2]

THE HISTORY OF WOMEN'S HISTORY

Women's history did not begin in the 1970s. Just as there was a "first wave" of feminism, stretching from the 1830s to 1920, so there was a "first wave" of women's scholarship. This first wave produced primarily what women's historians today refer to as "contributions" history: narratives detailing the unrecognized contributions that women made to cultural and economic life. In 1853, for example, Sarah J. Hale published a "Record" of "All Distinguished women from 'the Beginning' till A.D. 1850"! Also in the 1850s, Elizabeth Ellet published books on women in the American Revolution and on pioneer women. Toward the end of the century, as some women won access to higher education, women's history became more sophisticated. Scholars began writing "social history"; that is, they attempted to describe the lives of the majority of women, not just the elite or the exceptional, and doing so meant they used a great variety of sources to describe women's daily lives, their work, health practices, cookery, and so on. For example, Alice Earle wrote several volumes on women's life in the colonies.

Early in the twentieth century, American women's scholarship expanded greatly. More sociological than historical, it was part of a flowering of work committed to progressive social change, much of it remarkable in its combination of readability and meticulous empirical research. Today it forms vital primary source material for the second wave of women's historians. The Russell Sage Foundation supported a number of projects, including Margaret Byington's study of a steel town, *Homestead: The Households of a Mill Town* (1910), Katherine Anthony's *Mothers Who Must Earn* (1914), and Louise Odencrantz's *Italian Women in Industry* (1919). Numerous journalists and novelists of the period found a popular voice in which to denounce the exploitation of working women and ethnic minorities.[3] In this spirit of concern for poor women, several historians produced work that combined social commitment with high scholarly standards. Lucy Maynard Salmon's *Domestic Service* (1897) and Edith Abbott's *Women in Industry* (1913) are examples.[4] These early twentieth-century scholars argued that the subordination and exploitation of women formed an essential part of the society and economy. Focusing now on the masses of women—rather than the exceptional, privileged few who had made "contributions"—these new scholars showed that the low status of women was not a matter of outdated customs but a continuing feature of modern society.

During the long hiatus in the power of feminism, between World War I and the 1960s, one historian, Mary Beard (1876–1958), produced a rather different interpretation of women's social and political role. Beard's thesis, described in her 1946 book *Woman as Force in History*, was that women have always been a major, if unrecognized, power in the construction of society and culture. Her point of view was an advance over that of the old "contributions" school because she was discussing the contributions of ordinary women, not exceptional heroines or wives of great men; but unlike the Progressive era's social scientists, she emphasized women's influence as well as their subordination. When women's historians of the late 1960s and 1970s rediscovered and reclaimed their historical legacy, they repeated the pendulum swing, emphasizing first women's victimization, then their activism or "agency." Historian Gerda Lerner was influential in calling for a "woman-centered" history, and today the best historians have created a balanced portrayal of the interaction of women's oppression and women's power.

Women's historians usually approach their scholarship from a feminist perspective. The definition of "feminism" is contested and has changed throughout the history of the women's rights movement. I use it here, in its most inclusive and historical sense, to mean those who disapprove of women's subordinate status, who believe that women's disadvantaged position is not inevitable and can be changed, and who doubt the "objectivity" of history as it has been previously written in a male-dominated culture.[5] But just as the women's movement is composed of different tendencies, so has women's history become a field of debate as well as consensus. There are many "feminisms." The common denominator among women's historians is the insistence that gender must be an important category of analysis. Women's historians do not expect to agree or always to produce the answers expected by feminist political activists. They do, however, insist that scholarship take into account the different situations of men and women, and they criticize scholarship that draws its evidence exclusively from male sources and then interprets that evidence as representing the entire society.

No brief overview of women's history today could cover more than a selection of the best work (a broader scope is reflected in the bibliography). This essay offers a sampler, designed to indicate something of the range of the field, just as many eighteenth-century girls once embroidered designs that exhibited the many stitches they had learned. Following a summary of some major themes, I describe two particularly influential areas of new scholarship—first, historical changes in the concept of female gender, or "femininity"; and second, women's work—which will serve as examples of how the new historians have constructed a balance between women's victimization and women's power.

THEMES OF THE NEW WOMEN'S HISTORY

The central claim of the new women's history is that a focus on women not only adds to but alters earlier pictures of the past, exposing what was inaccurate and misleading in those depictions. There is no unified subject matter or unified approach in the new women's history, but several major themes have characterized much of the best work in the field. One is the question of "difference"—gender difference between women and men. By "gender" I mean the socially acquired characteristics of femaleness and maleness, as distinct from "sex," the biological attributes of women and men. The distinction between sex and gender is basic to all modern feminist critical thought, for it challenges assumptions that differences between women and men are "natural" and immutable. Historians have had to take on the double task of criticizing exaggerations of sexual difference, particularly characteristic of late eighteenth- and nineteenth-century thought, and identifying uniquely female modes of work, relationships, and thought where they do exist. The study of gender in women's history has begun to stimulate analysis also of the historical meanings of masculinity. This development, though embryonic, has already given rise to a controversy about whether a gender studies emphasis might provide the basis for yet another evasion of research and writing focused on women.[6]

A second theme of the new women's history redefines the word "difference" to emphasize the variety of women's experiences. It criticizes a tendency in historical scholarship, including that about women, to generalize from the experience of dominant class and racial groups. Historians have begun to reconstruct the experience of the least privileged women of our society—Native American, African American, Hispanic American, Asian American, immigrant, working-class, and farm women—and the results have altered or at least questioned older historical interpretations. Gerda Lerner led the way with her influential 1969 article "The Lady and the Mill Girl," calling attention to class differences in women's experience. Soon other women's historians laid out major challenges to the history of labor organizing by showing how male workers and their unions sometimes excluded women and fought to confine women workers to inferior and underpaid jobs. In immigration history, the failure to study women led to misleading generalizations, such as the notion that immigration eroded family ties. The most recent example of the exploration of diversity, perhaps, has been in western women's history. In its first decades the new women's history examined primarily East Coast sources but it has moved steadily westward to the Great Plains, the Rocky Mountains, the Southwest, and the Pacific, and in doing so has brought a greater variety of minority groups into the center of its attention. Women's history has been continuously self-critical of its own generalizations.

In undermining old generalizations, perhaps the richest single field has been African American women's history. Scholarship in this area has shown, for example, that black women by no means followed whites in accepting economic dependence on husbands as the only ideal; and that a combination of poverty, discrimination, and a unique African American culture honored women's labor and professional achievements. Historians have demonstrated that black women were deliberately excluded from many women's organizations, including women's rights and feminist groups. The questions historians ask in their scholarship always derives from the intellectual and political influences they themselves encounter; thus African American women's historians observed both about the contemporary and the historical women's movement that many groups conventionally referred to as "women's organizations" were really white women's organizations. On the basis of untold labor in interviewing, preserving personal papers, and exploring forgotten archives, historians have documented a broad and rich record of black women's activism and organization in the fields of health, welfare, religion, education, and civil rights. New studies of women have also produced different pictures of slave family life and of the economic basis of the system.

Third, women's historians have demonstrated how the exclusion of women from political and economic power was accomplished. There are remarkable continuities in the patterns thus revealed—such as the fact that the ratio of women's to men's wages (averaging fifty-nine cents to the dollar) has remained relatively constant for over a century; and the fact that as occupations rose in status, they tended to be taken over by men, as in the case of medicine. At the same time, there have been changes, and not always for the good: for example, from the eighteenth to the nineteenth century, the number of self-employed women operating farms and small businesses declined, and in the 1920s many professions had a higher proportion of women than they do today. Historians have also found substantial evidence that women now have more power in family life than they once did, because of divorce rights, birth control, maternal custody of children, and the delegitimation of wife beating. Babysitting and child-care centers are neither adequate nor fairly distributed, but they still represent important tools for women's autonomy.

The feminist analysis of political power has shown that it cannot be measured strictly by legal rights. Although women won equal legal rights with the suffrage amendment, only the renewed women's movement more than four decades later substantially increased their political participation and challenged legal and economic discrimination in education, insurance, employment, welfare benefits, and marriage and family law. Despite the concern with women's power and powerlessness, women's historians at first slighted political history—the development of legislation and judicial rulings affecting women. Few historians studied the women's-rights movement, for example. Instead, most women's historians focused on social, economic, and cultural matters, including work, health, sexuality, and relationships. Most recently, there has been a return to political history as women's historians pioneered a critique of the old division of the private from the public. First women's historians expanded the concept of the political—showing, for example, how some groups of women were able to influence state policy even before they were enfranchised. Women's historians today are among those active today in developing what is being called a "new political history," which seeks to examine the mutual influence of state policy and nongovernmental activities and ideologies.

Also among the challenges of the new women's history has been its focus on phenomena that were previously considered ahistorical or trivial. We have studies of friendship and love, birth control and child-birth, child-raising, prostitution, women's clubs, sexual activity, housework. These interests, plus the search for women of the past who have so often been apparently silent and invisible, have inspired creativity in finding evidence. Dolores Hayden used architectural blueprints to interpret the power relations in domestic life. Paula Giddings focused on a sorority and on black college newspapers to illuminate black women's activism. Several historians turned to social workers' case records to investigate domestic relations. Judith Leavitt used physicians' diaries to find evidence about women's behavior during childbirth. Many learned to map different groups of records upon each other in order to learn from the omissions.

WOMEN'S CULTURE, GENDER, AND SEXUALITY

One of the first areas to attract the new women's historians, and one that has yielded a rich harvest of reinterpretation, was the study of nineteenth-century norms of femininity: that is, the social and ideological construction of the female gender among elite whites. In the process of studying this construction, women's historians worked out much of their use of the concept of "gender," now perhaps the most basic building-block concept in women's history. Tracing how this examination of Victorian middle-class white femininity proceeded also illustrates the debate about "difference" and the transcendence of the exclusive emphases on women's victimization and on elite women.

In 1966 one of the first authors of the new wave of women's history, Barbara Welter, published "The Cult of True Womanhood," an account of how ministers and other male moralists attempted to impose an ideology of "true womanhood" in the mid-nineteenth century. They prescribed for women four virtues: piety, purity (meaning sexual purity), domesticity, and submissiveness. Welter's analysis did not include, but could have included, maternalism—the notion that women were uniquely destined for motherhood. This ideology defined, at least among the urban middle class, the borders of respectability for women and punished those who deviated by branding them "unfeminine." Welter showed that women were encouraged to internalize their subordination and that the notion of femininity served as a club to keep them in line. Her work historicized these ideologies, demonstrating that they were not eternal, had changed, and by implication could change yet again. Although Welter did not theorize the term "gender," historians now would describe her work as demonstrating how different meanings can be attached to sexual differences, both physical and social—and these meanings constitute what most scholars today mean by "gender."

The criticism stimulated by Welter's article is a mark of its great influence. First, it was criticized for using prescriptive literature (material prescribing how women *should* act, such as sermons) as evidence of how women *did* act. How do we know, some historians asked, that women really accepted this model of behavior? Few people actually behave in conformity to such ideal models. And some historians soon showed that many white privileged women did in fact deviate considerably from normative standards of "true womanhood." Consequently, by the mid-1970s many women's historians were drawing on the methods of the "new social history," emphasizing the search for more reliable evidence about how ordinary people actually lived and behaved.

In addition, other historians disputed the consequences of "true womanhood" for women. The first influential critique was implicit in Carroll Smith-Rosenberg's article "The Female World of Love and Ritual" (1975).[7] Welter had posited a system of rigidly separated male and female spheres, internalized through a set of rigidly gendered female virtues and imposed on women by moral authorities. Smith-Rosenberg, looking at another aspect of the same phenomenon, suggested that those separate spheres—particularly women's domesticity—gave women a space of their own, an autonomy. She showed the intense and fulfilling relationships women had with one another, and the control that women exercised over such familial rites of passage as births and deaths. Soon several other historians explicitly articulated this reinterpretation, challenging the simple victimization script and emphasizing women's own agency in the construction of their lives. In 1976 Linda Gordon's history of birth control showed that women's emphasis on the right to refuse their husbands' sexual demands was by no means simply an expression of prudishness and hostility to sex in general but a resistance to male sexual norms. It was part of a political demand raised by the feminist movement, an assertion of women's power and dignity in general and of reproductive control (then called "voluntary motherhood") in particular. In 1978 Nancy Cott, in "Passionlessness: An Interpretation of Victorian Sexual Ideology, 1790–1850," argued that women themselves had helped construct at least one of the four cardinal virtues cited by Welter: women promoted the notion of female purity as a means of empowerment, allowing them to claim a moral superiority to men.[8] Some historians began to speak of a special woman's culture, which included a specifically female style of perception, relationships, communication, and activism. Temma Kaplan's 1982 article about working-class women's economic struggles in Europe influenced many American historians with its concept of a "female consciousness," as distinct from a feminist consciousness: the latter is a critical political perspective, challenging existing gendered power relations, while female consciousness might accept such relations but nevertheless support greater respect and power for women within them.[9]

Around the women's culture idea arose a swirl of debate, however, because others feared that it tended to romanticize women's subordinate position—or gloss over the subordination altogether—and to deny women's aspirations to play a greater part in male culture, which after all dominated in all the spheres of power. Smith-Rosenberg's article provoked the criticism that such a benign story of how women had organized their "sphere" disguised the fact that the sphere was a kind of prison. Perhaps the concept of a "female world of love and ritual" romanticized virtues that were simply adaptations to the lack of political and economic rights. Perhaps it ignored the cost to women of being prevented from aspiring to other virtues—such as assertiveness, adventurousness, sexiness, and irreverence—or to a place in the public sphere.[10] Responding from a slightly different angle, Estelle Freedman looked at the implications of an autonomous female culture for women's political power. In "Separatism as Strategy," she argues that women's insistence on separate organizations and institutions, such as women's colleges, has given them a basis of power and self-development that they lost when they fought instead for integration into institutions dominated by men.[11]

Yet another critique of generalizations about women's culture was that they did not apply, or not in the same way, to women of minority groups, to the poor, to farm women, to lesbians—and when one added up the exclusions they constituted the majority of women! Both sides of the debate had been at first guilty of treating the experience of privileged women as universal. Nevertheless, a new theoretical premise had emerged from this tangle of related works—that gender and a separate female culture had not been simply imposed on women but created by men and women both; and that the degree of women's separateness from men was itself variable, representing the results both of domination and of resistance to it. Collectively, historians engaged in this debate demonstrated the multifaceted nature of femininity, its function simultaneously in women's oppression and in women's struggle for autonomy. From the mid-1970s on, the best women's history has offered this complex view.

Work on nineteenth-century femininity also developed in another direction, toward a preliminary history of women's sexuality. Welter's work had implied that women accepted a sense of themselves as less lustful than men. Cott had suggested that women used "passionlessness" as an ideological base for increasing political power. Gordon's history of birth control had showed that for nineteenth-century feminists, the right to limit their pregnancies was fused with the right to say no to husbands' sexual demands; that before women could "find" their own sexual yearnings, they had to get themselves out from under the wifely obligation to submit to men on demand. The feminist tradition had always contained two currents of thought about sexuality—one prudish, but another asserting women's right to sexual pleasure and to defining their own sexual needs independently of male desire or reproductive purpose.[12]

In the historical discussion of sexuality, as in the discussion of gender, the same controversies emerged regarding differences between the sexes and the effectiveness of attempts to make "respectable" women actually conform to official standards of behavior and feeling. The earlier work tended to assume that Victorian sexual repression had actually created asexual identities in women. Gordon and Cott questioned whether the model of repression was right in assuming that male sexual appetite was the norm of "natural" human yearnings. If, as nineteenth-century feminists charged, men had become "oversexed" as a result of the pressures of a cult of true manhood, was it not possible that the female style of lesser sexual drive was the "natural" one—or, more likely, that there is no such thing as a natural human sexuality, since sexuality exists only in contexts of the cultural norms that form it?

Then a challenge emerged from another perspective, based on new evidence: that Victorian women may not have been so sexually quiescent after all. Since there are very few data on the actual sexual behavior of the period, historians had to be reminded once again not to rely on prescriptive literature for their evidence. Carl Degler found one turn-of-the-century physician-sexologist who reported that many "Victorian" women claimed frequent orgasms.[13] Thus, in the work on sexuality the quintessential debate among women's historians reemerges in slightly different form: are women molded or have they been able to create their own identities? The answer, it is now clear, will be—both.

The works cited above focused primarily on heterosexual sexual relations, but Smith-Rosenberg's examination of women's friendships uncovered relationships whose emotional intensity and physical intimacy seemed to the late twentieth-century reader like lesbianism. The discussion about whether these nineteenth-century relationships should be called lesbian had several dimensions. One was definitional: was lesbianism a name to be applied only to sex between women, or should nonsexual but emotionally loving relations be called lesbian? If the latter, then how were married women with beloved women friends to be distinguished from unmarried women who formed lifelong partnerships with other women? In the nineteenth century, intense female friendships, expressed verbally and physically, were considered proper, even conventional, and were in no way in conflict with heterosexual marriage. Then, as historian Nancy Sahli first showed, the turn-of-the-century heterosexual "sexual revolution" stigmatized such homosexual (or homosocial) relationships, reinterpreting them as juvenile crushes, and insisting that women "grow out" of them. In the 1920s heterosexual dating became the norm for teenagers. Devaluing female friendship, as Christina Simmons showed, experts began to advocate "companionate marriage" as an ideal in which husbands and wives were to be each other's best friends and to build an emotional intensity and intimacy that had not been normative in Victorian marriage.[14]

This development stripped the "camouflage" from women who were attracted to other women, depriving their intense female friendship of legitimacy and labeling their attachments "deviant." The most important factor in the development of modern lesbianism was women's wage labor and the possibility of supporting themselves without dependence on men. Gradually over the first half of this century, some women-loving women began to take on a separate identity as lesbians and to reject marriage. (And today, at the end of this century, some lesbians are beginning to reclaim marriage and to insist on redefining it in a way that can encompass lesbian relationships.) We see here a vivid example of how similar or even identical behaviors—love affairs between women—took on vastly different social (and therefore personal) meanings over a century's time. Most recently, Madeline Davis and Elizabeth Kennedy, in their history of the lesbian community of Buffalo, used oral history to take a close look at the evolution of a lesbian sexual and social subculture. They showed how "closet" lesbians, fearing persecution, constructed a new kind of community for themselves by frequenting bars, laying the basis for the lesbian liberation movement of the 1970s. Davis and Kennedy also found that the conditions allowing lesbians to reject marriage and "come out" included employment opportunities and thus the possibility of economic independence from men.

WOMEN HAVE ALWAYS WORKED

In labor history, one of the largest subfields of women's history, the controversies about women's "difference" and the balance between their victimization and assertion have been worked out in slightly different ways. In identifying and interpreting women's work, women's labor historians proceeded less through debate than through a collective process similar to an archeological dig: they exposed individual artifacts of the buried past and then hazarded guesses at the design of the whole edifice.[15]

Studies of women's labor began with the task of dispelling the notion, dating from the Victorian era, that women did not work. This delusion derived, first, from the white and elite bias that took as typical the lives of a minority of prosperous housewives who employed servants. It grew also from the Victorian norm that hard work was unfeminine, a norm that made child care and housework invisible as forms of labor; they appeared rather as emanations of love and of a female nestmaking that was instinctual, not learned or laborious. Historians have demonstrated that the majority of American women did not lead privileged lives and that all except the most wealthy women worked. Before the current revival of feminist scholarship, historians of labor who mentioned women usually limited themselves to documenting the segregation of paid women workers into low-status, low-wage jobs. More recent women's labor historians have confirmed this picture but have produced a far more complex overview. They stress the variety of women's unpaid but essential labor: housework, farm labor, needlework, healing, cooking, child-raising, baby-sitting. For example, at the beginning of the nineteenth century, factories made only 65,000 yards of cloth a year, as compared to 230,000 produced in women's homes.[16] Once "work" became defined as wage labor—a process defined notably by Jeanne Boydston—women were widely considered to be part of the nonlaboring population, so that historians had to be virtual detectives to seek out the true division of labor. Women's work was often unrecognized as such even by the women themselves. Virginia Yans-McLaughlin discovered that many women who told census-takers they were not employed were in fact contributing not marginally but substantially to the family economy. So strong became the norm that adult women were not to be employed that even when women were active as wage laborers they were often overlooked by their contemporaries and by historians.

The increasing recognition that women's labor has always been indispensable to the economy raised several interpretive questions. What exactly was the impact of capitalism and then industrialization on women? It soon appeared to be more uneven, complex, and sometimes indirect than on men. Who was to blame for women's inferior position in the labor market? The new evidence quickly revealed how employers profited by hiring women for lower wages than they would have had to pay men and by using women workers to divide and thus weaken the collective efforts of workers. But the evidence also suggested that women's "dual role" or "double day"—their primary responsibility for domestic labor—made them less committed to wage labor. For many women workers, even those who had full-time jobs, household labor responsibilities always loomed larger both in time demands and in emotional importance. Another line of inquiry raised critical questions about the influence of male workers in holding women at the bottom of the labor market. Still another debate concerned the overall impact of women's entrance into the labor force. Did it reduce the differences between the sexes? If so, did that affect further the cause of sexual equality? These questions are still being debated but the vibrant field of women's labor history has amassed evidence and interpretations that have greatly raised the level of the debate over what it was twenty-five years ago.

At one time it appeared that women might become a dominant part of the industrial working class. At the beginning of the nineteenth century, when the first factories began to produce textiles, women were in the majority among the 4 percent of U.S. citizens who worked in manufacturing. Women working in the early New England textile mills—the "mill girls"—were a favorite subject of historians for some time, their factory jobs interpreted to support a view of women's labor experiences as unique and marginal. Virtually all were unmarried teenagers or young women, daughters of farmers who were motivated simultaneously by a need to help their families economically and a desire to escape the narrow constraints of their farm homes. In the textile towns of Massachusetts and New Hampshire they lived in boardinghouses and created for themselves something resembling a college dorm experience—a premarriage interlude of relative freedom. They were a remarkably well-educated group of workers who felt socially and culturally the equal of their employers. But more revisionist history has shown, by contrast, that in many ways their experience was typically proletarian. Contrary to the claims of the mill owners, the mill girls were severely exploited, putting in fourteen- to sixteen-hour days in terrible working conditions for very low pay. They quickly became militant in their demands for better pay and conditions, creating not only wildcat strikes but the beginnings of labor organization. They had some grievances unique to women—notably sexual harassment—but they also fought speedups and arbitrary foremen and dangerous conditions, just as men have done.[17]

The important role of women as factory workers in the early stages of industrialization in this country was, however, an aberration. In contrast to the pattern in Europe, where poor women continued to be a major part of the industrial working class, in the United States the vast majority of women never worked at industrial jobs outside their homes. For employed women of all groups, the most common jobs were service and clerical, not industrial. As late as 1940 the most common women's occupation was domestic service. One of the richest areas of women's history in the last two decades has been the study of the millions of women doing the common "women's jobs"—typists and other clerical workers, waitresses, retail saleswomen, prostitutes, seamstresses, librarians, social workers, nurses, midwives, schoolteachers, and, of course, domestic servants.

One reason women did not continue to enter industrial employment in large numbers is that male workers did not want them. Both as husbands and as employees, men worked to protect their privileges as heads of family (that is, as the suppliers of money) and their monopoly on the better jobs. Labor historians such as Ava Baron have made some of the best contributions to the new field of the history of masculinity in demonstrating how fundamental work identities have been to men, how men often define manhood partly in terms of their skill, mastery, or employment status, so that their efforts to exclude women from their own job categories could be extremely determined indeed. Women's historians and feminist economists have shown that the very concepts of and measurements of labor skills have encoded masculinity. Comparable worth investigations of the 1970s revealed that many women's jobs of greater difficulty than men's, requiring greater training than men's, such as preschool teacher, were systematically ranked much lower than male jobs such as janitor.

Women's historians, scrutinizing critically the history of labor unions, questioned an old belief among unionists and labor historians that women made poor unionists: that they were hard to organize and became unreliable union members because they viewed themselves as temporary workers and would accept substandard wages. Reconstructing the history of two periods of intense union activity, 1905–20 and 1932–45, women's labor historians found no evidence for such a notion and substantial evidence to the contrary: women workers had a sterling record of militance and perseverance in labor struggles.

The fact remains that even in relation to the low proportion of male workers who were unionized in the United States, women had lower rates of unionization. In seeking explanations, women's historians developed a second criticism of unions: that union members themselves, and often the union leaders officially, sometimes worked against the organization of women. Alice Kessler-Harris has argued this vividly, pointing out that because many unions functioned like men's clubs, their members felt, partly unconsciously, that a female presence would have a chilling effect on their camaraderie. Economist Heidi Hartmann pointed to the benefits men got from excluding women. Many unionists actively tried to keep women out, even though unionizing women would have protected male workers against wage reductions. And the sexual harassment, from both supervisors and male co-workers, that has been a consistent grievance of working women for at least 150 years also made women feel unwelcome in "men's" jobs.[18]

Women's employment did not necessarily reduce gender difference or promote women's rights. The new women's history found that the transformations effected by industrialism were limited by the tenacity of many aspects of the sexual division of labor. There has been remarkably little change in the assignment of child care, cooking, cleaning, and general homemaking responsibility to women. Nonetheless, the content and meanings of the sexual division of labor did change substantially. For example, the ideal of the "family wage"—the premise that men should be able to earn alone enough to support a family—turned out to be more myth than reality. There was never a time in U.S. history when most working-class men could earn enough to become the sole providers for their families.[19] Yet the family-wage premise purveyed a popular notion of housewives as idle, masking the vital contributions of women to the family economy.[20] It affirmed the association of femininity with dependence. The prosperous, urban "home"—no longer a place of production or labor but, with respect to the economy, merely a parlor and bedrooms, the scene of women's and children's isolation from power—became the idealized home for all.

Yet women continued to contribute to the family economy, adapting to the new urban setting their rural strategies for adding to the family income. In smaller cities they long continued to raise and sell chickens, eggs, and vegetables; in Muncie, Indiana, in the early 1920s, 40 to 60 percent of families had their own vegetable gardens. Everywhere women delivered babies, took in laundry and ironing, minded children for disabled or employed women, manufactured and sold home brew and spirits, peddled, saved, and pawned. Between 20 and 30 percent of mid-nineteenth-century women took in paying boarders. Among early twentieth-century immigrant women the figure reached over 50 percent—and immigrants represented the majority of the working class in the big eastern cities at that time. Keeping boarders was not simply renting space; it meant cooking and cleaning for them, doing their laundry and sewing, and, not least, looking after them emotionally. In other words, it was hard labor, however unrecognized. Moreover, in the nineteenth century many working-class mothers could remain at home only because their children worked. (Later, the increase in married women's employment was to a considerable degree the way families made up for the loss of family income resulting from compulsory education and the prohibition on child labor.)

Many mothers, too, did industrial work at home. Women's history has required the revision of one of the major previous understandings of the impact of industrialism, that it removed production from the household. In certain industries, notably garment and hat manufacture, mechanization actually increased the demand for hand finishing, and contractors farmed out this work to women in their homes. Many of the poorest urban women did this industrial piecework—called home-work—because it enabled them to earn while minding their children. Manufacturers used homework to increase their profits: it cost them no overhead or workers' benefits, and the home workers put in the longest hours in the worst conditions for the lowest pay of any industrial work-ers. Home workers' isolation from other workers made it harder for them to organize or be organized into unions. (Recent efforts to deregu-late such work foreshadow similar mixed effects: many women wel-come a chance to be able to earn while staying at home, but renewed homework will certainly lower wages and worsen working conditions.)

Women's work, then, was substantially transformed by industrial-ism, without any noticeable convergence between men's and women's work experience. Women who combined housework, child care, and income-producing work, putting in eighteen-hour days, were as much the characteristic laborers of industrial society as were miners, construc-tion workers, and factory hands. Women's history thus requires a re-definition of who the working class is.

Historian Leslie Woodcock Tentler argued that the prevailing ideol-ogy that woman's true place was at home and that domesticity meant idleness influenced women workers themselves. Well into the twentieth century the typical woman worker was young, unmarried, and childless; she regarded work as a mere interlude between school and marriage. Furthermore, Tentler argued, the age segregation of most female jobs—by and large, young women were separated from older—meant that the unmarried workers did not learn about the unromantic, unleisured real-ities of marriage and motherhood. Tentler's findings imply that women's preference for domesticity reflected their indoctrination by a romantic ideology. Other evidence suggests, however, that terrible working condi-tions gave most working-class women a real, material reason to prefer housework. Tentler's argument elicited criticism that once again re-vealed the diversity of women's experience.

For no group of women was the ideology of the nonlaboring woman such a falsehood as for African Americans. The scholarship on this question creates some of the sharpest challenges to conventional historical understanding. For slave women as for men, the right balance between victimization and resistance is much in debate. The historiogra-phy of slave women, like the general history of slavery, began by em-phasizing the cruelties experienced and the damage done. At first the focus was on women's sexual and reproductive exploitation and on the "destruction" of black families in the slave system.[21] Even sympathetic histories ignored the importance of slave women's labor to the planta-tion economy. But Jacqueline Jones and Deborah White have detailed the heavy labor required of slave women: not only were they responsible for field- and housework for their masters, but the family life of the slaves also depended on women's labor—after the hours owed the master—in cooking, spinning, weaving, sewing, cleaning, nursing, child care, educating. In the 1970s Herbert Gutman demonstrated black resistance in defending family ties against slavery, and several black feminist scholars have explored the possibility that slave women's strong confidence in themselves as workers may also have enabled them to build a culture of resistance.

Historians have found different labor patterns among black and white working-class women as well as among middle-class women. Higher proportions of African-American mothers of all classes have worked outside their homes. Black women have faced a doubled labor-market discrimination and have had access only to the lowest-paying and least desirable jobs: for poor black women this has meant mainly domestic service, industrial cleaning, laundry, meat-packing, field labor. Yet at the same time, higher proportions of black than of white women have been professionals, especially in teaching, social work, and the other helping professions. And higher proportions of black families have been female-headed. There is less consensus, however, about the causes of these differences. Is the legacy of slavery mainly responsible, or post-slavery institutionalized racism? Do the differences result mainly from victimization or from the resistance to it? The answers must avoid assuming that high levels of female employment and single-mother families are always bad. It seems likely that the situation of black women is a result of both oppression and resistance and that they have reason for pride as well as bitterness in interpreting their history: their successes have often been the result of adaptation to adversity, of learning that they had only themselves to rely on, of shouldering a greater share of family and community burdens than they might have chosen.

Scholarship on many other racial/ethnic groups is still very scarce. What exists shows a complex pattern. In some ways, the diversity of women's labor experience seems to rest on substantial commonalities. For women of all backgrounds, industrialization often meant migration from farm to city and some loss of extended family and community. For transoceanic immigrants, world-scale industrialization meant the impoverishment of certain areas (such as southern and eastern Europe), flight to the New World, and sharp breaks with kinfolk and tradition. Their conditions of life and labor created important common experiences among all immigrants: saving money to send to the old country, attempting to reunite family members, establishing mutual aid societies. And they created common problems: generational conflicts as the youth became "Americanized" faster than their parents, increased desertion by fathers, and high rates of single motherhood.

Yet in some ethnic groups behaviors differed sharply. Hasia Diner has identified among Irish American women's expectations, brought from Ireland, of late marriage and economic independence. These expectations help explain, for example, their disproportionate representation both as domestics and as labor organizers, positions that might at first seem opposed. Many historians have attributed Jewish immigrant women's readiness to seek employment and education at least in part to their primarily urban backgrounds in Europe and the tradition of male dedication to religious study. By contrast, the greater paternalism of Italian men, and traditions of strong chaperonage of women's fidelity, kept Italian women more homebound. Still, Elizabeth Ewen's *Immigrant Women in the Land of Dollars,* which compares Jewish and Italian women in New York at the beginning of the twentieth century, shows that despite the virtually complete separation of ethnic neighborhoods, the universal impact of the money economy had far outweighed cultural tradition by the second generation.

In the last half-century the homogenization of the white ethnic groups was accelerated by trends in patterns of women's labor. Many white working-class women were pulled out of their ethnically homogeneous neighborhoods into "downtown" jobs (and schooling as preparation for jobs). This experience involved two related processes: a massive increase in the numbers of women who worked, and a shift in where they worked. These two developments were connected in both cause and effect, and the resultant new conditions of work have been the subject of excellent historical studies. Several historians have turned their attention to the new women's jobs of the early part of this century—nurse, secretary, retail store clerk, telephone operator. "Feminization" studies have looked at jobs that changed gender—such as clerical work, which was predominantly male in the last century—and challenged the view that women "chose" their inferior jobs. The shift in the gender of certain occupations from male to female virtually always reduced their status and pay. Moreover, despite the universal sex segregation of the labor market, studies show how quickly the sex-typing of jobs can be changed when profits depend on it.

Studies of these new types of jobs reveal the variety of working-class experience, implicitly criticizing the image of *the* worker as male and blue-collar. This image derives not only from men's experience exclusively but also from that of a relatively small number of skilled workers. Studies of "pink-collar workers" (waitresses, beauticians, and so on) and domestic and clerical workers have expanded our sense of what the working class is and how it behaves. Studies of department store clerks by Susan Porter Benson, cannery workers by Vicki Ruiz, waitresses by

Dorothy Sue Cobble, and domestic servants by Tera Hunter and Evelyn Nakano Glenn found intense and effective solidarity, resistance, militance, and often self-organization, challenging the tendency to look primarily to men in heavy industry for labor leadership.

The cumulative effect of job transformation, however, has not been to lessen sex segregation. The large-scale economic transformation of the United States from a primarily industrial to a primarily service and bureaucratic economy has drawn millions of women into the labor force but kept them mainly in jobs earmarked as female. When women first entered the labor force, they were often doing paid work for strangers that they had once done free for family and friends—weaving, sewing, caring for children, nursing, and generally nurturing. With more people working outside their homes, still more of the services once performed without pay—mainly by women—in home or community have become commercial. More people eat food in restaurants, buy ready-to-wear clothing, shop in markets, pay for entertainment, and all these enterprises hire service workers, primarily women. Further, as corporations conglomerate and grow, clerical work increases geometrically, and women are hired to do it. Because the labor market remains extremely segregated by sex, women's employment by no means entails entry into a "male world." Nor has the ratio of women's to men's wages improved much as the proportion of women working has grown. There is little evidence of overall improvement in women's employment status.

The new female service jobs have been created much more rapidly than new jobs for men in the manufacturing sector. At the same time, men's real wages (wages measured in terms of buying power) relative to community standards of living have fallen in this century, so that more families need the wages of two adults. Thus the female labor force is very different from what it used to be. When the early twentieth-century pattern of girls working briefly between school and marriage could no longer supply the labor needs of the growing economy, married women were pulled into the labor force. In 1890, 5 percent of all married women were in the labor force; in 1987, 56 percent. (Twenty-three percent of black married women worked in 1890, more than ten times the white rate of 2 percent; by 1980 the figure for black women was 48 percent, only 12 percent more than the white rate.) The typical woman worker of the nineteenth century was single, an immigrant, and a garment, factory, or domestic service worker. Today's typical female worker is married, has schoolage children, and works as a waitress or saleswoman or in a clerical post. Today most young women expect to be employed virtually all their lives; wage labor is no longer a mere interlude.

CONCLUSION

Both areas of women's history discussed here—nineteenth-century gender, labor—confront similar questions. Historians have argued both the values of women's unique qualities and the function of those traits in constricting women's options and holding them in a subordinate position. Historians have debated also the origin of norms of the feminine—how they were constructed, to what extent they have been imposed on women, to what extent invented by women. Moreover, historians have found evidence both of cross-cultural and transhistorical patterns in women's experience and of immense diversity in women's experiences—by class, race, ethnic group, religion, sexual orientation, family status—indeed, by a probably endless variety of factors. Moreover, this diversity is by no means composed only of benign differences; some groups of women have dominated and exploited other groups of women. The field of women's history has neither consensus nor much desire for one. Indeed, the exploration, doubting, and challenging of previous conclusions is pervasive. This is clearly related to the fact that the subjects of women's history—women—are themselves changing fast, discovering new possibilities in themselves and for themselves, redefining their individual versions of what it is to be a woman.

NOTES

Only works *not* listed in the bibliography are fully cited in the notes.

1. See, e.g., Donald Mathews, "Women's History/Everyone's History," in Hilah F. Thomas and Rosemary Skinner Keller, eds., *Women in New Worlds: Historical Perspectives on the Wesleyan Tradition* (Nashville, Tenn.: Abingdon, 1981), 33–34. I am grateful to Joyce Follet for this reference.

2. Barbara Leslie Epstein, *The Politics of Domesticity: Women, Evangelism, and Temperance in Nineteenth-Century America* (Middletown, Conn.: Wesleyan University Press, 1981), 109–10; Elizabeth Pleck, "Feminist Responses to 'Crimes against Women,' 1868–1896," *Signs* 8, no. 3 (1983): 451–70; and Gordon, *Heroes of Their Own Lives.*

3. For samples of this popular writing in nonfiction, see Clara Laughlin, *The Work-a-Day Girl* (1913); Dorothy Richardson, *The Long Day* (1905); Josephine Donovan, *The Woman Who Waits* (1920) and *The Saleslady* (1929). Mary Antin's *The Promised Land* (1912) is an excellent example of an autobiography; Anzia Yezierska's *Breadgivers* (1925) is a powerful novel of this sort.

4. The best histories produced in this period appeared, however, in Europe—notably Alice Clark's analysis of the impact of capitalism on women's work, *Working Life of Women in the Seventeenth Century* (1919; New York: Augustus M. Kelley, 1968).

5. Historians disagree about the best way to define "feminism." Nancy Cott, in her *Grounding of Modern Feminism*, prefers to use the term in a more historically specific way, referring to a new vision of women's place arising in the early twentieth century, one that included an affirmation of economic independence as a goal for women.

6. For a discussion of this issue, see the women's history journal *Gender and History* 1, no. 1 (1989), esp. the editorial (pp. 1–6), and Gisela Bock's "Women's History and Gender History: Aspects of an International Debate," 7–30.

7. This article has been reprinted in several anthologies, including Smith-Rosenberg, *Disorderly Conduct*, 53–76; and Cott and Pleck, *Heritage of Her Own*, 311–42.

8. In Cott and Pleck, *Heritage of Her Own*.

9. Temma Kaplan, "Female Consciousness and Collective Action: The Case of Barcelona, 1910–1918," *Signs* 7, no. 3 (1982): 545–66.

10. See "Politics and Culture in Women's History: A Symposium," *Feminist Studies* 6, no. 2 (1980): 28–64.

11. Estelle B. Freedman, "Separatism as Strategy: Female Institution Building and American Feminism, 1870–1930," *Feminist Studies* 5, no. 3 (1979): 512–29.

12. In addition to Gordon's *Woman's Body, Woman's Right*, see DuBois and Gordon, "Seeking Ecstasy on the Battlefield."

13. Carl Degler, "What Ought to Be and What Was: Women's Sexuality in the Nineteenth Century," *American Historical Review* 79, no. 5 (1974): 1467–90.

14. Nancy Sahli, "Smashing: Women's Friendships before the Fall," *Chrysalis* 8 (summer 1979); Christina Simmons, "Companionate Marriage and Lesbian Threat," *Frontiers* 4, no. 3 (1979): 54–59.

15. For a collection of documents on women's work in U.S. history, see Baxandall and Gordon, *America's Working Women*.

16. Mary Ryan, *Womanhood in America*, 3d ed. (New York: Franklin Watts, 1983), 75. This is an excellent textbook but out of print.

17. Thomas Dublin, *Women at Work: The Transformation of Work and Community in Lowell, Massachusetts. 1826–1860* (New York: Columbia University Press, 1979); Jonathan Prude, *The Coming of Industrial Order: Town and Factory Life in Rural Massachusetts, 1810–1860* (New York: Cambridge University Press, 1983); Lise Vogel, "Hearts to Feel and Tongues to Speak: New England Mill Women in the Early Nineteenth Century," in Milton Cantor and Bruce Laurie, eds., *Class, Sex, and The Woman Worker* (Westport, Conn.: Greenwood Press, 1977), 64–82.

18. Kessler-Harris, "Where Are the Organized Women Workers?" Heidi Hartmann, "Capitalism, Patriarchy, and Job Segregation by Sex," in Zillah Eisenstein, ed., *Capitalist Patriarchy and the Case for Socialist Feminism* (New York: Monthly Review Press, 1979), 206–47; Mary Bularzik. "Sexual Harassment at the Workplace: Historical Notes," in James Green, ed., *Workers' Struggles, Past and Present: A "Radical America" Reader* (Philadelphia: Temple University Press, 1983), 117–35.

19. A good summary of the references on this point is in Winifred D. Wandersee, *Women's Work and Family Values, 1920–1940* (Cambridge, Mass.: Harvard University Press, 1981), 141 n.2.

20. Martha May, "Bread before Roses: American Workingmen, Labor Unions, and the Family Wage," in Milkman, *Women, Work, and Protest*, 1–21.

21. Angela Davis, *Women, Race, and Class* (New York: Random House, 1981).

BIBLIOGRAPHY

There are hundreds of books and thousands of articles on U.S. women's history. To make this list useful to a wide audience, I have been highly selective and have excluded biographies, specialized monographs, and most anthologies and articles.

Surveys

Albers, Patricia, and Beatrice Medicine, eds. *The Hidden Half: Studies of Plains Indian Women*. Washington, D.C.: University Press of America, 1983.

Armitage, Susan, and Elizabeth Jameson, eds. *The Women's West*. Norman: University of Oklahoma Press, 1987.

Baker, Paula. "The Domestication of Politics: Women and American Political Society, 1780–1920." In Linda Gordon, ed., *Women, the State, and Welfare*. Madison: University of Wisconsin Press, 1990.

Banner, Lois. *In Full Flower: Aging Women, Power, and Sexuality: A History*. New York: Random House, 1992.

Baron, Ava, ed. *Work Engendered: Toward a New History of American Labor*. Ithaca, N.Y.: Cornell University Press, 1991.

Baxandall, Rosalyn, and Linda Gordon, eds. *America's Working Women: A Documentary History*. New York: Random House, 1976. 2d ed., revised, 1990.

Cott, Nancy F., and Elizabeth H. Pleck, eds. *A Heritage of Her Own: Towards a New Social History of American Women*. New York: Simon & Schuster, 1979.

Del Castillo, Adelaida R., ed. *Between Borders: Essays on Mexicana/Chicana History*. Encino, Calif.: Floricanto Press, 1990.

DuBois, Ellen Carol, and Vicki L. Ruiz, eds. *Unequal Sisters: A Multicultural Reader in U.S. Women's History*. 2d ed. New York: Routledge, 1994.

Etienne, Mona, and Eleanor Leacock, eds. *Women and Colonization: Anthropological Perspectives*. New York: Praeger, 1979. (Includes four of the best historical articles on Native American women.)

Evans, Sara M. *Born for Liberty: A History of Women in America*. New York: Free Press, 1989.

Giddings, Paula. *When and Where I Enter: The Impact of Black Women on Race and Sex in America*. New York: Bantam Books, 1984.

Gordon, Linda. *Woman's Body, Woman's Right: A Social History of Birth Control in America*. New York: Penguin, 1976. 2d ed., 1990.

Groneman, Carol, and Mary Beth Norton, eds. *"To Toil the Livelong Day": America's Women at Work, 1780–1960*. Ithaca, N.Y.: Cornell University Press, 1987.

Harley, Sharon, and Rosalyn Terborg-Penn, eds. *The Afro-American Woman: Struggles and Images.* Port Washington, N.Y.: Kennikat Press, 1978.

Hewitt, Nancy, and Suzanne Lebsock, eds. *Visible Women: New Essays on American Activism.* Urbana: University of Illinois Press, 1993.

Hine, Darlene Clark, Wilma King, and Linda Reed, eds. *"We Specialize in the Wholly Impossible": A Reader in Black Women's History.* New York: Carlson, 1995.

Jensen, Joan M., and Sue Davidson, eds. *A Needle, a Bobbin, a Strike: Women Needleworkers in America.* Philadelphia: Temple University Press, 1984.

Jensen, Joan M., and Darlis A. Miller, eds. *New Mexico Women: Intercultural Perspectives.* Albuquerque: University of New Mexico Press, 1986.

Jones, Jacqueline. *Labor of Love, Labor of Sorrow: Black Women, Work, and the Family from Slavery to the Present.* New York: Basic Books, 1985.

Kerber Linda, Alice Kessler-Harris, and Kathryn Kish Sklar, eds. *U.S. History as Women's History: New Feminist Essays.* Chapel Hill: University of North Carolina Press, 1995.

Kerber, Linda, and Jane Sherron De Hart, eds. *Women's America: Refocusing the Past.* 4th ed. New York: Oxford University Press, 1995.

Kessler-Harris, Alice. *Out to Work: A History of Wage-Earning Women in the United States.* New York: Oxford University Press, 1982.

Leavitt, Judith Walzer. *Brought to Bed: Child-Bearing in America, 1750–1950.* New York: Oxford University Press, 1986.

———, ed. *Women and Health in America: Historical Readings.* Madison: University of Wisconsin Press, 1984. Revised, 1996.

Lerner, Gerda, ed. *Black Women in White America: A Documentary History.* New York: Pantheon, 1972.

Matthews, Glenna. *The Rise of Public Woman: Woman's Power and Woman's Place in the United States, 1630–1970.* New York: Oxford University Press, 1992.

Milkman, Ruth, ed. *Women, Work, and Protest: A Century of U.S. Women's Labor History.* Boston: Routledge & Kegan Paul, 1985.

Mirande, Alfredo, and Evangelina Enriquez. *La Chicana: The Mexican-American Woman.* Chicago: University of Chicago Press, 1983.

Mora, Magdelena, and Adelaida R. Del Castillo, eds. *Mexican Women in the United States: Struggles Past and Present.* Los Angeles: University of California Chicano Studies Research Center, 1980.

Pico Vidal, Isabel. "The History of Women's Struggle for Equality in Puerto Rico." In June Nash and Helen Icken Safa, eds., *Sex and Class in Latin America.* South Hadley, Mass.: Bergin & Garvey, 1980.

Rosenberg, Rosalind. *Beyond Separate Spheres: The Intellectual Roots of Modern Feminism.* New Haven, Conn.: Yale University Press, 1982.

Schlissel, Lillian, Vicki L. Ruiz, and Janice Monk, eds. *Western Women: Their Land, Their Lives.* Albuquerque: University of New Mexico Press, 1988.

Scott, Anne Firor. *Natural Allies: Women's Associations in American History.* Urbana: University of Illinois Press, 1991.

Solomon, Barbara Miller. *In the Company of Educated Women: A History of Women and Higher Education in America.* New Haven, Conn.: Yale University Press, 1985.

Strasser, Susan. *Never Done: A History of American Housework*. New York: Pantheon, 1982.

Wiener, Lynn Y. *From Working Girl to Working Mother: The Female Labor Force in the United States, 1820–1980*. Chapel Hill: University of North Carolina, 1985.

Colonial Period and Eighteenth Century

Brown, Kathleen M. *Good Wives, Nasty Wenches, and Anxious Patriarchs: Gender, Race, and Power in Colonial Virginia*. Chapel Hill: University of North Carolina Press, 1996.

Dayton, Cornelia Hughes. *Women before the Bar: Gender, Law, and Society in Connecticut, 1639–1789*. Chapel Hill: University of North Carolina Press, 1995.

Gutiérrez, Ramón A. *When Jesus Came, the Corn Mothers Went Away: Marriage, Sexuality, and Power in New Mexico, 1500–1846*. Stanford, Calif.: Stanford University Press, 1991.

Karlsen, Carol F. *The Devil in the Shape of a Woman: Witchcraft in Colonial New England*. New York: Norton, 1987.

Kerber, Linda K. *Women of the Republic: Intellect and Ideology in Revolutionary America*. Chapel Hill: University of North Carolina Press, 1980.

Norton, Mary Beth. *Founding Mothers and Fathers: Gendered Power and the Forming of American Society*. New York: Knopf, 1996.

———. *Liberty's Daughters: The Revolutionary Experience of American Women, 1750–1800*. Boston: Little, Brown, 1980.

Ulrich, Laurel Thatcher. *Good Wives: Images and Reality in the Lives of Women in Northern New England, 1658–1750*. New York: Oxford University Press, 1983.

———. *A Midwife's Tale: The Life of Martha Ballard. Based on Her Diary, 1785–1812*. New York: Vintage, 1991.

Nineteenth Century

Boydston, Jeanne. *Home and Work: Housework, Wages, and the Ideology of Labor in the Early Republic*. New York: Oxford University Press, 1990.

Cott, Nancy F. *The Bonds of Womanhood: "Woman's Sphere" in New England, 1780–1835*. New Haven, Conn.: Yale University Press, 1977.

Diner, Hasia. *Erin's Daughters in America: Irish Immigrant Women in the Nineteenth Century*. Baltimore, Md.: Johns Hopkins University Press, 1983.

DuBois, Ellen Carol. *Feminism and Suffrage: The Emergence of an Independent Women's Movement in America, 1848–1869*. Ithaca, N.Y.: Cornell University Press, 1978.

DuBois, Ellen Carol, and Linda Gordon. "Seeking Ecstasy on the Battlefield: Danger and Pleasure in Nineteenth-Century Feminist Thought." *Feminist Studies* 9 (1983): 7–25.

Dudden, Faye E. *Serving Women: Household Service in Nineteenth-Century America*. Middletown, Conn.: Wesleyan University Press, 1983.

Faragher, John Mack. *Women and Men on the Overland Trail*. New Haven, Conn.: Yale University Press, 1979.

Faust, Drew Gilpin. *Mothers of Invention: Women of the Slaveholding South in the American Civil War*. Chapel Hill: University of North Carolina Press, 1996.

Flexner, Eleanor. *Century of Struggle: The Woman's Rights Movement in the United States*. 1959. New York: Atheneum, 1970. (Still the best survey of the suffrage and women's movement, 1800–1920.)

Ginzberg, Lori D. *Women and the Work of Benevolence: Morality, Politics, and Class in the Nineteenth-Century United States*. New Haven, Conn.: Yale University Press, 1990.

Gonzalez, Deena. *Refusing the Favor: Spanish-Mexican Women of Santa Fé, 1820–1880*. Forthcoming.

Hewitt, Nancy A. *Women's Activism and Social Change: Rochester, New York, 1822–1872*. Ithaca, N.Y.: Cornell University Press, 1984.

Jensen, Joan. *Loosening the Bonds: Mid-Atlantic Farm Women, 1750–1850*. New Haven, Conn.: Yale University Press, 1986.

Lebsock, Suzanne. *The Free Women of Petersburg. Status and Culture in a Southern Town, 1784–1860*. New York: Norton, 1984.

Lerner, Gerda. "The Lady and the Mill Girl: Changes in the Status of Women in the Age of Jackson, 1800–1840." *Midcontinent American Studies Journal* 10 (spring 1969): 5–14. Reprinted in Cott and Peck, *A Heritage of Her Own*.

McCurry, Stephanie. *Masters of Small Worlds: Yeoman Households, Gender Relations, and the Political Culture of the Antebellum South Carolina Low Country*. New York: Oxford University Press, 1995.

Pascoe, Peggy. *Relations of Rescue: The Search for Female Moral Authority in the American West*. New York: Oxford University Press, 1990.

Ryan, Mary. *Cradle of the Middle Class: The Family in Oneida County, New York, 1790–1865*. New York: Cambridge University Press, 1981.

———. *Women in Public: From Banners to Ballots, 1825–1880*. Baltimore, Md.: Johns Hopkins University Press, 1990.

Scott, Anne Firor. *The Southern Lady: From Pedestal to Politics, 1830–1930*. Chicago: University of Chicago Press, 1970.

Smith-Rosenberg, Carroll. *Disorderly Conduct: Visions of Gender in Victorian America*. New York: Knopf, 1985. (A collection of essays.)

Stansell, Christine. *City of Women: Sex and Class in New York, 1789–1860*. New York: Knopf, 1986.

Welter, Barbara. "The Cult of True Womanhood, 1800–1860." In *Dimity Convictions*, 21–41. Athens: Ohio University Press, 1976.

White, Deborah Gray. *Ar'n't I a Woman? Female Slaves in the Plantation South*. New York: Norton, 1985.

Twentieth Century

Bederman, Gail. *Manliness and Civilization*. Chicago: University of Chicago Press, 1995.

Benson, Susan Porter. *Counter Cultures: Saleswomen, Managers, and Customers in American Department Stores, 1890–1940*. Urbana: University of Illinois Press, 1986.

Blackwelder, Julia Kirk. *Women of the Depression: Caste and Culture in San Antonio, 1929–1939*. College Station: Texas A&M University Press, 1984.

Boris, Eileen. *Home to Work: Motherhood and the Politics of Industrial Homework in the United States*. Cambridge: Cambridge University Press, 1994.

Boris, Eileen, and Cynthia R. Daniels, eds. *Homework: Historical and Contemporary Perspectives on Paid Labor at Home*. Urbana: University of Illinois Press, 1989.

Brumberg, Joan Jacobs. *Fasting Girls: The Emergence of Anorexia Nervosa as a Modern Disease*. Cambridge, Mass.: Harvard University Press, 1988.

Cahn, Susan K. *Coming On Strong: Gender and Sexuality in Twentieth-Century Women's Sport*. New York: Free Press, 1994.

Cameron, Ardis. *Radicals of the Worst Sort: Laboring Women in Lawrence, Massachusetts, 1860–1912*. Urbana: University of Illinois Press, 1993.

Chafe, William H. *The American Woman: Her Changing Social, Economic, and Political Roles, 1920–1970*. New York: Oxford University Press, 1972.

Cobble, Dorothy Sue. *Dishing It Out: Waitresses and Their Unions in the Twentieth Century*. Urbana: University of Illinois Press, 1991.

Cott, Nancy. *The Grounding of Modern Feminism*. New Haven, Conn.: Yale University Press, 1987.

Davies, Margery. *Woman's Place Is at the Typewriter: Office Work and Office Workers, 1870–1930*. Philadelphia: Temple University Press, 1982.

Davis, Madeline D., and Elizabeth Lapovsky Kennedy. *Boots of Leather, Slippers of Gold: The History of a Lesbian Community*. New York: Routledge, 1993.

De Hart, Jane Sherron, and Donald Mathews. *Sex, Gender, and the Politics of ERA: A State and the Nation*. New York: Oxford University Press, 1990.

Deutsch, Sarah. *No Separate Refuge: Culture, Class, and Gender on an Anglo-Hispanic Frontier in the American Southwest, 1880–1940*. New York: Oxford University Press, 1987.

Echols, Alice. *Daring to Be Bad: Radical Feminism in America, 1967–1975*. Minneapolis: University of Minnesota Press, 1989.

Evans, Sara. *Personal Politics: The Roots of Women's Liberation in the Civil Rights Movement and the New Left*. New York: Vintage, 1979.

Ewen, Elizabeth. *Immigrant Women in the Land of Dollars: Life and Culture on the Lower East Side, 1890–1925*. New York: Monthly Review Press, 1985.

Faderman, Lillian. *Odd Girls and Twilight Lovers: A History of Lesbian Life in Twentieth-Century America*. New York: Penguin, 1991.

Gilmore, Glenda. *Gender and Jim Crow*. Chapel Hill: University of North Carolina Press, 1996.

Glenn, Evelyn Nakano. *Issei, Nisei, War Bride: Three Generations of Japanese American Women in Domestic Service*. Philadelphia: Temple University Press, 1986.

Gonzalez, Rosalinda H. "Chicanas and Mexican Immigrant Families, 1920–1940: Women's Subordination and Family Exploitation." In Lois Scharf and Joan M. Jensen, eds., *Decades of Discontent: The Women's Movement, 1920–1940*. Westport, Conn.: Greenwood Press, 1983.

Gordon, Linda. *Heroes of Their Own Lives: The Politics and History of Family Violence, Boston, 1880–1960*. New York: Penguin, 1988.

———. *Pitied but Not Entitled: Single Mothers and the History of Welfare*. New York: Free Press and Harvard University Press, 1994.

Hartmann, Susan M. *The Home Front and Beyond: American Women in the 1940s.* Boston: Twayne, 1982.

Higginbotham, Evelyn Brooks. *Righteous Discontent: The Women's Movement in the Black Baptist Church, 1880–1920.* Cambridge, Mass.: Harvard University Press, 1993.

Hine, Darlene Clark. *Black Women in White: Racial Conflict and Cooperation in the Nursing Profession, 1890–1950.* Bloomington: Indiana University Press, 1989.

Hunter, Tera. "Domination and Resistance: The Politics of Wage Household Labor." *Labor History* 34 (spring–summer 1993).

Kessler-Harris, Alice. "Where Are the Organized Women Workers?" *Feminist Studies* 3 (fall 1975): 92–110.

Kunzel, Regina. *Fallen Women, Problem Girls: Unmarried Mothers and the Professionalization of Social Work, 1890–1945.* New Haven, Conn.: Yale University Press, 1993.

Leavitt, Judith Walzer. *Typhoid Mary.* Boston: Beacon Press, 1996.

Matsumoto, Valerie. "Japanese-American Women during World War II." *Frontiers* 8 (1984).

May, Elaine Tyler. *Homeward Bound: American Families in the Cold War Era.* New York: Basic Books, 1988.

Meyer, Leisa. *Creating G.I. Jane: Sexuality and Power in the Women's Army Corps during World War Two.* New York: Columbia University Press, 1996.

Meyerowitz, Joanne J. *Women Adrift: Independent Wage Earners in Chicago, 1880–1930.* Chicago: University of Chicago Press, 1988.

———, ed. *Not June Cleaver: Women and Gender in Postwar America, 1945–1960.* Philadelphia: Temple University Press, 1994.

Muncy, Robyn. *Creating a Female Dominion in American Reform, 1890–1935.* New York: Oxford University Press, 1991.

Neth, Mary. *Preserving the Family Farm: Women, Community, and the Foundations of Agribusiness in the Midwest, 1900–1945.* Baltimore, Md.: Johns Hopkins University Press, 1995.

Neverdon-Morton, Cynthia. *Afro-American Women of the South and the Advancement of the Race, 1895–1925.* Knoxville: University of Tennessee Press, 1989.

Palmer, Phyllis. *Domesticity and Dirt: Housewives and Domestic Servants in the United States, 1920–1945.* Philadelphia: Temple University Press, 1989.

Peiss, Kathy. *Cheap Amusements: Working Women and Leisure in Turn-of-the-Century New York.* Philadelphia: Temple University Press, 1986.

Petchesky, Rosalind Pollack. *Abortion and Woman's Choice: The State, Sexuality, and Reproductive Freedom.* New York: Longman, 1984.

Ruiz, Vicki. *Cannery Women, Cannery Lives: Mexican Women, Unionization, and the California Food Processing Industry, 1930–1950.* Albuquerque: University of New Mexico Press, 1987.

Ruiz, Vicki, and Susan Tiano, eds. *Women on the United States–Mexico Border: Responses to Change.* Westminster, Mass.: Allen & Unwin, 1987.

Sanchez Korrol, Virginia. "Survival of Puerto Rican Women in New York before World War II." In Clara E. Rodriguez, Virginia Sanchez Korrol, and Jose Oscar Alers, eds., *The Puerto Rican Struggle: Essays on Survival in the United States.* New York: Puerto Rican Migration Research Consortium, 1980.

Shaw, Stephanie J. *What a Woman Ought to Be and to Do: Black Professional Women Workers during the Jim Crow Era.* Chicago: University of Chicago Press, 1996.

Smith, Susan L. *Sick and Tired of Being Sick and Tired: Black Women's Health Activism in America, 1890–1950.* Philadelphia: University of Pennsylvania Press, 1995.

Tentler, Leslie Woodcock. *Wage-Earning Women: Industrial Work and Family Life in the United States, 1900–1930.* New York: Oxford University Press, 1979.

Ware, Susan. *Holding Their Own: American Women in the 1930s.* Boston: Twayne, 1982.

Yung, Judy. *Unbound Feet: A Social History of Chinese Women in San Francisco.* Berkeley: University of California Press, 1995.

A Sampler from the "First Wave" of Women's History

Beard, Mary R. *Mary Ritter Beard: A Sourcebook.* Edited by Ann J. Lane. New York: Schocken, 1977.

Dexter, Elizabeth Anthony. *Colonial Women of Affairs.* 1931. New York: Augustus M. Kelley, 1972.

Donovan, Frances. *The Saleslady.* Chicago: University of Chicago Press, 1929.

————. *The Woman Who Waits.* Boston: Richard G. Badger, 1920.

Laughlin, Clara E. *The Work-A-Day Girl.* New York: Revell, 1913.

Richardson, Dorothy. *The Long Day: The Story of a New York Working Girl.* New York: Century, 1905.

Spruill, Julia Cherry. *Women's Life and Work in the Southern Colonies.* 1938. New York: Norton, 1972.

12

■ THE HISTORY OF THE FAMILY AND THE HISTORY OF SEXUALITY

Estelle B. Freedman

THE RISE OF THE NEW SOCIAL HISTORY IN THE 1960S HELPED DIRECT SCHOLARLY attention to the "private side" of history, in contrast to traditional accounts of political, economic, and intellectual life. Inspired by the political concerns of groups largely neglected in studies of elites, and facilitated by quantitative methods borrowed from the social sciences, the new social history explored in depth both personal life and social institutions. One result was the creation of several new subfields, including the histories of the family, of women, and of sexuality.

While women's, family, and sexual history often overlap, they also have distinctive subjects. Since the 1960s, historians of the family have looked closely at changing household structure, demographic trends, and the impact of large-scale economic change on family units and family members. The field of women's history, which has flourished since the 1970s, often explores family life, with special attention to women's unpaid work within the household, including child rearing and housework. Women's history, however, is equally concerned with the gendered meanings of nonfamilial life, including politics, wage labor, and social movements. Similarly, the more recently established history of sexuality overlaps with family studies—for example, in its concern with courtship, marriage, and reproductive sex—while it simultaneously addresses subjects usually beyond the confines of the household, including rape, prostitution, and homosexuality.[1]

The shifting location of the history of sexuality—from its origins within family history to its development as a distinctive subfield—parallels the chronological narrative told within these two scholarly literatures. In early American culture, sexuality was largely subsumed within the family and for the purpose of procreation. Over the course of the nineteenth century, sexuality gradually emerged as a concept in its own right, apart from reproduction, both within families and outside of them. By the mid-twentieth century, most Americans considered sexuality as much an individual as a familial matter, and sex had become a subject of intense political debate as well.

As separate histories of the family and sexuality have developed since the 1970s, new questions have replaced older ones. An initial focus of family history was the shift from a "traditional" (large, extended, patriarchal) family to a "modern" (small, nuclear, companionate) family. Scholars explored when, how, and why this long-term change occurred. Drawing on demographic sources, they paid close attention to changing age at marriage, family and household size, patterns of inheritance, and rates of divorce and of out-of-wedlock births. Family historians also argued about the process of historical change, particularly how industrialization and migration affected the family, and the extent to which the family served as an active agent of change or proved resistant to change.

Early histories of sexuality tended to explore ideology, relying heavily on sources of elite opinions, such as prescriptive literature written by clergy and doctors. A major focus was the Victorian sexual system, which was closely associated with sexual repression and contrasted to a twentieth-century sexual revolution that expanded opportunities for physical pleasure. Gradually scholars sought closer social historical evidence of actual sexual behavior. Using private records—such as diaries, letters, and early sex surveys—they began to emphasize the sexual enthusiasm of middle-class couples in the nineteenth century, pushing backward in time earlier notions of a modern sexual "revolution."

Increasingly, however, historians have turned away from such broad generalizations about both family and sexual history, distinguishing more carefully among diverse regional and cultural patterns and recognizing the multiple histories of families and sexualities. For example, some historians question whether a "traditional" family ever predominated, at least in the large, extended, patriarchal form of historical myth. At the same time, taking race and class differences into account has made more apparent that many groups continued to rely on "traditional" family economic strategies during the era of industrialization.

Recognizing that families contain individuals who may have conflicting interests has made the family unit appear less monolithic. Finally, both family and sexual historians now pay more attention to the social and cultural construction of their subjects, and they read prescriptive literature less literally and more critically. Influenced by the work of Michel Foucault, they ask questions about when, how, and why new sexual categories (such as homosexuality) have emerged, whether through medical or political discourse. These studies help make important connections between public meanings and seemingly private acts.

Indeed, recent studies of family and sexuality have challenged the very notion of the "private side" of history by showing how private acts have deeply political import and inspire heated public controversies. Reviewing historical studies of the family and sexuality thus helps to illuminate contemporary public policy dilemmas, ranging from abortion and unwed motherhood to the rights of lesbians and gay men to military service and marriage. The historical literature also suggests how metaphors of race, sex, and family both inform and obscure our contemporary political rhetoric.

This essay introduces the growing and complex literatures of family and sexual history, first by synthesizing recent studies to provide an overview of historical change from pre-industrial to modern America, and then by highlighting three fruitful areas of recent scholarship: race and class dynamics within family and sexual history; the recurrent controversies over reproductive policies; and the emergence of the identity categories of homosexuality and heterosexuality.

THE CONTOURS OF CHANGE

The image of the American family constructed in the years after World War II—privatized, suburban, white, nuclear, middle-class households in which fathers worked for pay and mothers nurtured children in the home—could not long withstand the scrutiny of the generation of historians who came of age in this period. The shattering of the postwar ideal during the 1960s raised questions about continuity and discontinuity in family life, while the rapidly changing sexual mores of the era helped raise questions about past sexual systems. Although family and sexual history initially focused on the white middle classes—the group that still dominates most studies—themes of diversity increasingly characterize the literature, which questions the universality of western European family patterns and illustrates the malleability of family and sexual norms in the face of historical change.

Studies of early America reveal an especially wide range of familial arrangements, from various Native American cultures, to the divergent New England and Chesapeake regions of European settlement, to the African American family that emerged after the institutionalization of slavery. Over the course of the colonial era, although a European family and sexual system increasingly predominated, important regional and cultural distinctions continued.

For most Native American peoples, kin and clan ties were more important than immediate family relations, given the economic interdependence and social permeability of families. As Stephanie Coontz suggests, the absence of private property in these preclass, prestate societies produced a more egalitarian social system based on principles of reciprocity and cooperation. Men and women formed unions, and a clear sexual division of labor existed, yet women shared economic and political authority in their tribes, many of which had matrilineal systems of descent. Marriage was largely an individual choice and could be dissolved at will. All adults were responsible for raising children, not only their own offspring. Both children and adults, including prisoners of war, could be adopted easily into a tribe.

Native American ideas about sexuality were often embedded in a spiritual context and did not have the negative associations of sinfulness common among Europeans. Many groups accepted polygamy, premarital intercourse, or institutionalized cross-gender dressing, and children grew up with few restrictions on sexual experimentation. Among the preconquest Pueblos, Ramón Gutiérrez explains, sexuality provided women with an important source of symbolic power, while neither the naked body nor sexual intercourse was considered shameful. Once married, however, most native peoples formed exclusive unions, and while infidelity was not sanctioned, couples could easily separate and form new unions. Among Eastern tribes, as European captives of war recounted, rape was not tolerated.

Most European settlers expressed shock at the sexual habits of the native inhabitants and proselytized what they believed to be the superior Christian morality of nuclear families grounded in both private property and patriarchal authority. In New England, for example, both John Demos and Mary Beth Norton have explored the ways that the family represented a "little commonwealth," providing a microcosm for society. Adult male heads of household held political authority, while women, children, servants, and slaves remained subordinate. As Norton points out, this hierarchical family ideal could not easily accommodate independent women, such as widows who headed households and thus stood outside of patriarchal control. So important was the symbolic rule of fathers that when women did gain religious or economic authority, like Ann Hutchinson, they often provoked political crises.

The colonial-era family provided, in addition to its exemplary political function, the basic economic unit for European settlers. As in pre-modern Europe, the family was the locus of both production and consumption, and thus critical to survival; everyone lived in families, which grew rapidly. A scarcity of laborers and abundance of land encouraged a "high" reproductive strategy, easily enacted in New England, where families migrated together. In contrast to the European marriage pattern, few of these colonists remained single, and they married at a much younger age, allowing more years for childbearing. Natural increase largely accounted for the doubling of the colonial population from the seventeenth to the eighteenth century, and married women could expect to bear more than eight children.

In this "reproductive society," the appropriate locus of sexual activity was either in courtship or in marriage. Sexual intercourse was an important duty of married couples, a necessity to reproduce but a form of physical pleasure as well. Premarital sex often took place during courtship; though prosecuted heavily by church and state in early New England, it might be forgiven as long as marriage and repentance followed. Most men and women who challenged the reproductive norm—by acts of rape, sodomy, adultery, fornication, and miscegenation—could expect severe, often public punishment and the pressure to repent. Both genders participated in the regulation of sexuality, especially in New England, intruding into the behavior of neighbors and kin and testifying in court about the illicit sexual relations of others.

In the Chesapeake, as both Mary Beth Norton and Lorena Walsh have shown, a shortage of women migrants delayed family formation, while high mortality rates prevented the rapid population growth that would otherwise have produced more even sex ratios. Indentured servants and, later, slaves filled the need for laborers. Since indentured servants could not wed until they had fulfilled their labor contracts, the childbearing years of many women were curtailed by late marriage. Sexual regulation focused less on maintaining morality than on preventing the economic burden of children born to single women servants.

As slavery began to supplant indentured servitude after 1670, importation of African men predominated, delaying the formation of slave families. Southern colonies outlawed interracial marriage, but the births of mixed-race children made evident the persistence of illicit unions. By the mid-eighteenth century, Allan Kulikoff has shown, the African American population began to reproduce itself. As sex ratios evened out, it became easier to form unions, even though legal marriage was not possible. Slaves tended to create stable, monogamous families with high birth rates. Slave women, however, remained vulnerable to sexual advances from owners, who knew that the offspring of these unions would become valuable slave property.

Among free white settlers, a new sexual and family system began to emerge in the eighteenth century, along with population pressure on available land. With greater geographical mobility and the growth of commercial towns in the late eighteenth century, and in the light of the social disruptions brought on by years of warfare, the relatively stable communities of the early colonial period could not survive intact. As a result, in both New England and the Chesapeake, Daniel Scott Smith and Robert Wells have each shown, the proportion of single women giving birth rose during this period, a sign of the breakdown of traditional familial regulation of sexuality and marriage.

Some scholars link a decline of patriarchal authority within families to the emergence of republican ideals in political thought. Parental power over marriage choice became less enforceable without land for children to inherit. Personal attraction and not just duty increasingly justified marriage, and individuals became accustomed to exercising choice. The beginnings of conscious family limitation also appeared in the late eighteenth century, as did an overall decline in state and church control of morality. Self-regulation and individual choice now played a larger role in personal life, creating a mentality that rejected older, hierarchical controls. Over the next century, government regulation of personal life declined, paralleling laissez-faire attitudes toward economic life.

In the process, however, women, who had long been both constrained and protected by community enforcement of moral codes, faced new sexual risks. It was harder to ensure that premarital intercourse would lead to marriage in the event of pregnancy. Because once favorable sex ratios had reversed themselves, women had more difficulty marrying or remarrying, especially in older settled areas like New England. Women had few alternatives to marriage, since it was virtually impossible for them to be economically self-supporting. As marriage and premarital virtue took on greater significance for most women, the prospect of abandonment by a lover or of an illegitimate birth became even more problematic than in the past. This economic and sexual vulnerability coincided with anxieties about individual morality generated by republican ideals of self-government. One result, Nancy Cott has suggested, was a new emphasis on female purity at the close of the eighteenth century, pointing toward the further association of women with morality in an increasingly gendered sexual system.

Historians have applied various labels to the new family ideal that emerged among the white middle class in the nineteenth century, from "companionate marriage" to "separate spheres." However termed, families changed as households became smaller, the result of declining marital fertility rates and fewer non-kin living within the households of their employers. Northern community studies by Paul Johnson and Mary

Ryan provide concrete examples of how a growing wage-labor system, which attracted young, single workers into towns and cities, meant that more and more individuals lived beyond family governance, whether by parents or employers. At the same time, historians such as Carl Degler emphasize that new social and political ideals born of the Enlightenment and the American revolution rejected the patriarchal model of the family. These democratic ideals first applied to adult white males, but notions of individual rights would eventually extend to blacks, women, and children.

In the northern states, a new model of romantic love and companionate relations between spouses gradually emerged, as did an emphasis on child rearing as woman's vocation. As the productive economic functions of the family shifted to the market place, the middle-class home became a more specialized, and more privatized, arena associated with emotional life. An abundant historical literature analyzes the middle-class home as a "female sphere" in which women assumed the tasks of nurturing children and providing a refuge from the rapidly changing public world of male economic and political activity.[2]

Recent studies have been influenced by feminist theoretical critiques that emphasize the interdependence of public and private spheres. In practice, historians now argue, women in the home contributed significantly to economic life, while the family continued to provide economic as well as emotional sustenance. Jeanne Boydston explores the contributions of women's unwaged housework, health care, and continued production of food and clothing; Joan Jensen discusses the contributions of rural women to household economies. For urban working-class families, women's wage labor, as well as their household duties, were critical to economic survival, and, as Christine Stansell shows, social life spilled out from private families into urban tenement neighborhoods. For both the urban immigrant and native-born working classes, and for rural families that combined self-sufficient agriculture and domestic production with wages earned through outwork or young women's domestic service, the family remained critical to survival. Fathers, mothers, and children often contributed wages to the family economy, and as Tamara Hareven and others explain, kin networks were critical for finding employment, especially among immigrants.

Despite these continuities with a pre-industrial past, in those areas where wage labor became common, especially in the northern states, individual family members were increasingly drawn into the market, providing some measure of independence from parents. Not only sons but also some daughters gained economic independence, Thomas Dublin argues in his studies of New England working women. Family historians also recognize that conflict, as much as cooperation, took place in families of all classes. In the case of domestic violence, women and children left families, or, as both Elizabeth Pleck and Linda Gordon have shown, they turned to newly established public agencies for protection.

Family life in the antebellum South, however, continued to resemble pre-industrial patterns, taking unique forms for whites and for blacks. For white slaveowners, Elizabeth Fox-Genovese argues, the household remained the unit of both production and reproduction. Although white women had some authority within the household, they remained subordinate to their husbands. Carol Bleser and other historians suggest a tension between the patriarchal structure of southern white family life and newer ideals of companionate marriage, which appeared among courting couples even in the South. Although fewer studies explore the white yeoman class, Stephanie McCurry argues that this group drew heavily on family metaphors in constructing a southern white defense of slavery.

For slaves, family formation remained difficult. Couples might live on separate holdings in "abroad" marriages, while extended family or fictive kin were essential for child rearing. Although free black households were likely to be male headed, Brenda Stevenson explains, the law of slavery defined the African American family as matrilineal by basing slave status on the mother, rather than the father. Deborah Gray White shows how slave women's reproductive labor contributed to the economic wealth of their white owners, while their emotional and productive labor in the slave quarters helped sustain their families.

For white Americans, the meaning of sexuality was shifting from its earlier mooring in marital, reproductive relations. A key indicator of change was the declining white marital fertility rate, which dropped by 50 percent over the course of the nineteenth century (from more than seven children in 1800 to fewer than four in 1900--black rates remained higher but paralleled the direction of change a generation or two later). Historians once argued that couples limited family size by managing their sexual lives through periodic continence, but more recent studies, such as Janet Brodie's comprehensive account of family limitation in the nineteenth century, document that couples used contraception and that when it failed, some turned to abortion.

At the same time, for both men and women, sex became less associated with reproduction and more important as a form of personal intimacy, especially within courtship and marriage. According to both Ellen Rothman and Karen Lystra, white, middle-class courting couples sought love before, rather than after, marriage and embraced sexual union as a means of enhancing the bond between husband and wife. The once popular notion that Victorian-era women suppressed their erotic desires has been supplanted by a rich literature detailing the passionate relations between middle-class couples. According to Steven Seidman, however, sexuality was primarily a path to romantic or spiritual union, rather than a form of eroticism in its own right.

Even as the romantic meanings of sexual intimacy flourished within middle-class courtship and marriage, sexuality itself moved beyond the family and into the public sphere. Like other traditional family functions drawn into the market, female sexuality increasingly became available for hire. Men whose wages and geographic mobility allowed them access to nonreproductive sex outside marriage sought urban, working-class prostitutes. In the West, several studies show, enterprising madames set up brothels near mining camps or military forts and Chinese business agents imported impoverished young women from their homeland to provide sexual services to single male immigrants.

Men's extramarital relationships were condoned by a double standard that condemned and heavily penalized either "fallen" or adulterous white women. Historians now recognize that rather than merely victimizing women, the double standard often inspired them to mobilize politically. Works by Carroll Smith-Rosenberg, Mary Ryan, and Peggy Pascoe argue that white middle-class women drew upon the moral authority derived from female purity ideals to try to impose their standards of morality on single and married men, and upon working-class and immigrant women. Beginning in the antebellum period, women in the Northeast established moral reform associations to keep men from going to brothels or seducing working women; they also tried to uplift and redeem prostitutes. Women in the abolitionist movement considered the sexual abuse of female slaves an affront to all womanhood and justified their antislavery activism on this ground. In the late nineteenth century, middle-class black women also drew upon an ideology of women's purity to organize within their communities.

Ryan argues that white middle-class women, after their initial reform efforts, retreated to the private family; other studies suggest, however, that the next generation revived the expansion of maternal authority outside the home. After the 1870s, the Women's Christian Temperance Union attacked not just male drinking but also male impurity in the name of "home protection." Pascoe shows how white women's organizations in the West tried to instill middle-class values by establishing rescue homes aimed at unwed mothers, Indian women, and Chinese prostitutes, as well as the ways residents resisted or appropriated these efforts.

By the turn of the twentieth century, the middle-class ideal of a companionate family that contained sexuality within marital intimacy flourished. But, according to Steven Mintz and Susan Kellogg, revolutionary challenges confronted American families, including soaring divorce rates and declining marital fertility rates. Elaine Tyler May argues that marital expectations were changing from the Victorian system of duty to a modern quest for personal satisfaction. At the same time, both working and middle-class women—drawn into an economy that was expanding in service and clerical jobs considered appropriate for women— increasingly sought education and employment before, or instead of, marriage. Some urban bohemians engaged openly in nonmonogamous and homosexual relationships. Massive immigration from southern and eastern Europe, and the initial migration of southern blacks to northern cities, heightened middle-class fears that white families were committing "race suicide" by failing to reproduce rapidly enough. All of these changes provoked efforts to channel sexuality back into the home and keep it tied to marital intimacy.

Several historians have analyzed the late nineteenth-century campaigns to suppress "obscenity," including information about contraception and abortion, emphasizing the role of the newly established medical profession in shifting authority over sexual matters from women to physicians. James Mohr illustrates this process in his study of the criminalization of abortion after 1860. While women continued to use contraception and seek abortions, legal obstacles made it harder to do so, especially when families did not have access to doctors. The role of race suicide fears in the criminalization of abortion and contraception suggests that sexual issues were often symbols of nonsexual social concerns. Campaigns against prostitution and venereal disease, for instance, revealed deep anxieties about the implications of women moving out of the home, as well as about the ways that immigrants and the urban working class were reshaping American institutions and values. Similarly, as Jacquelyn Dowd Hall, Darlene Clark Hine, and others have argued, the image of the black man as rapist, which took hold in the South during this era along with the epidemic of lynching allegedly meant to contain him, served to mask the rape of black women by white men and to justify a new system of racial subordination—segregation— in the South.

Political efforts to regulate sexuality illustrate one way that social, as well as economic, functions were moving outside the family. Public schools offered basic education, reformatories retrained errant youth, and courts rather than private religious institutions adjudicated divorce. Thus agencies of the state increasingly responded to concerns about family instability. During the Progressive Era, divorce laws tightened, juvenile courts emerged to enforce the role of *parens patriae*, and municipalities waged anti-vice campaigns. Although families continued to socialize individuals, government agencies increasingly set the terms for familial and moral order, reversing the nineteenth-century trend and, in some interpretations, attempting a new form of social control to shore up a "traditional" private family—one that had emerged only in the nineteenth century.

Despite these efforts, modern American economic and social life reinforced the continued separation of sexuality from the family. By the 1920s, white Americans were embracing a new set of sexual values. Instead of "sexual revolution," historians John D'Emilio and Estelle Freedman refer to "sexual liberalism"—an overlapping set of beliefs that detached sexual activity from the instrumental goal of procreation, affirmed heterosexual pleasure as a value in itself, defined sexual satisfaction as a critical component of personal happiness and successful marriage, and weakened the connections between sexual expression and marriage by providing youth with room for some experimentation as preparation for adult status. Sexual liberalism rested upon the shift from families to individuals as the basic economic unit, and from women's increasing participation in both wage labor and a sexualized commercial and popular culture.

In response to these new values and roles, the reproductive strategy of family limitation intensified. In the Progressive Era, radicals like Margaret Sanger demanded access to contraception for working-class families; by the mid-twentieth century, most families aimed for two children, and even Roman Catholics increasingly used birth control as "planned parenthood" became the norm for both black and white middle-class families. As both black and white married women increasingly worked for pay, fertility control became even more critical for their families. The decriminalization of abortion in 1973 and the extensive use of oral contraceptives reflected these new concerns. By the 1980s, the separation of sexuality and reproduction deepened even further as new reproductive technologies—such as artificial insemination and in vitro fertilization—made possible reproduction outside of the family and apart from heterosexual relations, as Elaine Tyler May has shown. Increasingly, sexual pleasure, rather than reproduction, though usually alongside intimacy, became a primary value for both women and men.

Both the growing commercialization of sexuality and the rise of a science of "sexology" reinforced the relocation of sexuality from the family to both the commercial marketplace and the individual consumer. Works by Kathy Peiss and Lewis Erenberg illustrate that a sexual service industry flourished after 1900, including not just prostitution but also legitimate bars, clubs, movies, and dance halls, part of the growth of mass leisure industries. At the same time, within the new discipline of sexology, doctors, psychologists, and psychiatrists devised intricate categories and scales to measure the individual in terms of his or her sexuality.

Although historians are just beginning to write about recent family and sexual history, several works raise important questions about the new sexual boundaries that emerged by mid-century, emphasizing the legal, political, and cultural policing of nonmarital sexuality. Books by Mary Odem and Ruth Alexander focus on the identification of adolescent female sexuality as a form of deviance and the criminal prosecution of working-class youth for their sexual activities. John D'Emilio and Allan Berube each show how the emerging homosexual community became the target of political attacks after World War II. Elaine Tyler May argues that post–World War II American popular culture associated female sexuality with the threat of atomic war. A recurrent theme in this literature is the need to regulate nonmarital sexuality when a norm of female purity no longer served to channel sexuality into marriage and family.

In addition, recent work on the decade of the 1950s suggests that the era of suburbanization and the Baby Boom represented a deviation from long-term trends in family history. For a short period, marriage age fell, fewer people remained single, and fertility rates rose. May argues that specific historical circumstances, particularly a reaction to the fears of depression and war and the political uncertainty of the Cold War, escalated calls for "domestic security" through middle-class family life. Joanne Meyerowitz summarizes an alternative view of the 1950s in the title of her anthology, *Not June Cleaver,* suggesting that only a minority of American families approximated the cultural ideal of the suburban household represented by the television family of her title. The eruption of sexual radicalism in the 1960s, along with rising divorce and falling marital fertility rates, places the earlier decade in perspective as a temporary departure from the trends of declining family and household size, the separation of sexuality and reproduction, and the emergence of individuals rather than families as the basic economic and social units in modern American society.

RACE, CLASS, AND SOCIAL HIERARCHIES

Overviews of historical change necessarily slight the complexities of diverse social processes. Some of the most exciting work in family and sexual history asks two sets of questions about diversity. First, how would a multicultural account of race, class, and ethnic difference reshape historical interpretations? Second, how have Americans drawn upon ideologies of the family and sexuality either to enforce or to modify social hierarchies among diverse groups?

The most developed historical literature addresses the ways that race has constructed our understandings of both family and sexuality. Studies of the conquest of Native American and Spanish-speaking populations highlight how beliefs in the superiority of the white, European family and sexual practices provided a justification for the appropriation of land and the cultural devaluation of conquered peoples. Joan Jensen has shown how even sympathetic settlers like Quaker missionaries tried to impose upon Native Americans a European model of the family, in which husbands worked the fields and women remained in the home. Similarly, the Dawes Act of 1887 attempted to enforce a nuclear family model for Native Americans through a land allotment system that imposed patrilineal inheritance, while federal Indian schools removed children from their tribal cultures and taught them the superiority of European American family customs.

Throughout the process of settlement, cultural stereotypes of Indian, Mexican, and black women as lascivious or promiscuous helped create a myth that these women sought sexual contact, masking the extent of sexual exploitation that accompanied all forms of racial conquest. Albert Hurtado offers abundant and painful evidence that white settlers purposefully raped native women to undermine tribal resistance to conquest. As Evelyn Brooks Higginbotham explains, sexual fantasies about African Americans helped rationalize both slavery and the rape of slave women. Indeed, the belief in white moral superiority surfaced in relation to all racial and ethnic groups—including the Chinese in California and the Irish in eastern cities.

Long-standing historiographical controversies over the nature of the African American family illustrate well questions of diversity and social dominance. Was the black family destroyed by slavery; did it survive in a form that approximated the white, middle-class ideal; or did African Americans create a family system of their own that drew upon African traditions and their resistance to slavery? Herbert Gutman's influential work refuted earlier claims, popularized by Daniel Patrick Moynihan, that slavery undermined the black family by separating its members through sale, creating a lasting pathology of female-headed black households. Despite prohibitions to legal matrimony, slaves courted, held marriage ceremonies, sustained lineages over generations, and reunited families after emancipation whenever possible. To some scholars, however, Gutman seemed to portray slaves as if they were white, middle-class Americans, ignoring uniquely African American family patterns, such as the role of extended kin networks in raising children. More recently, feminist historians have criticized Gutman's work for accepting the categorization of the "normal" two-parent and "deviant" single-parent family. Studies of slavery by Deborah Gray White and by

Brenda Stevenson stress the importance of mother-child bonds and suggest that a women's community in the slave quarters provided a critical source of strength. Fewer studies address the African American family in the twentieth century, although northern black community studies suggest the importance of extended kin networks for migration and for economic survival.[3]

The racially charged discussions of sexuality in the late nineteenth and early twentieth centuries affected both blacks and whites in important ways. In response to the southern lynchings that helped justify segregation, black women organized to expose the injustices of lynching and to defend their own reputations by upholding an ideal of black female sexual purity. At the same time, Jacquelyn Dowd Hall has pointed out, the use of rape accusations to maintain white political dominance kept white southern women in need of male protection. Both Peggy Pascoe and Nancy Cott have observed that marriage law helped enforce racial segregation by outlawing interracial unions, or "miscegenation," not only between whites and blacks but also between whites and Asian Americans, Native Americans, or East Indians. In addition, racial thought strongly influenced gender relations. The concept of "white manhood," Gail Bederman argues, added racial power to male gender identity at a time when older notions of manly self-restraint had become less salient.

Among white Americans, beliefs about the family and sexuality contributed significantly to the process of class formation. Mary Ryan's study of an upstate New York community in the nineteenth century explores how middle-class status came to be defined in large part by the presence of a wife/mother in the home. The moral reform campaigns spearheaded by middle-class men and women enforced class identity by labeling as inadequate the families of many workers and immigrants, in which wives and children necessarily worked for wages. Some scholars have accused juvenile courts and reform schools of targeting children from working-class homes for removal to reformatories, although Barbara Brenzel and others have found that working-class families often sought the intervention of state agencies to help with troubled children.

Studies of ethnicity echo these conflicts over family and sexual values. An earlier historiography, like the literature on slavery, portrayed the destruction of traditional family life among immigrants to the United States. Oscar Handlin's *The Uprooted* epitomized this view, but subsequent scholarship portrayed a more resilient immigrant family that imported traditional values and both resisted and adapted to American culture. Virginia Yans McLaughlin, in her study of Italian Americans, argues that southern Italian family values persisted even when women and children became wage earners. Like Italians, Judith Smith has shown, eastern European Jewish immigrants combined family traditions and economic necessity by encouraging mothers to earn within the household, taking in boarders or piece work, while daughters usually contributed their factory wages to the family economy.

Recent studies tend to emphasize selective acculturation by immigrants rather than complete resistance to American family and sexual patterns. Among Mexican Americans, George Sanchez explains, "familism" helped migrants survive economically and culturally, but increasingly their goal was to become Mexican American, a blend of two cultures. Although a large, patriarchal family structure characterized many Mexican immigrants, by the 1940s, Karen Anderson suggests, an ideal of companionate marriage became popular within the second generation. Among Japanese American immigrants, the family was a critical institution for pooling economic resources; yet, as Valerie Matsumoto has found, its traditional form of parental authority could not persist under the stress of internment during World War II and with the acculturation of the nisei and sansei generations.

Finally, attention to class and ethnicity can revise historical interpretations of changing sexual practices in the twentieth century. According to historians such as Kathy Peiss, the sons and daughters of immigrants pioneered in the transformation of work and leisure, as they socialized on factory breaks or in urban amusement parks and dance halls. Native-born reformers often associated these behaviors with prostitution, but working-class young women distinguished between commercialized sex and consensual sexual relations within a system of "treating" or dating. White middle-class women eventually adopted these standards. Similarly, the pattern of single motherhood first evident among African American women became more widespread among white women by the late twentieth century.

REPRODUCTIVE PRACTICES AND POLITICS

Race and class issues figure importantly in the historical literature on reproduction, much of which explores the social implications of the demographic transition from large to small family size. In addition to asking why and how private families limited their fertility, historians look at the public policies that responded to, and sometimes shaped, those decisions. These policies often rested on race and class assumptions about childbearing.

Most historians accept both economic and ideological explanations for the marital fertility decline. As a commercial economy expanded, first in agriculture and then in manufacturing and service industries, children increasingly represented an economic liability, costly to raise and educate, rather than an asset, as they had been as farm workers. At the same time, ideals of individualism and social mobility placed more weight on the nurture and education of each child. Some historians credit married women in the nineteenth century with taking control of fertility by refusing to have intercourse as a way of reducing childbearing. But smaller family size benefited husbands as much as wives. Moreover, abstinence from intercourse was not the only means for limiting conception. Practices ranging from folk remedies to male and female contraceptive devices help explain the decline in marital fertility rates. As James Mohr has shown, by the mid-nineteenth century, married, middle-class women increasingly sought abortions to limit family size.

African American fertility rates remained higher than those of whites, since slaveowners encouraged reproduction and postemancipation blacks remained largely rural farmers. Slave women, however, sometimes induced miscarriage, a practice some historians consider a form of resistance to forced reproduction. After blacks migrated to northern cities in the twentieth century, a small middle class sought contraceptive information to limit family size. Similarly, family size declined for immigrant families only after an initial period of high fertility.

As Elaine Tyler May points out, reproduction has been as much a public as a private concern in American culture. The decline in the size of native-born white families fueled fears of "race suicide"—the theory that higher reproductive rates among immigrant and black families meant that the white middle-class would be overrun by a population they considered, in Darwinian and eugenic terms, less fit to rule society. Encouraging white births while discouraging others might reverse the trend. The race suicide scare fueled the criminalization of abortion, ushering in a century of illegal abortion that lasted until the 1970s. Contraception also went underground after the Comstock Act of 1873 outlawed the circulation of contraceptive information or devices through the U.S. postal service. Linda Gordon has shown how birth control began as a radical movement and then, during the 1920s, sought acceptability through alliance with doctors. Only persistent leadership and the poverty of the depression of the 1930s lifted the obstacles to legalizing birth control by the mid-twentieth century.

Eugenic ideas about the superiority of the white race also fueled public policies that limited reproduction among certain social groups. Recent studies argue that state reformatories incarcerated working-class and immigrant girls who were labeled sexual delinquents, thus preventing them from becoming pregnant. Courts and reformatories often diagnosed sexually active young women as "feebleminded," sending them to special institutions and allowing their sterilization. Widespread state sterilization of Native American and African American women continued well into the twentieth century, often without the knowledge of the woman or her family. Mexican American women, too, became subject to actual or virtually compulsory sterilization at public hospitals, often after they gave birth. In short, sterilization prevented childbearing for poor women, particularly from minority groups, while criminalization of contraception and abortion tried to enforce childbearing for white, middle-class families.

Recent studies of single pregnancy by Regina Kunzel and Rickie Solinger reiterate the relationship between reproductive policies and race and class hierarchies. Before World War II, single women who became pregnant were often considered by definition socially undesirable, if not feebleminded, and liable to pass their bad habits on to their offspring. After World War II, although biological explanations persisted for black single pregnancy, new psychological theories depicted white single mothers as curable; their babies now became candidates for adoption, and they might start life over without the stain of having a fatherless child. These policies served both material and symbolic ends. Infertile white couples, long stigmatized for failing to reproduce, benefited from the availability of adoptable white babies. At the same time, a new racial stereotype emerged, identifying the black unwed mother as a symbol of the price to be paid for too much sexual expression. This symbol was particularly potent given the significant African American northern migration and the social costs of the recently established program for Aid to Families with Dependent Children. Contemporary rhetoric about welfare draws on this history of highly racialized stereotypes of single mothers.

HOMOSEXUALITY AND SEXUAL IDENTITIES

What began as a small historical literature on the emergence of homosexual identity in the mid-twentieth century has recently expanded to provide a wide-angle lens for viewing the process of the historical construction of sexualities, including heterosexuality. One of the major contributions of these studies has been to show the malleability of the social organization of sexuality in response to historical forces, including changes in economic and family life. This social constructionist approach, which contrasts with the essentialism of biological and psychoanalytic theories of sexuality, reveals how the concept of sexuality itself is both a historical product and an intriguing subject of both intellectual and social historical research.

The first studies to explore the formation of homosexual identity and community concentrated on the 1940s and 1950s as a turning point in this process. John D'Emilio dated the origins of the first gay rights, or homophile, movement to just after World War II. He found the roots of this small political mobilization in both the social changes of wartime, when an urban gay subculture nourished homosexual identity, and in the "bonds of oppression" forged during the anti-gay atmosphere of the 1950s. Allan Berube's study of lesbians and gay men during World War II recounts in depth the ways that wartime single-sex environments created opportunities for young men and women to explore their same-sex desires. Both of these studies find a shift from relative tolerance during the war to social stigma and political harassment during the subsequent era of McCarthyism. Yet gay culture continued to thrive in the 1950s. Ethnographers of lesbian culture in this period have identified working-class bars as a key source of identity and community formation, and D'Emilio also found that bars provided a prepolitical form of community for gay men. The eruption of the gay liberation movement in 1969, when Greenwich Village bar patrons resisted a police raid, thus had roots in an earlier working-class bar culture.

Taken together, these works on midcentury identity and community add another corrective to the cultural stereotype of the suburban postwar family. In most cities, homosexual subcultures flourished in the 1940s and 1950s, and a nascent political movement took shape. This literature also points toward the increasing importance of sexuality as a form of personal identity and social life in modern America. The work of D'Emilio and Berube on the mid-century, and of George Chauncey on earlier decades, locates the historical source of identity not simply within medical and psychiatric discourses but in larger social processes as well, including wage labor and urban growth, which allowed individuals to establish identities outside of traditional families.

Historians of women have written about two distinct patterns, differentiated largely by class, that provide historical perspectives on lesbian identity. Carroll Smith-Rosenberg's classic study, "The Female World of Love and Ritual," identifies nineteenth-century white, middle-class women's intense bonds of romantic friendship, which bordered on the erotic. In the late nineteenth century, educated and professional women sometimes established lifelong partnerships, known as "Boston marriages." Some scholars question whether these loving relationships included physical sexual expressions, while others claim that women's intimate friendships could be labeled lesbian, a term not yet in use at that time. The literature suggests that women's friendships, whether sexual or not, came under medical scrutiny with the emergence of sexology in the late nineteenth century and the naming of lesbianism as a pathological condition, forcing many women to hide or reject formerly acceptable female intimacies. Although a medical model of perversion was popularized in the early twentieth century, subsequent studies question whether it actually suppressed women's same-sex relationships. Biographies by Blanche Cook and Susan Ware reveal social networks of lesbians within the reform circles surrounding Eleanor Roosevelt in the 1920s and 1930s. These partners, however, remained discrete about their private lives and did not publicly claim a lesbian identity.

A second pattern of identity emerges in studies of working-class women. In the nineteenth and early twentieth centuries, some working women who adopted masculine clothing in order to earn men's wages also adopted male identity and married other women. Joanne Meyerowitz's study of working women who lived outside of families located early twentieth-century female partnerships that resembled those of married couples. Within working-class subcultures, both in prisons and in urban bars, a gendered sexual system developed in which "butch" women were often considered true lesbians, while their "femme" partners were not. For decades before the modern feminist and gay rights movements, charges of "mannishness" could be used to stigmatize women of all classes as lesbians, whether athletes or politicians, thus jeopardizing their livelihoods and reputations.

The organization of working-class sexuality around gender identity is also a central theme in George Chauncey's study of male homosexuality in New York City. In the late nineteenth and early twentieth centuries, before the popularization of concepts of homosexuality and heterosexuality, masculine working men, whether single or married, engaged in sexual relations with "passive" effeminate men, but only the latter were considered "queer." These "fairies" populated an openly gay public subculture, including dances and other meeting places, which interacted with mainstream popular culture, at least until the 1930s. Chauncey has also argued that sexologists initially emphasized gender, rather than sexual object choice, as the mark of "inversion." Thus both masculine men and feminine women were considered normal, no matter who they pursued sexually.

Understanding the shift from gender inversion to same-sex desire, or homosexuality, requires a broader perspective on cultural change. Chauncey hypothesizes that a crisis in middle-class men's gender identity resulted from men's narrowing economic opportunities and women's encroachments on the public sphere. A stronger assertion of masculine identity undermined tolerance for effeminate men, leading to the era of the "closet" and a decline in public gay culture. Other historians, such as

Anthony Rotundo, point to crises of middle-class masculinity that would support the view that in the twentieth century, men increasingly defined themselves in opposition to the feminine. Gail Bederman notes a new fear of effeminate men, or "sissies," as white middle-class men sought new sources of power, coining the term "masculinity" to describe their character. Similarly, Jonathan Ned Katz argues that both heterosexual and homosexual identities emerged at the turn of the century, when these terms first appeared in medical discourse. Katz explains that as new forms of self-consciousness, sexual identities derived from nineteenth-century views of true love as both a physical and an emotional expression, as well as from the new Freudian definitions of libido, or sex drive. In short, sexuality itself became more important as a form of personal identity.

As all Americans began to have self-consciously sexual selves, a variety of medical, popular, and political discourses elaborated a heterosexual norm and labeled homosexuality as a pathological or subversive deviation. This era of intolerance, and of the homosexual closet, lasted until the late twentieth century. Since the 1960s, feminist and gay rights activists have vocally challenged the institutionalization of "hetero-normativity." Current policy debates over the incorporation of lesbians and homosexuals into mainstream American institutions result from these efforts to normalize homosexuality.[4]

Current issues in lesbian and gay history point toward broad future questions for the study of both sexuality and the family. For one, contemporary efforts to extend the legal right of marriage to gay couples forces a redefinition of the family. Once assumed to be based on heterosexual reproductive relationships, families now include same-sex as well as opposite-sex parenting, whether by couples or within networks of fictive kin. Thus what was once thought to be a deviant form of sexuality is now becoming a means of reproducing traditional family forms, suggesting both the continued significance of the family and its diverse manifestations. Future studies will no doubt pay close attention to historical examples of nonbiological familial ties, whether same or opposite sex, and to the multiple forms of kinship and extended-family communities that have characterized diverse groups within American society.

CONCLUSION

The literature on family and sexual history has clearly changed from an older, fairly monolithic account of the transition from traditional to modern families, and from a simple narrative of sexual progress from repression to revolution. Scholars now recognize that multiple family forms coexist in various historical periods, often related to race, ethnicity, and economic class, and that family norms can serve to enforce political and social dominance. In addition, sexual history has come to be seen less as a linear progression toward greater freedom than as a tangle of power relations that constantly reconstruct sexual norms. Both family and sexuality are considered not merely personal but central to politics and social policy debates. Beginning in the colonial period, when the family represented the ideal for political and social order, and continuing through the late twentieth century, when the terms "sexual politics" and "family values" have become codes for liberal or conservative political agendas, the nature of Americans' intimate lives has been at the core of public discourse about how society should be organized.

Two sources for historical study may prove especially useful for future explorations of the links between the private and public meanings of the family and of sexuality. First, studies of the law can illustrate how public policy constructs personal life by defining who can marry whom, the terms for dissolving marriage, the state's interest in reproduction and child rearing, the guidelines for enforcing sexual norms, and the penalties for sexual violence. Second, cultural studies can offer insights into the use of language and metaphor, especially about processes that connect race, family, and sexuality and construct social hierarchies.

Finally, studies of families and sexualities can contribute to broader historical analyses by the application of social construction theory. Understanding the family and sexuality as neither theologically nor biologically "natural" opens possibilities for denaturalizing other concepts central to American culture, such as race, class, gender, and ethnicity.[5] Exploring how these constructs intersect and reinforce one another to create complex social hierarchies is a major challenge for future historical studies. By linking the rich new fields of family and sexual history to the traditional political concerns of historians, scholars can show how seemingly private subjects are critical to understanding power in all of its forms.

NOTES

1. A rough chronological measure of the establishment of these historical subfields is provided by the founding of journals that specifically address their concerns: the *Journal of Family History* was founded in 1976, the *Journal of Women's History* in 1988, and the *Journal of the History of Sexuality* in 1990. Earlier review essays on the family (by Mary P. Ryan) and on sexuality (by Estelle B. Freedman) can be found in *Reviews in American History*, December 1982. See also

Tamara K. Hareven, "Family History at the Crossroads," *Journal of Family History* 12, nos. 1–3 (1987): ix–xxiii.

2. For an excellent review of the literature on the female sphere, see Linda Kerber, "Separate Spheres, Female Worlds, Woman's Place: The Rhetoric of Women's History," *Journal of American History* 75 (June 1988): 9–39.

3. The study of the black family has engaged both historians and sociologists since the early twentieth century. For a review of the controversy over Moynihan, see Lee Rainwater and William Yancey, *The Moynihan Report and the Politics of Controversy* (Cambridge, Mass.: MIT Press, 1967); for a useful recent survey of the literature, see Karen Anderson, "African American Families," in Joseph M. Hawes and Elizabeth I. Nybakken, eds., *American Families: A Research Guide and Historical Handbook* (Westport, Conn.: Greenwood Press, 1991), 259–90.

4. An alternative to this normalizing approach appears in the contemporary reformulation of the term "queer" to represent an oppositional political identity. For historians' perspectives on these terms, see Lisa Duggan, "Making It Perfectly Queer," *Socialist Review* 22, no. 1 (1992): 11–31, and Donna Penn, "Queer: Theorizing Politics and History," *Radical History Review* 62 (spring 1995): 24–42.

5. A growing field of "critical race theory," primarily in literary and legal studies, has been influential in this effort. See, e.g., Henry Louis Gates Jr., *"Race," Writing, and Difference* (Chicago: University of Chicago Press, 1986), and Thomas Holt, "Marking: Race, Race-Making, and the Writing of History," *American Historical Review* 100 (February 1995): 1–20.

BIBLIOGRAPHY

Alexander, Ruth. *The "Girl Problem": Female Sexual Delinquency in New York, 1900–1930.* Ithaca, N.Y.: Cornell University Press, 1996.

Anderson, Karen. *Changing Woman: A History of Racial Ethnic Women in Modern America.* New York: Oxford University Press, 1996.

Bardaglio, Peter. *Reconstructing the Household: Families, Sex and the Law in the Nineteenth-Century South.* Chapel Hill: University of North Carolina Press, 1995.

Bederman, Gail. *Manliness and Civilization: A Cultural History of Gender and Race in the United States, 1880–1917.* Chicago: University of Chicago Press, 1995.

Berube, Allan. *Coming Out under Fire: The History of Gay Men and Women in World War II.* New York: Free Press, 1990.

Bleser, Carol, ed. *In Joy and in Sorrow: Women, Family, and Marriage in the Victorian South.* New York: Oxford University Press, 1991.

Boydston, Jeanne. *Home and Work: Housework, Wages, and the Ideology of Labor in the Early Republic.* New York: Oxford University Press, 1990.

Brandt, Allan M. *No Magic Bullet: A Social History of Venereal Disease in the United States since 1880.* New York: Oxford University Press, 1985.

Brenzel, Barbara. *Daughters of the State: A Social Portrait of the First Reform School for Girls in North America, 1856–1905.* Cambridge, Mass.: MIT Press, 1983.

Brodie, Janet. *Contraception and Abortion in Nineteenth-Century America.* Ithaca, N.Y.: Cornell University Press, 1994.

Cahn, Susan K. *Coming On Strong: Gender and Sexuality in Twentieth-Century Women's Sport.* New York: Free Press, 1994.

Chauncey, George, Jr. *Gay New York: Gender, Urban Culture, and the Making of the Gay Male World, 1890–1940.* New York: Basic Books, 1994.

Cook, Blanche Wiesen. *Eleanor Roosevelt.* Vol. 1, *1884–1933.* New York: Viking, 1992.

Coontz, Stephanie. *The Social Origins of Private Life: A History of American Families, 1600–1900.* London: Verso, 1988.

———. *The Way We Never Were: American Families and the Nostalgia Trap.* New York: Basic Books, 1992.

Cott, Nancy. *The Bonds of Womanhood: "Woman's Sphere" in New England, 1780–1835.* New Haven, Conn.: Yale University Press, 1977.

———. "Giving Character to Our Whole Civil Polity: Marriage and the Public Order in the Late Nineteenth Century." In Linda K. Kerber, Alice Kessler-Harris, and Kathryn Kish Sklar, eds., *U.S. History as Women's History: New Feminist Essays.* Chapel Hill: University of North Carolina Press, 1995.

D'Emilio, John. *Sexual Politics, Sexual Communities: The Making of a Homosexual Minority in the United States, 1940–1970.* Chicago: University of Chicago Press, 1983.

D'Emilio, John, and Estelle Freedman. *Intimate Matters: A History of Sexuality in America.* New York: Harper & Row, 1988.

Degler, Carl. *At Odds: Women and the Family in America.* New York: Oxford University Press, 1980.

Demos, John. *A Little Commonwealth: Family Life in Plymouth Colony.* New York: Oxford University Press, 1970.

———. *Past, Present, and Personal: The Family and the Life Course in American History.* New York: Oxford University Press, 1986.

Dublin, Thomas. *Women at Work.* New York: Columbia University Press, 1979.

Erenberg, Lewis. *Steppin' Out: New York City Nightlife and the Transformation of American Culture, 1890–1930.* Westport, Conn.: Greenwood Press, 1981.

Faderman, Lillian. *Odd Girls and Twilight Lovers: A History of Lesbian Life in Twentieth-Century America.* New York: Columbia University Press, 1991.

———. *Surpassing the Love of Men: Romantic Friendship and Love between Women from the Renaissance to the Present.* New York: Morrow, 1981.

Foucault, Michel. *The History of Sexuality.* Translated by Robert Hurley. Vol. 1, *An Introduction.* New York: Pantheon, 1978.

Fout, John, and Maura Shaw Tantillo. *American Sexual Politics: Sex, Gender, and Race since the Civil War.* Chicago: University of Chicago Press, 1993.

Fox-Genovese, Elizabeth. *Within the Plantation Household: Black and White Women of the Old South.* Chapel Hill: University of North Carolina Press, 1988.

Frazier, E. Franklin. *The Negro Family in Chicago.* Chicago: University of Chicago Press, 1932.

Gilfoyle, Timothy. *City of Eros: New York City, Prostitution, and the Commercialization of Sex, 1790–1920.* New York: Norton, 1992.

Gordon, Linda. *Heroes of Their Own Lives: The Politics and History of Family Violence.* New York: Viking, 1988.

————. *Woman's Body/Woman's Right: A Social History of Birth Control in America.* New York: Grossman, 1976.

Gutiérrez, Ramón. *When Jesus Came, the Corn Mothers Went Away: Marriage, Sexuality, and Power in New Mexico, 1500–1846.* Stanford, Calif.: Stanford University Press, 1991.

Grossberg, Michael. *Governing the Hearth: Law and the Family in Nineteenth-Century America.* Chapel Hill: University of North Carolina Press, 1985.

Gutman, Herbert G. *The Black Family in Slavery and Freedom, 1750–1925.* New York: Pantheon, 1976.

Hall, Jacquelyn Dowd. *Revolt against Chivalry: Jessie Daniel Ames and the Women's Campaign against Lynching.* New York: Columbia University Press, 1979.

Handlin, Oscar. *The Uprooted.* Boston: Little, Brown, 1951.

Hareven, Tamara. *Family Time and Industrial Time: The Relationship between the Family and Work in a New England Industrial Community.* New York: Cambridge University Press, 1982.

————, ed. *Transitions: The Family and the Life Course in Historical Perspective.* New York: Academic Press, 1978.

Hareven, Tamara, and Adrejs Plakans, eds. *Family History at the Crossroads: A Journal of Family History Reader.* Princeton, N.J.: Princeton University Press, 1987.

Higginbotham, Evelyn Brooks. *Righteous Discontent: The Women's Movement in the Black Baptist Church, 1880–1920.* Cambridge, Mass.: Harvard University Press, 1993.

Hine, Darlene Clark. "Rape and the Inner Lives of Black Women." *Signs* 14 (summer 1989): 912–20.

Hirata, Lucie Cheng. "Free, Indentured, Enslaved: Chinese Prostitutes in Nineteenth-Century America." *Signs* 5, no. 1 (autumn 1979): 3–29.

Hurtado, Albert. *Indian Survival on the California Frontier.* New Haven, Conn.: Yale University Press, 1988.

Jensen, Joan. *Loosening the Bonds: Mid-Atlantic Farm Women, 1750–1850.* New Haven, Conn.: Yale University Press, 1986.

————. "Native American Women and Agriculture: A Seneca Case Study." In Ellen Carol DuBois and Vicki L. Ruiz, eds., *Unequal Sisters: A Multicultural Reader in U.S. Women's History.* New York: Routledge, 1990.

Johnson, Paul E. *A Shopkeeper's Millennium: Society and Revivals in Rochester, New York, 1815–1837.* New York: Hill & Wang, 1978.

Katz, Jonathan Ned. *The Invention of Heterosexuality.* New York: Dutton, 1995.

Kulikoff, Allan. "A 'Prolific' People: Black Population Growth in the Chesapeake Colonies, 1700–1790." *Southern Studies* 16 (winter 1977): 391–428.

Kunzel, Regina. *Fallen Women, Problem Girls: Unmarried Mothers and the Professionalization of Social Work, 1890–1945.* New Haven, Conn.: Yale University Press, 1993.

Lystra, Karen. *Searching the Heart: Women, Men, and Romantic Love in Nineteenth-Century America.* New York: Oxford University Press, 1989.

Matsumoto, Valerie. *Farming the Home Place: A Japanese American Community in California, 1919–1982.* Ithaca, N.Y.: Cornell University Press, 1993.

May, Elaine Tyler. *Barren in the Promised Land: Childless Americans and the Pursuit of Happiness.* New York: Basic Books, 1995.

————. *Great Expectations: Marriage and Divorce in Post-Victorian America*. Chicago: University of Chicago Press, 1980.

————. *Homeward Bound: American Families in the Cold War Era*. New York: Basic Books, 1988.

McCurry, Stephanie. *Masters of Small Worlds: Yeoman Households, Gender Relations, and the Political Culture of the Antebellum South Carolina Low Country*. New York: Oxford University Press, 1995.

McLaughlin, Virginia Yans. *Family and Community: Italian Immigrants in Buffalo, 1880–1930*. Ithaca, N.Y.: Cornell University Press, 1977.

Meyerowitz, Joanne, ed. *Not June Cleaver: Women and Gender in Postwar America, 1945–1960*. Philadelphia: Temple University Press, 1994.

————. *Women Adrift: Independent Wage Earners in Chicago, 1880–1930*. Chicago: University of Chicago Press, 1988.

Mintz, Steven, and Kellogg, Susan. *Domestic Revolutions: A Social History of American Family Life*. New York: Free Press, 1988.

Mohr, James C. *Abortion in America: The Origins and Evolution of National Policy*. New York: Oxford University Press, 1978.

Norton, Mary Beth. *Founding Mothers and Fathers: Gendered Power and the Forming of American Society*. New York: Knopf, 1996.

Odem, Mary. *Delinquent Daughters: Protecting and Policing Adolescent Female Sexuality in the United States, 1885–1920*. Chapel Hill: University of North Carolina Press, 1995.

Pascoe, Peggy. "Race, Gender, and Intercultural Relations: The Case of Interracial Marriage." *Frontiers* 12, no. 1 (1991): 5–18.

————. *Relations of Rescue: The Search for Female Moral Authority in the American West, 1874–1939*. New York: Oxford University Press, 1990.

Pleck, Elizabeth. *Domestic Tyranny: The Making of American Social Policy towards Family Violence*. New York: Oxford University Press, 1987.

Peiss, Kathy. *Cheap Amusements: Working Women and Leisure in Turn-of-the-Century New York*. Philadelphia: Temple University Press, 1986.

Peiss, Kathy, and Christina Simmons, with Robert A. Padgug. *Passion and Power: Sexuality in History*. Philadelphia: Temple University Press, 1989.

Rosen, Ruth. *The Lost Sisterhood: Prostitution in America, 1900–1918*. Baltimore, Md.: Johns Hopkins University Press, 1982.

Rothman, Ellen K. *Hands and Hearts: A History of Courtship in America*. New York: Basic Books, 1984.

Rotundo, Anthony. *American Manhood: Transformations in Masculinity from the Revolution to the Modern Era*. New York: Basic Books, 1993.

Ryan, Mary P. *Cradle of the Middle Class: The Family in Oneida County, New York, 1790–1865*. New York: Cambridge University Press, 1981.

Sanchez, George. *Becoming Mexican American: Ethnicity, Culture, and Identity in Chicano Los Angeles, 1900–1945*. New York: Oxford University Press, 1993.

Seidman, Steven. *Romantic Longings: Love in America, 1830–1980*. New York: Routledge, 1991.

Shoemaker, Nancy, ed. *Negotiators of Change: Historical Perspectives on Native American Women*. New York: Routledge, 1995.

Smith, Daniel Scott. "Family Limitation, Sexual Control and Domestic Feminism in Victorian America." In Mary S. Hartman and Lois Banner, eds., *Clio's Consciousness Raised*, 119–36. New York: Harper & Row, 1974.

———. "The Long Cycle in American Illegitimacy and Prenuptial Pregnancy." In Peter Laslett, Karla Oosterveen, and Richard M. Smith, eds., *Bastardy and Its Comparative History*, 362–78. Cambridge, Mass.: Harvard University Press, 1980.

Smith, Judith. *Family Connections: A History of Italian and Jewish Immigrant Lives in Providence, Rhode Island, 1900–1940.* Albany: State University of New York Press, 1985.

Smith-Rosenberg, Carroll. *Disorderly Conduct: Visions of Gender in Victorian America.* New York: Knopf, 1985.

Solinger, Rickie. *Wake Up Little Susie: Single Pregnancy and Race Before Roe v. Wade.* New York: Routledge, 1992.

Stansell, Christine. *City of Women: Sex and Class in New York, 1789–1860.* New York: Knopf, 1986.

Stevenson, Brenda. *Life in Black and White: Family and Community in the Slave South.* New York: Oxford University Press, 1996.

Walsh, Lorena S. "'Till Death Do Us Part': Marriage and Family in Seventeenth-Century Maryland." In Thad W. Tate and David L. Ammerman, eds., *The Chesapeake in the Seventeenth Century: Essays in Anglo-American Society*, 126–52. Chapel Hill: University of North Carolina Press; 1979.

Ware, Susan. *Partner and I: Molly Dewson, Feminism, and New Deal Politics.* New Haven, Conn.: Yale University Press, 1987.

Wells, Robert V. *Revolutions in Americans' Lives: A Demographic Perspective on the History of Americans, Their Families, and Their Society.* Westport, Conn.: Greenwood Press, 1982.

White, Deborah Gray. *Ar'n't I a Woman? Female Slaves in the Plantation South.* New York: Norton, 1985.

13

■■ AFRICAN-AMERICAN HISTORY

Thomas C. Holt

THE STUDY OF AFRICAN-AMERICAN HISTORY WAS INITIATED BY AFRICAN-AMERICAN intellectuals and activists in the latter half of the nineteenth century. William Wells Brown in *The Black Man: His Antecedents, His Genius, and His Achievements* (1863), William C. Nell in *The Colored Patriots of the American Revolution* (1855), and George Washington Williams in *History of the Negro Race in America* (1882) all chronicled the black experience in war and peace and black contributions to America. Toward the end of the century W. E. B. DuBois published his Harvard University doctoral thesis, *The Suppression of the African Slave-Trade* (1896), a work still relevant to contemporary studies of slavery. The early twentieth century saw additional work by African-American historians such as Carter G. Woodson, Charles Wesley, William Leo Hansberry, A. A. Taylor, Du Bois, and others.

Ironically, however, it was a sociological work published during World War II that probably introduced black history to most white Americans. In 1944 Gunnar Myrdal's *American Dilemma* detailed not only the current conditions and future prospects but much of the history of blacks in America. It was at once a work of scholarship and a protest, a brutally objective examination of the black condition and a passionate call for national action. It won general acceptance as the major work of the century on American race relations and black life in America.

Myrdal's report also attracted critics, however. Among them was Ralph Ellison, soon to be a prizewinning novelist. In a review published several years later, Ellison applauded many of Myrdal's findings but took exception to the overall theme and tone of the report. Its effort to move the nation to action by highlighting the cruel oppression of blacks had the unintended effect of rendering a portrait of black life that Ellison could not recognize. After the oppressions and "meannesses" of white racism had been detailed, all that remained was "a sociological Negro," or what Ellison referred to in another context as "an image drained of humanity." Surely, he protested, black life was more than the sum of white oppression. "Can a people," he asked, "live and develop for over three hundred years simply by *reacting*? Are American Negroes simply the creation of white men, or have they at least helped to create themselves out of what they found around them?"

Anyone reviewing the historiography of African-American history in the post–World War II period might be surprised by the pervasive influence of Ellison's protest on historical scholarship. The novelist's query struck home, especially with the generation of white and black scholars emerging from the tumultuous 1960s. Consequently, in sharp contrast with the century of scholarship that preceded it, that of the 1970s and 1980s gave its attention almost exclusively to the problem of understanding black history as black people experienced it. No longer would black history be simply the history of relations between the races or of black contributions to the nation's life and progress. It would be the history of black communities, churches, schools, businesses, families, and folk culture. In that history blacks would no longer be relegated to nonspeaking roles, the passive victims of white hostility or beneficiaries of white benevolence. They would be actors with top billing, creating institutions, sustaining communal values, and passing on a legacy of struggle and creativity to their posterity.

The result has been a veritable explosion of histories on almost every conceivable facet of black life, by no means all of which can be examined here. But there are three major watersheds in the history of blacks in America: enslavement and forced migration from Africa, followed by almost a century and a half of bondage; emancipation, followed by more than a half-century of sharecropping and tenancy; and finally, the great twentieth-century northern migrations that produced the contemporary black urban communities and a second emancipation. Although the subject matter of African-American history has grown voluminous and tremendously complex, these three periods provide the essential contexts for the black experience; at the same time, they are key to any comprehensive study of the American experience generally. The black experience has ceased to be a peripheral topic in American history; it is now among the central phenomena of the national experience.

SLAVERY

Arguably, slavery was the central and determining phenomenon shaping the first century of American history. Of course, one might also make claims for the Constitution, the ideology of freedom and equality, the expanding frontier, and immigration, but each of these was profoundly shaped by the fact that the nation was half slave and half free. Consequently, much of American historical literature is devoted to the study of the institution of slavery, its origins, and the causes of its destruction in the nation's bloodiest war.

Because slavery is obviously central to the black experience in America, students of African-American history are concerned with many of the same issues regarding slavery's rise and fall as are students of general American history: the work regime on slave plantations; the profitability of slavery as an investment of capital; the nature of the master's relation with the slave; the conditions of material and social life in the slave quarters; and the nature and incidence of slave resistance. But the focus of African-American history is often different. In a general American history survey the objective might be to discern the personality and motives of the slavemaster in order to explain, for example, the causes of the Civil War. African-American history is more likely concerned to explain how slavery affected the slave or, more broadly, to examine slavery as the formative experience of African-American life and culture. The two lines of inquiry are necessarily interrelated and mutually dependent; there can be no adequate history of the master that neglects the slave, and vice versa. Nevertheless, it is important to bear these different tendencies in mind as one surveys the historiography of slavery, because the emphasis has shifted perceptibly over the past quarter-century.

Modern scholarship on slavery in the United States begins with U. B. Phillips's *American Negro Slavery* (1918). Drawing on meticulous research into a vast repository of plantation records, Phillips's treatment was long considered the definitive interpretation. That interpretation, however, reflected Phillips's own southern racist convictions as much as it did his research. He portrayed slavery as a benign institution. The masters were kindly, interested less in making a profit than in a way of life. The slaves did not work hard, did not suffer material deprivations, did not miss the pleasures—in their fashion—of leisure. Resistance was insignificant and rebellions infrequent; when they did occur, the former reflected merely the laziness and malingering characteristic of a childlike race, the latter its criminal tendencies when not properly disciplined. Writing at the height of European colonial expansion into Africa, Phillips justified slavery as a rescue of blacks from African barbarism. It was a kind of "school" in which they would be readied for civilized life.

Although a number of black historians took exception to such an interpretation, it was not until Kenneth Stampp published *The Peculiar Institution* in 1955 that Phillips's views came under systematic, full-scale attack. With scholarship even more meticulous and thorough, Stampp demolished each of his predecessor's arguments. Slavery was a labor system above all else, he declared; it was "a systematic method of controlling and exploiting labor." Slaveowners were calculating capitalists out to make a killing, and they frequently did. The food, clothing, housing, and medical care given to slaves was inadequate by any standard of decency. They were driven to work under the lash from sunup to sundown, and there was little time left for leisure activities after the long, grueling day. Their family, religious, and community life was practically destroyed by the all-pervasive and systematic power of masters who sought only "to make them stand in fear." The slave plantation was not a schoolhouse; it was a factory run with prison labor. Yet despite—indeed because of—the harshness and hopelessness of the system, slaves did resist, frequently and with effect. They broke tools, malingered, struck work, ran away, and not infrequently raised their hands in violence against their owners.

Seldom has the historical profession witnessed such a thorough and completely successful revision of a major work of scholarship. Stampp's success must be credited not solely to his scholarship, however, but to the fact that the prevailing ideology of the time was ripe for his message. Europe was fast losing its grip on its African colonial empire; racist theories of human behavior were in retreat; and American segregation was under assault in federal courts and on southern streets. The racist assumptions that shaped Phillips's inquiry were replaced by a "race blind" creed in Stampp's. At the outset, Stampp declared his intellectual and personal faith: "I have assumed that the slaves were merely ordinary human beings, that innately Negroes *are*, after all, only white men with black skins, nothing more, nothing less."

Stampp's assumption expressed an admirable sentiment that resonated with contemporary black struggles to be recognized as "just like whites," deserving basic civil rights and decent treatment. His announced purpose was to understand "what slavery meant to the Negro and how he reacted to it [in order to] comprehend his recent tribulations." Thus Stampp shifted the focus of slavery studies away from questions of sectional conflict toward a concern for its meaning for African-American history and its legacy to black Americans. Given his starting point—the assumption that blacks shared the motivations and aspirations of white men and women—the legacy he found was heroic resistance to a brutal system.

Four years later Stanley Elkins made entirely different assumptions and posed different questions in *Slavery: A Study of American Institutional and Intellectual Life* (1959). Blacks could not be just like whites because the experience of enslavement had to have changed them. Contemporary observers—planters and northern travelers—had left descriptions of a slavish personality type, a "Sambo" character who lied, stole, shirked work, played the fool, and generally acted like a child before his master. There must be some truth to such a ubiquitous portrait, Elkins thought, so he set out to demonstrate how such a personality could have been formed.

In striking and deliberate contrast with Phillips and Stampp, Elkins did no new research into plantation archives. Instead, he drew on existing comparative studies of slavery in the United States and Latin America, which generally concluded that U.S. slavery was the harshest, most oppressive system in the Western Hemisphere. This he coupled with findings about the effects of the Nazi concentration camps on Jewish inmates. The concentration camp, he argued, provided an appropriate analogy to the slave plantation, and the psychological damage inflicted on the camps' inmates was a good guide to the impact of slavery on the slave. The camps created infantilized, docile Jews; the plantations produced infantilized, docile blacks. Like SS guard and Jewish inmate, master and slave were bound in a closed circle with the former exercising total power. Slaves were stripped of their African culture, their family life, or any other institution that might have checked the master's power or held a different mirror in which the slave could catch more than a distorted image of himself. The only person of significance in the slave's world was his master. Impressed with the neatness of his paradigm, Elkins insisted that only exceptional slaves were able to escape the psychological distortion that resulted from the calculated brutality of the system. To their descendants slaves bequeathed not a legacy of resistance but broken families, damaged minds, and a perverted culture.

Much of the recent literature on slavery has been stimulated, directly or indirectly, by the controversies provoked by Elkins's book. Detailed and thorough studies of slavery in Latin America and the Caribbean as well as in the United States have demolished key parts of his thesis. The contrasts between North and South America were not as great and the relations between masters and slaves were much more complex than Elkins had portrayed them. Nevertheless, his contribution had been to frame slave *mentalité* as a problematic research question. Rising to his challenge, historians have sought out new sources and new methods of investigation. There have been quantitative studies not only of plantation economies but of runaways and family life. Sources have been uncovered that give a better approximation of what slaves thought, felt, and valued: their songs and stories, their autobiographies and oral histories.

Emerging from these studies is a consensus that despite the harshness of the system, slaves were able to create communities beyond their masters' total control. They fashioned institutions and a cultural ethos that were functional to their needs, that enabled them to survive the rigors of slavery and bequeath a legacy of resistance to their posterity. The reexamination of two key institutions—the family and the church—provided much of the evidentiary basis for this consensus. In *Slave Community* (1972), John Blassingame reported Freedmen's Bureau statistics from the 1860s showing that most slaves lived in two-parent households. In *The Black Family in Slavery and Freedom* (1975), Herbert Gutman went much further, showing not only that most slaves grew up with two parents but that their parents were often joined in enduring, though unlegalized, unions. Obviously, marriage and family were valued realities of slave life, despite the system. But more important, Gutman saw evidence suggesting complex relationships and networks of kinship within plantation quarters. Contrary to Elkins's assumptions, slaves identified with one another, not the master. The names they chose for their children, the affection they expressed for their families, the bonds they forged among kin and non-kin alike could not be reconciled with a thesis that the white master was the only "significant other" in the slave's world.

Studies of slave religious life have reinforced this view. Albert Raboteau and Eugene Genovese describe a rich and complex belief system from which slaves gained dignity and purpose in the world. Theirs was not a masters' Christianity, justifying racial subordination, but a slaves' Christianity, affirming that they were the children of God. Some historians argue further that their religion provided the basis for collective resistance and revolt. Others, especially Genovese, assert on the contrary that religion turned the slave's resistance into channels that were basically nonpolitical and nonviolent. It reaffirmed their sense of worth and blunted the master's racist message, but it did not provide the millennial or even political consciousness that might have authorized revolution. Religion made slaves men, but it did not make them fight.

Beyond the consensus that slaves succeeded in creating a semi-autonomous community with alternative values and sanctions, there are conflicting interpretations about the nature and functioning of the slave system. Historians have arrived at the consensus view by different routes. Blassingame argued that the masters recognized their pecuniary interests in encouraging slave families, and the slaves seized the resultant opportunity to forge a network of family and community. In that community, like any other, lived diverse personality types in addition to "Sambo," including "Nat" the rebel and "Jack" the pragmatist, who accommodated to the system when he had to and fought it when he could. In *Time on the Cross* (1972), Robert Fogel and Stanley Engerman went much further. The productivity of slave labor showed that the system functioned efficiently, they argued. Therefore, planters must have been rational managers who relied on incentives and good treatment to get the best work out of their charges. In return for protection of their families, above-average subsistence, and various rewards and incentives, slaves worked hard and well. This portrait has much in common with that of U. B. Phillips, except that the result is black Horatio Algers instead of Sambos.

To date, the most coherent and comprehensive thesis is that offered by Eugene Genovese in *Roll, Jordan, Roll* (1974). In contrast with slaveowners in many other parts of the hemisphere (except colonial Brazil), American planters lived on their estates and developed personal relations with their bondsmen. That relationship was basically paternalistic, with both master and slave recognizing a reciprocity of duties and rights. Paternalism in this usage does not imply kindness or benevolence, however; Genovese finds a great deal of cruelty and sadism on plantations. But cruelty was not the norm. The norm was defined by an implicit bargain in which masters accepted responsibility for the slave's welfare (food, housing, medical care) in return for their labor. For the planters this bargain justified their predominant place in society, their life-style, and slavery itself; theirs was a view similar to that presented by U. B. Phillips. But slaves interpreted the bargain by their own lights. For them the linkage of their subsistence with their labor was not apparent. Often, what planters saw as payments for work or gifts for faithful service, slaves came to regard as rights and entitlements.

The virtue of Genovese's work is that it attempts to comprehend both master and slave within the same system. Indeed, it was the struggle between master and slave that defined the system. It was, of course, an uneven struggle. But for Genovese, not only was the masters' power predominant in the slaves' world, but the masters determined the terms in which the world was seen. Thus, the slaves' world view emerges as merely a mirror reflection of the masters'. Slaves did not simply accommodate to the paternalistic ethos; they internalized it. But despite Genovese's impressive dialectical reasoning, this part of his argument remains an inference rather than an established fact. The letters and diaries he consults give us a better view of the master's thought than the slave's. For the latter he consults the recollections of former slaves collected by the WPA in the 1930s. Among the problems of these sources is that they do not convey the slave's thought and experience with the same immediacy as does a master's diary; they present a world not as it was lived but as it was remembered.

In *Black Culture, Black Consciousness* (1977), Lawrence Levine evades this difficulty, finding more direct entrée into the slaves' construction and interpretation of their experiences through their stories, songs, riddles, and jokes. These sources evince "a far greater degree of self-pride and group cohesion than the system they lived under ever intended for them to [have]," writes Levine. "Upon the hard rock of racial, social, and economic exploitation and injustice black Americans forged and maintained a culture: they formed and maintained kinship networks, made love, raised and socialized children, built a religion, and created a rich expressive culture in which they articulated their feelings and hopes and dreams." Indeed, the best studies of slavery have focused on the plantation household and the roles of black women as the key architects of the culture Levine invokes. Though differing in perspective and approach, the works of Deborah Gray White (*Ar'n't I a Woman* [1985]), Jacqueline Jones (*Labor of Love, Labor of Sorrow* [1985]), and Elizabeth Fox-Genovese (*Within the Plantation Household* [1988]) together provide a detailed and highly nuanced portrait of life in the slave huts and the Big House, and the interaction between the two. Perhaps the black world they and Levine describe is one that Ralph Ellison would recognize.

The consensus that slaves played a crucial role in making their own world is the beginning point for most scholarship in African-American history since Elkins. For example, Charles Joyner's study of slavery in the Carolina low country, *Down by the Riverside*, details the economic and social environment that permitted slaves to fashion a distinctive culture. Barbara Fields's *Slavery and Freedom on the Middle Ground* shows how black initiatives during the Civil War set in motion the inexorable process of slavery's destruction. Moreover, by following the black experience from slavery through emancipation, Fields suggests the continuity into the post–Civil War era of a tradition of resistance fashioned under slavery conditions. Thus the consensus on slavery resonates throughout later periods of African-American history.

EMANCIPATION AND BLACK LIFE AFTER SLAVERY

For black Americans the decade following Lee's surrender at Appomattox was one of tremendous change. Not only was slavery destroyed, but freedpeople were granted civil and political rights and gained access to education and other public services previously denied them in the South. It was a season of hope. Thousands of northern blacks moved south seeking new economic opportunities and a better life. Yet the black child born on the eve of emancipation lived to see an almost complete reversal of this progress. By the end of the century, black Americans were being barred from the ballot box, segregated in practically all areas of public life, impoverished on southern plantations, and lynched in record numbers.

Few historians, if any, would dispute this description of black life between the Civil War and World War I. The actual conditions of black life in this period, in contrast with those of slave life, are generally not at issue. Most would agree with Rayford Logan's characterization of the decades following Reconstruction, a period during which the promise of freedom was mocked by the harsh realities of black life, as a "nadir" of African-American history. Historians have disagreed only about the origins or causes of these conditions. Was sharecropping merely a continuation from slavery of a system of racial domination? Was segregation a response to new conditions in the 1890s or a continuation of antebellum patterns? Some argue that these conditions reflect the former slaveholders' continued power over southern society; others, that powerful new classes responding to new conditions were responsible.

All these questions are relevant to the study of black history, because for half a century after emancipation the overwhelming majority of blacks continued to live in the South, working its farms and plantations. But African-American historians are concerned not only with the conditions of black life but with how black people experienced and responded to them. During the 1980s, therefore, studies of emancipation and Reconstruction emphasized the role blacks played in the unfolding events. Four decades earlier, few historians accepted W. E. B. Du Bois's claim in *Black Reconstruction* (1935) that the slaves had staged "a general strike," which eventually led to emancipation. Now, most historians accept the view that together with military and diplomatic pressures, it was the black war refugees who forced Lincoln to abandon his hands-off policy toward southern slavery. Many also see black participation in the Union war effort as preparation for the political struggles of the postwar period. Collectively and individually, former slaves tested the limits of their former masters' authority. Their initiatives during and immediately after the war laid the basis for the Reconstruction political agenda. Blacks met in state conventions to demand equal rights and economic justice; in numerous cities they protested racial discrimination and injustice. Their Union military experiences and these protests produced many of the Reconstruction's prominent leaders, who would play major roles in its successes and failures.

The Origins of Sharecropping

The emergence of sharecropping and tenancy was one of the failures of Reconstruction. The sharecropping-tenant system evolved during the postwar period and held both blacks and many whites in its grip until it finally gave way under economic and political pressures created by New Deal agricultural policies in the 1930s and population changes stimulated by the two world wars. The planter paid the sharecropper with part of the crop (usually half) at the end of the year. Tenants, who owned their stock and tools, rented the land from the planter, paying him a share of the crop (usually a fourth). Both tenants and croppers were supplied food, clothing, and other necessities by the planter or a local merchant until the crop was harvested. Given falling cotton prices and extraordinary interest charges on their provisions, neither cropper nor tenant was likely to make ends meet at the end of the year. Most economists agree that the system contributed to southern poverty and underdevelopment.

There is less agreement on freedpeople's role in the origins of this oppressive system. A traditional view held that the former masters were able to impose the system on former slaves because the Congress and Republican state governments failed to provide freedpeople with land after the war. More recently, historians have found evidence that blacks themselves played a role in the creation of the share system, that it took shape during the first decade after the Civil War as the result of a kind of standoff in the struggle between planters and their former slaves. Planters sought to maintain maximum control over their laborers, a control in which blacks saw uncomfortable similarities to slavery. For their part, the newly freed blacks wanted to escape the plantation, to have a farm, and to make choices for the first time about where, when, and how their families lived and worked.

These themes first appeared in two works published almost simultaneously in the 1960s: Joel Williamson's *After Slavery* (1965) and Willie Lee Rose's *Rehearsal for Reconstruction* (1964). In different ways, Williamson and Rose make black life and thought central to their study. In *After Slavery*, South Carolina freedpeople are portrayed as shaping and helping define the content and meaning of their freedom in both its interpersonal and its social dimensions, including the evolution of sharecropping and the development of separate black institutions. *Rehearsal for Reconstruction* shows freedpeople's initiatives helping to shape the wartime labor arrangements on government-run plantations, and their confrontation with the free-labor ideologues from the North prefiguring the broader postwar confrontations throughout the South. Rose makes it clear that the freedpeople were motivated by their concerns for family, community, and basic dignity and sought working and living arrangements approximating a family farm rather than wage labor.

The mark of these two books is evident in the styles, themes, and general approaches of some of the most important work that followed. One might say, for instance, that Leon Litwack's prizewinning *Been in the Storm So Long* (1979) is in the Williamson tradition; it explores in meticulous detail the infinite variety of arenas and modes of contest by which freedpeople attempted to define their freedom—interpersonal, familial, and finally political. In the Rose tradition, Lawrence Powell's *New Masters* (1980) highlights the clash between northern objectives and the aspirations of the freedpeople for control of their lives and work: most northerners felt that former slaves should be content to work on the plantations for wages; most black families aspired to own their own farms and work for themselves. James Roark's *Masters without Slaves* (1977) looks at the same sort of interpersonal contest and ideological clash from the perspective of the southern planters.

Clearly, postemancipation studies have been influenced by and to some extent have taken their cues from the trends in slavery studies. The emphasis on the development of a semiautonomous slave community and on the varied forms of resistance to the dehumanizing tendencies of slavery suggested parallel approaches to the period that followed. Those whole, healthy, assertive human beings found in slave cabins could hardly have just disappeared after the Civil War. Indeed, many recent studies of postemancipation black life draw on similar, if not the same, sources as the slavery studies—the WPA slave narratives, detailed plantation records, and contemporary diaries—to construct a picture of social structure and patterns of work-force participation. Scholars have also consulted the voluminous records of the Freedmen's Bureau and other federal agencies created by the crisis of Civil War and postemancipation adjustments. Recently, Ira Berlin and his colleagues in the Freedmen and Southern Society Project at the University of Maryland have made many of these documents more readily accessible in the multivolume series *Freedom: A Documentary History of Emancipation* (1982–).

Throughout the 1980s, therefore, scholars accepted the argument that sharecropping was a kind of compromise between planters who could not pay wages (because they had either no money or no credit) and freedpeople who resisted gang labor and wanted the closest possible approximation to a family farm. This interpretation was summarized most succinctly in Roger Ransom and Richard Sutch's *One Kind of Freedom* (1977), which tells the story of how blacks' refusal to sign contracts and, most of all, their withdrawal of labor—especially that of women and children—created a crisis to which the solution was sharecropping.

Still, this view has been significantly modified by more recent work. First, case studies of various plantation regions (especially in Mississippi and South Carolina) have shown that sharecropping as such did not emerge immediately after the Civil War but was preceded by a period of experimentation with several intermediate systems of payment and work organization. The most interesting of these were labor squads, work groups of two to ten laborers who were assigned certain tasks or sections of the crop and shared the proceeds of the harvest. There appears to be no consensus on how long this transition period of experimentation lasted; three, five, and ten years are all suggested by different scholars.

There is no consensus either on whose idea any of this was, on whose initiative the share system or labor squads or sharecropping originated. Ronald Davis, in *Good and Faithful Labor* (1982), states emphatically that freedpeople had a primary role in the creation of the system. Sharecropping was definitely *not* a compromise, he writes, because among all the actors involved—planters, freedmen, and Yankees—only the freedmen wanted it. "Planters literally were dragged kicking and screaming into the system. Unable to force the freedmen to work for fixed wages in a gang setting [which the blacks associated with slavery], planters accepted sharecropping because they had no choice in the matter."

Economic historian Gerald Jaynes's *Branches without Roots* (1986) makes a different set of corrections: freedmen, he writes, did not willingly accept the risks of sharecropping; they wanted the certainty of earning a livelihood, like all other agricultural workers and peasants, and would actually have preferred money wages—if they could have been certain of receiving the money. It was the uncertainty of payment that prompted their acceptance of shares of the crop, not any inherent attraction of shares over wages. According to Jaynes, it was the planters who had a preference for sharecropping; laborers preferred short-term wage contracts, which the planters refused.

On the other hand, Jaynes is very much in the tradition I have described in his emphasis on the prominent role of black workers in creating each of the systems that preceded sharecropping. He calls the refusal of share-laborers to work on various maintenance tasks (fencing and the like) *after* the harvest a "general strike" that forced changes in the pay system. The workers themselves preferred the squad system, because it allowed more equitable distribution of the work among the group, and the shares received could more nearly correspond to the actual effort of individuals. Eventually, the labor squads evolved into family-based units because that arrangement provided the best solution to incentive and control problems. Jaynes also describes many situations in which blacks asserted a voice in the management of their fields, although the planters disavowed such influence. Sharecropping as such, he says, did not become dominant until ten years after the Civil War.

In any case, share arrangements were beneficial only as long as workers had legal ownership of the share and cotton prices were high. The loss of Republican control of state legislatures vitiated the first condition, and the falling world market price of cotton negated the second. So despite all the evidence of worker initiative and militancy during the first decade of freedom, Jaynes insists that sharecropping emerged at the planters' initiative as a means of *sharing economic losses* with their tenants, given the falling price of cotton.

But whatever party—planters or freedpeople—primarily initiated the sharecropping system, clearly both acquiesced in it at the outset because each felt there was something to be gained. Furthermore, while it may be that the system was not yet *dominant* in the early 1870s, it is true that it coexisted with all the other forms of labor organization and payment.

Segregation

In some ways, discussions of the black role in the origins of segregation and Jim Crow parallel the debates over the origins of the economic system. On the eve of the Supreme Court's decision outlawing school segregation, C. Vann Woodward offered the persuasive thesis that legal segregation was a creation of the 1890s. In *The Strange Career of Jim Crow* (1955), Woodward argues that disfranchisement and segregation were southern reactions to the political ferment of the 1890s, when conservative Democrats and radical Populists competed for the black vote. Since neither group could be certain of winning this competition, they both made blacks the political scapegoats, agreeing to exclude them from the ballot box and segregate them in public life.

This thesis was challenged by Joel Williamson, who argued that racial separation and white supremacy were not new in the 1890s but had ample precedents in Reconstruction laws and in practice during the antebellum period in the North as well as the South. But as John Cell points out in *The Highest Stage of White Supremacy* (1980), his comparative study of American and South African racism, critics of Woodward's thesis often missed the point: that racial separation intensified and was institutionalized in law during the last decade of the century. The question of why this should have been so, of whether the causes were primarily economic, political, or sociological, remains to be resolved. Cell does offer a persuasive argument that the rise of segregation as a specific form of racial oppression was more likely to occur in urbanizing, modernizing areas of the American South than in traditional, rural areas. The racial tensions and anxieties stimulated by job competition from blacks and their social mobility encouraged repression in the form of discrimination and segregation.

In *Race Relations in the Urban South* (1978), Howard Rabinowitz takes an entirely different tack. He suggests that much of the debate over the origins of segregation is irrelevant to the situation most blacks found themselves in during the late nineteenth century. What blacks actually protested was not the segregation of public facilities but their complete or partial exclusion from schools, hospitals, and jobs outside agriculture. Under these conditions they might, indeed did, welcome segregated facilities as an improvement over what they had. The fact that southern and northern "liberals" were largely responsible for the development of such institutions underscores Rabinowitz's point. During this period blacks themselves demanded that white teachers be replaced by blacks in public schools. Furthermore, their withdrawal from white churches to form their own Baptist and Methodist congregations and their organization of mutual aid societies (some of which had evolved into insurance and banking companies by the 1890s) indicate initiatives toward institutional separation coming from within black communities.

Rabinowitz's findings also suggest that the celebrated debate between Booker T. Washington and W. E. B. Du Bois, over whether the best course for blacks was to accommodate to segregation or to protest it, should be reevaluated. Even before Washington's 1895 Atlanta Exposition speech there seems to have been strong sentiment favoring self-segregation and self-help. Of course, the respective portraits of Washington and Du Bois have acquired more complex shadings in recent studies. Louis Harlan's two-volume biography of Washington shows that he was "a multiple personality" who secretly supported attacks on Jim Crow while publicly advocating accommodation. And Du Bois, at times during his long career, enunciated views on self-help and segregation not entirely dissimilar to Washington's. The response of the larger black community to segregation suggests similar complexities and apparently contradictory tendencies. August Meier and Elliott Rudwick, in *Along the Color Line* (1976), describe a southern protest movement during this period, including boycotts and demonstrations, comparable in some respects to that of the 1950s and 1960s. Clearly, blacks could embrace voluntary separation in some areas of life, for strategic purposes, while emphatically rejecting it in others as an offense against their humanity.

BLACK LIFE IN THE
TWENTIETH CENTURY

Studies of black life in the twentieth century have emphasized protest and resistance to racial oppression, and the civil rights movement of the 1950s and 1960s is the central event. A consensus is emerging among scholars that that movement was not merely a creation of the Supreme Court's *Brown* decision of 1954 but had roots in the three previous decades of political and cultural change. Certainly, a case can be made that the origins of its leadership and the basis for its mobilization owe much to the dramatic urbanization of the black population during those decades. The first census following the Civil War showed that 90 percent of blacks were southerners, most of them farmers. The census taken on the eve of World War II showed just 77 percent of the black population still living in the South. Equally important, the percentage of blacks living in cities had jumped from 22 percent in 1900 to 34 percent in 1920 to 40 percent in 1930. By 1960 only half the black population lived in rural areas; less than one in ten still worked on a farm.

These demographic and economic changes laid the basis for the greatest political mobilization of black Americans since Reconstruction. Freed from the constraints of the rural South, blacks began to organize in both formal and informal political arenas. In the North during the 1920s and in southern cities by the 1940s and 1950s, blacks organized once again to protest segregation, Jim Crow, and job discrimination. With the advent of the New Deal, blacks became an important factor in national politics, and federal executive and judicial policies reflected the change. These political changes, together with a greatly augmented black intelligentsia and the revival of racial liberalism in the aftermath of Nazism, were essential precursors to the southern civil rights movement that seemingly exploded full-blown in the late 1950s. Before that movement had run its course the face of southern institutions had been radically transformed: voting and holding office in unprecedented numbers, blacks decisively influenced presidential politics and enticed erstwhile foes, among them Governor George Wallace of Alabama, to recant their earlier racist views.

The urbanization of the black population in the twentieth century was of critical importance, therefore, to the destruction of southern segregation. But it is the impact of urbanization on blacks themselves that has traditionally attracted most scholars' attention. Social scientists—sociologists, psychologists, and anthropologists—began studying the northern migration during the 1920s and 1930s. In contrast with black community leaders, who had encouraged the migration during World

War I as a liberation from southern oppression, most of these scholars emphasized its negative impact on northern communities. The black "peasant," moving from southern plantation to northern ghetto, was ill prepared for urban life. The increased black population exacerbated racial tensions in the cities, leading to intensified discrimination and residential segregation. Crime, disease, overcrowded tenements, and family disorganization characterized the expanding black ghettos. Some works, such as St. Clair Drake and Horace Cayton's *Black Metropolis* (1945), present a more complex and vital community life, but the dominant imagery emerges in the pathology described forcefully in works by E. Franklin Frazier, Robert Weaver, and Kenneth Clark. Like those in some of the slavery studies during this same period, these depressing portraits were stimulated, at least in part, by the need to call the nation to remedial action.

The explosion of urban rioting between 1964 and 1968 focused even more attention on the problem of the cities and indiscriminately fastened the pejorative "ghetto" label on black urban neighborhoods. In this context there appeared two new historical studies of the black migration to New York City and to Chicago: Gilbert Osofsky's *Harlem: The Making of a Ghetto* (1966) and Allan Spear's *Black Chicago: The Making of a Negro Ghetto, 1890–1920* (1967). Unlike most of the sociological literature that preceded them, these studies describe the role blacks themselves played in the emergence of ghettos. In New York City black realtors and community leaders, influenced by Booker T. Washington's self-help, accommodationist philosophy, initiated a veritable crusade that transformed Harlem from an exclusive white suburb into an all-black ghetto. In Chicago a similar group of Washington-inspired black leaders seized upon the southern migration to create a black clientele for their racially based businesses and civic enterprises.

Despite their emphasis on the initiatives and internal dynamics of black communities, however, both Osofsky and Spear still saw the emergence of ghettos as a consequence of white hostility and emphasized the pathologies induced by racial oppression. Indeed, two years after *Harlem*, Osofsky published an article suggesting, in effect, that if you had seen one ghetto, you had seen them all. The reasons for their "unending and tragic sameness," he contended, were poverty and racial discrimination. Osofsky's conclusion has been severely criticized for being neither systematic nor comparative. He did not draw on any black urban experience outside Harlem and Philadelphia, and he did not place his findings about blacks in the context of other ethnic groups. Indeed, his contentions are interesting mainly as expressions of then popular views and beliefs about "the ghetto," but in some ways they have affected other studies the way Elkin's Sambo thesis influenced slavery scholarship.

Almost as if in answer to Osofsky's critics, Kenneth Kusmer published *A Ghetto Takes Shape* (1976). Cleveland's black community was shaped by external forces (such as racism), internal forces (such as black pride and self-help), and the structural forces emerging from the urbanization process itself (transportation, communications, commercial zoning). Like his predecessors, Kusmer describes increasing white hostility as the black population exploded during the early twentieth century. Like Spear, he describes a Booker T. Washington–influenced faction among black leaders, which contested the older, integrationist group for community power. Since Kusmer extends his study to 1930, he sees also an eventual synthesis of these two strains into "the New Negro" of the 1920s. But Kusmer's major contributions are his comparison of changes in black occupational and residential patterns, *over time*, with those of other ethnic groups, and his suggestion that the changing urban infrastructure was a crucial arbiter of the choices available to whites and blacks alike. Such developments as the rise of department stores and new technologies like the telephone encouraged racial exclusion of white immigrants as well as blacks. Similarly, the separation of commercial and residential areas and the creation of better transportation systems made residential segregation more feasible. Indeed, Kusmer's discussion of the rise of the ghetto parallels John Cell's description of the rise of southern Jim Crow: modernization—generally considered a progressive force—emerges as the main culprit.

But despite aiding our comprehension of the subtleties and complexities of black urbanization, Kusmer, like his predecessors, frames his study against the backdrop of the 1960s preoccupation with urban unrest and its associated social pathologies; he still refers to the process as "ghettoization." The very term, Lawrence Levine suggests in *Black Culture and Black Consciousness* (1977), "invites us to see blacks always as passive victims and makes it difficult to ever perceive them as actors in their own right." Thus an ahistorical and pathological perspective is engrafted on the very language.

But for contemporaries (at least until the 1950s) these were not "ghettoes" but "communities" that symbolized a positive break with a history of oppression. Harlem was the locus of a cultural and literary renaissance and of the Garvey movement; Chicago gave birth to "a Black Metropolis." Osofsky, Spear, and Kusmer, approaching the subject from the perspective of a "rising ghetto model," provide little help in explaining such developments, unless one wishes to accept an implicit thesis of mass self-delusion.

Several later studies break decisively with the theme of victimization depicted in "the rise of the ghetto" school of black urban history. James Borchert's *Alley Life in Washington* (1980) shows that during much of the nineteenth century and well into the twentieth, substantial numbers of black migrants to northern cities settled in housing built within the interiors of city blocks. Generally considered "the poorest of the poor," these alley dwellers felt the full brunt of urban pathologies: inadequate income and housing, victimization by disease and crime, poor education. But, Borchert argues, alley dwellers were able to construct viable communities despite their adversity. Their families did not break down but grew more complex and supportive in response to urban conditions. The very harshness of life and the difficulties of survival encouraged a cooperative ethos. With courage and ingenuity, these southern migrants adapted their rural folk culture to the demands of the new environment.

Of course, it is not yet clear how representative Borchert's alley dwellers are of southern migrants generally. Peter Gottlieb's study of Pittsburgh, *Making Their Own Way* (1987), suggests that those coming north were not rural folk fresh off the farm but southern urbanites who, like some European immigrants, engaged in back-and-forth movement between old home and new rather than making an immediate permanent break. Even permanent settlers continued to have strong familial and cultural ties to "down home." Meanwhile, Joe William Trotter's *Black Milwaukee* (1985) argues that the entire ecological fixation of urban studies is misleading; far more important, he believes, is the process of proletarianization that urbanization entailed. For the first time, large numbers of blacks became wage workers rather than sharecroppers or tenants.

James Grossman's study of the migration to Chicago, *Land of Hope* (1989), brings to black urban studies the sensibilities and insights that have characterized the best studies of slavery and emancipation. He argues that in order to understand fully the migrants' experience and both the successes and failures of their adjustment to urban life, one must try to view the entire process from the perspective of the migrants. When we cease to treat blacks as mere victims of that process, we will better understand the terribly complex responses and developments of that era. Migration was a process, not a historical inevitability. Black southern migrants were bearers of a deeply ingrained and distinctive culture; from their southern experience a race-conscious world view emerged that informed both their choice to migrate and their responses to the urban environment—responses necessarily different from those of both northern-born blacks and white ethnic immigrants. More than any previous student of this era, Grossman demonstrates the extent and the mechanisms by which communal and kinship networks shaped the decision and the process of migration. He describes in convincing detail how these same forces influenced settlement and adjustment patterns: for example, the transfer almost intact of churches, barber shops, and other social institutions from specific southern communities. He makes a plausible case that black southern migrants responded to unionization and politics differently from white ethnics because unions were a cultural force with institutional roots in white ethnic communities but represented an external force in black communities. And finally, he provides a compelling and original frame of reference for the issue of race and class forces in the black experience: from the black perspective, class differences shaped social relations within the black community; outside that community, race was the dominant variable. All this suggests connections between early twentieth-century migrations and midcentury liberation movements, connections that are ripe for further exploration.

Deeply rooted in the urbanization and proletarianization of blacks during the interwar period, the civil rights movement and its aftermath form the latest chapter in the contemporary narrative of the African-American experience. Although the explicit links still have to be worked out, it is already clear from studies detailing the organizational life of the movement (Meier and Rudwick's *CORE* and Carson's *In Struggle*) and its personal and sociological basis (Morris's *Origins of the Civil Rights Movement* and Chafe's *Civilities and Civil Rights*) that earlier labor struggles were important predecessors and southern cities and towns essential crucibles of that resistance. It is clear as well that the problematic conclusion of that movement is linked to its failure to address effectively the problems associated with urban life and work in the second half of the twentieth century.

Ironically, the seemingly intractable problems of black unemployment and urban devastation have encouraged a resurgence in popular and sociological literature of the tone of victimization that Ellison complained about half a century ago. Closing the circle with this essay's point of departure into the study of modern African-American history, that literature suggests the continued relevance of such study. Throughout their history, blacks have found space within the system and resources within themselves to respond creatively to their oppression. They have been bludgeoned but not beaten, degraded but not destroyed. As slaves, as sharecroppers, as urban dwellers, black Americans have been able to make of themselves more than the sum of their oppression, more than "an image drained of humanity."

These are important and necessary correctives to the earlier historical traditions in which black history was largely the history of race relations and black people appeared mainly as victims of white meanness.

They suggest different perspectives on contemporary problems as well. But the meanness cannot be forgotten either. The present challenge of African-American history is to reintegrate these important materials on the internal black world and the black perspective on that world into the larger social, economic, and political forces that shaped it. In short, it is to realize that—"just like whites"—blacks have made their history, but they have not been free to make it any way they pleased. Just like all of humankind, African Americans are both the actors in and victims of their history.

BIBLIOGRAPHY

These are some of the recent works in African-American history.

Berlin, Ira, et al., eds. *Freedom: A Documentary History of Emancipation, 1861–1867.* Vol. 1, *The Destruction of Slavery.* Vol. 2, *The Black Military Experience.* New York: Cambridge University Press, 1982.
———. *Slaves No More: Three Essays on Emancipation and the Civil War.* Cambridge: Cambridge University Press, 1992.
Blassingame, John. *The Slave Community: Plantation Life in the Antebellum South.* Rev. ed. New York: Oxford University Press, 1979.
Borchert, James. *Alley Life in Washington: Family, Community, Religion, and Folklife in the City, 1850–1970.* Urbana: University of Illinois Press, 1980.
Carson, Clayborne. *In Struggle: SNCC and the Black Awakening of the 1960s.* Cambridge, Mass.: Harvard University Press, 1981.
Cell, John W. *The Highest Stage of White Supremacy: The Origins of Separation in South Africa and the American South,* New York: Oxford University Press, 1980.
Chafe, William H. *Civilities and Civil Rights: Greensboro, North Carolina, and the Black Struggle for Freedom.* New York: Oxford University Press, 1980.
Dittmer, John. *Black Georgia in the Progressive Era, 1900–1920.* Urbana: University of Illinois Press, 1977.
Fields, Barbara J. *Slavery and Freedom on the Middle Ground: Maryland during the Nineteenth Century.* New Haven, Conn.: Yale University Press, 1985.
Fox-Genovese, Elizabeth. *Within the Plantation Household: Black and White Women in the Old South.* Chapel Hill: University of North Carolina Press, 1988.
Franklin, John Hope, and August Meier, eds. *Black Leaders of the Twentieth Century.* Urbana: University of Illinois Press, 1982.
Genovese, Eugene D. *Roll, Jordan, Roll: The World the Slaves Made.* New York: Pantheon, 1974.
Gerber, David A. *Black Ohio and the Color Line, 1860–1915.* Urbana: University of Illinois Press, 1976.
Gilmore, Glenda Elizabeth. *Gender and Jim Crow: Women and the Politics of White Supremacy in North Carolina, 1896–1920.* Chapel Hill: University of North Carolina Press, 1996.

Gottlieb, Peter. *Making Their Own Way: Southern Blacks' Migration to Pittsburgh, 1916–1930.* Urbana: University of Illinois Press, 1987.

Grossman, James R. *Land of Hope: Chicago, Black Southerners, and the Great Migration.* Chicago: University of Chicago Press, 1989.

Gutman, Herbert G. *The Black Family in Slavery and Freedom, 1750–1925.* New York: Pantheon, 1976.

Higginbotham, Evelyn Brooks. *Righteous Discontent: The Women's Movement in the Black Baptist Church, 1880–1920.* Cambridge, Mass.: Harvard University Press, 1993.

Hine, Darlene Clark, ed. *The State of Afro-American History: Past, Present, and Future.* Baton Rouge: Louisiana State University Press, 1986.

Hirsch, Arnold R. *Making the Second Ghetto: Race and Housing in Chicago, 1940–1960.* New York: Cambridge University Press, 1983.

Jaynes, Gerald David. *Branches without Roots: The Genesis of the Black Working Class in the American South, 1862–1882.* New York: Oxford University Press, 1986.

Jones, Jacqueline. *Labor of Love, Labor of Sorrow: Black Women, Work, and the Family from Slavery to the Present.* New York: Basic Books, 1985.

Joyner, Charles. *Down by the Riverside: A South Carolina Slave Community.* Urbana: University of Illinois Press, 1984.

Kelley, Robin D. G. *Hammer and Hoe: Alabama Communists during the Great Depression.* Chapel Hill: University of North Carolina Press, 1990.

Kusmer, Kenneth. *A Ghetto Takes Shape: Black Cleveland, 1870–1930.* Urbana: University of Illinois Press, 1976.

Levine, Lawrence W. *Black Culture and Black Consciousness: Afro-American Folk Thought from Slavery to Freedom.* New York: Oxford University Press, 1977.

Lewis, Earl. *In Their Own Interests: Race, Class, and Power in Twentieth-Century Norfolk, Virginia.* Berkeley: University of California Press, 1991.

Litwack, Leon. *Been in the Storm So Long: The Aftermath of Slavery.* New York: Knopf, 1979.

Meier, August, and Elliott Rudwick. *Along the Color Line: Explorations in the Black Experience.* Urbana: University of Illinois Press, 1976.

———. *CORE: A Study in the Civil Rights Movement, 1942–1968.* Urbana: University of Illinois Press, 1975.

Morris, Aldon D. *The Origins of the Civil Rights Movement: Black Communities Organizing for Change.* New York: Free Press, 1985.

Payne, Charles M. *I've Got the Light of Freedom: The Organizing Tradition and the Mississippi Freedom Struggle.* Berkeley: University of California Press, 1995.

Powell, Lawrence N. *New Masters: Northern Planters during the Civil War and Reconstruction.* New Haven, Conn.: Yale University Press, 1980.

Rabinowitz, Howard N. *Race Relations in the Urban South, 1865–1890.* Urbana: University of Illinois Press. 1978.

———, ed. *Southern Black Leaders of the Reconstruction Era.* Urbana: University of Illinois Press, 1982.

Raboteau, Albert J. *Slave Religion: The "Invisible Institution" in the Antebellum South.* New York: Oxford University Press, 1978.

Rachleff, Peter J. *Black Labor in the South: Richmond, Virginia, 1865–1890.* Philadelphia: Temple University Press, 1984.

Rose, Willie Lee. *Rehearsal for Reconstruction: The Port Royal Experiment.* New York: Vintage, 1967.

Saville, Julie. *The Work of Reconstruction: From Slavery to Wage Laborer in South Carolina, 1860–1870.* Cambridge: Cambridge University Press, 1994.

Shaw, Stephanie J. *What a Woman Ought to Be and to Do: Black Professional Women Workers during the Jim Crow Era.* Chicago: University of Chicago Press, 1996.

Sitkoff, Harvard. *A New Deal for Blacks: The Emergence of Civil Rights as a National Issue—The Depression Decade.* New York: Oxford University Press, 1978.

Sobel, Mechal. *The World They Made Together: Black and White Values in Eighteenth-Century Virginia.* Princeton: Princeton University Press, 1987.

Trotter, Joe William, Jr. *Black Milwaukee: The Making of an Industrial Proletariat, 1915–45.* Urbana: University of Illinois Press, 1985.

White, Deborah Gray. *Ar'n't I a Woman? Female Slaves in the Plantation South.* New York: Norton, 1985.

Williamson, Joel. *After Slavery: The Negro in South Carolina during Reconstruction, 1861–1877.* Chapel Hill: University of North Carolina Press, 1965.

———. *A Rage for Order: Black-White Relations in the American South since Emancipation.* New York: Oxford University Press, 1986.

14

■ AMERICAN LABOR HISTORY

Leon Fink

HISTORIANS OVER THE PAST GENERATION HAVE REDISCOVERED THE AMERICAN working class. In doing so, they have focused less on official labor organizations (although such studies have played their part) than on the larger processes of social and economic change as these affect workers. The definition of "labor" itself has expanded beyond wage work in factories and workshops to encompass the lives of slaves on plantations and women at home; the subject of study also includes new or relatively unorganized groups such as department store employees, nurses, and migrant farm laborers. While the work experience itself still receives central attention, some labor historians give at least equal consideration to the dimensions of cultural identity, politics and governmental policy, and the structure of the labor market.

Such departures have given a distinctive new feel to a field that long took a more modest and self-restricted view of its purpose and direction. Originally growing out of the dedicated scholarship of early twentieth-century labor economists following John R. Commons, labor history traditionally concentrated on the impact of the economic marketplace on workers' skills, living standards, and organizing capacity. The trade union itself, the main subject of analysis, was regarded primarily as an economic institution; political activity, competing organiza-

333

tional models, and biographies of labor leaders received secondary emphasis.

The "new labor history," though encompassing many different thematic currents, has generally emphasized the ordinary worker as subject. Without denying the influence of markets, outside political events, and other forces, historians have attempted to reconstruct not only the behavior but the motivations and understandings of the common people. A major initiative in this direction (and one that inspired much subsequent work in the United States) was the publication of E. P. Thompson's *Making of the English Working Class* in 1963. Of the American works that followed Thompson's, probably none were more influential than those of the late Herbert Gutman. In wide-ranging community studies of worker protest and in a massive study of African American slaves, Gutman, like Thompson, focused on the question of how workers respond to situations and circumstances not of their own choosing.

In the hands of Gutman, David Montgomery, David Brody, and others whose published work began appearing during the 1960s, labor history left its niche on the sidelines of American historiography to enter into major debates about the nature of the American historical experience. Branching out creatively toward social and cultural analysis, the new labor history has necessarily involved forays into immigration, African American, and women's history. Industrial relations, urban geography, and popular culture have also become vital subjects. Even standard political topics such as the American Revolution, the Civil War, and political party development have been reshaped by this "history from the bottom up."

The new work rests on an implicit appreciation of diverse social forces operating in a country once considered a "classless" or, except for black-white divisions, a middle-class society. To be sure, no single, unified picture of an American working class has emerged from history's shadows as a result of this new work. This essay sketches some of the major themes, arguments, and questions raised by labor historians with an eye toward fitting them into a larger chronological and thematic treatment of American history. My aim is to illuminate the kind of work being done in one of the most dynamic arenas of American historiography.

COLONIAL ARTISANS AND THE AMERICAN REVOLUTION

Early American society might usefully be interpreted as a history of contending labor systems. From such a perspective one can focus on the varieties of colonial social-economic development and also gain insight into the ideology of the world's first revolutionary republic. At least three distinct types of econonic enterprise were widespread in North America by 1800: plantation production of agricultural commodities (tobacco, rice, indigo, sugar); family-based farming with limited relation to circumscribed markets; and artisan production tied to mercantile port cities. The first type spawned the North American version of Caribbean slavery and with it the defense of paternalistic controls by owners over laborers. The second type—classically centered in New England but scattered throughout the colonies—fostered a de facto independence from traditional centralized authority, which would become deeply rooted in American thought and culture. The third, closely tied to the second, generated values that would inform much of the country's later labor history.

Together, the scarcity of labor in the New World and relatively easy access to land had an almost immediate effect on the opportunities for servants, day laborers, and especially skilled mechanics. Within a few years of the founding of the colonies, servants' communications with their masters already bespoke a certain *Realpolitik* of leverage behind a traditional mask of deference. Throughout the colonies, employers complained as well of the high cost of artisan labor. Contracts for indenture rarely ran out their full seven-year tenure; in many cases the bonded servants simply left their assigned place for the open country. Well before the development of open divisions with the mother country, many colonists had thus already established an independence and personal liberty not accorded persons of their rank in Europe.

It was in the port cities that the developing ethos and the self-interest of the American colonists first clashed with those of the mother country. The renewed attempts by Britain in the 1760s to impose tight mercantile controls, raise taxes, and consolidate political authority over the formerly loosely self-governing colonies set off a series of confrontations with a disenchanted populace. Leading directly into the revolutionary upheaval itself, Alfred Young has persuasively argued, the colonists' resistance relied heavily on artisan crowds and the militant, sometimes violent activity of tightly organized lower-class gangs. Although we recognize few individuals below the rank of silversmith Paul Revere in the official pantheon of revolutionary heroes, the historical record makes clear that without the sympathetic printers, carpenters, cordwainers, navvies, and common laborers—who composed the main membership of such vanguard groups as the Sons of Liberty—American independence might have remained little more than an idle dream.

Although political leadership during the American Revolution rested for the most part with upper-class patriots, the self-conscious, if not autonomous, role of the artisan classes should not be overlooked.

The rationalist and radical democratic propaganda of a Tom Paine (himself a former staymaker) bore close ties with an artisan culture that maintained its own channels of association and communication. Identification of public virtue with the active participation of independent citizens in the affairs of state, the cornerstone of the republican message, fit perfectly with the artisan classes' ideals of liberty and small property.

The passionate commitment of the urban working classes to the ideals of the Revolution—a commitment that went beyond any calculus of self-interest—is evident from Jesse Lemisch's study of American sailors trapped in British prisons for much of the war. Faced with a choice of serving in the imperial forces or languishing behind bars, most not only remained in confinement but openly expressed their political loyalty to the Revolution. Celebrations of the Fourth of July, the formation of little "republics" replete with formal constitutions, and numerous escape attempts and acts of sabotage marked the resistance efforts of the captured seamen. Generally speaking, revolutionary events brought the artisan classes into more active and prominent public roles; politically, they would constitute a force to be reckoned with in the postrevolutionary decades of nation-building and attendant social conflict.

WORKERS IN A MARKET SOCIETY

The organization of journeymen artisans *as workers* beginning in the late 1820s confronted Americans with the unexpectedly contradictory implications of their much celebrated revolution. The artisan revolutionaries of the port cities assumed that both abundance and freedom might flow simultaneously from a society whose laws and economy liberated the individual from the impositions common to the aristocratic states of Europe. Combining a political faith in democracy with economic trust in a free market, the Paineites of the revolutionary era anticipated a more egalitarian social order based on small property. Consolidation of a federal constitutional order, enthusiastically greeted by the artisan constituency, did indeed strengthen the power of the new nation and appeared to insure its survival as a democratic republic. Soon, however, the prized republican virtues of liberty and independence again seemed threatened, in the eyes of many Americans, not by a tyrannical state but by forces generated within the marketplace itself. The Jacksonian fight over the Second Bank of the United States and access to credit, for example, arose directly from this sense of the Revolution imperiled from within. A crisis, both political and intellectual, was at hand for the artisan classes.

Skilled tradesmen in particular had begun to feel the severe pressures that would push the old master artisan either upward toward the ranks of merchant-manufacturers or, more commonly, back into wage labor. Consistently if unevenly, trade after trade fell victim to dilution through division of labor, a "bastardization" of craft that was in fact the first sign that the Industrial Revolution had indeed arrived on new shores.

The boot and shoe trade (the nation's largest manufacturing industry before the Civil War)—examined both by "old labor historians" like Commons and more recently by Alan Dawley, Paul Faler, and Mary Blewett—provides an excellent example. In 1800 a household served as the basic unit of shoe production. The master shoemaker—head of the household—purchased leather and supervised production in a small workshed behind the family cottage. A couple of younger journeymen who brought their tools with them received not only wages but firewood, clothing, and room and board from the master. Wives and daughters worked in the house as binders, hand-stitching the upper part of the shoe, while younger sons served as apprentices. Although each household contained an internal hierarchy, interdependence and a rough equality characterized relations among shoeworking households and indeed between shoeworking and most other households (those of farmers, craftsmen, shopkeepers) of the "republican" community.

By the 1830s household shoe production had given way to the centralized shop. The master, who had previously fashioned his goods on customer order or sold them to a small shopkeeper, now either transformed himself into an entrepreneur or fell victim to his merchant supplier. Taking advantage of credit and a protected national market, the general store (or "central shop") became the center of a vast putting-out system. This form of merchant manufacturing expanded the scale and lowered the cost of shoe production. In the process, however, the journeyman shoemaker, whether working at home or in a large workshop, had become a wage laborer.

Typically, this middle passage of merchant manufacturing, based on division of labor rather than technical innovation, ultimately gave way to more advanced factory production. In the shoe trade, for example, the application of sewing machines and mechanical stitching in the 1860s produced a further productive explosion.

The modern factory—a center of mass production based on a single power source—was not entirely absent from the antebellum American landscape. It was not the traditional artisanry that first came to grips with the rigors of the factory system, however, but a new labor force recruited from farms and villages. America's first "industrial proletariat" was in fact largely composed of young women and children either living in family settings (common among employees of most smaller mills) or boarding with peers in supervised dormitories (as practical in the first large, integrated spinning and weaving center, established at Lowell, Massachusetts, in 1821). In part to placate the fears of an anxious, suspicious citizenry over the importation of "British" methods into the American workplace, the celebrated Lowell owners offered a carefully planned, protective, and educational environment for Yankee farm girls recruited from northern New England. The supervised boardinghouses around the mills also nourished a community of sewing circles, reading groups, and a new, more urbane life-style among the farm women. The correspondence between millworkers and their home communities reveals an unmistakable ambivalence about the new industrial workplace; a sense of excitement, opportunity, and new openings in life existed side by side with complaint over the incessant repetition of tasks and the clatter of mill machinery.

While wage cuts and market compression would spark dissent in these "model" mill communities by the mid-1830s, the specific conditions of the mill labor force pointed generally to a more individual than collective escape from wage work. For the majority of these early American factory workers, millwork represented a short stage in a life course; it soon gave way to marriage, motherhood, and child rearing. The replacement of the rural Yankee recruits by impoverished Irish laborers in the late 1840s and 1850s presaged a new chapter in American industrial history: it introduced an immigrant labor force that could anticipate lifelong tenure in wage labor.

EARLY NINETEENTH-CENTURY WORKER PROTEST

Not surprisingly for a nation raised on doctrines of liberty and independence, the changing conditions and status of the American worker in the age of early manufacturing capitalism provoked organized protest. As historians have integrated political and cultural influences with economic explanations, popular protest has emerged less as an instinctive response to market stimuli than as a measure of the deep cleavages of interests and values in American society. Recent scholarship has particularly stressed the significance of an ethic of civic virtue or "republican" values in early worker protest. Again and again the voices of Jacksonian-era worker-activists in early trade unions, workingmen's parties, and popular broadsides decried the nation's growing gap in wealth and power as a betrayal of democratic citizenship. Boston labor leader Seth Luther, for example, warned workingmen in 1832 not to be "deceived by those who produce nothing and who enjoy all, who insultingly term us—the farmers, the mechanics and labourers—the Lower Orders, while the Declaration of Independence asserts that 'All Men Are Created Equal.'" Similarly, when the shoeworkers of New England struck in 1860—the largest labor protest to that day—it was not by accident that they selected Washington's Birthday as the day to begin the strike.

Although the young women of Lowell did not enjoy full citizenship in the republic, as Thomas Dublin has explained, they did claim rights deriving from a republican heritage. Calling themselves "daughters of freemen," the women protested worsening conditions at work. During the early 1840s the women's tactics centered on petitions for shorter hours, organized by the Lowell Female Labor Reform Association. Echoing the words of Tom Paine, the women warned employers that "we will show these drivelling cotton lords, this mushroom aristocracy of New England, who so arrogantly aspire to lord it over God's heritage, that our rights cannot be trampled upon with impunity; that we will no longer submit to that arbitrary power which has for the last ten years been so abundantly exercised over us."

Early nineteenth-century workers also sought political as well as industrial remedies to stem the development of a permanently class-divided society in America. Whether through workingmen's parties or factional influence within the Democratic party, the artisans, Sean Wilentz demonstrates, pushed for shorter-hours legislation, universal suffrage (for white men), free public education, cheap access to federal lands (a demand that would come to fruition in the 1862 Homestead Act), and an end to the private "monopoly" banking system.

SLAVES AS WORKERS

One large class of American workers could scarcely lay claim to the various social, industrial, and political remedies sought by freeborn American citizens. These were the African American slaves who sustained the vital plantation economy and its tributary urban marketplaces in the southern states. Of course, the means of redress open to slaves were severely restricted. Nevertheless, even without formal political and legal rights and denied the dignity of recognized marriage and family ties, the enslaved labor force exerted subtle checks on the power of the masters.

Although plantation production was officially entrusted to overseers and drivers, its pace was effectively in the control of the field hands themselves. Generally, as Eugene Genovese has argued, a de facto accommodation was attained, combining the slaves' pragmatic, provisional resignation to the system of servitude with the masters' acceptance of the fact they could wrest only so much effort from their "lazy" charges. Arbitrary and excessive (even by the informal code of slavery) treatment by masters occasioned various, if usually individual, acts of resistance—from breaking tools to running away to attempting violent revenge. From the slaves' oral tradition, however, we know that this African American laboring class was both conscious of its oppression and shrewd in its response: overt resistance and acts of hostility were less common than a more quiet communal forebearance and collective survival ethic. Unbeknown to most white observers, the African Americans carved out a distinctive, messianic Christianity and devoted exhaustless energies to the maintenance of family ties even in the face of sale and dispersal.

With the Civil War and emancipation, the former slaves showed that the political ideals of white America had not escaped their attention either. During the Reconstruction period their representatives universally voiced a demand for land and a free ballot—for access to that vaunted "independence" and "liberty" so long denied them. In 1865, when federal authorities ordered Sea Island blacks to turn back war-conscripted plantation lands to their former owners, a committee of freedmen angrily protested: "This is our home, we have made These lands what they are. . . . We have been always ready to strike for Liberty and humanity yea to fight if needs be to preserve this glorious union. Shall not we who are freedmen and have been always true to this Union have the same rights as are enjoyed by Others?"[1]

WORKERS IN THE GILDED AGE AND PROGRESSIVE ERA

Much that we think of as modern America was first consolidated during the late nineteenth century. The spread of the business corporation as the country's basic economic unit, the accompanying rise of large-scale factories, the growth of cities, and the urban culture of consumption based on mass marketing were all products of what Mark Twain called the Gilded Age. We normally picture the period as one that celebrated the businessman as the mover and shaker of America's progress and established a dominant intellectual climate sanctioning unrestricted free enterprise. In this fiercely middle-class culture, according to the conventional historical wisdom, American working people were simply middle-class citizens without money and education. Possessed of the same desires as everyone else, they lived with Horatio Alger dreams of "moving on up" the economic ladder by individual effort. Both the stepladder of immigrant upward mobility and a labor movement geared to craft-based demands for "more!" offered evidence of the fundamental unity and stability of a business-dominated culture by the turn of the century.

Such a gloss on the late nineteenth century requires correction if we are to grasp the real play of social conflict and historical possibility at the time. The Gilded Age witnessed the last and most significant attempt by American workers to fashion an alternative to corporate capitalism from within traditional political and social values. During recent years labor historians have explored the workers' world during the late nineteenth and early twentieth centuries from a variety of angles. One of the most popular approaches has been the community study used to examine industrializing towns and immigrant communities in large cities such as Chicago, New York, and Philadelphia. A second focus has been on the study of the work process itself, with attention to specific occupational subcultures. A third emphasizes worker organizations and labor politics during the period. Together, these studies have reconstructed a lost world of working-class America.

Within the workers' world the work experience itself generated an ethic of mutuality foreign to the emphasis on individualism that is often assigned to the period. Amid changing technological and managerial constraints imposed from above, workers—first as autonomous craftsmen, then through union work rules, and finally through sympathy strikes—struggled to maintain or regain control over decisions on the shop floor. The craftsman's notion of the work "stint" (the self-imposed limit on worker output), a visceral resistance or defiant "manliness" toward unwarranted exactions from employers or supervisors, and a disciplined solidarity with fellow workers defined a workplace ethic enveloping not only skilled craftworkers but unskilled, immigrant factory workers as well. David Montgomery's study of "workers' control" has emphasized the strength of the early twentieth-century labor ethic; other studies have drawn attention to the divisions within the labor force occasioned by the heterogeneity of skill, gender, and ethnic background of American workers.

American workers' organizing efforts in the age of Carnegie, to be sure, drew on more than the daily fight for "control" at the workplace. A popular republicanism questioned the effects, indeed the very morality, of a corporate industrial order in which one class of citizens would have so much power over others. As a philosophical Ohio farmer put it, "In Europe labor is accustomed to oppression, and it's a hard part of God's destiny for them, to be borne patiently as long as they can get enough to hold body and soul together"; in America, however, "our people have been carefully educated to consider themselves the best on earth, and they will not patiently submit to privation such as this system is leading to. They not only feel that they are the best of the earth, but there is no power, no standing army, no organized iron rule to hold them down." The responsibility of democratic citizenship required workers to earn a "competence," enough income and time to sustain a healthy family, educate the children, and stay personally abreast of worldly affairs. In 1885 one labor agitator declared that lumbermen who toiled fourteen or fifteen hours a day were "not free men—they had no time for thought, no time for home."

Efforts to transcend "wage slavery," evident in much of the political and industrial activity of organized workers since the 1860s, peaked with the rise of the Knights of Labor in the mid-1880s. The Knights, numbering more than three-quarters of a million members by 1886 and aspiring to a universal crusade of the "producing classes" (excluding only "social parasites"—lawyers, bankers, and liquor salesmen), reflected the full range of social and political initiatives in Gilded Age laboring communities. Unlike the older view of the Knights, which relegated the organization to the dustbins of history as impractical and backward-looking, recent treatments have shown renewed respect for the Great Upheaval, labor's serious and rational challenge to the consolidation of corporate capitalism in the 1880s. Under the vast social umbrella of the Knights of Labor (skilled and unskilled, men and women, native and immigrant, white and black joined as equals), Leon Fink has argued, moral and political education, producer cooperatives, land resettlement schemes, and Greenback-labor politics mixed uncertainly with trade union organization and the weapons of the strike and boycott. Reading rooms and family picnics as well as Labor Day parades and independent political tickets defined the socialization of individuals, families, and communities into the labor culture. Drawing on the traditions of fraternal lodges such as the Masons and Odd Fellows, the Knights began as a secret society, cloaking its activities in a rich veil of ritual and formal ceremony.

It was not only in formal organizations or overtly political activity, however, that the tensions of working-class versus middle-class values registered at the turn of the century. In popular leisure as well, historians have discovered a record of conflict, resistance, and, finally, adaptation by the immigrant working classes to outside pressures. Mid-nineteenth-century recreation among the laboring classes generally centered on local neighborhoods; it was loosely self-organized; and because of both a traditional unruliness among working men and a self-styled brashness among young working women, it tended to affront middle-class Protestant standards of proper decorum. Neighborhood saloons, raucous celebrations of holidays such as the Fourth of July, untamed behavior in the public parks, and defiance of the quiet Sabbath all came in for critical scrutiny by middle-class reformers. Sunday closings, prohibition, museums, libraries, and supervised recreation were all prescribed from on high as ways to "civilize" the working-class immigrants. Just as certainly, such impositions were either politically resisted or, sometimes more effectively, simply ignored by their would-be beneficiaries.

But while the genteel leisure reformers generally failed to remake the behavior and values of American workers, another set of changes did have lasting effects on the popular culture. These involved the commercialization of leisure time, or the creation of what has come to be called mass, consumer culture. Higher incomes combined with a generally shrinking work week had created, by the turn of the century, a mass audience for professional sports and entertainment industries. By 1910 the nickel theaters showing silent motion pictures (featuring talents usually drawn from the immigrant working class itself) could be labeled "the academy of the workingman," and by the 1920s some fifty million, or half the U.S. population, could be counted in weekly attendance at the movies. Initially catering to working-class audiences with a tolerant indulgence of drinking and casual family comings and goings, the movie theaters began to take on more lavish, disciplined, middle-class standards only in the 1920s. In the end the new mass culture, argues Roy Rosenzweig, would be neither an autonomous creation of the common people nor a product created and packaged entirely apart from them. Drawing originally on popular and democratic impulses, leisure in America—like politics—would involve a continuous if often contested quest to harness the public impulse for private ends.

The examination of leisure and popular culture suggests the breadth of themes now invoked by the study of labor history. The transformation of work and the workers' community, the consequent struggle not only for material standards of living but for a voice in the direction of American society, and the changing meanings that working people themselves gave to their actions lend the study of labor history a broad territorial claim within the larger discipline. Indeed, much of the social and cultural history of the American people may be observed through these lenses.

LABOR IN THE TWENTIETH CENTURY

Labor history in the twentieth century—with the exception of specific influences from immigration history, women's history, and black history —has continued to concentrate on political, economic, and institutional subject matter. The social and cultural focus common to much recent nineteenth-century labor history has received less emphasis. Still, recent historiography of the modern period reflects the general attempt to relate labor history to larger changes in American life. As a result, even the "political" or "organizational" histories of labor—the synthetic efforts of David Brody, Mike Davis, Ronald Filipelli, James Green, Alice Kessler-Harris, and Robert Zieger are particularly worthy of mention— offer perspectives that might well lend themselves to general treatments of the period.

A basic question running through much work on the early twentieth century concerns the relative weakness of organized labor and its political influence in the United States. Why were American workers unable to breach the barriers of skill (or craft) that divided them? Why did they not, as in European countries, develop a more corporate consciousness as workers? And why did they not seek a political vehicle for themselves in the form of a socialist or labor party?

Needless to say, such questions receive diverse answers. Some scholars emphasize the structural constraints of American society. The very strength of an expansionary American capitalism, they argue, fended off social polarization by creating jobs and raising living standards and, at the same time, won over the vast reaches of the middle class to an acceptance of corporate power. Others argue that the heterogeneity of the American working class reinforced ethnic and racial identities at the expense of classwide solidarity. Employers, who tended to be fiercely antagonistic to collective bargaining agreements, were able to play skillfully on the inner divisions among the workers. The combination of segmented (or separate) labor markets for men and women, blacks and whites, and even different immigrant groups; company welfarism for select employees; and the ready use of the "stick" against would-be organizers allowed the major mass-production industries to escape organization. Even when the defenses of the corporations themselves were breached—as in the famous battles at Homestead (1892), Pullman (1894), and Ludlow (1914)—employers, as Sidney Lens documents, were able to call on the good offices of the courts or on armed troops to put down the rebellion.

Within this generally hostile climate, of course, workers and their organizations faced the question of what strategy and actions to pursue. Samuel Gompers and the national leadership of the AFL represent, by most accounts, the line of pragmatic, conservative adaptation to the status quo. Disabused of the "illusions" of the socialists and the false panaceas of "reform unionists" such as the Knights of Labor, the national trade unions in the Gompers era stuck to a self-protective agenda, eschewing industrywide workplace initiatives as well as any ambitious political challenge to corporate power. A business unionism geared only to the immediate workplace interests of each craft; an exclusive disregard for the plight of minority, women, and unskilled immigrant workers;

and a commitment to voluntaristic self-help versus government protective legislation defines, by standard measurement, the dominant outlook of organized labor (excluding the socialists and the IWW, or Wobblies) prior to the Great Depression. "Americanism," the dominant national political culture as promulgated by business, political, and judicial authorities, appears in this period to have been successfully narrowed from its broader "republican" origins to a focus on national economic growth and individual rights in property. Within these limits organized labor sought only to be seated at the "bourgeois" supper table, a mere "interest group" with no great influence.

Without disturbing this overall image of labor's political weakness, recent work—exemplified by Montgomery's magisterial *Fall of the House of Labor*—nevertheless considerably complicates the picture. Looking below the national leadership of the AFL, one sees a great deal more variety of social and political response during the period. In industrial centers such as Chicago and San Francisco, for example, citywide labor federations exerted both industrial and political muscle and also readily extended themselves in campaigns to organize the unorganized. Foreshadowing the great industrial union struggles waged by the CIO, immigrant women successfully wrested union recognition from employers in the garment industry in 1910; skilled metalworkers in manufacturing centers across the nation from 1909 to 1922 spearheaded recurrent sympathy strikes aimed at wresting control of the work process from arbitrary managerial authority; western shipyards and midwestern packinghouses and steelworks erupted in the turbulent year of 1919; and southern textile workers rose en masse in fierce but losing struggles in 1928–29 and 1934. The socialist movement under the leadership of Eugene V. Debs, Nick Salvatore suggests, also tapped indigenous radical roots among both urban and western agrarian laborers. Finally, historians have begun to qualify the very "conservatism" of AFL figures such as Gompers and Adolph Strasser, emphasizing an abiding Marxist influence on their thought and the pragmatic nature of their political cautiousness. Within the two-party system, and especially at the state and municipal level, some have noted, labor was a vigorous and progressive actor.

LABOR AND THE NEW DEAL SETTLEMENT

If, during the early twentieth century, organized labor rested on the margins of social and political influence, the upheaval of the 1930s combined with wartime mobilization to alter the picture. The rise of industrial unionism in the CIO, labor's role in the New Deal coalition and social welfare legislation, and the institutionalization of collective bargaining during World War II and the postwar boom (1945–73) have, not surprisingly, formed a primary topical agenda for contemporary historians. Studies of the postwar labor force, however, including the expanding (and largely female) clerical and service sectors and the southern black exodus to northern industrial centers, have also added a few social history counterweights to a primarily "political" narrative.

Studies of labor in the era of the New Deal offer perhaps the most convincing argument for the integration of American political and labor history. On one hand, we cannot understand the emergence of an American welfare state without taking into account the extraordinary activation of the industrial citizenry in the strike waves of 1934 and 1936–37 and their electoral mobilization around the party of Roosevelt. This mobilization—still to be thoroughly examined at the grassroots level—involved an interconnected chain of circumstances. The economic collapse revived the more radical minority tendencies (socialism and Communism, as well as industrial unionism) that had developed earlier within the trade union movement. Then, too, the 1930s witnessed the political coming of age of the second-generation New Immigrant communities that dominated the nation's industrial heartland. Italians, Poles, Jews, and African Americans whose jobs, income, and education as well as their racial and ethnic endowment had banished them from the centers of decision-making in America—in politics, in business, and even within organized labor—now publicly asserted their own version of the national interest. Thus, both the success of New Deal legislation and labor's new institutional clout may be seen to reflect popular transformations, centered on the grassroots stirring within the working class.

On the other hand, no adequate explanation of labor in mid-twentieth-century America could focus on workers' history by itself. Organized labor was lifted out of its twentieth-century doldrums by the active intervention of the federal government in the form of the anti-injunction Norris-LaGuardia Act (1932); section 7a of the National Industrial Recovery Act (NIRA) of 1933, which sanctioned collective bargaining; and the Wagner Act (1935), which placed the full weight of the state behind labor's right to organize. By rolling back the obstructionist arm of the labor law and laying the foundations as well for both social welfare and employment policy, the New Deal (especially as consolidated during World War II) inaugurated a new era of American industrial relations.

Just as the Great Depression conditioned the social transformation of the 1930s and 1940s, so would the nation's changing economic circumstances influence the role and responses of workers in the postwar world. Resting on America's worldwide economic expansionism, American business accommodated in the boom years as never before to collective bargaining. As long as union recognition and collective bargaining contracts did not disturb opportunities for profit and investment, the conciliation of organized labor appeared secure.

Still, to be accepted by both business and government, unions would have to renounce the solidaristic strategies of sympathy strikes as well as any larger, critical political role. This was the lesson learned, and generally accepted, by the AFL and CIO (united in 1955) from both the Taft-Hartley Act (1947) and a range of postwar industrial conflicts. Thus, while both union membership and workers' living standards soared during the boom years, "labor" became less and less a social movement of rank-and-file workers. An effective agent of social insurance for those who were organized (and this still excluded the vast reaches of the growing service, clerical, and high-tech sectors as well as the underemployed "underclass"), unions came to appear to much of the public and even to some of their own members as a collection of "special interests."

Such changes of function and perception would take their most destructive toll only after the collapse of the boom (roughly, in 1973), amid the rise of international economic competition and the fraying of the liberal New Deal coalition—a process that culminated in the free-market, anti-union conservatism of the Reagan years. At the workplace, the ballot box, and the bar of public opinion, organized labor has suffered a precipitous decline since the boom years. Yet even as traditional centers of labor strength, including mine, steel, and construction unions, were enervated by steadily declining bargaining power, other groups such as hospital workers and teachers showed a new-found dynamism.

RECENT REVISIONS OF THE WORKER AS HISTORICAL SUBJECT

Since 1990 the writing of American labor history has experienced a subtle shift in emphasis. Together, the impact of a more conservative political climate and the extension of historians' curiosities to previously marginalized subjects has contributed to a decidedly more sober assessment of past labor movements. On the one hand the very logic of the new labor history, by extending investigation to women, minority workers, and the less skilled, has led to more critical judgments of the limited vision and exclusive practice of white, male-breadwinner-dominated trade unions. On the other hand, the continuing diminution in numbers and influence of organized labor in our own day has led historians to focus on ways in which working people have regularly been buffeted, if not openly manipulated, by forces beyond their control. Recent "revisionist" studies have thus emphasized the effects of structural economic change, managerial strategy, and the coercive power of the law and the courts on industrial relations, as well as the disfiguring patterns of violence and alcoholism on laboring communities.

The question of when—and how—working people have affected American society remains one of the most basic motivations for the work of recent labor historians. Of course, almost any aspect of American history may be analyzed from the opposite angle: how did it affect the working classes? Political, economic, even diplomatic history may be subjected to such scrutiny. But it has been the project of historians since the 1970s to go beyond the question of how labor fit into American conditions and how it was acted upon. As Herbert Gutman wrote, quoting Jean-Paul Sartre, what is important is "not what 'one' has done to man, but what man does with what 'one' has done to him." With an eye on the American worker at work, at home, and at play, historians have acted energetically on Sartre's injunction. In so doing they have also repeatedly demonstrated the centrality of the labor movement itself—by reason of both its actions and its defaults—in the character of American democracy. The American working class, to paraphrase E. P. Thompson, has been present at its own several makings—and unmakings. As a lengthy and unending record of resistance, advances, and setbacks for the welfare of ordinary citizens, the "labor question" holds the key to explaining much of what is peculiarly American about American history.

NOTE

1. I thank Ira Berlin for this citation from a letter by Henry Brum et al. to "the President of these United States," October 28, 1865 (from the National Archives as collected and edited by the Freedmen and Southern Society Project, University of Maryland).

BIBLIOGRAPHY

These are recent works on general American labor history and its sequential eras as indicated in the text.

General

American Social History Project. *Who Built America? Working People and the Nation's Economy, Politics, Culture, and Society.* New York: Pantheon, 1989.

Brody, David. *Workers in Industrial America: Essays on the Twentieth-Century Struggle*. New York: Oxford University Press, 1980.

———. *In Labor's Cause: Main Themes on the History of American Labor*. New York: Oxford University Press, 1993.

Buhle, Paul, and Alan Dawley, eds. *Working for Democracy: American Workers from the Revolution to the Present*. Urbana: University of Illinois Press, 1985.

Davis, Mike. *Prisoners of the American Dream: Politics and Economy in the History of the U.S. Working Class*. London: Verso, 1986.

Filipelli, Ronald L. *Labor in the U.S.A.: A History*. New York: McGraw-Hill, 1984.

Fink, Leon. *In Search of the Working Class: Essays in American Labor History and Political Culture*. Urbana: University of Illinois Press, 1994.

Foner, Philip. *Organized Labor and the Black Worker, 1619–1981*. New York: International Publishers, 1973.

———. *Women and the American Labor Movement*. New York: Free Press, 1982.

Gordon, David M., Richard Edwards, and Michael Reich. *Segmented Work, Divided Workers: The Historical Transformation of Labor in the United States*. New York: Cambridge University Press, 1982.

Green, James. *The World of the Worker: Labor in Twentieth-Century America*. New York: Hill & Wang, 1980.

Kessler-Harris, Alice. *Out to Work: A History of Wage-Earning Women in the United States*. New York: Oxford University Press, 1982.

Montgomery, David. *Citizen Worker: The Experience of Workers in the United States with Democracy and the Free Market during the Nineteenth Century*. New York: Cambridge University Press, 1993.

———. *The Fall of the House of Labor*. New York: Cambridge University Press, 1987.

Wertheimer, Barbara M. *We Were There: The Story of Working Women in America*. New York: Pantheon, 1977.

Zieger, Robert H. *American Workers, American Unions, 1920–1985*. Baltimore, Md.: Johns Hopkins University Press, 1986.

America to the Civil War

Dawley, Alan. *Class and Community: The Industrial Revolution in Lynn*. Cambridge, Mass.: Harvard University Press, 1976.

Dublin, Thomas. *Farm to Factory: Women's Letters, 1830–1860*. New York: Columbia University Press, 1983.

———. *Women at Work: The Transformation of Work and Community in Lowell, Massachusetts, 1826–1860*. New York: Columbia University Press, 1979.

Foner, Eric. *Tom Paine and Revolutionary America*. New York: Oxford University Press, 1976.

Gutman, Herbert G. *The Black Family in Slavery and Freedom, 1750–1925*. New York: Pantheon, 1976.

Nash, Gary B. *The Urban Crucible: Social Change, Political Consciousness, and the Origins of the American Revolution*. Cambridge, Mass.: Harvard University Press, 1979.

Prude, Jonathan. *The Coming of Industrial Order: Town and Factory Life in Rural Massachusetts, 1810–1860*. New York: Cambridge University Press, 1983.

Rediker, Marcus. *Between the Devil and the Deep Blue Sea: Merchant Seamen, Pirates, and the Anglo-American Maritime World, 1700–1750*. New York: Cambridge University Press, 1987.

Smith, Billy G. *The "Lower Sort": Philadelphia's Laboring People, 1750–1800*. Ithaca: Cornell University Press, 1990.

Stansell, Christine. *City of Women: Sex and Class in New York, 1789–1860*. New York: Knopf, 1986.

Wilentz, Sean. *Chants Democratic: New York City and the Rise of the American Working Class, 1788–1850*. New York: Oxford University Press, 1984.

Late Nineteenth Century

Fink, Leon. *Workingmen's Democracy: The Knights of Labor and American Politics*. Urbana: University of Illinois Press, 1983.

Gutman, Herbert G. *Work, Culture, and Society in Industrializing America: Essays in American Working-Class History*. New York: Vintage, 1977.

Kaufman, Stuart. *Samuel Gompers and the Origins of the American Federation of Labor, 1848–1896*. Westport, Conn.: Greenwood Press, 1973.

Keyssar, Alexander. *Out of Work: The First Century of Unemployment in Massachusetts*. New York: Cambridge University Press, 1986.

Krause, Paul. *The Battle for Homestead, 1880–1892: Politics, Culture, and Steel*. Pittsburgh, Pa.: University of Pittsburgh Press, 1992.

Levine, Susan. *Labor's True Woman: Carpet Weavers, Industrialization, and Labor Reform in the Gilded Age*. Philadelphia: Temple University Press, 1984.

Montgomery, David. *Beyond Equality: Labor and the Radical Republicans, 1862–1872*. New York: Knopf, 1967.

Oestreicher, Richard J. *Solidarity and Fragmentation: Working People and Class Consciousness in Detroit, 1875–1900*. Urbana: University of Illinois Press, 1986.

Rachleff, Peter. *Black Labor in the South: Richmond, Virginia, 1865–1890*. Philadelphia: Temple University Press, 1984.

Ross, Steven J. *Workers on the Edge: Work, Leisure, and Politics in Industrializing Cincinnati, 1788–1890*. New York: Columbia University Press, 1985.

Stromquist, Shelton. *A Generation of Boomers: The Pattern of Railroad Labor Conflict in Nineteenth-Century America*. Urbana: University of Illinois Press, 1987.

Twentieth Century

Barrett, James R. *Work and Community in the Jungle: Chicago's Packinghouse Workers, 1894–1922*. Urbana: University of Illinois Press, 1987.

Bensman, David, and Roberta Lynch. *Rusted Dreams: Hard Times in a Steel Community*. New York: McGraw-Hill, 1987.

Benson, Susan Porter. *Counter Cultures: Saleswomen, Managers, and Customers in American Department Stores, 1890–1940*. Urbana: University of Illinois Press, 1986.

Bernstein, Irving. *The Lean Years: A History of the American Worker, 1920–1933.* Baltimore, Md.: Johns Hopkins University Press, 1966.

———. *The Turbulent Years: A History of the American Worker, 1933–1941.* Boston: Houghton Mifflin, 1970.

Brody, David. *Steelworkers in America: The Non-Union Era.* Cambridge, Mass.: Harvard University Press, 1960.

Cooper, Patricia. *Once a Cigar Maker.* Urbana: University of Illinois Press, 1987.

Deutsch, Sarah. *No Separate Refuge: Culture, Class, and Gender on an Anglo-Hispanic Frontier in the American Southwest, 1880–1940.* New York: Oxford University Press, 1987.

Dubofsky, Melvin. *We Shall Be All: A History of the Industrial Workers of the World.* Urbana: University of Illinois Press, 1988.

Dubofsky, Melvin, and Warren Van Tine. *John L. Lewis: A Biography.* Ann Arbor: University of Michigan Press, 1969.

Fink, Leon, and Brian Greenberg. *Upheaval in the Quiet Zone: The History of Hospital Workers' Union, Local 1199.* Urbana: University of Illinois Press, 1989.

Fraser, Steve. *Labor Will Rule: Sidney Hillman and the Rise of American Labor.* New York: Free Press, 1991.

Hall, Jacquelyn, et al. *Like a Family: The Making of a Southern Cotton Mill World.* Chapel Hill: University of North Carolina Press, 1987.

Kazin, Michael. *Barons of Labor: The San Francisco Building Trades and Union Power in the Progressive Era.* Urbana: University of Illinois Press, 1987.

Lens, Sidney. *The Labor Wars: From the Molly Maguires to the Sitdowns.* Garden City, N.Y.: Doubleday, 1973.

Lichtenstein, Nelson. *Labor's War at Home: The CIO in World War II.* New York: Cambridge University Press, 1982.

———. *The Most Dangerous Man in Detroit: Walter Reuther and the Fate of American Labor.* New York: Basic Books, 1995.

Meier, August, and Elliott Rudwick. *Black Detroit and the Rise of the UAW.* New York: Oxford University Press, 1979.

Milkman, Ruth, ed. *Women, Work, and Protest: A Century of U.S. Women's Labor History.* Boston: Routledge & Kegan Paul, 1985.

Montgomery, David. *Workers' Control in America: Studies in the History of Work, Technology, and Labor Struggles.* Cambridge: Cambridge University Press, 1979.

Rosenzweig, Roy. *Eight Hours for What We Will: Workers and Leisure in an Industrial City, 1870–1920.* New York: Cambridge University Press, 1983.

Salvatore, Nick. *Eugene V. Debs: Citizen and Socialist.* Urbana: University of Illinois Press, 1982.

Schatz, Ronald W. *The Electrical Workers: A History of Labor at General Electric and Westinghouse, 1923–60.* Urbana: University of Illinois Press, 1983.

Zieger, Robert H. *The CIO, 1935–1955.* Chapel Hill: University of North Carolina Press, 1995.

Zunz, Olivier. *The Changing Face of Inequality: Urbanization, Industrial Development, and Immigrants in Detroit, 1880–1920.* Chicago: University of Chicago Press, 1983.

Recent Revisions on the Worker as Subject

Blewett, Mary H. *Men, Women, and Work: Class, Gender, and Protest in the New England Shoe Industry, 1780–1914*. Urbana: University of Illinois Press, 1988.

Faue, Elizabeth. *Community of Suffering and Struggle: Women, Men, and the Labor Movement in Minneapolis, 1915–1945*. Chapel Hill: University of North Carolina Press, 1991.

Fones-Wolf, Elizabeth. *Selling Free Enterprise: The Business Assault on Labor and Liberalism, 1945–60*. Urbana: University of Illinois Press, 1994.

Forbath, William E. *Law and the Shaping of the American Labor Movement*. Cambridge, Mass.: Harvard University Press, 1991.

Frank, Dana. *Purchasing Power: Consumer Spending, Gender, and the Seattle Labor Movement, 1919–1929*. New York: Cambridge University Press, 1994.

Roediger, David R. *The Wages of Whiteness: Race and the Making of the American Working Class*. New York: Verso, 1991.

Tomlins, Christopher L. *Law, Labor, and Ideology in the Early American Republic*. New York: Cambridge University Press, 1993.

Way, Peter. *Common Labour: Workers and the Digging of the North American Canals, 1780–1860*. New York: Cambridge University Press, 1993.

15

■■ ETHNICITY AND ■■ IMMIGRATION

James P. Shenton
and Kevin Kenny

IMMIGRATION IS ONCE AGAIN A SIGNIFICANT ASPECT OF AMERICAN LIFE. THE LATINO population of the United States has almost tripled since 1960, reaching 20 million in 1990. The Asian population reached 7.3 million in the same year, the majority from Korea, China and, more recently, India. In the 1980s alone, 7 million immigrants entered the United States legally, more than for any decade in American history except 1901–10, when 8.8 million arrived. And, if an estimated average of 300,000 to 500,000 undocumented aliens a year is added to the figures, the total for the 1980s exceeds that for 1901–10 and becomes the highest in American history. These new immigrants are not as high a proportion of the total population as they once were (12 percent in the 1850s, 11 percent in the 1900s, and at most 3 percent in the 1980s), but an era of mass migration to the United States has returned and with it a national debate over culture, history, language and immigration restriction.

In the light of these developments, historians have begun to reappraise the history of American immigration and ethnicity as a whole. Considerable attention has been paid to the newest immigrants from Asia and Latin America. The history of immigration in the colonial period and in the nineteenth and early twentieth centuries has also been reconsidered and revised. In place of an old picture dominated by the

353

"breakdown" of immigrant cultures and their assimilation into a dominant Anglo culture, new models of ethnicity and assimilation are beginning to emerge, calling into question traditional two-dimensional accounts of race as white versus black, of ethnicity as native-born American
versus foreign-born "ethnic," and of assimilation as citizen versus alien.

THE FIRST IMMIGRANTS

According to the first federal census, taken in 1790, there were 3,172,444
whites and 757,208 blacks in the original states plus Vermont, Kentucky, and Tennessee. It is estimated that 56 percent of this population
of almost 4 million were of English and Scottish origin, 19 percent of
African origin, 8 percent Irish (just over half of whom were Scotch-Irish
Protestants from Ulster), 7 percent German, and the remainder from
Holland, France, Sweden, and elsewhere. Estimates of the total number
of people who migrated to the United States before 1819, when the
federal government first required ships' captains to report the number of
debarking passengers, have been educated guesses at best.

There were significant differences between the immigrants who
settled the Chesapeake Bay area and those who settled New England.
The Puritan migration of the 1630s generally consisted of stable, relatively prosperous family groups. The Chesapeake, by contrast, attracted
larger numbers of single males, typically poorer than their northern
peers, and lacking the discipline and social cohesiveness provided by Puritanism. If they were not the "whores, rogues and vagabonds" described
by a previous generation of historians, significant numbers of the immigrants to the southern colonies came from the lower orders of British
society. Desperate for men and women who could work, these colonies
were prepared to import convict labor, as Roger Ekirch has described in
his study of 50,000 convicts transported to the American colonies in the
eighteenth century. But convicts were the exception; and, even in the
southern colonies, immigrants were not the "dregs" of British society
but a representative cross-section of its lower and middle orders. David
Galenson, for example, has demonstrated that the indentured servants
who made up the bulk of the immigrant population in the colonial period were skilled artisans, healthy teenage boys, practicing farmers, and
landless laborers in need of work.

Immigrants may have been "pushed" out of their homelands for
economic, political, religious, military, and even biological reasons, but
there was an equally strong set of "pull" factors enticing them to come
to the United States. Many of these pull factors were simply the mirror
images of the forces pushing the immigrants out of their homelands: the

possibility of becoming rich or at least economically comfortable, the availability of land, religious and political freedom. Some of these expectations proved exaggerated, others illusory. A genuinely transatlantic approach to the history of American immigration in the colonial era must start with a thorough understanding of the push factors at home; move from there to the pull factors and the extent to which they were real; and, on that basis, examine patterns of settlement, culture, and assimilation. One step in that direction is the recent work of Bernard Bailyn on the lives and aspirations of tens of thousands of anonymous emigrants who left Britain for America in the 1770s. Most of them did so, he concludes, less for reasons of war, plague, poverty, or persecution than out of attraction to "this strange world" across the Atlantic Ocean.

The British and Irish domination of immigration from Europe in the colonial period should not blind us to the considerable diversity and contentiousness among the newcomers. While more indentured servants settled in the southern than the northern colonies, the fundamental fact about the former region is that servants coexisted with large numbers of slaves, brought to the United States involuntarily from the Caribbean and Africa. And, if Puritan New England was the most homogenous American region until the arrival of the Irish in the 1830s, it retained its purity only at the price of banishing heretics and hanging proselytizing Quakers. As for other ethnic groups, there were about 100,000 Americans of Dutch birth or descent in the United States in 1790, 80,000 of them within a fifty-mile radius of New York City. Between 75,000 and 100,000 German immigrants are estimated to have arrived during the colonial period, concentrating in Pennsylvania but settling along the East Coast as far south as Georgia. And, though the number of French immigrants in the colonial period is unknown, it included 14,000 Huguenot refugees who came to the future United States and another 10,000 Roman Catholics who settled in Canada. During the French Revolution, 10,000 more refugees came to the United States, many from the Caribbean islands.

The Middle Colonies were the most ethnically diverse and religiously tolerant. If this was true of William Penn's Philadelphia, it was all the more true of New York City, as Randall Balmer has explained. Tensions between the Dutch and the English residents of the city peaked in 1664 and again in 1689–91, when Dutch artisans and small shopkeepers fought unsuccessfully against English rulers and their allies in the Dutch merchant class. Thereafter, New York was to be an English colony, but it lost none of its diversity. According to one report, eighteen languages were being spoken there as early as 1643.

Despite its diversity and its centrality in subsequent national development, excessive attention to the Northeast obscures the nature of migration and ethnicity in colonial North America as a whole. While the position of Native Americans and African Americans in the colonial period is considered elsewhere in this volume, greater attention is needed to Spanish colonization and, above all, to people of Spanish and Mexican Indian origin in the Southwest. The standard work is still John Bannon's history of the Spanish borderlands from the sixteenth through the early nineteenth centuries. Among the most readable accounts of the deep-rooted Mexican presence in the Southwest is John Chavez's account of the Chicano image of a "Lost Land." But the outstanding work on this early period is Ramón Gutiérrez's powerful and evocative account of the Pueblo Indians of New Mexico from the arrival of the Spanish in the sixteenth century to the Anglo conquest three centuries later, viewed through the lens of power, religion, sexuality, and marriage. With themes as rich as these, the history of the borderlands is fast becoming one of the most exciting subfields in American ethnic history.

THE "OLD" IMMIGRANTS

Historians typically use the term "old" immigration for the period 1820 and 1880, and "new" immigration for the period 1880 to the 1920s. This terminology has recently become outdated, as the genuinely "new" immigration is the one that has occurred in the United States since 1965. Nonetheless, it retains some usefulness for historiography by differentiating the two great waves of immigration to the United States in the century after 1820.

The "old" immigration brought more than 10 million immigrants to the United States in a sixty-year period, with the greatest activity between 1840 and 1860, when almost 4.5 million arrived. The first to arrive in large numbers were the Irish, almost 5 million of whom traveled to the United States between 1820 and 1920, a figure exceeded only by the Germans. Their passage to America has been memorably portrayed by Kerby Miller, whose work throws down a gauntlet to historians of American immigration and ethnicity in general by insisting that the immigrants' world in America makes little sense unless we begin with a thorough understanding of the world they left behind. This Miller does to great effect for the Irish, though not without formulating a thesis guaranteed to ruffle the feathers of many Irish Americans. The Irish, Miller argues, were deeply damaged by the forces of "modernization" (colonial conquest, capitalist agriculture, the beginnings of industry and urbanization) and arrived in the United States ill-equipped to cope with the harsh and often bewildering nature of industrial life. Falling back on a rich, preliterate Gaelic culture, they tended to interpret their emigration not as voluntary self-improvement but as exile and banishment. It was a short step from there to blaming the British for the whole thing, and it was no accident that the United States became in the late nineteenth century the most fertile source of ideas, munitions, men, and money for the struggle to win independence in Ireland.

The other group that accounted for significant numbers of the "old" immigrants were the Germans. They typically arrived in family units, in contrast to the young single men and women who came from Ireland. And they arrived through New Orleans as well as the eastern cities, generally moving on into the interior. About 1 million Germans came to the United States in the 1840s and 1850s; more than 3 million between 1860 and 1900; and another 1.3 million by 1924. Catholics dominated the first wave, but Protestants, especially from Prussia, were increasingly numerous thereafter. The Germans tended to arrive with some money and skills, unlike the Irish, many of whom had neither, especially in the 1840s and 1850s. Thus, while the typical German immigrant became a farmer, artisan, or shopkeeper, the typical male Irish immigrant (Paddy) became an unskilled laborer and the typical female Irish immigrant (Bridget) became a domestic servant or, later, a factory worker. German immigration lacks a synthesis in the grand style produced by Kerby Miller for the Irish. But fine regional studies have been written by Walter Kamphoefner on Westfalians in Missouri and by Stanley Nadel on German ethnicity, religion, and class in New York City's kleindeutschland. Bruce Levine's work examines the impact of German immigrants, infused with the revolutionary spirit of 1848, on the antebellum labor movement and the antislavery crusade.

The great anomaly among the old "immigrants" were the Chinese, 322,000 of whom arrived in the United States between 1850 and 1882. Nearly all of them were males between the ages of 14 and 35; they worked primarily on railroad construction on contracts drawn up before they arrived; and they settled on the West rather than the East Coast. The typical Chinese railroad laborer contracted to work for six to eight years, with the hope of accumulating cash and returning to China. The Contract Labor Law of 1865 had allowed for such contracts, but they were outlawed by the Contract Labor Law of 1885. The importance of the Chinese to the history of American migration lies partly in the labor they performed on railroad construction and partly in the precedent they set as the first immigrant group to be excluded from entry to the United States. The impetus to restrict the Chinese came in part from a widespread and deeply racist belief that they could never assimilate into American life. Related to this, as Alexander Saxton has explained, was a fear on the part of organized labor, led ironically enough by recent immigrants from Ireland, that cheap Chinese labor was a major threat to the welfare of "American" workers. The Chinese Exclusion Act of 1882 suspended the entry of Chinese laborers for ten years; it was re-enacted in 1892 and 1902, and in 1904 the ban was extended indefinitely.

The nineteenth century also witnessed ongoing struggles between the Mexican residents of the Southwest and migrating Anglo-Americans, culminating in the annexation of half of Mexico's national territory (including Texas) in the 1840s. Arnoldo de Léon has written an impressive account of the racial discrimination faced by Texans of Mexican origin (*tejanos*); while David Montejano places the categories of race and class at the center of Texan history since 1836, in an ambitious and influential work of revisionist history. Useful community studies for the nineteenth and twentieth centuries include Albert Camarillo's work on Santa Barbara and southern California from 1848 to 1930; Gilberto Hinojosa's account of the transformation of the border town of Laredo from 1755 to 1870; Mario Garcia's work on the Mexicans of El Paso between 1880 and 1920; and studies of East Los Angeles by Rodolfo Acuña and Ricardo Romo. Perhaps the most theoretically innovative work has been on issues of gender and the family. Rebecca Craver's work, for example, deals with Mexican-Anglo intermarriage in New Mexico in the early nineteenth century. Richard Griswold del Castillo examines the tensions accompanying migration and assimilation in the Chicano family since 1848. And Sarah Deutsch analyzes the cultural interaction, particularly in terms of gender, between Latinos, Anglos, and Native Americans in New Mexico and Colorado from 1880 to 1940.

THE "NEW" IMMIGRANTS

Between 1880 and 1924, almost 27,000,000 white immigrants entered the United States. Locating this great migration in the context of global movements of labor and capital, John Bodnar has provided something of a blueprint for studying this "new" immigration as a whole. Two-thirds of the "new" immigrants came from parts of central, eastern, and southern Europe that were economically underdeveloped and politically regressive. Most were drawn to the booming industrial sector of the American economy, where they performed unskilled labor; but many brought skills that were vital to industries as diverse as construction and garment production. With the exception of John Bodnar's work and that of a handful of others (notably Caroline Golab, Victor Greene, Paul Krause, and Ewa Moraskawa), the literature on Slavic immigrants is surprisingly sparse.

Of all the "new" immigrants, Jews have received the most comprehensive treatment by historians. Moses Rischin's account of the social and intellectual life of New York's eastern European Jews has become a classic, thirty-five years after it was published. Irving Howe offers a massive and exuberant treatment of radicalism in the same community, while Sydney Weinberg in his recent work explores "how Jewish women sought and found meaning for their lives within the framework of their own system and values." Stephan Brumberg has demonstrated how public schools acted as an agent of "Americanization" for newcomers from central and eastern Europe. Deborah Dash Moore deals sympathetically with the stresses endured by the generation obliged to straddle two worlds, arguing that divisions between parents and children have been overstated. By contrast, John Bukowczyk's study of another "new" immigrant group, the Poles, concludes that intergenerational stresses were considerable. Elizabeth Ewen's work finds striking similarities in the lives of Jewish and Italian women on the Lower East Side. Both groups belonged to a patriarchal immigrant culture that nonetheless accorded them an autonomous women's sphere; both were rapidly "Americanized" through initiation into a consumer society that undermined traditional gender roles and opened up new, and sometimes double-edged, ways of life, work, and womanhood.

The literature on the Italians is almost as ample as that on the Jews. About 4 million immigrants came from Italy to the United States between 1899 and 1924 alone. Most arrived with a firmly rooted regional or provincial identity and came predominantly from the south. These considerations have shaped much of the recent scholarship, especially the argument that assimilation into the American environment involved a simultaneous recognition, for the first time, of a common Italian heritage. Silvano Tomasi offers a judicious account of the strains between Italian immigrants and the Irish Americans who dominated the Roman Catholic Church in New York; while Robert Orsi offers a colorful portrait of the religion practiced and performed on the streets of Italian Harlem. Betty Boyd Caroli's work examines repatriation, remarkably common among the Italians; many arrived in the United States as "birds of passage" and about 1.5 million returned to Italy in the first fifteen years of the twentieth century. Virginia Yans-McLaughlin's work on the Italians of Buffalo between 1880 and 1930 offers a detailed and sympathetic portrait of work, family life, and community in a single city, concluding that despite initial discrimination the transition from Italy to America was "relatively smooth." Finally, Donna Gabaccia's work on Sicilian labor and immigration demonstrates with great effectiveness Kerby Miller's point that the immigrants' experience cannot properly be understood without a detailed examination of the world they left behind.

Gabaccia's work raises one of the central questions in the study of immigration, its intersection with the history of labor. For most of American history it is impossible to write the history of one without writing the history of the other. This point was influentially made in the 1970s by Herbert Gutman, who demonstrated how the American working class, in contrast to the putative English model, did not undergo a single "making" but was instead repeatedly transformed by infusions of pre-industrial immigrants. The importance of a detailed knowledge of European social and political history in any account of American immigration and labor has been emphasized in a series of works by the German historian Dirk Hoerder. In a similar vein are Bruce Levine's work on mid-nineteenth-century German immigrants and Susan Glenn's study of work, family, womanhood, and trade unionism among Jewish immigrants.

The relation between ethnicity and class has been the subject of fruitful inquiry, especially in the historiography of the late nineteenth and early twentieth centuries. David Emmons emphasizes the ethnic exclusiveness and working-class "pragmatism" of Irish immigrant workers in Butte, Montana. Similarly, John Bodnar argues that east European immigrants tended to eschew radicalism by putting concerns of family, ethnic kin, and religion before larger social interests. David Montgomery concedes that the exclusion from the organized labor movement of unskilled immigrants from central, southern, and eastern Europe gravely damaged the cause of labor as whole. On the other hand, Bruce Levine, Eric Foner, David Goldberg, and others all demonstrate, in different ways, how ethnic consciousness could serve as a catalyst rather than an obstacle to class consciousness. Gary Gerstle's study of the textile town of Woonsocket, Rhode Island, explains how twentieth-century "Americanism" could be defined in working-class as well as middle-class terms, allowing French Canadians and Franco-Belgian immigrants to overcome their ethnic differences.

Some of the best recent work on the intersection of labor and immigration history examines the history of Mexican workers in the United States. Vicki Ruiz, for example, examines the struggle for unionization by Mexican women in the California cannery industry between 1930 and 1950. Zaragosa Vargas offers a penetrating analysis of Mexican industrial workers in Detroit and the Midwest between World War I and the New Deal. Emilio Zamora presents a wide-ranging account of rural and urban Mexican workers in early-twentieth-century Texas. And Camille Geurin-Gonzalez covers the world of Mexican immigration, farm labor, and repatriation in California. For Mexicans in the twentieth century, as for groups like the Irish and the Italians in the nineteenth, issues of work and class have been the essence of the immigrant experience.

NATIVISM AND
IMMIGRATION RESTRICTION

One thing the "old" immigrants and the "new" faced in common was the onslaught of nativism, defined by its leading historian, John Higham, as "intense hostility to an internal minority on the grounds of its foreign (or 'un-American') connections." As the first substantial group of non-Anglo Protestants to arrive as immigrants in the United States, the Irish bore the brunt of the early attacks, a development most recently examined by Dale Knobel. The general pattern of nativism throughout American history has been analyzed by David Bennett, who argues that what "tied these movements to one tradition was the common vision of alien intruders in the promised land—people who could not be assimilated in the national community because of their religion or ethnicity."

The customs, cultures, languages, religions, and dress of the "new" immigrants struck many native-born Americans as exotic and threatening. Could they ever be assimilated into American life? This question was asked with increasing frequency beginning in the 1890s, and the attitude behind it is typified by one congressman's warning: "There may have been a time when we could assimilate this undesirable immigration—the ignorant, the pauper, and the vicious class. That time has passed. . . . They strain our public and our private charities, fill our charitable institutions, and are a constant menace to our free institutions." The varieties of nativist thought deployed against the new immigrants—anti-Catholic, antiradical, anti-Semitic, and Anglo-Saxon racist—have been delineated by John Higham in one of the classic works of American immigration history.

The movement to regulate and eventually restrict immigration grew slowly from the 1890s, eventually achieving its goals in the 1920s. The Immigration Act of 1891 excluded people with contagious diseases and mental disorders and established Ellis Island as the principal clearinghouse for the new arrivals. Certain classes of political radical were excluded under new legislation in 1903. During the next thirteen years, thirteen separate legislative acts were passed, each closing the Golden Door bit by bit. The year 1917 was a turning point, with the codification of the existing legislation and the classification of thirty-three types of aliens to be denied entrance, among them "feeble-minded" persons, persons of "constitutional psychopathic inferiority," and those who held "subversive" political views. The same year, Congress passed a literacy test for immigrants over President Woodrow Wilson's vehement veto, and a national campaign against radicalism and "un-American" sympathies reached its peak.

An unrestricted system of immigration could not have stayed in place indefinitely. But the striking thing about immigration restriction is the extent to which it was formulated in terms of racial nativism. In 1921, Congress passed an emergency immigration act, establishing a quota system by which annual immigration from any country could not exceed 3 percent of the number of persons of that nationality present in the United States in 1910. This law reduced immigration from about 800,000 to about 357,000 a year. But the nativists remained unsatisfied, demanding a 2 percent quota, based on the 1890 census, when there had been far fewer "new" immigrants in the United States. In 1924 the National Origins Act (or Johnson-Reed Immigration Act) banned immigration from East Asia entirely, reduced the quota from 3 to 2 percent (about 165,000 a year, reduced to 150,000 in 1927), and pushed the base year back from 1910 to 1890. Future immigration, in other words, was to be primarily "Nordic" or "Teutonic" in composition, and the numbers were drastically reduced. The new "national origins" system stayed in place until 1965.

ASSIMILATION AND ANGLO-CONFORMITY

The virulence of American nativism calls into question the category of "assimilation" that has typically lain at the heart of debates over immigration and ethnicity, both popular and scholarly. Early interpretations of immigrant history accepted as a given the migration of people from all over the world and considered their assimilation into American life as the central problem to be studied. At the turn of the twentieth century, as today, the prevailing ideal of a "melting pot" could be either restrictive or progressive. In one sense, it entailed the imposition of Anglo-conformity on the immigrants, who were urged to cast off their "old world" cultures and embrace Americanism without delay. In a second, more liberal sense, this process of assimilation was capable of leveling the differences of ethnicity and religion between the various peoples of the United States; and, perhaps more important, it could transcend divisions of class between and within immigrant populations.

If the idea of a melting pot was always somewhat ambiguous, a more coherent version of the liberal ideal of assimilation was that of "cultural pluralism," a term coined by Horace M. Kallen in 1915, when the pressure for assimilation had hardened into a highly intolerant brand of "100 percent Americanism." The idea of cultural pluralism is usually expressed by the metaphor of a salad bowl or a symphony orchestra. In a salad, the lettuce is distinct from the tomatoes and the carrots, but together they make up a whole; in a symphony orchestra, all the instruments make different and even discordant sounds, but in unity they achieve harmony.

This central theme of assimilation is evident in the writings of the pioneer historian of U.S. immigration history, Marcus Hansen. He began his work on immigration by applying Frederick Jackson Turner's frontier thesis to the shaping of "the American character" as it absorbed diverse ethnic strains and immigrant groups. But, struck by the remarkable diversity of what he was describing, Hansen moved steadily to a position of cultural pluralism. Earlier Americans, he argued, had "made a bad blunder, when consciously or unconsciously they decreed that one literature, one attitude toward the arts, one set of standards should be the basis of culture." Why was the continent being reserved for one strain of Anglo-American culture, which had simply happened to settle in America first? Where this line of inquiry would have led Hansen is unclear, since he died young. But his fears and questions were certainly prescient, identifying dilemmas faced by the United States as the twentieth century draws to a close.

The Irish, among the most intensively studied of American immigrant groups, provide an example of the often contradictory choices facing a historian trying to understand the assimilation of a single ethnic group. Oscar Handlin, in his seminal social history of the Boston Irish, argues that the immigrants had a damaged, dysfunctional culture and their only hope of redemption was to cast off their old world customs and assimilate into the dominant mode of Anglo-conformity. There could be little room for cultural pluralism in this model. For Thomas Brown, on the other hand, the very commitment of Irish-Americans to the nationalist cause of freedom for Ireland insured their assimilation into the middle-class mainstream of American life. Pointing to the narrow social base of Brown's work, Eric Foner argues that Irish immigrant working men and women (in other words, the great majority of the immigrants) were assimilated into a radical, working-class alternative definition of America. This interpretation has been challenged by David Emmons, who finds little genuine or lasting radicalism among the Irish copper-workers of Butte, Montana; and by Kerby Miller, who concludes pessimistically, but on the basis of abundant and persuasive evidence, that a respectable Catholic middle class came to dominate the Irish community as a whole, overpowering more radical alternatives and insuring assimilation in an essentially bourgeois rather than radical manner.

Issues of race, gender, and culture enrich and complicate the debate still further. Hasia Diner and Janet Nolan have added a new dimension to the debate by explaining the distinctive way in which Irish women migrated, worked, and assimilated. More recently, David Roediger and Noel Ignatiev have argued that the precondition for Irish assimilation was to embrace the identity of "whiteness," thereby precluding potential interracial alliances among the most disadvantaged members of the labor force. The point here is not to blame the Irish so much as to expose the dilemmas facing immigrants and workers seeking to make a life for themselves in a society defined by race. Finally, Peter Way has added a radical, if still deeply pessimistic, twist to the Handlin thesis, emphasizing the damage inflicted on Irish culture by imperialism at home and capitalism abroad. Irish canal laborers in early-nineteenth-century America were so degraded and oppressed, Way concludes, that for them assimilation was not even an option.

The essential features of this debate are clearly relevant in understanding the assimilation of any immigrant group in America, not just the Irish. None of the models proposed will stand alone, and some are incompatible. What is needed is an account that pays due attention to the importance of religion; poverty and social mobility; pattern of migration and settlement; the interaction between newcomers and established members of the ethnic community; the hegemony of the middle class, both inside and outside the immigrant community; the potential for radical challenges to that hegemony; and the central questions of race and gender that recent historiography place at the heart of the study of immigration and ethnicity. In this respect, the work of Roediger and others suggests a particularly useful model for the study of ethnic and class identities, emphasizing how they were constructed in racial terms of "whiteness" and gendered terms of "masculinity." It is a model that can be applied as effectively to Mexicans in the twentieth century as to the Irish in the nineteenth.

It was difficult for the Irish to assimilate in nineteenth-century America, but clearly it was not impossible. By the time of the "new" immigration, they had been accorded, albeit grudgingly, the somewhat anomalous status of full Nordic Americans. But for other groups in American society in the late nineteenth and early twentieth centuries, most notably Latinos and Asians, "assimilation" took the form of subjugation and segregation, or was denied altogether through a policy of exclusion. By 1970, for example, one-third of all Puerto Ricans (almost 1.5 million) lived on the mainland, 817,712 of them in New York City, compared to only 463,242 in the island's capital, San Juan. Puerto Ricans have had U.S. citizenship since 1917, but this has not prevented them from being one of the most economically disadvantaged ethnic groups in the United States.

A similar, though quite distinctive pattern of discrimination is evident against Mexican Americans. The last century of Mexican American immigration has transformed the social, cultural, and political landscape of the Southwest. It has also been a period of systematic discrimination not only against Mexican immigrants but also against established Mexican Americans. Mexican labor quickly lost its indispensability when the American economy collapsed in the 1930s. Nearly half a million Mexicans were repatriated, some voluntarily and some coercively, as Camille Guerin-Gonzales and Abraham Hoffman have explained. In Texas and elsewhere, Mexican American citizens of the United States were subject to disfranchisement and a de facto Jim Crow system of segregation. In 1954, thousands of undocumented Mexican *braceros* were deported, under a government-organized program called "Operation Wetback."

Since 1960, Mexican immigration to the United States has grown at a faster pace than ever before. In 1990, the 20 million Latinos in the United States accounted for 9 percent of the country's population; 13.4 million of them were of Mexican origin, up from only 3.5 million in 1960. As the recent work of David Gutiérrez has persuasively demonstrated, the ongoing interaction between Chicanos and repeated waves of immigrants from Mexico calls into question the traditional dichotomy between citizen and alien at the heart of all models of assimilation. Mexican Americans have had a deeply ambivalent attitude toward newcomers from Mexico, on one hand embracing them in a transnational identity, on the other hand experiencing their presence as a cause of discrimination against themselves and an obstacle to assimilation. Within these tensions lie the makings of new, more fluid and dynamic categories of citizenship and ethnicity on both sides of the border.

That citizenship alone is no guarantee of civil and political rights is made clear in the history of Mexican Americans, Puerto Ricans, and African Americans, and even more starkly in the history of the Japanese Americans during World War II. In 1940 there were about 127,000 Americans of Japanese ancestry. Roughly one-third of them were unnaturalized first-generation immigrants, or issei; the other two-thirds were naturalized or native-born citizens of the United States, or nisei. Most Japanese Americans lived in California, others in Oregon, Washington, and Hawaii. John Modell has demonstrated the fragility of their position in society, a position that was to be severely undermined after war broke out between the United States and Japan in 1941. More than 100,000 Japanese Americans were forcibly "evacuated" to "relocation centers" in the interior during World War II, on the grounds that they represented a threat to national security. This harrowing tale, told most recently by Yuji Ichioka, Page Smith, and Michi Weglyn, offers a grim demonstration of the limits of tolerance and assimilation in twentieth-century America.

A WORLD IN MIGRATION: THE NEWEST IMMIGRANTS

As the United States approaches the twenty-first century, immigration has once again become a significant aspect of its history. Inspired by the Civil Rights and Voting Rights Acts, the Hart-Celler Act of 1965 abolished the old racial quota system; at the same time, however, it looked to the future by placing a limit on Latin American immigration for the first time. Under the new system, which went into effect in 1968, the annual ceiling was increased to 290,000: 170,000 from the Eastern Hemisphere (i.e., the rest of the world other than the Americas), with no more than 20,000 from any single county, and 120,000 from the Western Hemisphere. Provisions were made for special visas for refugees fleeing racial, political, and religious persecution (though not economic hardship), and more than 1 million refugees from Cuba and Indochina had arrived by 1980.

Before 1965, 90 percent of the annual immigrants to the United States were Europeans; by 1985, that figure had dropped to 10 percent. Between 1980 and 1990 alone, the number of Asians in the United States doubled, reaching more than 7 million. But the main source of immigration has been Latin America. Demographers estimate that by 2030, Americans of European origin will be in a minority, a situation that already pertains in New York City and in the California school system. This new wave of immigration is already receiving considerable scholarly attention. To take the ethnic mosaic of New York City as but one example, recent works attest to the continuing remarkable diversity of the metropolis: Hsiang-Shui Chen on immigrants from Taiwan, Philip Kasinitz on Caribbean immigrants and the politics of race, Illsoo Kim on the city's burgeoning Korean community, Peter Kwong on the new Chinatown, Michael Laguerre on the new Haitian community, and Nancy Foner's edited collection on immigrants, including Koreans, Chinese, Haitians, Soviet Jews, Dominicans, and Jamaicans and other Caribbean peoples. With a steady, two-way movement along the "Caribbean corridor," especially from Haiti, Jamaica, Puerto Rico, and the Dominican Republic, New York City—like the United States as a whole—is ethnically and racially more diverse than ever before.

Hand-in-hand with the proliferation of new immigrant groups since the 1960s has come a discovery of the concept of ethnicity by white Americans descended from previous immigrants. The more dogmatic versions of this "new white ethnicity" insist that the descendants of the Irish, the Italians and the Slavs have retained distinctive cultural and ethnic values without assimilating into the dominant Anglo-American culture. Inherent in this position, as Orlando Patterson has pointed out, is a reaction against the heightened race consciousness of African Americans and the social and political gains they have made since 1960.

While this form of ethnic chauvinism sees ethnicity as a fixed, almost primordial, essence, a final but as yet undeveloped strand of the historiography argues that ethnicity is a constructed and contested element of subjective identity. Compared to other fields in American history, the history of immigration and ethnicity has borrowed surprisingly little from discourse theory and the general "linguistic turn." Given the centrality of ethnicity as a category of subjective identity, however, the time is certainly ripe for such an approach. Werner Sollors has suggested a useful approach for analyzing ethnicity as a cultural construct, but the work has yet to go from a theoretical to an empirical level (in the writing of history at least, if not in literary studies).

At its most effective, the move to destabilize and historicize the category of ethnicity offers historians a powerful new tool, allowing them to expose the dynamics of power whereby immigrant communities are formed and reformed and ethnic identities defined and redefined. In particular, the ideological and discursive processes through which particular ethnic identities are constructed into categories of race and gender demand further attention. The best work in the future is likely to focus on the definition of ethnicity and assimilation by examining conflicts over resources, power, and culture between immigrants and the larger society they enter, between different ethnic and racial groups, and between different members of the same immigrant communities.

BIBLIOGRAPHY

Apart from older works discussed in the text, this list consists of a representative selection of works published since 1980.

General Studies and Surveys

Archdeacon, Thomas. *Becoming American: An Ethnic History.* New York: Free Press, 1983.
Bayor, Ronald H., and Timothy J. Meagher, eds. *The New York Irish.* Baltimore, Md.: Johns Hopkins University Press, 1996.
Bennett, David H. *The Party of Fear: From Nativist Movements to the New Right in American History.* Chapel Hill: University of North Carolina Press, 1988.

Bodnar, John E. *The Transplanted: A History of Immigrants in Urban America.* Bloomington: University of Indiana Press, 1985.

Buckowczyk, John J. *And My Children Did Not Know Me: A History of the Polish-Americans.* Bloomington: Indiana University Press, 1987.

Chan, Sucheng. *Asian-Americans: An Interpretive History.* Boston: Twayne, 1991.

Daniels, Roger. *Asian America: Chinese and Japanese in the United States since 1850.* Seattle: University of Washington Press, 1988.

Del Castillo, Adelaida R., ed. *Between Borders: Essays on Mexicana/Chicana History.* Encino, Calif.: Floricanto Press, 1990.

Golab, Caroline. *Immigrant Destinations.* Philadelphia: Temple University Press, 1977.

Hansen, Marcus. *The Atlantic Migration, 1607–1860.* Cambridge, Mass.: Harvard University Press, 1940.

———. *The Immigrant in American History.* New York: Harper Torchbooks, 1940.

Ichioka, Yuji. *The Issei: The World of the First-Generation Japanese Immigrants, 1885–1924.* New York: Free Press, 1988.

Miller, Kerby A. *Emigrants and Exiles: Ireland and the Irish Exodus to North America.* New York: Oxford University Press, 1985.

Montejano, David. *Anglos and Mexicans in the Making of Texas, 1836–1986.* Austin: University of Texas Press, 1987.

Patterson, Orlando. *Ethnic Chauvinism: The Reactionary Impulse.* New York: Stein & Day, 1977.

Sollors, Werner, *Beyond Ethnicity: Consent and Descent in American Culture.* New York: Oxford University Press, 1986.

———, ed. *The Invention of Ethnicity.* New York: Oxford University Press, 1989.

Takaki, Ronald T. *Strangers from a Different Shore: A History of Asian Americans.* Boston: Little, Brown, 1989.

Thernstrom, Stephan, Ann Orlov, and Oscar Handlin, eds. *Harvard Encyclopedia of American Ethnic Groups.* Cambridge, Mass.: Harvard University Press, 1980.

Yans-McLaughlin, Virginia, ed. *Immigration Reconsidered: History, Sociology, and Politics.* New York: Oxford University Press, 1990.

Immigration and Ethnicity in Early America

Bailyn, Bernard. *The Peopling of British North America: An Introduction.* New York: Knopf, 1985.

———. *Voyagers to the West: A Passage in the Peopling of America on the Eve of the Revolution.* New York: Knopf, 1986.

Bailyn, Bernard, and Philip D. Morgan, eds. *Strangers within the Realm: Cultural Margins of the First British Empire.* Chapel Hill: University of North Carolina Press, 1991.

Balmer, Randall H. *A Perfect Babel of Confusions: Dutch Religion and English Culture in the Middle Colonies.* New York: Oxford University Press, 1989.

Bannon, John F. *The Spanish Borderlands Frontier, 1513–1821.* Albuquerque: University of New Mexico Press, 1974.

Butler, Jon. *The Huguenots in America: A Refugee People in a New World Society.* Cambridge, Mass.: Harvard University Press, 1983.

Ekirch, A. Roger. *Bound for America: The Transportation of British Convicts to the Colonies, 1718–1775.* New York: Oxford University Press, 1987.

Fischer, David Hackett. *Albion's Seed: Four British Folkways in America.* New York: Oxford University Press, 1989.

Galenson, David W. *White Servitude in Colonial America: An Economic Analysis.* New York: Cambridge University Press, 1981.

Goodfriend, Joyce D. *Before the Melting Pot: Society and Culture in Colonial New York City, 1664–1730.* Princeton, N.J.: Princeton University Press, 1992.

Gutiérrez, Ramón A. *When Jesus Came, the Corn Mothers Went Away: Marriage, Sexuality, and Power in New Mexico, 1500–1846.* Stanford, Calif.: Stanford University Press, 1991.

Kettner, James H. *The Development of American Citizenship, 1608–1870.* Chapel Hill: University of North Carolina Press, 1978.

Swierenga, Robert. *The Dutch in America: Immigration, Settlement, and Cultural Change.* New Brunswick, N.J.: Rutgers University Press, 1985.

Nineteenth Century to 1890

Brown, Thomas N. *Irish-American Nationalism, 1870–1890.* Philadelphia: Lippincott, 1966.

Craver, Rebecca. *The Impact of Intimacy: Mexican-Anglo Intermarriage in New Mexico, 1821–1846.* El Paso: Texas Western Press, University of Texas, 1982.

De Léon, Arnoldo. *They Called Them Greasers: Anglo-American Attitudes toward Mexicans in Texas, 1821–1900.* Austin: University of Texas Press, 1983.

Diner, Hasia. *Erin's Daughters in America: Irish Immigrant Women in the Nineteenth Century.* Baltimore, Md.: Johns Hopkins University Press, 1983.

Dolan, Jay P. *The Immigrant Church: New York's German and Irish Catholics, 1815–1865.* Baltimore, Md.: Johns Hopkins University Press, 1987.

Foner, Eric. "Class, Ethnicity, and Radicalism in the Gilded Age: The Land League and Irish America." *Marxist Perspectives* 1 (summer 1978): 6–55.

Gutman, Herbert. *Work, Culture, and Society in Industrializing America: Essays in American Working-Class History.* New York: Vintage Books, 1977.

Handlin, Oscar. *Boston's Immigrants, 1790–1880: A Study in Acculturation.* Rev. ed. Cambridge, Mass.: Belknap Press of Harvard University Press, 1959. Reprint, New York: Atheneum, 1976.

Hinojosa, Gilberto. *A Borderlands Town in Transition: Laredo, 1755–1870.* College Station: Texas A&M University Press, 1983.

Ignatiev, Noel. *How the Irish Became White.* New York: Routledge, 1995.

Kamphoefner, Walter D. *The Westfalians: From Germany to Missouri.* Princeton, N.J.: Princeton University Press, 1987.

Knobel, Dale T. *Paddy and the Republic: Ethnicity and Nationality in Antebellum America.* Middletown, Conn.: Wesleyan University Press, 1986.

Levine, Bruce. *The Spirit of 1848: German Immigrants, Labor Conflict, and the Coming of the Civil War.* Urbana: University of Illinois Press, 1992.

Nadel, Stanley. *Little Germany: Ethnicity, Religion, and Class in New York City, 1845–1880.* Urbana: University of Illinois Press, 1990.

Roediger, David. *The Wages of Whiteness: Race and the Making of the American Working Class.* New York: Verso, 1991.

Saxton, Alexander P. *The Indispensable Enemy: Labor and the Anti-Chinese Movement in California.* Berkeley: University of California Press, 1971.

Takaki, Ronald. *Iron Cages: Race and Culture in Nineteenth-Century America.* New York: Oxford University Press, 1990.

Trommler, Frank, and Joseph McVeigh, eds. *America and the Germans: An Assessment of a Three-Hundred-Year History.* 2 vols. Philadelphia: University of Pennsylvania Press, 1985.

Turbin, Carole. *Working Women of the Collar City: Gender, Class, and Community in Troy, New York, 1864–86.* Urbana: University of Illinois Press, 1992.

Way, Peter. *Common Labour: Workers and the Digging of North American Canals, 1780–1860.* New York: Cambridge University Press, 1993.

Late Nineteenth and Twentieth Century

Acuña, Rodolfo. *A Community Under Siege: A Chronicle of Chicanos East of the Los Angeles River.* Los Angeles: Chicano Studies Research Center, University of California, 1984.

Bodnar, John E. *Immigration and Industrialization: Ethnicity in an American Mill Town, 1870–1940.* Pittsburgh, Pa.: University of Pittsburgh Press, 1977.

———. *Workers' World: Kinship, Community, and Protest in Industrial Society, 1900–1940.* Baltimore, Md.: Johns Hopkins University Press, 1982.

Bodnar, John E., Roger Simon, and Michael Weber. *Lives of Their Own: Blacks, Italians, and Poles in Pittsburgh, 1900–1960.* Urbana: University of Illinois Press, 1982.

Bonacich, Edna, and Ivan Light. *Immigrant Entrepreneurs: Koreans in Los Angeles, 1965–82.* Berkeley: University of California Press, 1988.

Brumberg, Stephan F. *Going to America, Going to School: The Jewish Immigrant Public School Encounter in Turn-of-the-Century New York City.* New York: Praeger, 1986.

Camarillo, Albert. *Chicanos in a Changing Society: From Mexican Pueblos to American Barrios in Santa Barbara and Southern California, 1848–1930.* Cambridge, Mass.: Harvard University Press, 1979.

Caroli, Betty Boyd. *Italian Repatriation from the United States, 1900–1914.* New York: Center for Migration Studies, 1973.

Chan, Sucheng, ed. *Entry Denied: Exclusion and the Chinese Community in America, 1882–1943.* Philadelphia: Temple University Press, 1991.

Chavez, John. *The Lost Land: The Chicano Image of the Southwest.* Albuquerque: University of New Mexico Press, 1984.

Chen, Hsiang-Shui. *Chinatown No More: Taiwan Immigrants in Contemporary New York.* Ithaca, N.Y.: Cornell University Press, 1992.

Deutsch, Sarah. *No Separate Refuge: Culture, Class, and Gender on an Anglo-Hispanic Frontier in the American Southwest, 1880–1940.* New York: Oxford University Press, 1987.

Emmons, David M. *The Butte Irish: Class and Ethnicity in an American Mining Town, 1875–1925.* Urbana: University of Illinois Press, 1989.

Ewen, Elizabeth. *Immigrant Women in the Land of Dollars: Life and Culture on the Lower East Side, 1890–1925*. New York: Monthly Review Press, 1985.

Fawcett, James, and Benjamin Carino, eds. *Pacific Bridges: The New Immigration from Asia and the Pacific Islands*. New York: Center for Migration Studies, 1987.

Foner, Nancy, ed. *New Immigrants in New York*. New York: Columbia University Press, 1987.

Gabaccia, Donna R. *From Sicily to Elizabeth Street: Housing and Social Change among Italian Immigrants, 1880–1930*. Albany: State University of New York Press, 1983.

———. *Militants and Migrants: Rural Sicilians Become American Workers*. New Brunswick, N.J.: Rutgers University Press, 1988.

Garcia, Juan Ramón. *Operation Wetback: The Mass Deportation of Mexican Undocumented Workers in 1954*. Westport, Conn.: Greenwood Press, 1980.

Garcia, Mario T. *Desert Immigrants: The Mexicans of El Paso, 1880–1920*. New Haven, Conn.: Yale University Press, 1981.

———. *Mexican Americans: Leadership, Ideology and Identity, 1930–1960*. New Haven, Conn.: Yale University Press, 1989.

Gerstle, Gary. *Working-Class Americanism: The Politics of Labor in a Textile City, 1914–1960*. New York: Cambridge University Press, 1989.

Glenn, Susan. *Daughters of the Shtetl: Life and Labor in the Immigrant Generation*. Ithaca, N.Y.: Cornell University Press, 1990.

Goldberg, David W. *A Tale of Three Cities: Labor Organization and Protest in Patterson, Passaic, and Lawrence, 1916–1921*. New Brunswick, N.J.: Rutgers University Press, 1989.

Greene, Victor. *The Slavic Community on Strike: Immigrant Labor in Pennsylvania Anthracite*. Notre Dame, Ind.: University of Notre Dame Press, 1968.

Griswold del Castillo, Richard. *La Familia: Chicano Families in the Urban Southwest, 1848 to the Present*. Notre Dame, Ind.: University of Notre Dame Press, 1984.

———. *The Los Angeles Barrio: A Social History*. Berkeley: University of California Press, 1979.

Guerin-Gonzales, Camille. *Mexican Workers, American Dreams: Immigration, Repatriation, and California Farm Labor, 1900–1939*. New Brunswick, N.J.: Rutgers University Press, 1994.

Gutiérrez, David G. *Walls and Mirrors: Mexican Americans, Mexican Immigrants, and the Politics of Ethnicity*. Berkeley: University of California Press, 1995.

Hareven, Tamara. *Family Time and Industrial Time: The Relationship between Family and Work in a New England Industrial Community*. New York: Cambridge University Press, 1982.

Higham, John. *Strangers in the Land: Patterns of American Nativism, 1860–1925*. 1963. New York: Atheneum Books, 1977.

Hoerder, Dirk, ed. *Struggle a Hard Battle: Essays on Working-Class Immigrants*. DeKalb: Northern Illinois University Press, 1986.

———, ed. *European Migrants: Global and Local Perspectives*. Boston: Northeastern University Press, 1996.

———, ed. *Labor Migration in the Atlantic Economies: The European and North Amer-*

ican Working Classes during the Period of Industrialization. Westport, Conn.: Greenwood Press, 1985.

Hoffman, Abraham. *Unwanted Mexican Americans in the Great Depression: Repatriation Pressures, 1929–1939.* Tucson: University of Arizona Press, 1974.

Hosakawa, Bill. *Nisei: The Quiet Americans.* New York: Morrow, 1969.

Howe, Irving, with Kenneth Libo. *World of Our Fathers: The Journey of East European Jews to America and the Life They Found and Made.* New York: Harcourt Brace Jovanovich, 1976.

Ichioka, Yuji, ed. *Views from Within: The Japanese American Evacuation and Relocation.* Los Angeles: Asian American Studies Center, University of California, 1989.

Jensen, Joan M. *Passage from India: Asian Indian Immigrants in North America.* New Haven, Conn.: Yale University Press, 1988.

Kasinitz, Philip. *Caribbean New York: Black Immigrants and the Politics of Race.* Ithaca, N.Y.: Cornell University Press, 1992.

Keil, Hartmut, and John B. Jentz, eds. *German Workers in Industrial Chicago, 1850–1910: A Comparative Perspective.* DeKalb: Northern Illinois University Press, 1983.

Kim, Illsoo. *New Urban Immigrants: The Korean Community in New York City.* Princeton, N.J.: Princeton University Press, 1981.

Kitano, H. L., and Roger Daniels. *Asian-Americans: Emerging Minorities.* 2d ed. Englewood Cliffs, N.J.: Prentice-Hall, 1988.

Krause, Paul. *The Battle for Homestead, 1880–1892: Politics, Culture and Steel.* Pittsburgh, Pa.: University of Pittsburgh Press, 1992.

Kwong, Peter. *The New Chinatown.* New York: Hill & Wang, 1987.

Laguerre, Michael. *American Odyssey: Haitians in New York City.* Ithaca, N.Y.: Cornell University Press, 1984.

Modell, John. *The Economics and Politics of Racial Accommodation: The Japanese of Los Angeles, 1900–1942.* Urbana: University of Illinois Press, 1977.

Montgomery, David. *The Fall of the House of Labor: The Workplace, the State, and American Labor Activism, 1865–1925.* New York: Cambridge University Press, 1987.

Moore, Deborah Dash. *At Home in America: Second Generation New York Jews.* New York: Columbia University Press, 1981.

Mora, Magdalena, and Adelaida R. Del Castillo, eds. *Mexican Women in the United States: Struggles Past and Present.* Los Angeles: Chicano Studies Research Center, University of California, 1980.

Moraskawa, Ewa. *For Bread with Butter: Life-Worlds of East Central Europeans in Johnstown, Pennsylvania, 1890–1940.* New York: Cambridge University Press, 1986.

Muller, Thomas, and Thomas J. Espenshade. *The Fourth Wave: California's Newest Immigrants.* Washington, D.C.: The Urban Institute, 1985.

Novak, Michael. *The Rise of the Unmeltable Ethnics: Politics and Culture in the Seventies.* New York: Macmillan, 1972.

Nolan, Janet. *Ourselves Alone: Women's Immigration from Ireland, 1885–1920.* Lexington: University Press of Kentucky, 1989.

Orsi, Robert. *The Madonna of 115th Street: Faith and Community in Italian Harlem, 1880–1950*. New Haven, Conn.: Yale University Press, 1985.

Ostergren, Robert. *A Community Transplanted: The Transatlantic Experience of a Swedish Immigrant Settlement in the Upper Middle West, 1835–1915*. Madison: University of Wisconsin Press, 1988.

Patterson, Orlando. *Ethnic Chauvinism: The Reactionary Impulse*. New York: Stein & Day, 1977.

Rischin, Moses. *The Promised City: New York's Jews, 1870–1914*. Cambridge, Mass.: Harvard University Press, 1962.

Rodriguez, Richard. *Hunger of Memory: The Education of Richard Rodriguez*. Boston: D. R. Godine, 1981.

Romo, Ricardo. *East Los Angeles: History of a Barrio*. Austin: University of Texas Press, 1983.

Ruiz, Vicki. *Cannery Women, Cannery Lives: Mexican Women, Unionization, and the California Food Processing Industry*. Albuquerque: University of New Mexico Press, 1987.

Ruiz, Vicki, and Susan Tiano, eds. *Women on the U.S.-Mexico Border: Responses to Change*. Boston: Allen & Unwin, 1987.

Saran, Parmatma. *The Asian Indian Experience in the United States*. Cambridge, Mass.: Schenkman, 1985.

Smith, Page. *Democracy on Trial: The Japanese-American Evacuation and Relocation in World War II*. New York: Simon & Schuster, 1995.

Tomasi, Silvano. *Piety and Power: The Role of Italian Parishes in the New York Metropolitan Area, 1880–1930*. New York: Center for Migration Studies, 1975.

Vargas, Zaragosa. *Proletarians of the North: A History of Mexican Industrial Workers in Detroit and the Midwest, 1917–1933*. Berkeley: University of California Press, 1993.

Weglyn, Michi. *Years of Infamy: The Untold Story of America's Concentration Camps*. New York: Morrow, 1976.

Weinberg, Sydney. *The World of Our Mothers: Lives of Jewish Immigrant Women*. Chapel Hill: University of North Carolina Press, 1988.

Weisser, Michael R. *A Brotherhood of Memory: Jewish Landsmanshaftn in the New York World*. New York: Basic Books, 1985.

Yans-McLaughlin, Virginia. *Family and Community: Italian Immigrants in Buffalo, 1880–1930*. Ithaca, N.Y.: Cornell University Press, 1977.

Zamora, Emilio. *The World of the Mexican Workers in Texas*. College Station: Texas A&M University Press, 1993.

16

■ LIBERTY AND POWER: U.S. DIPLOMATIC HISTORY, 1750–1945

Walter LaFeber

AMERICAN DIPLOMATIC HISTORY BECAME A POPULAR CLASSROOM SUBJECT IN THE 1930s and 1940s. In those decades Americans began to realize that their overseas expansion after 1898 had made the nation a leading military power and the globe's greatest economic force. They were also discovering that events thousands of miles away directly shaped their own lives: a failed European banking system in 1931 forced people out of work in the American Midwest; Japanese aggression in China during 1940 led to the conscription of American men while the United States was officially at peace.

In 1783 George Washington proclaimed this new country "our rising empire." By the close of World War II it had fully risen. The United States was the globe's superpower militarily, economically, and culturally. When, after 1945, a U.S. president secretly decided to change a government in Italy, Iran, Vietnam, Lebanon, or the Belgian Congo, he possessed the power to enforce his decision and shape the lives of people in distant—and, to most Americans, unknown—nations. Such power raised central issues: What were the values and traditions that shaped and guided it? Could such power actually be used to benefit different peoples? Were Americans capable of becoming global policemen without endangering their own prosperity and constitutional liberties? The nation's diplomatic history had to be understood before such pivotal questions could be answered.

Diplomatic historians discovered that they were uniquely qualified to deal with such fundamental issues. They were uniquely qualified, that is, if they understood that diplomatic history is not simply a story of "what one clerk told another" (as a scholar once described it). American foreign relations are made up of the politics, cultures, and economic relationships that determine what a U.S. clerk tells a foreign counterpart. Properly crafted, diplomatic history analyzes the relationships not only between nations but between peoples within those nations that shape their foreign policies. It moves across both national boundaries and scholarly disciplines, using such a diverse and wide-reaching approach to attain a central goal: to discover and explain the *power* that determines those inter- and intranational relationships in a world increasingly interdependent. Thus the teaching of U.S. foreign policy can become the framework within which many other crucial events of American history must be understood. And such teaching can identify the points at which the everyday concerns of Americans interact with those of the global community in which they live.

The nature of that larger community, however, has constantly changed. The "world" that preoccupied Americans in the early nineteenth century was Spanish Florida, or British-Indian alliances in the Mississippi Valley. The world that preoccupies Americans in the late twentieth century stretches around the globe and into the heavens. The values, even the political system, that Americans employ in dealing with those different worlds have nevertheless remained remarkably constant. U.S. diplomatic history, therefore, should explain the nature of power in the international system, analyze America's reciprocal relationships within the international arena, and, in understanding this complex past, reveal the steps we took as a people to reach the position we occupy in our own time. It should also reveal how the past has determined the purposes we now have for using a power undreamed of even by Washington when he prophesied a rising American empire.

INTERPRETIVE OVERVIEWS

The most important general interpretations of U.S. diplomatic history have shared two characteristic approaches. The first has been to explain past foreign policy in order to provide insight into contemporary problems. The second has been to relate internal and external policies—so closely that the line between domestic and foreign affairs has frequently blurred.

The "realist" school of the 1950s aimed at reshaping Americans' views of their world by revising their views of the past. The realists argued that to survive in the modern world, Americans had to understand the realities of power (especially military power) and understand as well that the United States was not all that different from other nations. It was just one more player in a global diplomatic game whose rules were balance-of-power politics. The American system thus acted on the world stage much like other powers, such as eighteenth-century France or nineteenth-century England. Realist scholars emphasized that the Founders of 1776 and 1787 had scored their historic successes because they understood and acted upon these principles in carrying out early American foreign policy. But unfortunately, the realist historians continued, by the late nineteenth century the Founders' tough-minded world view had been replaced by "legalism and moralism." These new traits led U.S. officials to place their faith in such abstract ideals as international law and enlightened public opinion, rather than power politics, to preserve peace and American prosperity. These "idealists," the realists contended, mistakenly viewed the United States as unique and believed that this very uniqueness (such as the supposed good effects of democratic public opinion) could replace military force as the determinant of global affairs.

George F. Kennan's *American Diplomacy, 1900 to 1950* (1951) remains the best-known statement of the realist position. In Kennan's view, U.S. policy during the formative years between 1898 and 1920, when the United States became a great world power, was too often shaped by misplaced faith in legalisms and morality, or overly influenced by other nations who manipulated somewhat naive Washington officials. Kennan argued, for example, that the United States became an important power in Asia during 1898–1900 not because Americans understood their real interests in Asian affairs but because they were maneuvered by British officials to support an "open door" policy, defined by U.S. Secretary of State John Hay as a "fair field and no favor" for all nations competing in the China market. This policy, Kennan and other realists believed, primarily benefited the interests of Great Britain, not the United States. Kennan went on to argue that Woodrow Wilson was so taken with abstract legal and moral concerns (such as "making the world safe for democracy") that as president he misunderstood the realities of world power. Consequently, he helped the Allies destroy Germany between 1917 and 1920 and thereby also destroyed any hope of a healthy, long-term European balance of power; such a balance required a stable Germany at its center. Perhaps, Kennan suggested, Wilson's policies made Americans feel more righteous in the aftermath of World War I, but they created a power vacuum in central Europe that was soon filled by Nazi militarism and Soviet expansionism.

The realist approach has been refined and elaborated in a series of influential books by Norman Graebner. His studies span the length of U.S. diplomatic history, but he has focused on certain turning points: the 1840s expansionism into Mexico and to the Pacific, the Civil War, and the Cold War years. Graebner emphasizes what he calls the "means-ends" question: whether the United States had the means at a specific point to achieve its diplomatic ends. Too often, he concludes, Americans were guided not by a realistic understanding of the power they held but by unrealistic beliefs in the power of morality and legality. Such beliefs led officials such as Wilson to reach for foreign policy objectives that were unobtainable. Graebner worries especially about the tendency of Americans, when they become disillusioned by the failure of their morality to create a better world, to resort to dangerous military means. Thus, when President Wilson failed to make Mexico and the Caribbean nations democratic by preaching to them, he sent in the Marines. And thus, Graebner argues, when Americans forgot about the limits of their power and were guided instead by a simplistic and confused anti-Communism, they became immersed in Vietnam.

The realists concentrated their attention on elite officials, those few at the top level who made and carried out foreign policy. They showed less interest in the complex social and economic levels of American society that produced those officials and their ideologies. By the 1960s the realist approach was being challenged by scholars who were interested in examining the entire society, not just the elite. Going beyond the political and intellectual history employed by the realists, the new scholars also stressed the importance of the links between economic change and foreign policy. In the work of the "revisionists," as these younger scholars came to be known, the distinction between domestic and foreign affairs virtually disappeared.

Of special importance in the revisionist school were three books by William Appleman Williams. *The Tragedy of American Diplomacy* (1959) is a short book with a large thesis: since at least the 1890s the open-door approach shaped not only U.S. policy in China (as Kennan and most historians believed) but American diplomacy worldwide. Moreover, Williams directly contradicts Kennan by demonstrating that the open-door policy was engineered not by British officials but by U.S. leaders who fully understood, and were determined to expand, their nation's economic interests. Williams stresses the economic component, but he also reinterprets that component as the ideology for twentieth-century American policy in general. As Bradford Perkins observed in 1984, much of the work published in diplomatic history after 1960 has been a dialogue with Williams's book.

Williams expands his argument in *The Contours of American History*

(1961), in which he blends domestic and foreign affairs into one coherent interpretation of the entire American experience. In exploring the sources of power in an evolving American society, he divides the nation's history into three phases: the age of "mercantilism," from colonial times until the 1820s, when the state's power guided private enterprise; the age of "laissez-nous faire," from the 1820s to the 1890s, when power fragmented and the legend of American individualism appeared amid rampant continental expansionism; and the age of the corporation after the 1890s. In 1969 Williams published *The Roots of the Modern American Empire*, which asserts that agrarian interests, threatened by suffocating crop surpluses after the Civil War, framed the argument about how to dispose of this glut of goods and reached a solution that anticipated the twentieth-century policies of an industrialized America. That solution, Williams argues, was to conquer world markets and employ, if necessary, direct government help to do so. He concludes that this policy transformed John Winthrop's seventeenth-century Christian vision of a virtuous American "City on a Hill," radiating its power by its own example, into a worldwide empire extending its power by military and economic force. Williams's emphasis on the integral relationship between domestic and foreign policies influenced other historians, including many who disagreed with his emphasis on the economic sources of U.S. diplomacy.

The revisionists' concern with the domestic sources of diplomacy served as the starting point for a more recent attempt to provide a general framework for understanding the nation's foreign policy. Thomas J. McCormick believes that the concept of "corporatism" can reveal the forces that drove that policy. Within this concept the University of Wisconsin scholar includes the country's large functional groups—government, business, labor organizations—working in voluntary but close association. These groups, McCormick argues, have cooperated at a private rather than a governmental level to shape national policies; hence, their activities have often been missed by the media. Fundamental to the corporatists' power, he adds, has been their belief in and control over "productionism"—that is, maximum production that enlarges the economic pie for everyone. To the corporatists, emphasizing maximum production has been preferable to creating political mechanisms for redistributing wealth. The ultimate political mechanism for redistributing wealth, after all, is revolution.

Historians have used variations of corporatism to understand two pivotal eras: the Progressive years of 1913 to 1933, and the early Cold War years of 1945 to 1953. Woodrow Wilson and Herbert Hoover, the argument runs, were the central figures in the attempt to create a cooperative arrangement among government, labor, and business groups.

The aim of corporatism was not only to ameliorate problems in the United States but, by helping others produce ever greater amounts of wealth, to raise living standards and thus abort revolutionary movements in Latin America and central and eastern Europe. Revolutionary class warfare could be replaced with class cooperation. Wilson outlined such economic and political cooperation in his Fourteen Points speech of 1918. The address asked all powers to comply voluntarily with those diplomatic principles (the open-door policy, "freedom of the seas," self-determination) that he believed could most effectively increase production and trade, as well as distribute the resulting wealth in an orderly, nonrevolutionary manner.

The significance of Wilson as a seminal figure in modern American foreign policy and the importance of understanding the antirevolutionary theme in that policy is stressed by Arno Mayer in two influential works, *Political Origins of the New Diplomacy, 1917–1918* (1959) and *Politics and Diplomacy at Peacemaking: Containment and Counterrevolution at Versailles, 1918–1919* (1967). Emphasizing the close relationship of domestic politics and foreign policy, Mayer shows that severe internal problems had created fears in Europe and the United States that Bolshevism would triumph in the West. That fear in turn led Wilson and Europe's leaders to focus on containing Bolshevism rather than on building a healthy Europe. In more recent scholarship, Lloyd Gardner has agreed with Mayer that the Wilson presidency marks the place to begin understanding many of the problems that have plagued twentieth-century U.S. foreign policy. But the Rutgers University historian has taken the argument a step further. He believes (contrary to Kennan and other realists) that Wilson fully understood that United States interests required an orderly and open world system. The president assumed that his nation's liberal principles could best produce such a system, but when he attempted to apply them in such countries as Mexico, Russia, and Haiti, they seemed to produce more, not less, revolution. Wilson then resorted to military power to realize his dream of an orderly system. In *Covenant with Power* (1984), Gardner argues not only that Wilson's policy led him into repeated military interventions but that his successors—from Calvin Coolidge to Ronald Reagan—also found that a commitment to opposing revolutions and promoting democracy continually led them to use military force.

Robert Wiebe describes the Progressive era as *The Search for Order* (1967). Foreign policy leaders headed that search through both their efforts to achieve cooperation (corporatism) at home and their beliefs that productionism and antirevolutionary policies were prerequisites for order abroad. Michael Hogan's *Informal Entente* (1977) demonstrates how a variant of corporatism characterized American foreign policy–

making during the 1920s. In *The Marshall Plan* (1987), Hogan uses the corporatist approach to analyze fundamentals of the massive and historic effort to rebuild western Europe after World War II. That book is one of several published in the 1980s that takes corporatism to a quite different level. Whereas the term had been used to show the links between U.S. internal decision-making and the nation's foreign affairs, it has come to mean an approach that can open insights into policy-making in the entire Western capitalist world. Capitalism is viewed less as a national phenomenon than as a world system. Foreign policies follow the requirements of that system. Thus, American diplomatic history has become the discipline that can explain how pre-1945 U.S. foreign policy, shaped largely by domestic needs, was transformed into a foreign policy increasingly influenced by an international marketplace and a culture created by a new technology and late twentieth-century capitalism that have little respect for national borders. Thomas McCormick's *American Half-Century* (1990, 1995) is a key analysis of how that transformation occurred.

Having started with accounts of "what one clerk told another," American diplomatic history has moved on to demonstrate how a complex domestic system shapes foreign policy and, more recently, how an increasingly integrated world system (or what has been called "the global village") determines Americans' interactions with that system. No other field is better equipped to trace these fundamental changes, because only diplomatic history is able to trace the links between domestic and foreign affairs and, at the same time, properly place those relationships within the context of the constantly shifting power relationships in the international system. From this perspective, American history is largely, and increasingly, international history.

CHRONOLOGICAL OVERVIEW

If the "revisionist" historians have shaped the debate over post-1890 U.S. foreign policy, the "realists" continue to influence our view of the first generation of American diplomacy. But even studies of the Founders necessarily stress the importance of the larger international arena. As exemplified by James Hutson's *John Adams and the Diplomacy of the American Revolution* (1980), the realists have argued that throughout the 1776–1800 period, U.S. officials intelligently and profitably followed the principles of European power politics. Hutson demonstrates, for example, that the nation's commercial policy—its lifeline—was not based on any idealistic hope that foreign powers would unselfishly accept the American ideal of free trade. Instead, the policy rested on the principle of reciprocity: unless European nations welcomed U.S. exports of cotton and tobacco, Americans would not allow European goods into the United States. The Founders thus depended not on enlightened public opinion or morality but on economic self-interest and power politics.

Hutson applied this insight to the seminal document of U.S. foreign economic policy, John Adams's "model treaty" of 1776. Adams argued that the United States should use its economic power to enforce the treatment it wanted from other nations. If that economic weapon could be successfully employed, he continued, Americans would not have to protect themselves by entering dangerous political alliances with powerful European states. In Adams's hand, therefore, U.S. commerce became a weapon with two barrels: one would ensure that Americans had access to indispensable overseas markets, and the other would help guarantee that they could avoid entangling political alliances with more powerful nations. The United States would instead enjoy maximum freedom of action in world affairs (or what has become known in American history as "isolationism"). Adams's approach realistically utilized the nation's great strength, its commerce, to hide its political and military weaknesses.

Adams's generation, however, made one near-fatal mistake. It assumed that the loose confederation of American states could effectively regulate its commerce and also retaliate against Europeans who refused to treat Americans equitably. By 1786 the Europeans, led by the vengeful British, had declared economic warfare against the United States. Unable to exploit foreign markets, Americans sank into economic depression. That crisis in turn triggered internal riots, especially in western Massachusetts, and also threats from settlements beyond the Appalachians to leave the floundering United States and join the adjacent British and Spanish empires. In *Independence on Trial: Foreign Affairs and the Making of the Constitution* (1973, 1986), Frederick Marks III argues that these internal crises led directly to the calling of the Constitutional Convention in 1787. The delegates were determined to create a centralized government that could effectively regulate overseas commerce, conduct a vigorous foreign policy, and thus stabilize conditions at home. Domestic tranquillity depended so greatly on the capacity to carry out a successful foreign policy that the Founders had to design a new system possessing such a capability. In a world of cutthroat imperial rivalries, the United States had to develop its own more centralized imperial system in order to survive.

Once that system began operating in 1789, Americans fought bitterly over the question of which groups would control it. Again, the intimate relationship between domestic and foreign affairs appeared, for out of that fight arose the first American political party system. One faction organized around Alexander Hamilton's plan for centralizing power by, among other means, having the new government fund state debts. To pay off those debts, however, the central government needed revenue, especially from import taxes. Most U.S. imports came from Great Britain. Therefore, Hamilton urged a policy of friendship toward the British. That is, domestic needs dictated his foreign policy. But James Madison and Thomas Jefferson disagreed. They were more concerned with exports (especially from southern states) than imports. Consequently, they feared Great Britain, which heavily discriminated against U.S. goods, and preferred France, with whom the United States enjoyed a favorable balance of trade. The division between Hamiltonians and Jeffersonians was not simply along pro-British and pro-French lines but between factions that had different domestic interests. By 1796 the factions had begun to coalesce into Federalists and Democratic-Republicans. The first American party system was born.

A turning point in the history of the "rising empire" occurred with the War of 1812. In the 1960s historians viewed that conflict as an almost farcical war into which a weak President Madison was forced by fire-eating War Hawks from the West and South. J.C.A. Stagg's *Mr. Madison's War* (1983), however, has persuasively argued that it was the president, not Congress, who fully understood the vital U.S. interests at stake in 1810–12 and that Madison shrewdly led the nation into war to protect those interests. He believed that Americans required a large overseas commerce to survive and that they should be free to sell in any markets they wished. The British refused to recognize that right; to defeat Napoleon, London officials tried to cut off U.S.-European trade by seizing American ships and sailors. Madison concluded that a threat of war and, if necessary, a U.S. invasion of Canada (long viewed as a "hostage" that Americans could use to pry concessions out of London) would so endanger British colonies in the New World that Great Britain would be forced to recognize American rights. The War of 1812 thus became another struggle for basic U.S. commercial liberties.

Madison had badly miscalculated, however. By using new findings in social and political history, Stagg demonstrates that Americans' first allegiance was not to the national government but to local interests. Throughout much of New England those parochial interests influenced merchants to work with the British fleet that controlled the seas. New England therefore refused to support the war and in 1814 even threatened to leave the Union. The president was finally saved by the end of the Napoleonic wars in Europe and major U.S. naval victories on the Great Lakes, victories that discouraged the British from continuing the fighting. With the European conflict ended, London was able to recognize greater U.S. rights on the high seas. The New England secessionist movement collapsed, and the section's merchants turned from their traditional British connections to other markets (as in newly independent Latin America) or to investing at home in the rising manufacturing complex. Stagg's work spells out on several levels the intimate relationship between domestic and foreign affairs at a pivotal point in the nation's history.

After 1815, Americans turned inward to settle the vast lands they had acquired in the 1783 peace treaty that ended the Revolution and in Jefferson's purchase of Louisiana in 1803. A key figure of the 1814 to 1844 years was Andrew Jackson—war hero, Anglophobe, Indian fighter, and two-term president. Robert Remini's three-volume biography (1977–84) argues that Jackson's military exploits were primarily responsible for the U.S. ability to annex Florida between 1818 and 1821 and also for the 1819 Transcontinental Treaty with Spain that provided the first U.S. claim to the Pacific coast. Remini's interpretations have been questioned, however, from several directions. One criticism draws from older work showing that the shrewd diplomacy of Secretary of State John Quincy Adams was more important to these U.S. successes than Jackson's activities. Adams's handling of Spanish, British, and Russian threats in Florida and along the northwest coast, as well as his pivotal role in formulating the Monroe Doctrine's principles in 1823, have led scholars to rank him as the greatest secretary of state in the nation's history.

A second criticism of Remini's approach has come from scholars exploiting findings in literary criticism, social history, and even psychiatry. Michael Rogin's *Fathers and Children: Andrew Jackson and the Subjugation of the American Indians* (1975) uses insights from psychiatry to explain Jackson's brutal treatment of British agents in Florida and Native Americans in Florida and elsewhere. Richard Drinnon's *Facing West* (1980) places the violent white expansionism of the nineteenth century within a four-hundred-year context of warfare against races Americans considered inferior. In this newer literature, Jackson becomes only a more interesting and famous example in a long line of leading Americans who resolved personal and social problems by subjugating others. In the hands of these scholars the frontier has become less the birthplace of democracy and economic equality (as it was characterized, for instance, in Frederick Jackson Turner's classic work) than a killing ground where European settlers and Native Americans savaged each other until the brutality infused white American consciousness. U.S. expansion no longer remained a tale of encounters between foreign ministers.

The expansionism climaxed during the 1840s. As their critics claimed, Americans were "amphibious animals" who moved aggressively on both land and sea. On land, the James K. Polk administration

(1845–49) seized nearly half of Mexico, acquired the Oregon territory, and annexed the nine-year-old state of Texas, which had rebelled against Mexico. U.S. landholdings suddenly increased 50 percent. Overseas, the Whig leadership of Daniel Webster and other mercantile northeasterners worked out the first formal treaties with China in 1844 and with Japan a decade later. In the late 1840s U.S. officials began linking their continental conquests and Asian interests by staking out claims in Central America, where during the 1850s Americans built the first ocean-to-ocean railway.

This combination of mainland and transoceanic expansion has been labeled "American continentalism" by historian Charles Vevier, who provocatively insists that the two types of expansion have been closely related. Vevier demonstrates, for example, that the first ideas about building a transcontinental railroad in the United States came from men in the 1840s who understood the reciprocal relationship between expansion on land and by sea. Building such a rail system, they reasoned, would not only link eastern producers with Pacific coast ports but develop the nation's interior and thus increase the amount of goods that could be sold in Asian markets. The development of the American continent would lead to the development of American interests in Asia—and vice versa.

David Pletcher's *Diplomacy of Annexation* (1973), the standard work on the 1840s, argues that the war against Mexico was unnecessary. A booming American population was searching for new lands to settle, Pletcher argues, and by waiting for that expanding population to sweep over California and the Southwest, Americans could have obtained peacefully what Polk acquired by sacrificing thousands of lives. Pletcher disagrees with Charles Sellers, Polk's biographer, who had used fresh scholarship in political history to argue, in *James K. Polk: Continentalist, 1843–1846* (1966), that Polk had little choice but to wage war. Powerful economic and social factions, found especially in the president's Democratic party, created a wave of expansionism that Polk rode into the White House—and war. Pletcher and Sellers nevertheless agree in discounting the old belief that a small conspiracy led by Polk or by southern slave interests caused the Mexican War. Rather, larger internal dynamics generated the expansionism. The system, not one man or one group, shaped foreign policies in the climactic 1840s.

Historians have also concluded that the 1840s marked a turn in white–Native American relations. Reginald Horsman's *Race and Manifest Destiny* (1981) identifies a growing conviction among whites that they had wrongly believed non-Caucasians could be peacefully assimilated into "civilized" society. By the 1840s the whites had concluded that Indians and Mexicans had to be eliminated, rather than assimilated, if white settlement were to progress. Thomas Hietala's *Manifest Design* (1985) continues the story by demonstrating a vital relationship between expansionism in the 1840s and in the 1890s. Before the publication of Hietala's work, historians saw little continuity between the earlier decade (when land expansion was dominant) and the later years (when Americans moved across water to conquer bases in the Caribbean and the Pacific). Now it appears that the racial views and the policy of military conquest of the 1840s triggered a series of wars with the Indians that lasted for nearly a half-century. Those conflicts opened much of the trans-Mississippi region to white settlement, allowed the building of transcontinental railroads and other key transportation systems, and thus developed the coherent, continental base that enabled the United States to emerge as a world power in the War of 1898. Again, internal change helped explain overseas triumphs. The Indian wars of the 1870s and 1880s, moreover, were important in developing the U.S. military that seized Spain's colonies in the Pacific and the Caribbean in 1898. During the 1880s a leading British military officer declared that the U.S. Army was, man for man, the best fighting force in the world. As Hietala demonstrates, the post-1840 Indian policies helped make it that way.

Other studies have found similar continuity between American expansion into Asia in the 1840s and the 1890s. A common characteristic was that both periods of expansion followed economic depression in the United States. (Indeed, it seems that each time a severe economic downturn has struck the United States, Americans have become intensely interested in the China market—as in the 1780s, 1840s, 1890s, 1930s, and 1970s to early 1980s.) In both the 1840s and 1890s the search for profits was accompanied by a U.S. policy that tried to block European attempts to colonize parts of Asia. That policy emerged in part out of American pride in winning the first modern anticolonial struggle in 1776. This pride was complemented by the realization that any parts of Asia colonized by Europeans could be closed to American business and missionaries. U.S. officials consequently insisted on an open-door principle in Asia as early as the 1840s and finally obtained reluctant consent to the principle from Europeans and Japanese in 1899–1900. In *The Making of a Special Relationship* (1983), a work that provides an overall analysis of U.S.-China encounters to 1914, Michael Hunt argues that Washington's concern to keep China whole and noncolonized produced that "special relationship" but the relationship was complex: Americans were interested not merely in protecting the Chinese but in exploiting their markets.

Hunt's use of Chinese sources reveals, moreover, that China's officials shrewdly manipulated the foreigners, playing off American against European in an attempt to control all the intruders. Wrongly assuming that the Chinese were showing them special favor, Americans developed a too innocent view of China's foreign policy. In reality, the Chinese had long looked down on Americans as "second-chop Englishmen" who deserved little better treatment than other imperialists. Thus the Chinese fear of and antipathy to U.S. power in the post-1949 era had roots deep in the nineteenth century.

The 1890s were a watershed decade in American foreign policy. As noted above, its key events were parts of long-term developments that had begun much earlier in the century, but the decade also witnessed changes that mark the beginnings of modern American foreign policy. In those years the United States forced the British to recognize that it was now the paramount power in the Western Hemisphere. It was also during those years that newly powerful industrial and banking groups played the major role in shaping U.S. foreign policy for the first time. Instead of being preoccupied with finding overseas markets for raw cotton and wheat, as they had been for a century, U.S. exporters searched for customers of cotton textiles, agricultural machinery, and even locomotives that American factories were producing overabundantly. The first important U.S. multinational corporations appeared in the 1880s and 1890s, led by such well-known firms as Singer Sewing Machine (which established profitable subsidiaries in Russia), Eastman Kodak, and Standard Oil. The dynamic of American expansion was transformed: after four hundred years of seeking landed frontiers, it was looking for buyers of industrial goods and bank capital. If land was acquired, it was to be used not for farming but for naval bases in Hawaii, the Caribbean, and the Philippines that could protect the growing overseas commerce.

Finally, the 1890s produced a more centralized governmental apparatus to run foreign policy efficiently. Between 1897 and 1901 that apparatus was controlled by President William McKinley. Recent scholarly work has viewed McKinley as the first modern chief executive because of his ability to dominate Congress and his willingness to use military force overseas without congressional sanction. The military dimension of late nineteenth-century expansionism has gained special attention. In an original but neglected work, *Gray Steel and Blue Water Navy* (1979), B. Franklin Cooling demonstrates that domestic economic interests and foreign policy needs combined to build the first ships of the modern U.S. Navy. Officials realized that they needed a great fleet to protect growing overseas interests and understood that the nation's powerful iron and steel complex could create such a force. Thus emerged the military-industrial alliance. The relationship was not always smooth; Washington officials were not pleased, for example, when Andrew Carnegie tried to sell them steel at higher prices than he was charging the

Russians. But need dictated compromise, and by the War of 1898 the military-industrial alliance had produced the Great White Fleet that won the war and could project its power to the distant Pacific.

McKinley first utilized that power, but he did so with little public flair. Theodore Roosevelt, on the other hand, bragged that he used the White House as "a bully pulpit" to summon Americans to assume world power. The flamboyant New Yorker seldom tried to escape public attention, even if courting it meant making defiant demands on other (usually weaker) governments or going off to shoot wild animals in Africa. But since Howard K. Beale's pathbreaking *Theodore Roosevelt and the Rise of America to World Power* (1956), we have understood that the private diplomat was more cautious than the public president. After 1904, for example, he worried that the Japanese and Russians were violating open-door principles and shutting Americans out of large parts of China. But he also knew that the United States could never fight a successful war against other powers on the Asian mainland simply to uphold the open-door principle, so he tried instead to work out a settlement with the Japanese. In Latin America, where U.S. power did dominate, his use of force was less restrained. In his search for order and markets, he used naval power in 1904–5 to stop a revolution in Santo Domingo and protect U.S. shipping and banking interests. Those reasons for the intervention, which became known as the Roosevelt Corollary to the Monroe Doctrine, established important precedents for later chief executives who sent troops into the Caribbean region.

Roosevelt and Woodrow Wilson grew to hate each other, but the latter found he had to follow many of the former's policies, especially in Latin America, where Wilson used force on a half-dozen occasions to stop internal upheavals. The most important recent analyses of Wilson's foreign policies, however, have also focused on two other questions. The first is why the president decided, with great reluctance, to take the United States into the massive slaughter of World War I. In the 1950s historians believed that the German declaration in January 1917 of all-out submarine warfare forced Wilson into the conflict. That declaration now appears a necessary but not sufficient explanation for the American decision. Wilson's leading biographer, Arthur Link, has concluded that the determination to be a full participant at any postwar peace conference was of special importance in the decision. Link and others have shown that Wilson believed he could obtain agreement to principles critical to U.S. domestic interests (such as freedom of the seas and liberal international trade) only by becoming a full participant in the shaping of the postwar world. He thus entered the conflict not only to insure the defeat of Germany but to produce a peace that would truly make the world "safe for democracy" and other American interests.

There is less agreement among historians about the second question, how and why Wilson dealt with the first major twentieth-century revolutions. His most important challenge was handling the danger of Lenin's Bolshevik policies at the 1919 Paris Peace Conference. As the young journalist and presidential adviser Walter Lippmann observed at the time, Lenin was not invited to Paris, but his shadow hovered over every discussion because war-devastated Europe was a powder keg waiting to explode into Communist revolution. Most scholars now believe that Wilson failed to create the kind of democratic Europe he wanted because he was trapped between conservative (even reactionary) western European leaders and the eastern revolutionaries. No one could have developed a workable compromise between those two forces. More specifically, historians see Wilson trapped between Bolshevism and his faith in self-determination. He came to recognize that self-determination might actually lead to Communist states. When Hungarians and Germans threatened to elect Communists in 1919, the president chose to contain the threatened spread of radicalism, even if it meant sacrificing his ideal of self-determination.

The Republican officials who made U.S. foreign policy in the 1920s never resolved this growing tension between the principle of self-determination and the threat of radical revolution. Scholars agree that Washington policy-makers during this decade were little interested in Wilson's view of self-determination; they were dedicated instead to using the immense U.S. financial resources (many of which resulted from loans made to the belligerents during the Great War) to rebuild the world along capitalist lines. As noted above, the key word applied by historians to these policies is "corporatism" (or "associationalism"). U.S. bankers and exporters, for example, worked together to capture overseas markets—a combination that might have been illegal at home because of antitrust laws. But U.S. officials encouraged such cooperation overseas because only then could Americans compete with the giant "combines" and cartels of European business. This approach obviously did not resemble the ideal of nineteenth-century "free enterprise." It was a new approach formulated by Washington officials (especially Herbert Hoover) so that U.S. corporations could work together to obtain needed foreign markets—or exploit such vital raw material sources as Middle East oil reserves, which British and French firms threatened to monopolize.

Associationalism had another advantage: it functioned privately and outside the glare of domestic politics. The approach was worked out in corporate board rooms or in unnoticed discussions between corporate leaders and Washington officials. The business and political elites of the 1920s wanted no interference from Congress, public opinion, or foreign governments; their goal was maximum freedom of action—which also explains why they wanted nothing to do with the League of Nations or other international organizations that might tie American hands. In *American Business and Foreign Policy, 1920–1933* (1971), Joan Hoff Wilson calls this search for freedom-of-maneuver "independent international-ism." Given the expanding American interests, the term is much more accurate than the "isolationist" label usually pinned on the 1920s and 1930s.

American leaders believed that the nation's welfare depended on a healthy international system. That welfare, they assumed, included not only matters of economics but the survival of individual freedom within the United States. As Hoover declared dramatically in 1921, the American system of individualism "cannot be preserved in domestic life, if it must be abandoned in our international life." Events between 1929 and 1933 proved Hoover to be a prophet. The New York money market weakened in 1929 from overspeculation and corruption, and its weakening threatened to destroy fragile European and Japanese economic systems whose lifeblood in the 1920s had been U.S. capital. As those foreign systems collapsed, the international framework fell apart; U.S. overseas markets disappeared; and the number of unemployed Americans more than doubled between 1930 and 1933 until it reached an astronomical 25 percent. "Associationalism" and "independent internationalism" had failed to produce healthy systems at home or abroad.

Franklin D. Roosevelt moved slowly after 1933 to restore the American role in world affairs. He initially gave domestic problems priority and believed he could separate them from overseas events. His approach quickly collapsed. Because of American economic and potential military power, the United States was inevitably involved in world politics. Even the so-called isolationists in Congress from midwestern and Rocky Mountain states had spokesmen, such as Republican Senator William Borah of Idaho, who were willing to cooperate with the Soviet Union or the new Chinese government to stop Japanese aggression. But the isolationists wanted no major involvement in European affairs or in League of Nations actions that might suck the United States into a major war. By the time of the Munich agreement between Germany, Great Britain, and France in 1938 and the outbreak of war a year later, however, the question was not whether the United States would become drawn into World War II but how.

Scholars have argued bitterly whether Roosevelt trailed, led, or simply lied to American public opinion during 1940–41. A consensus has formed that he was sensitive to and restrained by isolationist strength, but that after his third-term election victory in 1940 he secretly and steadily pushed the United States into war. Especially revealing has been the recent discovery of British Prime Minister Winston Churchill's account of his talk with FDR at the Atlantic Conference in August 1941. Speaking more than three months before the Pearl Harbor attack, Roosevelt privately declared that he so fully supported the British that he was determined to send them increased supplies—and if Hitler tried to stop the ships, it would create an "incident" that could carry the United States fully into the war.

In studying the events that led to the Japanese attack on Pearl Harbor, historians have divided over the question of whether a settlement might have been possible with Japan. Akira Iriye's *Power and Culture: The Japanese-American War, 1941–1945* (1981) argues that Washington and Tokyo officials shared common views about restructuring the world community and, specifically, the appropriate development of China. John Dower, in *War without Mercy: Race and Power in the Pacific War* (1986), has vigorously disagreed. Dower concludes that each side held views based on indigenous racial, religious, and political prejudices that led to mutual hatred, not shared assumptions. Iriye's and Dower's work on racial stereotypes in the 1940s resembles the analyses by Horsman and Hietala, who explored racism to provide insights into mid-nineteenth-century diplomacy.

More work has been published on the emergence of the Cold War in the 1940s than on any other topic in American diplomatic history. The first accounts, appearing in the 1940s and 1950s, focused on political events (such as the Yalta and Potsdam summit conferences of 1945) and blamed the Soviets for starting the Cold War. Fresh scholarship in the 1960s, however, stressed the role of economic factors and argued that the United States—which enjoyed great economic advantages as well as a monopoly on the atomic bomb in the 1940s—bore heavy responsibility for the conflict. Washington officials were especially criticized for insisting on challenging Soviet security even in the Russian border regions of eastern Europe, Iran, Greece, and Turkey. Other historians emphasized the role of individuals: the inexperienced and insecure Harry Truman, who, some believe, reversed Roosevelt's policies that had been aimed at cooperating with the Soviets; or the brutal Joseph Stalin, whose growing paranoia made him irrationally determined to dominate Europe and Asia.

The most influential scholarship, however, has not stressed isolated political, economic, or individual causes; it has instead insisted that the Cold War arose out of the clash of two systems. The American system valued certain individual freedoms that U.S. officials believed required an open, capitalist world. As Truman declared in a major foreign policy speech of March 6, 1947, "freedom of worship" and "freedom of speech" are "related" to "freedom of enterprise." Because of that perceived relationship, the United States opposed the Soviet system, which destroyed many economic and personal freedoms in eastern Europe. Also because of that perceived relationship, U.S. officials moved to dismantle the French and British colonial empires that had long discriminated against American freedom of enterprise in such regions as French Indochina and British protectorates in the Middle East. The United States helped force the British and French to quit their colonial areas and find security in an American-dominated alliance system.

McCormick's *American Half-Century* and Thomas Paterson's incisive book *On Every Front: The Making of the Cold War* (1979, 1992) use different approaches to view the Cold War as a competition between two historical systems rather than as a result, say, of Truman's insecurity or political mistakes made at Yalta. Deep-rooted traditions in both the United States and the Soviet Union that closely tie domestic needs to foreign policies now seem a more helpful explanation of the Cold War than do individuals or individual events in the 1940s. And the effectiveness or ineffectiveness of those traditions in pushing forward Soviet or American national interests is now seen to have depended in turn on the evolving international arena—whose peoples in such countries as Vietnam and Afghanistan have, since the 1950s, increasingly pushed back.

Within the American tradition of foreign policy, scholars have recently paid special attention to two topics. The first is the role played by peace groups. Charles DeBenedetti's overviews trace the movement's importance back to the War of 1812. World War I, however, was again a turning point. During and immediately after that conflict, peace groups were directed by secular as well as religious concerns, attracted people from many sectors of the society, devised nonviolent methods for resisting war, and became a major force for cooperative, internationalist peace efforts. The antiwar movement received headlines during the post-1960 Vietnam and Central American conflicts, but it was shaped decades earlier.

A second topic that has drawn attention is the role of the changing Constitution and, especially, presidential powers in shaping foreign policy. Surprisingly, historians had devoted little attention to this fundamental relationship between constitutional rights and the execution of diplomacy until Richard Nixon blatantly abused his powers between 1970 and 1973. Abram D. Sofaer's *War, Foreign Affairs, and the Constitutional Power* (1976) demonstrates that 150 years before the "imperial" presidencies of Nixon and Lyndon Johnson, the first chief executives— especially Jefferson—began to upset the system's checks and balances.

No topic in U.S. diplomatic history is more important than the changing relationship between constitutionally guaranteed freedoms at home and the exercise of American power abroad. U.S. interests, confined to thirteen seacoast colonies in 1776, had shaped global affairs by 1945. American diplomatic history, once viewed as consisting of conversations between elite officials, has become the study of how a complex domestic political economy transformed a "rising empire" into an established global empire by the late 1940s. The effects of that empire on the larger international system and, especially, on the constitutional freedoms that the foreign policy was supposed to protect are, however, only beginning to be understood.

BIBLIOGRAPHY

These sources, in addition to those identified by title in the text, are selected from recent works in U.S. diplomatic history to 1945 and the early origins of the Cold War.

Becker, William H., and Samuel F. Wells, Jr., eds. *Economics and World Power: An Assessment of American Diplomacy since 1789.* New York: Columbia University Press, 1984.

Beisner, Robert L. *From the Old Diplomacy to the New, 1865–1900.* 2d ed. Arlington Heights, Ill.: Harlan Davidson, 1986.

Cohen, Warren, ed. *New Frontiers in American–East Asian Relations.* New York: Columbia University Press, 1983.

Costigliola, Frank. *Awkward Dominion: American Political, Economic, and Cultural Relations with Europe, 1919–1933.* Ithaca, N.Y.: Cornell University Press, 1984.

Crapol, Edward P., ed. *Women and American Foreign Policy: Lobbyists, Critics, and Insiders.* 2d ed. Wilmington, Del.: Scholarly Resources, 1992.

DeBenedetti, Charles, ed. *Peace Heroes in Twentieth-Century America.* Bloomington: Indiana University Press, 1986.

Fisher, Louis. *Presidential War Power.* Lawrence: University Press of Kansas, 1995.

Foglesong, David S. *America's Secret War against Bolshevism: U.S. Intervention in the Russian Civil War, 1917–1920.* Chapel Hill: University of North Carolina Press, 1995.

Gardner, Lloyd C. *Safe for Democracy: The Anglo-American Response to Revolution, 1913–1923.* New York: Oxford University Press, 1984.

Green, David. *Shaping Political Consciousness: The Language of Politics in America from McKinley to Reagan.* Ithaca, N.Y.: Cornell University Press, 1988.

Hogan, Michael J., and Thomas G. Paterson, eds. *Explaining the History of American Foreign Relations.* New York: Oxford University Press, 1991.

Hunt, Michael, *Ideology and U.S. Foreign Policy.* New Haven, Conn.: Yale University Press, 1987.

Iriye, Akira. *The Globalizing of America, 1914–1945.* New York: Cambridge University Press, 1993.

Kolko, Gabriel. *Century of War: Politics, Conflict, and Society since 1914.* New York: New Press, 1994.

Leffler, Melvyn P. *A Preponderance of Power: National Security, the Truman Administration, and the Cold War.* Stanford, Calif.: Stanford University Press, 1992.

Link, Arthur S., ed. *Woodrow Wilson and a Revolutionary World, 1913–1921.* Chapel Hill: University of North Carolina Press, 1982.

Little, Douglas. *Malevolent Neutrality: The United States, Great Britain, and the Origins of the Spanish Civil War.* Ithaca, N.Y.: Cornell University Press, 1985.

McCormick, Thomas J. "Drift or Mastery?: A Corporatist Synthesis for American Diplomatic History." *Reviews in American History* 10 (December 1982): 318–29.

Perkins, Bradford, *The Creation of a Republican Empire, 1776–1865.* New York: Cambridge University Press, 1993.

Remini, Robert V. *The Life of Andrew Jackson.* New York: Harper & Row, 1988.

Rosenberg, Emily. *Spreading the American Dream: American Economic and Cultural Expansion, 1890–1945.* New York: Hill & Wang, 1982.

Schoonover, Thomas. *The United States in Central America, 1860–1911: Episodes of Social Imperialism and Imperial Rivalry in the World System.* Durham, N.C.: Duke University Press, 1991.

Thorne, Christopher. *Allies of a Kind: The United States, Britain, and the War against Japan, 1941–1945.* New York: Oxford University Press, 1978.

———. *Border Crossings: Studies in International History.* New York: Oxford University Press, 1988.

Vevier, Charles. "American Continentalism: An Idea of Expansion, 1845–1910." *American Historical Review* 65 (January 1960): 323–35.

About the Contributors

THOMAS BENDER is University Professor of the Humanities and Professor of History at New York University. His *Toward an Urban Vision* (University Press of Kentucky, 1975; Johns Hopkins University Press, 1982), won the Frederick Jackson Turner Award of the Organization of American Historians. His recent books include *New York Intellect* (Knopf, 1987) and *Intellect and Public Life* (Johns Hopkins University Press, 1993).

ALAN BRINKLEY is Professor of History at Columbia University. He is the author of *Voices of Protest: Huey Long, Father Coughlin, and the Great Depression* (Knopf, 1982), which won the National Book Award in 1983. His most recent book is *The End of Reform: New Deal Liberalism in Recession and War* (Knopf, 1995).

WILLIAM H. CHAFE is Alice Mary Baldwin Professor of History at Duke University. His book *Civilities and Civil Rights: Greensboro, N.C., and the Black Struggle for Freedom* (Oxford University Press, 1980) won the Robert F. Kennedy Book Award in 1981. He is also the author of *The Unfinished Journey: America since World War Two* (Oxford University Press, 1986) and *Never Stop Running: Allard Lowenstein and the Struggle to Save American Liberalism* (Basic Books, 1993).

LEON FINK, Associate Professor of History at the University of North Carolina, Chapel Hill, is the author of *Workingmen's Democracy: The Knights of Labor and American Politics* (University of Illinois Press, 1983) and coauthor of *Upheaval in the Quiet Zone: A History of Hospital Workers' Union Local 1199* (University of Illinois Press, 1989). His most recent book is *In Search of the Working Class* (University of Illinois Press, 1994).

ERIC FONER is DeWitt Clinton Professor of History at Columbia University. His *Reconstruction: America's Unfinished Revolution, 1863–1877* (Harper & Row, 1988) won the Bancroft Prize and the Francis Parkman Prize, among others. His most recent book is *Freedom's Lawmakers: A Directory of Black Officeholders during Reconstruction* (Louisiana State University Press, 1996).

ESTELLE B. FREEDMAN, Professor of History at Stanford University, is the coauthor of *Intimate Matters: A History of Sexuality in America* (Harper & Row, 1988). Her most recent book is *Maternal Justice: Miriam Van Waters and the Female Reform Tradition* (University of Chicago Press, 1996).

LINDA GORDON is Florence Kelley Professor of History at the University of Wisconsin, Madison. Her *Heroes of Their Own Lives: The Politics and History of Family Violence* (Viking/Penguin, 1988) was awarded the Joan Kelly Prize of the American Historical Association. An earlier book, *Woman's Body, Woman's Right: A Social History of Birth Control in America,* now appears in a revised edition (Viking/Penguin, 1990). Her most recent book is *Pitied but Not Entitled: Single Mothers and the History of Welfare* (The Free Press, 1994).

THOMAS C. HOLT is Professor of History at the University of Chicago. In 1978 his *Black over White: Negro Political Leadership in South Carolina during Reconstruction* (University of Illinois Press, 1977) received the Charles Sydnor Award of the Southern Historical Association.

KEVIN KENNY, Assistant Professor of History at the University of Texas at Austin, is the author of *Making Sense of the Molly Maguires* (Oxford University Press, 1997).

LINDA K. KERBER, May Brodbeck Professor in the Liberal Arts and Professor of History at the University of Iowa, served as president of the American Studies Association in 1988–89. She is the author of *Women of the Republic: Intellect and Ideology in Revolutionary America* (University of North Carolina Press, 1980; Norton, 1986).

ALICE KESSLER-HARRIS is Director of Women's Studies and Professor of History at Rutgers University. Among her publications are *Out to*

Work: A History of Wage-Earning Women in the United States (Oxford University Press, 1982) and *A Woman's Wage: Historical Meanings and Social Consequences* (University Press of Kentucky, 1990).

WALTER LaFEBER is Noll Professor of History at Cornell University. His most recent book is *The American Age: The United States at Home and Abroad since 1750* (Norton, 1989).

RICHARD L. McCORMICK, President of the University of Washington and Professor of History, is the author of *The Party Period and Public Policy: American Politics from the Age of Jackson to the Progressive Era* (Oxford University Press, 1986) and other works.

JOHN M. MURRIN, Professor of History at Princeton University, is coeditor of *Saints and Revolutionaries: Essays on Early American History* (Norton, 1984) and the 1986–87 winner of the Society of Cincinnati (New Jersey chapter) Award for his work on the history of colonial New Jersey.

JAMES P. SHENTON is Professor of History at Columbia University. Among his books are *Robert John Walker: A Politician from Jackson to Lincoln* (Columbia University Press, 1961) and *A Historian's History of the United States* (Putnam, 1966).

RICHARD WHITE is Professor of History at the University of Washington. His most recent book is *The Organic Machine* (Hill & Wang, 1995).

SEAN WILENTZ, Professor of History at Princeton University, is the author of *Chants Democratic: New York City and the Rise of the American Working Class, 1788–1850* (Oxford University Press, 1984), which has won several honors, including the Albert Beveridge Award of the American Historical Association and the Frederick Jackson Turner Award of the Organization of American Historians. His most recent book, coauthored with Paul Johnson, is *The Kingdom of Matthias* (Oxford University Press, 1994).